Essays in CONTEMPORARY ECONOMIC PROBLEMS, 1985

Essays in CONTEMPORARY ECONOMIC PROBLEMS, 1985

The Economy in Deficit

Phillip Cagan, editor
Eduardo Somensatto, associate editor

American Enterprise Institute
Washington and London

The Library of Congress has cataloged this serial publication as follows:

Essays in contemporary economic problems. — 1981/1982 ed. —
   Washington, D.C. : American Enterprise Institute for Public
   Policy Research, c1981.

   1 v. : ill. ; 23 cm.

   Annual.
   Vol. for 1981/82 has subtitle: Demand, productivity, and population.
   Continues: Contemporary economic problems.
   ISSN 0732-4308 = Essays in contemporary economic problems.

   1. United States—Economic policy—1981-   —Periodicals. 2. Economic policy—Periodicals. 3. Economics—Periodicals. I. American Enterprise Institute for Public Policy Research.

   HC106.7.A45a   330.973′005   82-642433
                                                       AACR 2   MARC-S

ISBN 0-8447-1371-6 (cloth)
ISBN 0-8447-1372-4 (paper)

ISSN 0732-4308

Printed in the United States of America

CONTENTS

FOREWORD

The most important issue of economic policy today unquestionably concerns the federal budget deficit. It dominates public policy discourse, where it has generated a lively and serious debate on the likely economic consequences. The debate has brought forth competing explanations and raised questions about preconceived notions. Considerable confusion and uncertainty have surrounded the likely effects of the deficits.

Concern over the deficits heightened when it became apparent that they would not decline unless existing budgetary policies were altered and that a string of large deficits would pose a serious threat to long-run economic growth and stability. There arose fears that the deficits would reduce capital formation, produce an unsustainable accumulation of debt, and in time reignite inflationary pressures. Yet, since this persistence of large deficits is unprecedented in the peacetime history of the United States, past experience has been of little help in showing the possible effects.

We have now had two years of structural deficits over 4 percent of GNP. Many of the consequences are now becoming evident.

This eighth volume of AEI's annual series on *Contemporary Economic Problems* is devoted to an interim assessment of the economy in deficit. It contains twelve essays by AEI scholars and other experts on the various issues raised by the deficits. The topics range from a review of the reasons for the increase in the deficits to an evaluation of their various effects, covering an analysis of the economic consequences, an evaluation of tax policy options to reduce them, a discussion of the foreign experience with them, and the political difficulties of dealing with them.

This series of volumes on *Contemporary Economic Problems* is now edited by Phillip Cagan, professor of economics at Columbia University and visiting scholar at AEI. Dr. Cagan has been associated with this series from its inception, and we at AEI are pleased that he has agreed to direct the project. As editor he brings the expertise, broad knowledge, and high standards that ensure continuation of the past quality of this series. Eduardo Somensatto of AEI is working with him as associate editor.

The current volume reflects our commitment to the evaluation of the most pressing public policy issues. This volume, which contains a comprehensive set of studies on the issue of deficits, provides the background and analysis needed to understand the most important economic issue confronting our nation today.

WILLIAM J. BAROODY, JR.
President
American Enterprise Institute

Introduction

Phillip Cagan

With the enactment in 1981 of staged tax reductions, the economy developed large budget deficits, which rose to 6 percent of GNP by 1983 and continued at a high level. Discussion of the deficits focused at first on an expected crowding out of private investment and reduced economic growth. High interest rates accompanying the deficits and attributed to them threatened to abort the nascent business recovery in 1983 and complicated the servicing of the heavy debts of third world countries. A contrasting optimistic view held by "supply-side" economists saw the deficits disappearing through rapid economic growth stimulated by the reduction in taxes.

Confounding these initial prognoses, the outcome has been strikingly different. The large deficits have not disappeared; yet interest rates have come down considerably, the business recovery was not aborted, private investment has been strong, and the third world debtors have so far managed to avoid defaults.

This volume assesses the first two years of the economy under the large deficits. Various views of the effects of the deficits are discussed and appraised. All the contributors benefited from joint discussions that allowed a cross-fertilization of findings. In this introduction I survey the major conclusions that emerge from our studies.

The deficit was $175 billion in fiscal year 1984 (ending September 30), in contrast to President Reagan's original plan, when he took office in 1981, to balance the budget in 1984. The main reason for the difference was the administration's overoptimistic economic projection for the years between 1981 and 1985, in particular its failure to foresee the 1981–1982 recession. As a result, tax revenues were much less than originally anticipated. Increases in expenditures above the original proposals, however, were almost equally important in contributing to the discrepancy.

Projections for coming years vary with assumptions about expenditures; economic growth, which affects revenues; and interest rates, which determine the cost of servicing the federal debt. Without major spending reductions or tax increases, however, the deficit will remain about 4½ to 5 percent of GNP, given moderate rates of economic growth and little change in interest rates. The administration's projections of declining deficits are based on major spending cuts and the more optimistic assumptions that economic growth will be higher and interest rates lower. Higher economic growth appears remote, but the inflationary premium in interest rates might continue to subside. Interest rates are also held up by federal borrowing, however, and could come down to reduce interest payments on the debt if deficit borrowing is first cut by other means. It remains to be seen how much Congress cuts expenditures or raises taxes. The deficit might even increase, of course, if inflation escalated to raise expenditures faster than revenues or if a business recession developed.

The economic importance of the U.S. budget deficit appears to shrink when it is viewed as part of government deficits worldwide. Although most other government deficits have not risen as sharply, the aggregate deficit of governments worldwide, including the U.S. government, has nevertheless increased. Yet these deficits would have been much smaller but for the influence of the recession ending at the end of 1982 in the United States and later abroad. It can be argued that low levels of economic activity are accompanied by reduced private sector investment, which, despite large government deficits, makes the volume of total credit demands normal. Total credit demands have not been normal, however. The strong investment demand in the United States, in combination with the U.S. and other government deficits, has absorbed a significant part of world savings.

The strong U.S. investment demand, which contradicted forecasts that it would be reduced by federal borrowing, can be attributed to the vigorous cyclical recovery in 1983 and the substantial cut in business taxes, which were sufficient to lower the user cost of capital, even in the presence of high real interest rates. In effect, the investment tax credit and the accelerated cost recovery provision of the 1981 and 1982 tax acts served as an antidote for the negative effect on investment of high real rates of interest. Past research on the effects of similar tax stimulants to investment since the early 1900s suggests that much of their positive effect on investment wears off after several years. This happens because lower costs of capital stimulate a desired increase in capital that is finite. Once the new machinery is in place, investment slows to a level consistent with maintenance (depreciation) of the capital stock. Overall, if U.S. real interest rates remain high, the strong investment growth of 1983–1984 can be expected to atrophy as the effect of investment tax stimulants wears off. Deficits will have to fall to a level consistent with a stable ratio of debt to GNP (about $100 billion per year) as a minimum condition for avoidance of crowding out.

The financing of the increased U.S. credit demands has come from a combination of state and local government budget surpluses, business gross saving, household saving, and capital inflows from abroad. The state and local surpluses are likely to decline as they typically do in a business expansion when budget expenditures rise and taxes are reduced, and increases in household saving have so far been minor despite the tax incentives. Foreign capital inflows, which exceeded $80 billion in 1984, have financed a good part of the federal deficit attributable to the 1981 tax reduction. The capital inflow is in response to the strong demand for credit in the United States, which lies behind the large appreciation of the dollar in foreign exchange markets. The capital inflow is the counterpart of an equal deficit in foreign trade and services. The crowding out by the federal deficit has therefore fallen initially not on investment but on U.S. export and import-competing industries. The strong dollar has benefited the exports of foreign countries and has blunted the initial foreign criticism of high U.S. interest rates. The import competition in the United States has fostered pressures for trade restrictions, however, and created a major policy issue.

By intensifying the competition from imports, the strong dollar has helped hold down the U.S. inflation rate. This allowed monetary policy to ease after mid-1984 as the economic expansion slackened. The fear that monetary policy might be driven to monetize the deficits and reignite new inflationary pressures has so far subsided. But until high deficits are brought down, concern that future interest rates will remain high persists, as indicated by unusually high long-term rates. Future pressures on interest rates are made additionally uncertain by the expectation that the foreign acquisition of U.S. assets, mostly short-term bank deposits, must sooner or later slacken, thus reducing a major source of funds to finance U.S. credit demands and putting further upward pressures on U.S. real interest rates. An accompanying depreciation of the dollar would unleash inflationary forces and raise nominal interest rates as well. None of these developments seems likely to occur rapidly, but speculative activity in the foreign exchange market has the capacity to speed up otherwise slow adjustments.

Aside from the short-run disturbances, the long-range problem is that U.S. budget deficits are piling up a mountain of public debt. Interest payments on the debt add to future deficits, requiring ever larger budgetary adjustments to control the deficits at some later date, while growing debt and deficits tend to raise the interest rate. A long-range burden exists because the financing of the deficit tends either to crowd out domestic investment and reduce future economic growth or to mortgage an equivalent amount of future income to foreign holders of U.S. debt. In some other countries the burden of mounting debt has been reduced in real terms by an even more burdensome

3

policy of inflating it away, an unlikely possibility in the United States where the interest rate on the largely short-term debt can adjust to inflation and the capability of controlling the growth of debt exists.

With the problems of large budget deficits now widely recognized, a political battle has developed over how to reduce them. The battle reflects the various political priorities assigned to protecting existing expenditures and tax preferences and is exacerbated by changes in the structure of Congress in recent years that have reduced its ability to resolve budgetary disagreements, making a quick resolution unlikely. A growing dissatisfaction with the complexities of the federal tax system has also created political backing for simplifying the tax code. Yet all proposals for tax reform have disadvantages, and the disruptive process of changing the tax system can only add to the uncertainty of the legislative outcome. Large budget deficits could persist as the major economic problem for most of this decade. Without some resolution, however, the problem can only get worse.

1

Accounting for the Deficit

John C. Weicher

Summary

When he came into office, President Reagan projected a balanced budget by 1985. The FY1985 budget that he actually submitted, three years later, had a $180 billion deficit instead. This paper describes the differences between the two projections. It compares revenues and expenditures, category by category.

The discrepancy is composed of a $105 billion shortfall in revenues and $81 billion of outlays in excess of the original projection. (The revenue projection includes the administration's proposed tax cut; it is not part of the shortfall.) The major reason for both discrepancies is an overoptimistic economic forecast; in particular, the administration failed to foresee the 1981–1982 recession. This failure was not limited to the administration; most economic forecasters similarly did not expect it. The error in forecasting accounts for all of the revenue shortfall and perhaps half of the excess expenditures. Subsequent economic growth during the 1983–1984 recovery, while more rapid than the Reagan administration forecast in 1981, has not been enough to make up for the recession; real GNP is still well below the level projected four years ago. The tax increases approved in 1982 and 1983 were not large enough to offset more than a minor fraction of the lost revenues. On the outlay side, the additional deficits arising from the recession have resulted in a much larger interest burden; additional interest alone is about 40 percent of the discrepancy. Increases in some cyclically sensitive programs, such as unemployment compensation, have also contributed.

The rate of inflation has also been much lower than originally projected. This lower rate has mitigated the outlay increase, particularly in indexed programs; however, it has exacerbated the revenue shortfall.

A less important but not negligible contributing factor has been the administration's inability to win congressional approval of all its proposed spending cuts. Small changes across several program areas have added up to more than 10 percent of the expenditure discrepancy. The administration may also have originally wanted sharper reductions in social security and Medicare than it finally proposed. In a few areas, it has modified its original policy and asked for greater expenditures.

The economic forecasting inaccuracies should be kept in mind when evaluating the deficit situation for the next few years. The administration now assumes unusually rapid real economic growth for the 1985–1989 period. Failure to achieve that growth will result in larger deficits than those now projected.

Introduction

In March 1981, within a month of taking office, President Reagan projected a balanced federal budget in fiscal year 1985, at the end of his term.[1] In February 1984, when he submitted his actual 1985 budget to Congress, the president expected a deficit of $180 billion.[2] What happened in between?

This paper explains how the projected balanced budget turned into a projected deficit equal to almost 20 percent of expenditures. It traces the changes in federal revenue and expenditure projections for each major category of income and outlay.

The paper is basically an exercise in accounting, but in identifying the sources of the discrepancies it also identifies the economic and political factors that invalidated the original projections. Because long-term budget projections have consistently been wrong, and wrong in the same direction as President Reagan's 1982 projection, the paper may contribute to an understanding of this general pattern. It may also offer some insight into the probable accuracy of budget projections now being made for the future.

I emphasize that the paper analyzes the differences between two projections of the 1985 budget, both made by the Reagan administration. It does not describe, except incidentally, the extensive changes that President Reagan made in President Carter's last budget;[3] nor does it attempt to forecast the actual budget deficit in 1985 or to incorporate the changes in projections that have occurred since the president's 1985 budget was prepared.[4] Still less does it purport to *evaluate* the Reagan budget proposals or the changes actually approved by Congress.

There is a certain symmetry in the projection errors; they are composed almost equally of revenue shortfalls and of unanticipated expenditures. In the 1985 budget, President Reagan projects revenues that are $105 billion less than he expected them to be three years earlier ($745 billion compared with $850 billion) and expenditures that are $81 billion greater ($925 billion compared with $844 billion). The expenditure discrepancy in turn is almost equally divided between errors in individual budget categories ($38 billion) and a lump-sum of "additional savings to be proposed" ($44 billion), which was never subsequently specified. These expenditures are actual outlays rather than budget authority; unless otherwise indicated, all expenditure figures cited in the paper are outlays.

The next two sections of the paper take up revenues and outlays in turn.

Revenue Differences

President Carter's final budget projected revenues for FY1985 at $1,053 billion, which would have been the first trillion-dollar budget in U.S. history. President Reagan's "Program for Economic Recovery," proposed just two months later in March 1981, contained sweeping tax reforms that were projected to reduce revenues by $163 billion, almost one-sixth. In addition, the economic assumptions underlying the revenue projections were revised downward by $40 billion, primarily because the new administration projected a significantly lower inflation rate, averaging about 1.5 percentage points below the Carter projection. (The administration also projected faster economic growth between 1981 and 1985, but this growth was not enough to offset the effect of lower inflation.) The combined effect of the legislative proposals and changed economic assumptions was to lower the Carter projections by slightly more than $200 billion, to $850 billion. By February 1984, however, it was clear that the revenue projection was far too high. The FY1985 budget projected revenues of only $745 billion.

Table 1–1 explains the sources of the discrepancy. It demonstrates that economic forecasting errors are responsible for the entire difference—and more than the entire difference—between the 1981 and 1984 projections of 1985 revenues. Had the original economic forecast proved accurate, revenues would be $176 billion higher in FY1985 than they are now projected to be. This difference is partly offset by changes in the tax laws that the president did not propose in 1981; in the last four years, taxes have been higher than he originally wanted and are now projected to be $76 billion more than the 1981 projection for FY1985.

There are two reasons for the difference in tax policy. In 1981 Congress did not approve as large a tax cut as the president requested (at least for the 1981–1985 period). In addition, as the 1981–1982 recession deepened it became clear that revenues would fall short of the original projections much more than was desirable, and Congress passed two new tax bills in 1982 and one in 1984, all of which the president supported. The social security changes enacted in 1983 have also raised revenues slightly. The combined effect of the subsequent tax increases has been greater from FY1983 through FY1985 than the

TABLE 1-1
CHANGING REVENUE PROJECTIONS, 1981–1985
(billions of dollars)

	1981	1982	1983	1984	1985
CBO baseline (January 1981)	612	709	810	920	1,033
Reagan proposals (March 1981)	−9	−51	−97	−145	−182
Reagan projection (March 1981)	603	658	713	775	851
Differences between Reagan proposals and enacted law	5	11	24	52	76
Economic Recovery Tax Act of 1981	5	11	6	10	16
Tax Equity and Fiscal Responsibility Act of 1982	0	0	16	34	37
Surface Transportation Assistance Act of 1982	0	0	2	4	4
Social Security Amendments of 1983	0	0	0	6	9
Repeal of interest and dividend withholding	0	0	0	−3	−2
Deficit Reduction Act of 1984	0	0	0	1	11
Other	0	0	1	0	−1
Projected revenues, assuming no changes in the economy	608	670	738	828	927
Changes due to differences in economic performance and assumptions	−9	−52	−137	−154	−176
Projected revenues (August 1984)	599	618	601	673	751

NOTE: For tax law changes, positive numbers represent tax increases, and negative numbers represent tax cuts. The number 0 is used either when the amount is less than $500 million or when the legislation went into effect in a subsequent year.

SOURCES: Congressional Budget Office, *Baseline Budget Projections for Fiscal Years 1985–1989* (February 1984), app. D; *The Economic and Budget Outlook: An Update* (August 1984), chap. 3; additional unpublished material provided by Congressional Budget Office.

differences between the president's original tax proposals and the changes enacted by Congress in 1981. For FY1985, the 1982–1984 tax legislation has brought in $60 billion—$37 billion of it from the Tax Equity and Fiscal Responsibility Act of 1982 (TEFRA)—compared with only $16 billion resulting from President Reagan's Program for Economic Recovery, which embodied a larger tax cut than the Economic Recovery and Tax Act of 1981 (ERTA) actually provided.

The data in table 1–1 come from the Congressional Budget Office, rather than from the proposed budgets of the presidents.[5] They differ from the proposed budgets in several respects. The 1984 and 1985 revenue figures are taken from the August 1984 "Update." The economic recovery during the first half of 1984 was stronger than either CBO or the Office of Management and Budget (OMB) had anticipated at the beginning of the year. In addition, revenues are reported on a "current services" basis. They thus exclude tax-law changes proposed by President Carter in his FY1982 budget, which account for the full difference between his $1,053 billion revenue projection and the $1,033 billion in table 1–1. The FY1985 budget also omits most of the tax increase approved in 1984. But the similarities are more important than the differences. The CBO estimates of the revenue effects resulting from the various tax-law changes between 1981 and 1983 are quite close to those estimated by the administration; the aggregate estimates are $113 billion and $117 billion, respectively.[6] This statement suggests that the estimates of economic forecasting errors are similarly close. The CBO data are preferable because they provide more detail.

The numbers in the table should not be taken as precisely accurate. In fact, tax-law changes and economic developments interact with each other to produce the overall effect, and there is some element of arbitrariness in assigning the interactive effects to a single causal factor. But the table is certainly a reliable guide to the approximate order of magnitude.

Changes in the Economy. At the beginning of 1981, both President Carter and President Reagan foresaw continuing recovery from the 1980 recession, which had ended in the third quarter of the year. They expected real growth of about one percentage point during 1981, followed by much stronger growth during the next four years. President Carter's estimate was 3.5–3.7 percent annual real growth; President Reagan's, 4.2–5.0 percent. Both also anticipated that inflation would peak in 1981 and then decline steadily. Here President Carter was much more pessimistic; he assumed inflation of 10.5 percent in 1981 (measured by the gross national product deflator rather than by the

Consumer Price Index), gradually diminishing to 7.0 percent by 1985. President Reagan anticipated a peak inflation rate of 9.9 percent and a much sharper fall to 5.4 percent. The higher inflation rate more than offset the lower rate of real GNP growth, so that President Carter projected nominal GNP of just over $4.6 trillion in 1985, compared with $4.5 trillion by President Reagan.

Both projections were quite wide of the mark. The 1981–1982 recession and the concurrent restrained growth of the money supply held both real GNP growth and inflation well below either forecast. Real GNP declined by almost 2 percent during 1982 instead of rising by 3½ or 4 percent. At the same time, the inflation rate fell to 6 percent in 1982 (3 percent at an annual rate by the end of the year), 2.3 percentage points below the Reagan forecast and 3.3 points below President Carter's. Nominal GNP in 1982 was $220 billion below President Carter's projection and $250 billion below President Reagan's projection, both of which were made less than two years earlier.

The Reagan administration has often been criticized for its over-optimistic economic projection—its "rosy scenario"—at the beginning of 1981. Its estimates of tax revenue, however, were quite similar to those of the Congressional Budget Office at the same time.[7] Both forecast rather similar growth rates of nominal GNP; from 1980 to 1985, CBO expected an average annual growth rate of 11.65 percent compared with the administration's 11.40 percent. The administration anticipated higher real growth in GNP and lower inflation than CBO anticipated, but the differences almost canceled out. Like the administration, CBO did not then foresee the 1981–1982 recession. In this failure they were not alone. During the summer of 1981, several months after the administration's budget proposals and economic projections were published, two-thirds of the private economic forecasters participating in the annual survey of the National Association of Business Economists felt that the next recession would not begin until after the end of 1982.[8] At the time, however, the recession was actually just beginning.

The strong economic recovery of 1983 and the first half of 1984 have not been enough to offset much of the loss in tax revenue resulting from the recession. Real GNP in 1983–1984 has probably grown at about 5.2 percent annually, compared with the 4.75 percent projected by the Reagan administration in 1981. This growth is not enough to offset the effect of the recession. Nominal GNP has grown much more slowly than originally anticipated because the recovery has been accompanied by a very small upturn in the inflation rate from the cyclical trough. The annual inflation rates have remained well below the forecasts—about 3.8 percent as compared with 6.5 percent. Nominal

GNP during the recovery has therefore grown at an annual rate about 2½ percentage points below the 1981 projection—9.2 percent against 11.6 percent. Since tax revenues are a function of nominal GNP, the low inflation has meant that revenue growth is continuing to fall short of the original projections, despite the strength of the recovery.

As a result, the president's FY1985 budget forecasts a 1985 real GNP that is about 5.7 percent lower than his 1981 forecast, a price level that is 6.9 percent lower, and a nominal GNP that is 11.7 percent ($525 billion) lower. In terms of annual changes, actual and currently projected real growth averaged 1.3 percent less than the 1981 projection, inflation averaged 1.8 percent less, and nominal growth averaged almost 2.5 percent less.

It is tempting to try to disaggregate the resulting revenue shortfall into components attributable to the recession (for which the administration has often been blamed) and the reduction in inflation (for which it likes to claim credit), but this exercise is likely to be misleading. Economically, it is certainly questionable—at best—to treat the two phenomena as separate events that happened to occur at the same time. The reduction in inflation would not have been as great in the absence of the recession; the recession would not have been as severe—might not even have occurred—if the goal of reducing inflation had not been pursued as vigorously by the administration and the Federal Reserve.

There are various budgetary rules of thumb that give a rough measure of the changes in revenue resulting from changes in either real GNP or the inflation rate. Calculations by OMB indicate, for example, that a percentage point increase in either has the same effect on revenues because it has the same effect on nominal GNP, and revenue changes are assumed to be proportional to changes in nominal GNP. This rule would imply that slightly more than half the revenue shortfall in FY1985 is attributable to the inflation rate that is lower than originally assumed by the administration.[9] But the calculation is at best a rough guide to the approximate relative importance of errors in forecasting inflation and real GNP.

The 1981 Tax Cut: Proposal versus Accomplishment. President Reagan's original proposal to cut taxes in 1981 had two main features: a three-year reduction in the personal income tax rate schedule of 10 percent each year (the Kemp-Roth plan) and a liberalization of the depreciation rules for capital equipment, which applied to both the personal and the corporate income tax (the Accelerated Cost Recovery System, ACRS or "10-5-3"). The plan also included some minor increases in user fees for airports and waterways.

The bill actually passed by Congress modified these proposals in important ways and added several other changes. The reduction of the personal income-tax rate was smaller—5 percent rather than 10 percent in the first of the three years—and went into effect three months later than planned. The smaller first-year reduction and the delay of course reduced the magnitude of the tax cut, particularly in 1981. But in some other respects, ERTA lowered taxes more than the president had requested. The income tax brackets were indexed, beginning in 1985, eliminating the phenomenon of "bracket creep" by which inflation pushed taxpayers into higher marginal tax brackets and thereby raised their taxes, even if their before-tax incomes only kept pace with inflation. A deduction for two-earner married couples was also added, in an attempt to end the "marriage tax penalty"; previously, married couples with nearly equal earnings would pay more in taxes than if they were single. Other minor reductions were also included.

Most parts of the ACRS proposal were passed by Congress, but several changes resulted in larger tax cuts. Depreciation schedules for real estate were shortened. The president had proposed that unsubsidized rental housing should be depreciated over an eighteen-year period on a straight-line basis (that is, slightly more than 5½ percent a year), rather than the much longer periods under previous law. Congress instead permitted the write-off to occur over fifteen years at a faster rate, 175 percent of the declining balance (12 percent the first year, 10 percent the second, and smaller percentages in later years). It also liberalized the rules under which unprofitable firms could transfer unused depreciation deductions to profitable firms for tax purposes.

ERTA also included a small reduction in corporate income tax rates, several changes in the estate and gift taxes, and incentives to increase savings in the personal income tax (notably the universal Individual Retirement Account).

The net effect of all these changes was to reduce the tax reduction that was originally proposed, as table 1-1 shows. Postponing the first year of the personal income tax rate reduction and cutting it in half has more than offset all of the additional tax cuts combined, at least through 1985. (Sometime after 1985, when indexing goes into effect, ERTA will result in lower tax revenues than the 1981 proposal; the precise date depends on the inflation rate.) The effect was particularly strong in 1981 and 1982, as would be expected; less than half the original proposed tax cut was realized in the former year and about 80 percent in the latter.

The table also shows that the recession and the lower rate of inflation reduced tax revenues by much more than ERTA increased them over the president's original projections. The FY1984 budget asserts that the difference in inflation—5 percent less in the aggregate from 1981 through 1984—was enough in itself to reduce tax rates (presumably in terms of real income) to about the levels originally proposed. That is, ERTA plus lower inflation equaled Kemp-Roth.[10]

Tax Increases, 1982–1984. Because the recession reduced tax revenues much more than originally projected and the deficit was increasingly recognized as an economic and political problem, the administration and Congress agreed on four measures to raise tax revenues between 1982 and 1984. The revenue effects of these laws are shown in table 1–1.

The largest measure was the Tax Equity and Fiscal Responsibility Act of 1982 (TEFRA). This law modified the ACRS and the 1981 leasing provisions, raised several excise taxes and the federal unemployment tax on payrolls, and imposed withholding on interest and dividends. The most important revenue-raising provisions were those concerning depreciation.

At the trough of the recession, the postelection session of Congress also passed an increase in the gasoline tax, more than doubling it from four cents to nine cents per gallon. This money was earmarked primarily for highway construction and repair, but one cent was also set aside for mass transit construction projects. The tax was passed partly as an antirecession measure, to stimulate the economy through public works construction projects, and partly out of concern about the "decaying infrastructure" of older cities and rural areas.

Also at the end of 1982, the presidentially appointed National Commission on Social Security Reform presented a set of changes in the social security system designed to ensure its fiscal solvency for the foreseeable future. The commission's deliberations attracted great attention because of public awareness that the social security program would be unable to meet its obligations within a few months unless benefits were reduced or taxes were increased. The commission's recommendations were passed as the Social Security Amendments of 1983. The details of these amendments are discussed in the next section; here I merely point to the modest increases in revenue for 1985, as shown in table 1–1.

In 1983 one provision of TEFRA, withholding on interest and dividends, was repealed before it had a chance to go into effect. Withholding was controversial both when it was passed and when it was repealed after a strong lobbying effort by the banking industry. Its revenue effects, however, are also minor.

Most recently, as the deficit remained high despite the recovery, Congress passed the Deficit Reduction Act of 1984. This law changed the tax code in many ways. It repealed or postponed several of the 1981 tax provisions that had been scheduled to go into effect after 1984, limited the tax benefits available on property leased by tax-exempt organizations, tightened the requirements for and reduced the savings from income averaging, increased the depreciation period for real property investment from fifteen to eighteen years, and raised liquor taxes, among other changes. Not one of these changes is important by itself in 1985: only two are expected to increase revenues by as much as $1 billion; and the largest, income averaging, will bring in $2 billion. (In later years, however, the effects of several of the other provisions will become much more important.)

Outlays

The two outlay projections are presented in table 1–2. Before discussing them in detail, I will describe the structure of the table. The budget is presented primarily on the basis of the functional categories used by the Office of Management and Budget rather than on the basis of agency or congressional committee responsibility. In a few cases, however, the categorization changed between 1981 and 1984. Most notably, a new category of "social security and Medicare" has been created; previously the former was included in "income security" and the latter in "health." I have separated social security and Medicare and further subdivided the income security category into "other retirement," "unemployment compensation," and "low-income benefit programs." This division facilitates the identification of differences by category in the Reagan budget proposals and the subsequent projection errors. The low-income benefit term is also used in the 1985 budget, where it includes Medicaid as well as income security programs.[11] I have followed this convention in the table, leaving a small "other health" category. Another categorical change in the budget involves military retirement: in 1981 it was included in defense, in 1984 in income security. I have consistently reported it in the former category.

A glance at the table shows that the biggest dollar discrepancy by far is in the category of interest on the federal debt. This by itself accounts for nearly 90 percent of the total difference reported in the table. The second largest 1981 dollar underestimate of projected outlays, and the largest percentage underestimate, is in agriculture. Others in the $5 billion range include offsetting receipts ($7.0 billion), transportation ($6.2 billion), low-income benefit programs ($5.4 bil-

TABLE 1-2
PROJECTED FISCAL 1985 OUTLAYS, 1981 AND 1984
(billions of dollars)

Budget Category	March 1981	February 1984	Difference
National defense	303.9	289.3	−14.6
International affairs	12.2	17.5	5.3
General science, space, and technology	6.8	8.8	2.0
Energy	8.0	3.1	−4.9
Natural resources and environment	9.2	11.3	2.1
Agriculture	4.2	14.3	10.1
Commerce and housing credit	2.2	1.1	−1.1
Transportation	20.9	27.1	6.2
Community and regional development	7.2	7.6	0.4
Education, training, employment, and social services	24.0	27.9	3.9
Social security	201.1	190.6	−10.5
Other retirement	33.5	28.4	−5.1
Medicare	68.7	69.7	1.0
Other health	9.4	10.8	1.4
Unemployment compensation	16.7	20.1	3.4
Low-income benefit programs	65.0	70.7	5.7
Veterans' benefits and services	27.6	26.7	−0.9
Administration of justice	4.0	6.1	2.1
General government	4.5	5.7	1.2
General-purpose fiscal assistance	6.8	6.7	−0.1
Interest	83.4	116.1	32.7
Allowances	8.1	0.9	−7.2

(Table continues)

15

TABLE 1–2
(Continued)

Budget Category	March 1981	February 1984	Difference
Offsetting receipts	− 39.7	− 35.3	4.4
Total outlays	887.7	925.5	37.8

NOTE: Details may not add to totals because of rounding.
SOURCES: U.S. Executive Office of the President, Office of Management and Budget, *Fiscal Year 1982 Budget Revisions* (March 1981); *Budget of the United States Government, FY 1985* (February 1984).

lion), and international affairs ($5.3 billion). The changes in international affairs and transportation were also large as a percentage of the original projection. Other large percentage but small dollar errors occurred in the categories of administration of justice (52 percent, or $2.1 billion), general science, space, and technology (29 percent, or $2.0 billion), and unemployment compensation (27 percent, or $4.3 billion).

There are also a few categories in which the 1981 projection was thought to be too high by 1984. Most notable are national defense ($13.7 billion), social security ($10.5 billion), and energy ($4.9 billion, or 61 percent of the 1981 projection).

Table 1–2 identifies the categories in which projection errors have occurred but does not explain why those errors occurred. The reasons are basically the same as for the revenue shortfall: inaccurate economic forecasting, failure to achieve exactly what the administration proposed in 1981, and subsequent policy reversals. In the remainder of this section these factors are discussed in their approximate order of importance.

Economic Forecasting. As with revenues, the inability to forecast changes in the economy contributed more than any other factor to the discrepancy in expenditures. It is entirely responsible for the additional interest burden of the federal debt. The cumulative deficit between fiscal years 1981 and 1984 inclusive was projected in 1981 to be $122.2 billion; in 1984 it was projected at $547.6 billion. The total federal debt at the end of FY1984 was projected at $1,591.6 billion in the 1985 budget, an increase of more than 50 percent, more than $500 billion, from the debt level projected in March of 1981 ($1,036.5 billion). This is also an increase in the total debt outstanding of nearly

$700 billion in four years from the level of $914.3 billion at the end of FY1980.

With these higher deficits have come higher interest rates on the federal debt. In 1981 the ninety-one-day Treasury bill rate was projected to be 6.0 percent by 1985. In the 1984 budget, it is projected to be 7.7 percent. (In an arithmetic sense, the higher-interest outlays could be broken down into shares resulting from the higher burden of debt and the higher interest-rate structure; but since the latter is in large part the result of the former, the exercise would be somewhat misleading.)

Less important as a source of outlay discrepancy is the 1981–1982 recession. The Reagan administration did not forecast this recession when it prepared its original expenditure projections. While the recession is now over, it has had lingering budgetary consequences on the outlay side, as well as on revenues. The unemployment rate was originally projected to be 6.0 percent by 1985;[12] in the 1985 budget, that projection was raised to 7.6 percent. Unemployment compensation was therefore projected to be about $3 billion more than originally anticipated.[13] Some low-income benefit programs are also projected to have higher outlays as a result. Food stamps and Aid to Families with Dependent Children are particularly affected. Total outlays in this category are projected to be about $1 billion higher than they would have been had the administration's original economic forecast proved correct.[14]

The recession also deserves a significant part of the blame for the increase in agricultural price supports, amounting to more than $8 billion. Other factors have also contributed, notably the appreciation of the dollar which has reduced American food exports; a farm price-support bill enacted by Congress in 1981; and the Reagan administration's own change of program in 1983. The latter two changes, however, could be described as policy responses to the recession.

Partly offsetting these increases in projected outlays is the inflation rate, which has proven to be substantially lower than the administration originally projected and far lower than President Carter's last budget, or most economic forecasters, projected. The result has been lower nominal outlays for various programs than originally expected.

It is not feasible to trace through all the budget savings that result from the lower inflation, but table 1–3 offers a rather crude adjustment that may at least give some sense of the magnitudes. It adjusts each 1981 projection for the difference in the GNP deflator projection between 1981 and 1984. President Reagan originally forecast that the deflator would have a level of 252.4 in calendar year 1985; his 1985

TABLE 1–3
PROJECTED REAL FY1985 OUTLAYS, 1981 AND 1984
(billions of 1985 dollars)

Budget Category	March 1981	February 1984	Difference
National defense	284.3	289.3	5.0
International affairs	11.4	17.5	6.1
General science, space, and technology	6.4	8.8	2.5
Energy	7.5	3.1	−4.4
Natural resources and environment	8.6	11.3	2.7
Agriculture	3.9	14.3	10.4
Commerce and housing credit	2.1	1.1	−1.0
Transportation	19.6	27.1	7.5
Community and regional development	6.7	7.6	0.9
Education, training, employment, and social services	22.5	27.9	5.4
Social security	188.1	190.6	2.5
Other retirement	31.3	28.4	−2.9
Medicare	64.3	69.7	5.4
Other health	8.8	10.8	2.0
Unemployment compensation	15.6	20.1	4.5
Low-income benefit programs[a]	51.6	60.9	9.3
Veterans' benefits and services	25.8	26.7	0.9
Administration of justice	3.7	6.1	2.4
General government	4.2	5.7	1.5
General-purpose fiscal assistance	6.4	6.7	0.3
Interest	NA	NA	NA
Allowances	7.6	0.9	−6.6

(Table continues)

TABLE 1–3
(Continued)

Budget Category	March 1981	February 1984	Difference
Offsetting receipts	− 37.1	− 35.3	1.8
Total outlays[b]	743.1	799.6	56.5

NA = not applicable.

NOTE: Details may not add to totals because of rounding.

a. Omits bond payments on public housing and mortgage payments on Section 8 housing projects.

b. Omits payments fixed in dollars by previous commitment (public housing, Section 8, and interest on the federal debt).

SOURCES: Same as table 1–2. Outlays deflated by GNP deflator for calendar year 1985, as projected. The March 1981 projection was 6.9 percent greater than that made in February 1984.

budget projects a deflator of 236.1. The difference, 6.9 percent, is used to deflate the 1981 outlay projections in each budget category. The table omits the interest category, because a substantial share of it is paid on long-term bonds issued before 1981 and, therefore, unaffected by unforeseen changes in the inflation rate. For the same reason, interest and mortgage payments for subsidized housing are also omitted; these amounts are determined by interest rates and construction costs at the time the projects were built or subsidized.

Outlays in some program categories are much more sensitive to changes in prices of specific commodities than to changes in the general price level, and some of these prices have moved in quite divergent directions, as for example food and medical care. Table 1–3 does not attempt to adjust individual outlay category amounts by the prices most applicable to them. If this were done, it is clear that Medicare, for example, would be higher in March 1981 than is shown in the table and that the difference would be lower. Other budget categories are sufficiently broad that these adjustments would probably be minor. In the low-income-benefit category, for example, food stamps and nutrition programs would be lower in 1981, and Medicaid would be higher; the net effect would be little change.

Overall, the lower inflation rate may have held down projected outlays by about $15 to $20 billion, on the assumption that policy would have been made on the basis of the real value of the money spent in specific program categories. In some cases this assumption is questionable—elementary and secondary education, for example, were funded at close to a constant nominal dollar amount from 1982 through 1984—but in general it may not be unreasonable.

Social Security and Medicare. As noted previously, the 1981 budget revision contained a category of "additional savings to be proposed," which were not subsequently identified. Lawrence Kudlow, who served as chief economist at OMB at the beginning of the Reagan administration, has said that this category represented expected cuts in social security and Medicare but that the administration later decided that achieving significant reductions in these programs was politically impossible. When Health and Human Services Secretary Richard Schweiker proposed saving $9 billion per year by reducing social security benefits for earlier retirees, the Senate quickly and unanimously passed a resolution of disapproval.[15]

Some changes have been made in social security and Medicare, however. The 1981 Omnibus Budget Reconciliation Act contained several changes in Medicare, particularly increases in the deductibles for hospital insurance and supplementary medical insurance, which in the aggregate were projected to reduce outlays by slightly more than $1 billion in 1985.[16] The administration's 1983 budget proposal went much further, proposing additional budget cuts of $3.7 billion and a revenue increase of $900 million from integrating federal workers into the hospital insurance program. It also promised further reform proposals in the FY1984 budget to save an additional $4.1 billion by 1985. As part of TEFRA, Congress approved a rather different package of Medicare savings, focusing more on reduction in reimbursements to hospitals and amounting to $2.8 billion in 1985 outlays. It also approved the inclusion of federal employees in the hospital insurance program. Administration proposals in the FY1984 and FY1985 budgets have involved much smaller savings, about $2 billion and $1 billion, respectively. The 1984 proposals represented a significant redesign of the program, which some analysts have found conceptually preferable to the current approach, emphasizing more protection for catastrophic illness and more cost sharing for shorter hospital stays. These proposals were not repeated in 1985.[17]

The administration did originally propose several changes in social security as part of its March 1981 budget revisions. These changes included the elimination of three small components of the program: the minimum benefit, already mentioned; benefits for full-time adult students (aged 18–21 years) who are dependents of retired or disabled social security recipients; and the lump sum death benefit. President Reagan also proposed tighter administration of the disability insurance program, including a cap on benefits to any individual. These changes were projected to save $5.8 billion in 1985. Congress approved most of these changes as part of the Omnibus Budget Reconciliation Act and added further small reductions. The minimum benefit, however, was restored in separate legislation later in 1981. The net savings enacted in 1981 were therefore about $4 billion for FY1985, using the administration's original projections.[18]

The political objection to the social security proposals apparently caused the administration to decide against submitting further reform proposals in its FY1983 budget. Instead it appointed a bipartisan National Commission on Social Security Reform and incorporated the commission's recommendations in its FY1984 budget. These recommendations saved about $4.6 billion in 1985 outlays while adding about $5.4 billion in 1985 revenues.

Thus the administration did in fact eventually propose about $15 billion worth of savings in social security and Medicare, and Congress approved about $13.6 billion, although the specific reductions in Medicare were not identical to those proposed. This approved amount is about 30 percent of the original $43.7 billion of "additional savings to be proposed." In addition, the administration won approval of about two-thirds of its original proposed cuts in social security but at a political cost sufficient to discourage further efforts.

Later budgets do not mention the "additional savings" category nor identify any particular budget reductions as being intended to fulfill the March 1981 goal. The administration's FY1983 budget did propose about $5 billion of reductions in low-income benefit programs, $3 billion of it in the food stamp and child nutrition programs. These proposals were mostly rejected by Congress, however, and by and large have not been resubmitted. On balance, therefore, the category of "additional savings" appears to be a special case, and a large one, in which the Reagan administration subsequently changed its policy.

Congressional Rejection. Across many categories of the budget President Reagan was unable to persuade Congress to approve all of the cuts that he requested. Projected outlays therefore did not decline by 1985 as much as the president originally projected. In several instances the administration has subsequently decided not to resubmit the original proposals, thereby implicitly conceding that it is unable to cut the budget as much as it would like.[19]

The programs involved are quite diverse. Even a partial list of failures illustrates the range of budget-cutting efforts launched by the administration in its first months in office.

One of the largest categories—in terms of both success and fail-

21

ure—is education. The administration asked for cuts of $4.4 billion from the Carter budget for FY1982; it received $2.2 billion. For Title I of the Elementary and Secondary Education Act, which supports aid to educationally deprived children, the administration asked for a reduction of $1.4 billion and received $800 million. For vocational education assistance, it wanted to cut $270 million, and Congress approved $150 million. In the area of higher education, the administration wanted to limit eligibility for Pell grants to needy students, reducing outlays by $600 million; Congress accepted limitations that would save $300 million.

Also in the the budget category of education, training, employment, and social services, the administration sought to consolidate more than twenty programs into the social services block grant and reduce funding by $3.6 billion (from $5.8 billion to $2.2 billion). Congress rejected most of the consolidation and cut funds by $2 billion instead. Among the programs to be consolidated were those of the Community Services Administration, the last vestige of the original "war on poverty" agency, the Office of Economic Opportunity; this cut would have saved $540 million. Congress created a separate community services block grant, funded at $390 million, giving the administration $150 million of the savings it asked. It also abolished the agency.

The administration received most of the cuts that it sought from the low-income benefit programs, but Medicaid was a conspicuous exception. President Reagan proposed a limitation on the federal share of Medicaid funding in 1982 to no more than 5 percent above the amount in 1981, with future outlays rising only as rapidly as the GNP deflator. This limit would have saved more than $900 million in 1982 rising to $4.9 billion by 1985. Congress approved a much less stringent limitation, for only the years 1982 through 1984, which saved about a quarter as much as the administration wanted during those years. New proposals submitted in February 1982 as part of the FY1983 budget would have saved $3.6 billion in 1985. Congress approved savings of about $300 million as part of TEFRA.

The other fiscally important failure in this program category was the low-income home energy assistance program, which provides payments for heating bills. The administration wanted to cut this program by $500 million, more than 25 percent; Congress instead approved a reduction of $36 million, about 2 percent.

The president asked for changes in the unemployment compensation program that would have saved about $800 million. Congress approved several limitations on the extended benefits program (which provides thirteen weeks of additional support for those who have already received twenty-six weeks of payments) but rejected a plan to require beneficiaries to accept jobs at the minimum wage, outside their previous occupation, after thirteen weeks of regular benefits. The savings on extended benefits amounted to about two-thirds of the amount originally sought by the president.

In energy, the administration wanted to cut almost $700 million in FY1982, three-quarters of the total, from energy conservation programs, consisting of both technological development and "weatherization" assistance for the poor, for schools, and for hospitals. Congress approved a cut of about $500 million. The administration's original goal for 1985 was to cut more than $450 million from the Carter budget; by the time it drew up its own FY1985 budget, it was proposing to cut only about $225 million.

Several proposals in the category of natural resources and environment were only partially accepted or were totally rejected. The administration wanted to impose user fees for the inland waterway system, which it estimated would yield $640 million by 1985. Congress approved a much smaller program, which the FY1985 budget projected would produce only $170 million. The administration has continued to ask for additional charges; the FY1985 budget sought $200 million. The administration also tried to terminate three grant programs—for urban parks, historic preservation, and state and local recreation areas—saving about $300 million; Congress refused to make the cuts and continued full funding. Finally, Congress rejected a controversial proposal for a moratorium on land acquisition for the national parks and forests, which would have saved about $230 million in FY1982.

The administration was quite successful in trimming community and regional development, particularly economic development, but again did not get everything that it wanted. It sought to terminate the Economic Development Administration, saving about $900 million annually; Congress cut the budget to $300 million but would not abolish the agency. Similarly the administration was unable to end the Appalachian Regional Commission but did get the budget cut in half, from $400 million to $200 million.

In the category of administration of justice, President Reagan originally wanted to terminate two small agencies, the Office of Juvenile Justice and Delinquency Prevention ($200 million) and the Legal Services Corporation ($400 million). Congress refused. By the FY1985 budget, the administration had given up on the former, so its budget request was $200 million higher than it projected in 1981. It is still trying to get rid of the Legal Services Corporation.

In the science category, the administration originally wanted to cut the budget of the National Science Foundation by $200 million. Congress approved half of the reduction.

In the aggregate, the Reagan administration proposed budget cuts of about $15.3 billion for these diverse programs. It was able to win approval of only about $6.0 billion. The remaining $9.3 billion is about a quarter of the shortfall in the specific FY1985 budget savings proposed in March 1981 and more than 10 percent of the total specific cuts from President Carter's projected 1985 outlays. Moreover, this list omits certain categories, for example, transportation and agriculture, which will be discussed subsequently, as well as social security and Medicare.

In subsequent years, Congress has voted to increase outlays in many of the budget categories that it cut in 1981. The FY1984 budget approved by Congress, in particular, included some $10 billion more domestic expenditures than those requested by the administration. The largest increases were in education, training and employment, and social services ($3.0 billion), natural resources and environment ($2.7 billion), and commerce and housing credit ($1.8 billion). The total budget was only about $1 billion above the administration's request; the domestic increases were offset by a $5 billion cut in defense and the assumption of $5 billion savings in interest on the national debt (which did not materialize).[20]

There were very few offsetting instances in which the administration was able to get *more* budget cuts than it originally projected. Table 1–3 shows only three functional categories: energy, commerce and housing credit, and other health. Most of the reductions in energy are bogus; the Omnibus Budget Reconciliation Act put the Strategic Petroleum Reserve off budget, "in what members [of Congress] freely admitted was creative accounting,"[21] thereby reducing on-budget outlays in 1985 by about $2 billion. Another $1.5 billion of the reduction below the administration's original projection comes from stretching out construction of Tennessee Valley Authority power-generating plants; authorized construction has not been affected. There was, however, one real reduction: the administration cut energy research and development by an additional $1 billion annually in FY1983 after reducing it by about $400 million in its first year. In the category of commerce and housing credit, the additional saving is due to a change in the practices of the Federal Housing Administration. Beginning in 1983, FHA collects the entire premium for its mortgage insurance at the time the loan is approved; previously it collected the premium in monthly installments over the life of the loan.

These few instances of additional budget cuts hardly modify the general pattern. The administration was unable to win approval of a substantial minor fraction of its original cuts when it first proposed them, and it has subsequently been unable to persuade Congress to adopt them. These additions to the administration's proposed budget demonstrate the validity of words often attributed to the late Senator Dirksen: "A billion here and a billion there, and soon it adds up to real money."

Policy Reversals. Most of the greatest differences reported in tables 1–2 and 1–3 result from changes in policy by the administration after its first year in office. The largest reversal has occurred in the functional category of transportation.

The administration first sought to cut spending to $19.9 billion, some $1.7 billion or almost 8 percent below the Carter proposal for 1982. It planned to hold spending at about that level, rather than to allow increases, so that by 1985 the savings would have grown to some $6.9 billion. Congress approved most of the requested cuts for the 1982–1984 period as part of the Omnibus Budget Reconciliation Act.

Administration policy changed abruptly, however, at the trough of the 1981–1982 recession. In the postelection session of Congress, it embraced an increase in the gas tax of five cents per gallon for highway and mass transit construction. This was projected to add about $1.7 billion to highway trust-fund revenues in 1983 and $3.9 billion annually beginning in 1984. The administration correspondingly increased its projected outlays for highways by $3.4 billion in 1984 and $4.1 billion in 1985. (One cent of the additional tax was earmarked for mass transit projects, but this was approximately offset by changes in outlays from general revenue.) In the FY1984 budget, the administration also proposed an increase of $0.9 billion in budget authority for air transportation, financed from an increase in aviation user fees. The money is to be spent for capital modernization and airport improvement grants.

In agriculture the administration has also changed course, to a more modest extent and with much less effect on the budget. The first budget issue to come before Congress in 1981 was a reduction in dairy price supports. The administration fought for this reduction and was successful. At the same time it announced an intention to submit a farm bill that would reduce crop support outlays. The 1981–1982 recession, however, prompted Congress to enact its own price support bill, and the recession and the law combined to drive up farm income stabilization (price support) expenditures by $7.6 billion from FY1981 to FY1982, nearly tripling outlays in a single year. The administration then proposed a new payment-in-kind (PIK) program, in which farmers of key crops would receive commodities—the crops they had previously sold to the government—rather than cash in return for reducing their production. The administration estimated that PIK would generate $3.1 billion in savings in 1984 and $6 billion in 1985, because the commodities would be a replacement for money that would otherwise have to be authorized, appropriated, and spent as part of the federal budget.

The program has proved to be unexpectedly generous, however. More farmers chose to participate than the administration had anticipated, and the government was therefore forced to *buy* grain to fulfill its obligations; its stockpiles were inadequate. The government's costs also were increased because the stocks that it owned were often not located close to the farmers who were to receive them.[22] The FY1985 budget therefore projected that PIK would save only about half of the previous budget's estimate. A new farm bill must be approved by Congress this year, and the administration has indicated a continued intention to try to restrain farm price supports. It also blames the 1981 farm bill as well as the depressed economy for the high level of price supports.[23]

Nonetheless it seems clear that the administration has moderated its original intention to reduce price supports sharply. In the fall of 1984, the president also announced a plan to defer principal and interest payments on Farmers Home Administration loans to farmers with continuing financial problems; this will add slightly to the deficit by reducing repayments of the loans, but it is more important as a possible symptom of a shift in the administration's attitude toward agricultural programs.

Similar but smaller shifts have occurred in many other categories. In international affairs, about $2 billion of the differences between the projections in table 1–2 is due to expanded military equipment sales to foreign countries and aid to Central America. About $1 billion, however, is due to legislation passed in 1983 placing the foreign military sales credit loan program on budget beginning in FY1985. (The administration also sought and received additional budget authority of $8.5 billion for the International Monetary Fund in 1983, which it did not plan in 1981, but this amount does not show up in 1985 outlays.) In education, the administration, apparently reacting to the report of its National Commission on Excellence in Education, proposed to spend an additional $700 million. In science, proposed outlays have risen by about $1 billion between the FY1983 and FY1985 budgets; in the administration of justice category, they have risen by about $2 billion. These outlays amount to about 15 percent and 50 percent, respectively, of the FY1983 proposals. Again Senator Dirksen's comment seems appropriate.

Addendum: The Mid-Year Budget Revision. The discussion in this section and the data in tables 1–2 and 1–3 are based on the president's FY1985 budget, announced in February 1984. The budget contains more detail about individual programs and budget categories than any other document and is therefore the best guide to the changes in outlays from year to year. But it is not the most current picture of the 1985 fiscal year. In August 1984 the administration published its *Mid-Session Review of the 1985 Budget,* an annual update taking into account changes in economic assumptions and federal policy.[24] Expenditure estimates for FY1985 in the *Mid-Session Review* are $5.1 billion higher than in the FY1985 Budget. In most categories, however, the differences are minor.

The largest increase is for interest on the federal debt, projected at $130.2 billion, up $14.1 billion or 12 percent from six months earlier. This increase is entirely the result of changing economic assumptions; interest rates rose instead of falling.

The largest dollar decrease is for national defense, $9.8 billion or 3 percent. This decrease results primarily from changes in the administration's policy as part of the deficit reduction program, but the policy changes themselves apparently reflect the unwillingness of Congress to accept as rapid an increase in defense spending as the administration originally proposed. To a minor extent, also, the lower inflation rate has helped to hold down defense outlays.

The largest percentage decrease is for unemployment compensation, 21 percent or $4.3 billion. This decrease is entirely due to the unexpected strength of the economic recovery in the first half of 1984.

Most other budget categories show small increases.

The *Mid-Session Review* does not greatly change the overall pattern of differences between the March 1981 and February 1984 outlay projections. A greater share of the increase in projected expenditures is apparently due to the inaccurate economic forecast, particularly of interest rates. Congress also has shown more unwillingness to accept the administration's budget priorities, but this involves more of a shift between categories than an increase in total expenditures.

Conclusion

Failure to forecast the economy correctly is clearly the most important factor contributing to the discrepancy between the March 1981 and

FY1985 budget projections of the 1985 deficit. It accounts for more than the total $105 billion shortfall in revenues and probably slightly more than half of the $81 billion of expenditures in excess of the original projection.

The administration tried to mitigate the effect of the recession's lowering GNP and of the lower inflation rate by raising taxes in several ways during 1982–1984. These increases, however, have not been adequate to offset more than a minor fraction of the revenue shortfall from economic changes.

To a much lesser extent, failure to control domestic expenditures has contributed to the deficit. Apart from social security and perhaps Medicare, the sums involved in individual programs and even in functional budget categories are not large in the context of a near-trillion-dollar budget, but they do add up to about $10 billion more than the administration originally proposed to spend. Policy reversals in a few areas, unaccompanied by corresponding cuts elsewhere, have also contributed to the deficit.

Defense has not contributed to the discrepancy. Defense expenditures in the FY1985 budget are projected to be $14 billion less than originally expected. The reason is the lower rate of inflation; in constant (1985) dollars, the defense projection has increased by about $6 billion. But this figure is still not a large contributor to the outlay discrepancy. (The lower rate of inflation is also responsible for most of the reduction in social security.)

These findings have obvious implications for the deficit picture in the next five years. The administration's budget projects annual average real growth at 4 percent over that time. Growth at this rate would be well above the 3.3 percent average of the entire postwar period. It would be about the same as the country experienced during the corresponding period after the last five postwar recessions, on the average, and this may be the administration's basic rationale for the projection.[25] But this average includes one recovery, after the 1960–1961 recession, when there was no second recession during the following seven years. If that episode is set aside as atypical, the average growth for the other four periods is 3.7 percent, significantly enough below the administration's projection to result in substantially larger budget deficits than it now forecasts. Alternatively, the administration may believe that it can repeat the experience of the 1960s. That recovery, however, was strengthened and lengthened by an expansive monetary and fiscal policy beginning in 1965, as President Johnson sought to fight both the Vietnam War and the War on Poverty simultaneously and without raising taxes, a decision that was the source of the fifteen-year period of inflation that President Reagan has worked so steadily to bring to an end. The historical record is not encouraging to the administration's view that such growth can be sustained over so long a period without inflation.

The recent record also shows that deficits rise dramatically during recessions and are reduced only to a much lesser extent during the succeeding recovery. Such was the situation during the 1974–1975 recession, as the deficit rose from $15 billion in FY1973 to $66 billion in FY1976, and again in the course of the two recessions of the early 1980s, as the deficit went from $27 billion in FY1979 to more than $200 billion by FY1983. Another recession within the next two or three years would begin with a deficit already of more than $150 billion.

Notes

1. U.S. Executive Office of the President, Office of Management and Budget, *Fiscal Year 1982 Budget Revisions* (March 1981), p. 11. The president also projected a balanced budget in FY1984.

2. U.S. Executive Office of the President, Office of Management and Budget, *Budget of the United States Government: FY1985* (February 1984), p. 3–55.

3. For the record, it may be worth noting that President Carter projected a surplus of $85 billion in 1985. Both revenues and expenditures were projected to be much higher than President Reagan expected. President Carter did not propose a tax cut or indexation, and he anticipated much greater inflation; so revenues were projected to be $1.067 trillion.

4. For a discussion of budget projections for the next four years, see the paper by William Beamon, Jacob Dreyer, and Paul van de Water in this volume.

5. Congressional Budget Office, *Baseline Budget Projections for Fiscal Years 1985–1989* (February 1984), Appendix D. Additional data have been provided by Paul van de Water of CBO. Data provided by OMB indicate that about five-sixths of the deficit, rather than the entire deficit, can be attributed to incorrect economic forecasts. The difference does not greatly affect the argument in the text.

6. *FY1985 Budget*, pp. 4–8 to 4–9.

7. Congressional Budget Office, *Economic Policy and the Outlook for the Economy* (March 1981), summary table 3 and table 16.

8. Don R. Conlan and Grace E. Wickersham, "Highlights of the 1982 Economic Outlook Survey," unpublished paper presented at the September 1981 meeting of the National Association of Business Economists.

9. Data provided by Doug Norwood of OMB. Alternative rule-of-thumb estimates from CBO indicate that the effect of a percentage-point change in real economic growth is about 50 percent larger than that of a similar change in the inflation rate. This would imply that about 57 percent of the 1985 revenue shortfall resulted from the recession and the lower real growth during

the period. Congressional Budget Office, *The Economic and Budget Outlook: An Update* (September 1982), appendix B.

10. U.S. Executive Office of the President, Office of Management and Budget, *Budget of the United States Government: FY1984* (February 1983), p. 3–19.

11. *FY1985 Budget,* "Budget Program and Trends," pp. 3–27 to 3–30.

12. The assumption of 6.0 percent unemployment may have been unrealistic from the start. The CBO projection in March 1981 was that unemployment would be 7.5 percent in 1985. Congressional Budget Office, *Economic Policy and Outlook* (March 1981), summary table 3.

13. The strength of the economic recovery has caused the projected unemployment rate for 1985 to be lowered to 6.5 percent in the Mid-Session Review and projected outlays for unemployment compensation to be lowered correspondingly to $15.8 billion. U.S. Executive Office of the President, Office of Management and Budget, "Mid-Session Review of the 1985 Budget" (August 15, 1984), pp. 34–35.

14. This estimate is derived from an OMB Technical Staff Memorandum, "Sensitivity of Federal Expenditures to Unemployment," unpublished paper, April 18, 1980. Outlays for food stamps are calculated to rise by about $400 million for each percentage point increase in the unemployment rate; outlays for AFDC, by a little less than $200 million. Other benefit programs are much less sensitive. I have not attempted to adjust the OMB figures for programmatic changes since 1980.

15. Nicholas Lemann, "The Culture of Poverty," *The Atlantic* (September 1984), p. 29.

16. U.S. Executive Office of the President, Office of Management and Budget, *Budget of the United States Government: FY1983* (February 1982), pp. 5–129 to 5–132.

17. For a detailed discussion and evaluation of the Medicare changes since 1981, see Jack A. Meyer, "The Unfinished Agenda in Health Policy," in John C. Weicher, ed., *Maintaining the Safety Net: Income Redistribution Programs in the Reagan Administration* (Washington, D.C.: American Enterprise Institute, 1984), especially pp. 80–84.

18. In September 1984 Congress passed and the president signed a bill to set more stringent standards for terminating benefits in the Disability Insurance program. This came after widespread criticism of the administration's program for reviewing disability claims, begun under the Omnibus Budget Reconciliation Act of 1981. Critics charged that numerous Disability Insurance recipients had been unfairly and inappropriately dropped from the program, and several state courts limited the states' authority to conduct the reviews. It is not yet possible to estimate the additional outlays that will result from the looser standards approved in 1984. Pamela Fessler, "Disability Measure Wins Unanimous Approval," *Congressional Quarterly* (September 22, 1984), pp. 2332–2334.

19. It is difficult to be precise about the differences between the 1981 proposals and the administration's achievements. The Omnibus Budget and Reconciliation Act typically authorized funds only for FY1982, or at most through

FY1984. Thus it did not automatically represent either acceptance or rejection of the president's FY1985 proposals. In this section I have assumed that approval of the proposals for 1982 implied approval of those for 1985, unless Congress took action indicating otherwise at the same time; and similarly that rejection for 1982 implied rejection for 1985. Other reasonable approaches are possible; my sense is that they would not greatly affect the basic point of this section, although they would change the dollar values.

20. Dale Tate, "Congress Rebuffs President, Clears '84 Budget Resolution," *Congressional Quarterly* (June 25, 1983), pp. 1269–1274.

21. Andy Plattner, "Strategic Reserve Funding, First Energy Authorization in Reconciliation Measure," *Congressional Quarterly* (August 15, 1981), pp. 1507–1508. The quotation is on p. 1508.

22. Ronald Brownstein, "In Era of Record Deficits, Farm Price Supports Seem Likely Target for Cuts," *National Journal* (February 11, 1984), pp. 270–273.

23. *FY1985 Budget*, "Budget Program and Trends," pp. 3–35 to 3–37.

24. "Mid-Session Review of the 1985 Budget."

25. See *FY1984 Budget*, "Economic Assumptions and the Budget Outlook," pp. 2–13 to 2–16.

2

Dimensions of the Deficit Problem

William J. Beeman, Jacob S. Dreyer,

and Paul N. Van de Water

Summary

Since the mid-1960s federal spending has grown at a very rapid rate, far outpacing the growth of the economy. As economic performance deteriorated in the 1970s, popular dissatisfaction with the growing role of the federal government in the economy became apparent. In response to this dissatisfaction, the newly elected administration and the Congress undertook in the early 1980s measures aimed at reducing the role of the federal government in the economy. But it proved much easier for policymakers to restrain revenue growth than spending growth. The ratio of federal spending to GNP rose in FY1983 to a new post–World War II record, while the growth of revenues was restrained by tax cuts and recession. As a result, the federal deficit rose in FY1983 to a record 6.1 percent of GNP and remained at an exceedingly high level, 4.8 percent in FY1984.

One consequence of very large budget deficits in recent years has been a rapid build-up of federal debt. It reached a low point in 1974 and was relatively stable, as a percentage of GNP, through 1981 but has been rising steeply ever since. Ironically, the cost of financing the rapidly growing debt has been a major cause of spending growth in recent years; it also makes reducing growth in spending more difficult in future years.

Most budget projections indicate that very large budget deficits will persist at least through the 1980s unless major policy actions are taken. For example, the CBO "baseline" budget projections as of August 1984, which assume an extension of budget policies now in place, show deficits averaging 4.7 percent of GNP in the 1985–1989 period. Whether such large deficits would actually be realized and, if so, what their effect on the economy would be are two of the most hotly debated public policy issues today. This paper focuses on the former issue—the magnitude of the deficits, including the likely range of outcomes under alternative economic assumptions.

The first section below presents CBO projections of aggregate revenues, outlays, and the resulting budget deficit. These projections are based on assumptions about the performance of the economy in the second half of the 1980s, a performance that is only about average by post–World War II standards but quite good against the background of the past fifteen years. Yet, even under these relatively optimistic assumptions about the economy, the rate of growth of outlays over the next five years slightly exceeds that of revenues, so that the deficit as a percentage of GNP actually grows somewhat over this period. The first section also contains estimates of sensitivity of aggregate revenues and outlays to variations in three key economic variables influencing budgetary aggregates: real growth, interest rates, and the rate of inflation. One conclusion that can be drawn from this information is that, should the performance of the economy be inferior to that assumed by CBO, the growth of budget deficits would be much faster.

Section two places the deficit problem in a historical perspective. Data show that the seeds of large deficits of the 1980s were already sown in the 1970s, when the structural deficits—that is, deficits resulting from policies rather than attributable to the vicissitudes of the economic cycle—began to grow. The trend toward growing structural deficits has become accentuated in the last two years as the tax cuts of 1981 have been phased in and as the economy has rebounded from the 1981–1982 recession.

Section three looks in some detail at the revenue side of the federal budget. Personal income taxes, despite rate reductions in 1981–1983 and indexing provisions, will continue to provide the bulk of federal revenues. Social insurance receipts, which have risen over the post–World War II decades to some 35 percent of total revenues, will stabilize at their current levels both as a share of revenues and a percentage of GNP. Corporation income taxes, which, as a share of total revenues, are only one-third of what they were in the immediate postwar period, will continue to play their present, relatively modest, role as a source of revenues. The section on revenues contains estimates of sensitivity of revenues from various sources to the three key economic variables mentioned earlier. Should real growth and the rate of inflation be higher than assumed, the share of corporate income taxes will rise in relation to that of individual income taxes.

The last section examines the spending side of the budget. Until recently the only major spending category that was rising continuously was social security and Medicare. This category, as a percentage of GNP, has stabilized, however, and is not projected to rise noticeably in the second half of the decade. National defense has been the most volatile major spending category during past decades. As percentage of GNP it reached its trough in the late 1970s and has been gradually climbing through the first half of the 1980s. This climb is projected to continue until 1989, albeit at a slower pace than in recent years. The most rapid rate of increase has been displayed by the spend-

ing category "net interest." Just from 1980 to 1984, net interest spending as a share of GNP has risen by about two-thirds. Rapid growth in interest payments on the federal debt is projected to continue and rise in importance relative to other outlays. As a result, future deficits will become ever more influenced by the level of interest rates.

Budget Projections through the 1980s

The baseline budget projections of the Congressional Budget Office (CBO) for the second half of this decade show very large and rising budget deficits if budget policies remain unchanged. The federal deficit would fluctuate in the range of 4.5 to 4.9 percent of GNP, providing an unprecedented string of federal deficits and would cause the outstanding federal debt held by the public to rise from 36 to 46 percent of GNP. Both spending and revenues would rise faster than overall economic activity; budget outlays would rise from a near record 23.5 percent of GNP in fiscal year 1984 to 24.3 percent by the end of the decade, while revenues would rise from 18.7 percent to 19.4 percent of GNP (see table 2–1).

TABLE 2–1

FEDERAL BUDGET PROJECTIONS WITH UNCHANGED POLICIES,
FISCAL YEARS 1985–1989

	Actual	Base	Projections				
	1983	1984	1985	1986	1987	1988	1989
In billions of dollars							
Revenues	601	666	751	811	881	965	1,042
Outlays	796	842	929	1,006	1,097	1,203	1,305
Unified budget deficit	195	175	178	195	216	238	263
Debt held by the public[a]	1,142	1,312	1,497	1,706	1,936	2,189	2,466
As percentage of GNP							
Revenues	18.6	18.6	19.1	19.1	19.2	19.4	19.4
Outlays	24.7	23.5	23.7	23.7	23.9	24.2	24.3
Unified budget deficit	6.1	4.9	4.5	4.6	4.7	4.8	4.9
Debt held by the public[a]	35.4	36.7	38.1	40.2	42.1	44.1	46.0

a. End of year figures.
SOURCE: Congressional Budget Office.

Because no attempt is made to forecast policy changes, these budget projections should not be regarded as best-guess projections. Instead, they are conditional projections based upon the assumption of no policy change. Moreover, they provide only a rough order of magnitude of the deficit problem, even with fixed policies, because there is great uncertainty concerning the performance of the economy, especially several years into the future, which could have profound effects on the budget.[1]

The economic assumptions underlying the projections are shown in table 2-2. Given the uncertainty in the economic outlook and the extreme sensitivity of outlays and revenues to economic conditions, out-year economic projections are based on historical trends as far as possible. Thus real GNP increases by 32.2 percent in the seven-year period from the fourth quarter of 1982—the recession trough—to the fourth quarter of 1989. This increase equals precisely the average growth following the troughs of recessions in the postwar period. Whether this methodology will minimize errors is uncertain. Certainly a wide range of possible economic conditions in the second half of this decade cannot be rejected with a high degree of certainty. This uncertainty accounts for the debate concerning the extent to which rapid economic growth is likely to reduce budget deficits.

An illustration of the sensitivity of the budget to economic conditions is provided by comparing the administration and CBO budget

TABLE 2-2

ECONOMIC ASSUMPTIONS FOR CALENDAR YEARS 1986–1989

	Actual	Forecast		Projected			
Economic Variable	1983	1984	1985	1986	1987	1988	1989
GNP[a]	7.7	11.5	8.7	8.1	8.3	8.0	7.9
Real GNP[a]	3.7	7.3	3.6	3.1	3.3	3.1	3.0
CPI-U (all-urban)[a]	3.2	4.4	5.0	4.9	4.8	4.8	4.8
Civilian unemployment rate[b]	9.6	7.3	6.7	6.6	6.4	6.3	6.3
Three-month Treasury bill rate[b]	8.6	10.0	9.7	8.9	8.9	8.9	8.9
Corporate bond rate (Moody's AAA)[b]	12.0	13.1	12.3	11.5	11.5	11.5	11.5

a. Percent change year over year.
b. Percent.
SOURCE: Congressional Budget Office.

projections prepared in August 1984 (see table 2–3). The administration's projection shows the deficit declining gradually to $139 billion (2.6 percent of GNP) by fiscal year 1989, whereas CBO's projection shows the deficit rising to $263 billion (or 4.9 percent of GNP). Though there are some differences in assumed budget policies, $89 billion of the $124 billion differential in the deficit projections reflects different economic assumptions. About $59 billion of this difference reflects lower interest rates, while most of the remainder is due to the effect of faster growth on revenues. Although the administration's economic assumptions are more optimistic than CBO's, they are not completely without historical precedent. For example, the administration projection assumes 4.6 percent average annual growth over the seven-year period of expansion beginning with the 1982:IV trough, well below the 5.0 rate following the 1961 recession. (CBO assumes a lower average growth rate of 4.0 percent, precisely equal to the average postwar recovery). Thus, while the authors would attach a higher

TABLE 2–3

COMPARISON OF ADMINISTRATON AND CBO BUDGET PROJECTIONS,
1985–1989

	1985		1987		1989	
	Adminis-tration	CBO	Adminis-tration	CBO	Adminis-tration	CBO
Budget projections (fiscal years)						
(billions of dollars)						
Revenues	764	751	904	881	1,070	1,042
Outlays	931	929	1,077	1,097	1,209	1,305
Deficit	167	178	173	216	139	263
(percentage of GNP)						
Revenue	19.4	19.1	19.4	19.2	19.7	19.4
Outlays	23.6	23.7	23.1	23.9	22.3	24.3
Deficits	4.2	4.5	3.7	4.7	2.6	4.9
Economic assumptions (calendar years)						
GNP ($ billions)	4,030	4,004	4,747	4,687	5,521	5,466
Unemployment rate (%)	6.7	6.7	6.3	6.4	5.8	6.3
Treasury bill rate (%)	9.3	9.7	7.2	8.9	5.1	8.9
Inflation rate (%)	4.7	4.9	4.2	4.8	3.6	4.8

SOURCE: Congressional Budget Office.

probability to the CBO budget projections, the administration's economic and budget projection cannot be rejected as totally unrealistic.

Another way of gauging the effects of changes in economic assumptions on projections is by using rough orders of magnitude or rules of thumb. Table 2–4 illustrates the budgetary effects of a one-percentage-point change beginning in October 1984 for two variables: real economic growth and interest rates. These rules of thumb show the following:

• An increase in the real growth rate will increase revenues and decrease outlays and the deficit. If real growth is one percentage point higher than assumed for the CBO projections throughout the 1985–1989 period, the 1989 baseline deficit will be reduced by $105 billion.

• If interest rates are one percentage point higher than assumed by CBO, the baseline deficit for 1989 will be higher by $26 billion. Almost all of this change will be reflected in net interest outlays. Under the assumptions used by CBO, revenues will be little affected.

• An increase in inflation (not shown in the table) will have little effect on the deficit, if both discretionary spending and interest rates respond to the change.

These results should not be interpreted as alternative economic scenarios. Sustained changes in one economic variable do not generally occur without changes in other variables as well. Also, a one-percentage-point change in variables was assumed as a convenience

TABLE 2–4

THE EFFECTS ON BASELINE BUDGET PROJECTIONS
OF ONE-PERCENTAGE-POINT HIGHER ANNUAL RATES
BEGINNING OCTOBER 1984, FISCAL YEARS 1985–1989
(billions of dollars)

	1985	1986	1987	1988	1989
Real Growth					
Change in revenues	8	22	38	56	77
Change in outlays	−1	−4	−9	−17	−28
Change in deficits	−9	−26	−47	−73	−105
Interest Rates					
Change in revenues	1	1	1	1	1
Change in outlays	5	10	15	22	27
Change in deficit	4	10	14	21	26

SOURCE: Congressional Budget Office.

and not as a reflection of typical forecasting errors. Interest rates tend to be volatile and difficult to forecast, especially in recent years. Real growth rates, although they fluctuate greatly from year to year, tend to be more stable over five-year periods. Hence, a one-percentage-point average error in projecting interest rates for five years is more probable than a one-percentage-point error in projecting real growth rates.

Trends in Budget Aggregates

Federal spending as a proportion of GNP has risen sharply in the post–World War II period. Generally the upward trend has been interrupted only for short periods when wartime spending has wound down. Recently the growth in spending has slowed but, as a share of GNP, its growth appears to have accelerated. In the 1950s and 1960s revenues grew with outlays, but in the 1970s, revenues remained virtually constant as a share of GNP (see figure 2–1).

FIGURE 2–1
BUDGET TOTALS AS PERCENTAGE OF GNP, FISCAL YEARS 1950–1989

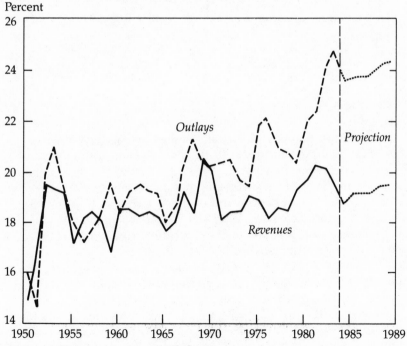

SOURCE: Congressional Budget Office.

FIGURE 2-2

FEDERAL DEFICIT AS PERCENTAGE OF GNP, FISCAL YEARS 1950–1989

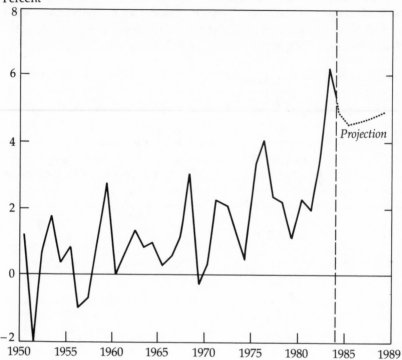

Percent

Projection

SOURCE: Congressional Budget Office.

As a proportion of GNP, federal outlays averaged 18.2 percent in the 1950s, 19.4 percent in the 1960s, 20.8 percent in the 1970s, and 23.4 percent in the first five years of the 1980s. The sharp rise in spending in the 1980s is surprising in view of the political efforts to reduce nondefense spending and of the fact that each of the earlier decades incorporated periods of wartime mobilization. Part of the explanation is the severity of the 1981–1982 recession, which was deeper than all other post–World War II recessions. Rapidly rising deficits also have been a major contributor to spending growth; about one-third of the increase in the spending-to-GNP ratio in this decade reflects the rising burden of financing increased deficits.

In the 1950s and 1960s the ratio of federal revenues to GNP was on a upward trend—similar to the growth in the spending-to-GNP ratio. The revenue-to-GNP ratio averaged 17.8 percent in the 1950s and 18.6 in the 1960s. As a result, deficits averaged less than 1 percent

FIGURE 2–3
PUBLIC DEBT AS PERCENTAGE OF GNP, FISCAL YEARS 1950–1989

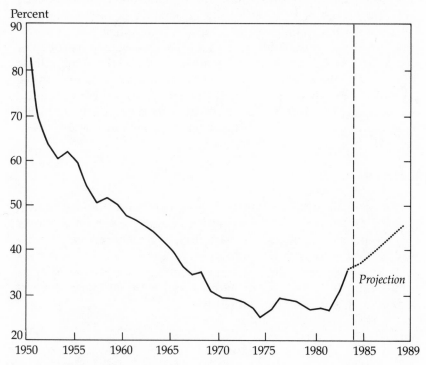

Percent

Projection

SOURCE: Congressional Budget Office.

of GNP in both decades. But in the 1970s there was no increase in the revenue-to-GNP ratio, and the deficit rose. Although revenues grew rapidly in FY1981 and FY1982 (revenues exceeded 20 percent of GNP), the ratio fell sharply in the following two years. Total revenues averaged about 18.6 percent of GNP during fiscal years 1983–1984, as the phased-in tax cuts reduced the tax burden back to the levels experienced in the 1960s and 1970s.

The combination of rising outlays and flat revenues (relative to GNP) caused deficits to rise to nearly 2.0 percent of GNP during the 1970s. After declining during the entire post–World War II period, the federal debt began to rise faster than GNP in the mid-1970s. With the recent acceleration of spending, the deficit-to-GNP ratio averaged 3.8 percent in the first half of the 1980s and, as indicated earlier, established a new record high in FY1983 (see figure 2–2). As a result, the outstanding federal debt held by the public has grown from 27.3 percent of GNP to 36.4 percent at the end of 1984 (see figure 2–3).

The rising deficits of the past few years are only partly explained by the cyclical behavior of the economy. Budget deficits that are not cyclical are said to be structural, that is, embedded in the policies rather than resulting from slack in the economy. Calculations showing what the deficits would have been at a constant unemployment rate show a rise in structural deficits in the 1970s and again in recent years (see table 2–5). In fact, as these estimates indicate, the standardized budget deficit realized in 1983 and 1984 was exceeded only once in the post–World War II period—during the 1968 Vietnam War build-up. But the rising structural deficit in recent years is not totally unrelated to economic conditions; the reduced rate of growth in productivity in the 1970s and 1980s contributed to rising structural deficits.

Federal Revenues

In the years since World War II, the composition of federal budget receipts has undergone considerable evolution. In fact, in many respects our present structure of budget receipts only remotely resembles the one in force in the immediate postwar years. The two most conspicuous trends in the postwar evolution of receipts are the spectacular growth of trust funds and a persistently declining share of corporate income taxes in total receipts.

TABLE 2–5

TRENDS IN BUDGET AGGREGATES, FISCAL YEARS 1950–1984

(percentage of GNP)

Period	Outlays	Revenues	Deficit	Structural Deficit	Publicly Held Debt
1950–1959	18.2	17.8	0.4	n.a.	60.2
1960–1969	19.4	18.6	0.8	0.5	40.2
1970–1979	20.8	18.9	1.9	1.2	28.2
1980–1984	23.4	19.7	3.8	1.5	31.5
1980	22.4	20.1	2.3	1.2	27.8
1981	22.8	20.8	2.0	0.5	27.6
1982	23.9	20.3	3.6	0.6	30.4
1983	24.7	18.6	6.1	2.4	35.4
1984	23.5	18.6	4.9	3.0	36.7

n.a. = not available.

SOURCE: Congressional Budget Office.

Growth of Trust Funds. In 1946, after taxes imposed during the war were reduced, receipts by trust funds, net of interfund transactions, amounted to less than 7.4 percent of total budget receipts. Until the mid-1950s the share of receipts by trust funds (net of interfund transfers) in total budget receipts was rising rather slowly. In the mid-1950s the growth of trust fund receipts accelerated rapidly, and already by 1961 their share in total budget receipts exceeded 20 percent. In 1971 their share stood at 28.5 percent, in 1981 at 31.5 percent, and in 1984 at more than 37 percent.

This unmistakable trend toward greater importance of trust funds is also reflected in surpluses of these funds, especially against the background of deficits incurred year after year in federal funds. During the first twenty years following World War II, trust funds typically enjoyed small surpluses, in the order of $1 billion to $3 billion annually. From the mid-1960s, surpluses of trust funds started growing, albeit erratically, thus partially offsetting consistent deficits of the federal funds (see figure 2–4). For 1984 the surplus of trust funds exceeded $25 billion, in contrast to the federal funds deficit of some $200 billion. By the end of this decade, annual surpluses of trust funds are projected to increase more than fourfold in current dollars from their 1984 levels.

For purposes of macroeconomic analysis, the distinction between federal funds and trust fund receipts is largely immaterial. Because trust fund surpluses are used for purchases of Treasury securities, they directly reduce demand for private savings by the federal government and hold down the rate of growth of government debt held by the public. From this perspective, the unified budget concept is the appropriate one for analyzing the effects of fiscal policy on the economy. To the extent that trust fund receipts are earmarked for funding specific programs or projects, however, their use is, by definition, more constricted than the use of general purpose receipts. Therefore, other things being equal, the trend toward an ever greater share of trust fund receipts in total budget receipts tends to reduce the flexibility of fiscal policy.

Trends in the Composition of Tax Revenues. On the eve of World War II, the two most important sources of federal government revenues were excise taxes and social insurance taxes and contributions. In 1940, receipts from these two sources were about equal in size and together accounted for 56 percent of total government revenues. Individual and corporate income taxes, also about equal in size, accounted for another 33 percent.

FIGURE 2-4
TRUST FUND SURPLUSES AND FEDERAL FUNDS DEFICITS,
FISCAL YEARS 1950–1989

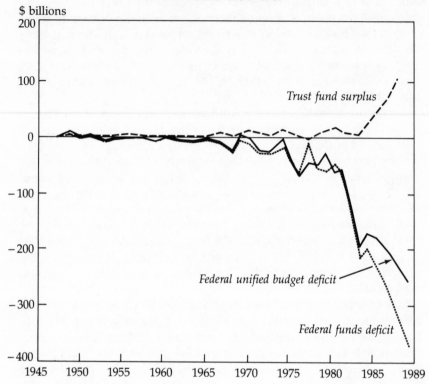

SOURCE: Congressional Budget Office.

The war changed this picture drastically. At the height of the war effort, in 1944, the combined share of excise taxes and social insurance taxes and contributions dropped to 17.5 percent, while income taxes, individual and corporate, provided 80 percent of total government revenues. Even as taxes came down after the war, the dominant importance of income taxes has remained a central feature of the U.S. tax system. In 1946, individual income taxes alone provided 41 percent of total receipts and corporate income taxes accounted for another 31 percent. Social insurance taxes and contributions amounted to only 7.8 percent of total receipts and all excise taxes to 16.9 percent.

Over the next two decades, the share of individual income taxes in total receipts, while fluctuating from year to year, started climbing (see figure 2–5). The respective shares of corporate income taxes and excise taxes displayed a discernible drift downward, while the share of

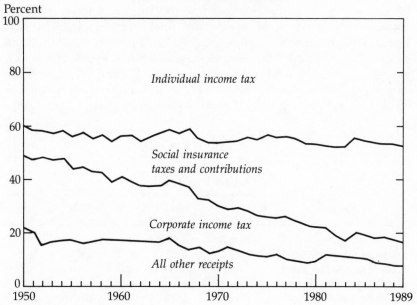

FIGURE 2–5
REVENUES BY SOURCE, AS PERCENTAGE OF TOTAL RECEIPTS,
FISCAL YEARS 1950–1989

Percent

Individual income tax

Social insurance
taxes and contributions

Corporate income tax

All other receipts

SOURCE: Congressional Budget Office.

social insurance taxes and contributions climbed quite rapidly. These trends of the first two postwar decades have become even more accentuated since the mid-1960s. First the tax surcharge of the Vietnam War era and then the inflation-induced bracket creep of the 1970s pushed individual income taxes as a share of total receipts into a higher range, hovering around 45 percent. In 1982 and 1983, the share of individual income taxes exceeded 48 percent of total revenues—the highest level ever. Social insurance taxes and contributions also reached a record level as a percentage of total government receipts—34.8 percent in 1983. Conversely, the share of corporate income taxes fell in 1983 to a record low of 6.2 percent. The share of excise taxes stabilized in recent years at around 6 percent of total receipts, and the share of miscellaneous receipts has also remained stable at about 5 percent (see table 2–6).

Changes in tax laws in 1981–1982 and economic expansion, which began at the end of 1982, combined to bring down, at least temporarily, the share of individual income taxes and to halt further slide in the share of corporate income taxes.

45

An analysis of receipts from various sources as a percentage of GNP would, for understandable reasons, uncover the same broad long-term trends as an analysis of these receipts in terms of their share of total revenues. Nonetheless, a few conclusions derived from the former analysis are worth a mention. Total receipts settled in their apparently permanent range of roughly 18–20 percent of GNP in the mid-1950s. On one hand, receipts from individual income taxes as a percentage of GNP, while fluctuating between 7.4 and 9.9 percent, are at present basically at the same level as they were thirty years ago (they were 8.1 percent in 1954 and 8.4 percent in 1984). On the other

TABLE 2–6

COMPOSITION OF FEDERAL REVENUES BY SOURCE,
FISCAL YEARS 1950–1984

Source	1950	1960	1970	1980	1984
In billions of dollars					
Individual income taxes	15.7	40.7	90.4	244.1	298.5
Corporate income taxes	10.5	21.5	32.8	64.6	56.9
Social insurance taxes and					
contributions	4.4	14.7	44.4	157.8	239.4
Excise taxes	7.5	11.7	15.7	24.3	37.4
All other receipts	1.4	3.9	9.6	26.4	34.4
Total receipts	39.5	92.5	192.8	517.1	666.5
As share of total receipts					
Individual income taxes	39.9	44.0	46.9	47.2	44.8
Corporate income taxes	26.5	23.2	17.0	12.5	8.5
Social insurance taxes and					
contributions	11.1	15.9	23.0	30.5	35.9
Excise taxes	19.1	12.6	8.1	4.7	5.6
All other receipts	3.4	4.2	4.9	5.1	5.1
Total receipts	100.0	100.0	100.0	100.0	100.0
As percentage of GNP					
Individual income taxes	5.9	8.2	9.3	9.5	8.3
Corporate income taxes	3.9	4.3	3.4	2.5	1.6
Social insurance taxes and					
contributions	1.7	2.9	4.6	6.1	6.7
Excise taxes	2.8	2.3	1.6	0.9	1.0
All other receipts	0.5	0.8	1.0	1.0	1.0
Total receipts	14.9	18.6	19.9	20.1	18.6

NOTE: Detail may not add to totals because of rounding.
SOURCE: Congressional Budget Office.

hand, social insurance taxes and contributions as a percentage of GNP rose almost three-and-a-half times. Over the same thirty years, corporate income taxes fell from some 6 percent of GNP to less than 2 percent, excise taxes from about 2.5 percent to 1 percent, and all other receipts doubled from 1/2 to 1 percent of GNP.

Revenue Projections. Baseline revenue projections are those that would accrue if current tax laws were to remain in effect throughout the projection period[2] and if the economy were to perform according to the economic assumptions summarized above. These projections are, therefore, conditional forecasts of the government receipts; both changes in tax laws and performance of the economy significantly different from the assumed pattern are most likely to affect considerably baseline revenue projections. Furthermore, the tax laws in force, and more generally the stance of fiscal policy reflected in spending and revenue projections, need not be consistent with the economic assumptions underlying those projections. Economic assumptions for the so-called out years, that is, years beyond the nearest two for which traditional economic forecast is made, are essentially derived from an adjusted average performance of the economy following a cyclical trough. These assumptions are, consequently, invariant with respect to changes in tax laws otherwise expected to have either macroeconomic or microeconomic effects. With these caveats in mind, table 2–7 summarizes baseline revenue projections for 1985–1989 disaggregated by major tax categories.

Perhaps the most conspicuous feature of these projections is the relative constancy of total revenues as a percentage of GNP. For comparison, it may be noted that variations in this particular measure of total revenues over a five-year period have been much greater, and year-to-year changes of more than one half of a percentage point have not been unusual. The relative constancy of projected revenues as a percentage of GNP is due to a smooth growth pattern embedded in the long-term economic assumptions and the postulated absence of changes in tax laws that may produce discrete large changes in the total receipts-to-GNP ratio.

Growth in projected receipts from 1985 to 1989 is more than fully accounted for by the climbing share of individual income taxes. Despite the tax-rate cutting provisions of the Economic Recovery Tax Act of 1981, individual income taxes as a share of GNP will climb back by 1989 to the levels prevailing in 1979–1980. Furthermore, as a share of total revenues, individual income taxes will, by 1989, reach once again the post–World War II record levels observed in the recession years

TABLE 2-7

PROJECTED COMPOSITION OF FEDERAL REVENUES BY SOURCE,
FISCAL YEARS 1985-1989

Source	1985	1986	1987	1988	1989
In billions of dollars					
Individual income taxes	342.2	374.8	410.9	454.3	498.0
Corporate income taxes	65.8	73.5	85.5	91.0	95.8
Social insurance taxes and contributions	267.6	289.8	310.7	345.1	372.3
Excise taxes	38.8	35.5	36.0	34.9	34.4
All other receipts	36.8	37.3	38.0	39.3	41.1
Total receipts	751.2	810.9	881.1	964.6	1,041.6
As share of total receipts					
Individual income taxes	45.5	46.2	46.7	47.1	47.8
Corporate income taxes	8.8	9.0	9.7	9.4	9.2
Social insurance taxes and contributions	35.7	35.7	35.2	35.8	35.7
Excise taxes	5.1	4.4	4.1	3.7	3.3
All other receipts	4.9	4.6	4.3	4.1	3.9
Total receipts	100.0	100.0	100.0	100.0	100.0
As percentage of GNP					
Individual income taxes	8.7	8.8	8.9	9.1	9.3
Corporate income taxes	1.7	1.7	1.9	1.8	1.8
Social insurance taxes and contributions	6.8	6.8	6.8	6.9	6.9
Excise taxes	1.0	0.8	0.8	0.7	0.7
All other receipts	0.9	0.8	0.8	0.8	0.8
Total receipts	19.1	19.1	19.2	19.4	19.4

NOTE: Detail may not add to totals because of rounding.
SOURCE: Congressional Budget Office.

1981 and 1982. By contrast, the second largest revenue category—social insurance taxes and contributions—after decades of virtually uninterrupted increases, have reached a plateau both as a share of total revenues and as a percentage of GNP.

Corporate income taxes are also projected to remain quite stable both as a share of total revenues and a percentage of GNP. In contradistinction to social insurance taxes and contributions, however, the relative importance of this revenue category is stabilized at the lower end of its post-World War II range.

Excise taxes, the role of which has been gradually declining for the last thirty years, will continue on a downward trend both as a share of total revenues and as a percentage of GNP. The combined share of remaining categories of receipts (estate and gift taxes, customs duties, earning by the Federal Reserve System) will decline from about 5 percent of total revenues in 1984 to some 4 percent in 1989, even though as a percentage of GNP its decline is less apparent.

Sensitivity of Revenues to Economic Assumptions. As was indicated earlier, projected budget outcomes are conditional upon postulated economic conditions prevailing during the period under consideration. Responses of aggregate revenues to departures in real growth, and nominal interest rates, are summarized in table 2–4.

It bears repeating that the computation of sensitivity of revenues to changes in a particular economic variable abstracts from interdependence between this and other economic variables. Acceleration of real growth, for example, is assumed in these exercises to occur without any change in either interest rates or the rate of inflation. Thus the purpose of such an exercise is to isolate the "pure differential effect" of an alternative path for a particular economic variable rather than to provide alternative revenue projections.

Depending on which economic variable departs from the path assumed in the baseline projection, the effect on revenues may be very different from that on outlays. Furthermore, different categories of revenues may react quite differently to a departure of a given economic variable from its baseline path. A case in point is the effect on revenues of higher nominal interest rates. Table 2–4 demonstrates that, while the effect of higher interest rates on outlays is immediate and cumulatively powerful, it has only a minor effect on revenues. The reason for such a low sensitivity of revenues to higher interest rates is, essentially, that higher interest income is about matched by higher interest-payment deductions. If it were not for higher earnings of the Federal Reserve System on Treasury securities (which are, of course, reflected dollar for dollar by higher Treasury payments), higher interest rates would have an almost imperceptible effect on revenues.

By contrast, the effect on revenues of a one-percentage-point higher annual rate of real growth is, understandably, large. As can be seen from table 2–4, initially almost the entire amount of deficit reduction due to higher growth can be accounted for by higher revenues. The sensitivity of outlays to a higher real growth rate becomes more pronounced over time, as the deceleration in the rate of growth of

TABLE 2–8

EFFECT OF ONE-PERCENTAGE-POINT HIGHER ANNUAL REAL GROWTH
RATE ON REVENUES BY SOURCE, FISCAL YEARS 1985–1989

(billions of dollars)

Revenue Source	1985	1986	1987	1988	1989	Total
Individual income	2.2	7.3	13.7	21.3	30.0	74.5
Corporate income	3.7	9.3	15.8	22.8	30.9	82.5
Social insurance taxes and contributions	1.8	4.5	7.4	11.0	14.6	39.3
Custom duties	0.1	0.2	0.3	0.5	0.7	1.8

SOURCE: Congressional Budget Office.

federal debt begins to be reflected in less rapidly rising interest payments.

Sensitivity of various categories of revenues to higher growth is quite uneven. Table 2–8 presents estimates of additional revenues by source attributable to a rate of real growth one percentage point above the path assumed in the baseline projection. While additional individual and corporate income-tax revenues generated by higher real growth are about the same, the sensitivity of corporate income-tax revenues is much higher than that of individual income-tax revenues. In 1989, higher real growth results in corporate income taxes 32.2 percent higher than in the baseline projection, while individual income taxes are only 6 percent above the baseline level. The much greater sensitivity of corporate income-tax revenues is almost entirely due to a larger economic profit share, that is a larger share of GNP accruing to the corporate sector.

Social insurance receipts are even less sensitive to real growth than individual income-tax revenues. A one-percentage-point higher annual growth rate by 1989 raises these receipts about 4 percent above the baseline projection. This is not surprising. Except under most unusual growth and employment patterns, growth of personal income is likely to be higher than growth of the wage bill. Furthermore, increased social insurance receipts initially reflect predominantly higher aggregate employment, not higher wages. Only in later years does higher real growth result in increased maximum levels of wages subject to social insurance taxes. (The taxable maximum is indexed to average earnings with a two-year lag.)

It is appropriate to add that sensitivity of various revenue categories to higher real growth rates is not invariant with respect to the sources and nature of higher growth. It is assumed in CBO projections that a one-percentage-point increase in real output is associated with a 0.4-percentage-point change in the unemployment rate. Additional tax revenues, summarized in table 2–8, are computed accordingly. Should additional real growth result entirely from more rapid productivity gains, however, the effect on revenues will be substantially different. The overall beneficial effect on revenues of a one-percentage-point higher growth rate would be greater, and the sensitivity of corporate income-tax revenues in relation to that of other revenue categories is likely to be even more pronounced.

A one-percentage-point higher rate of inflation generates about two-thirds of the amount of additional revenues generated by a one-percentage-point higher real growth. With the notable exception of corporate income tax, sensitivity of separate revenue categories to inflation is not substantially different from their sensitivity to real growth. A one-percentage-point higher rate of inflation will, by 1989, boost individual income-tax revenues about 6 percent above the baseline projection level—the same as a one-percentage-point increase in real growth. In other words, an increase in nominal GNP generates roughly the same amount of additional individual income-tax revenues irrespective of whether it results from higher real growth or from more rapid inflation. Similarly, the sensitivity of social insurance receipts to higher rates of inflation is almost the same as their sensitivity to real growth.

A one-percentage-point higher annual rate of inflation, however, produces only about one-third additional revenues from corporate income taxes as compared with an analogous increase in real growth. The difference in sensitivity of this tax category—about 11 percent above the baseline level by 1989 for higher inflation versus some 32 percent for higher real growth—is due to the fact that higher inflation leaves the share of GNP going to the corporate sector virtually unchanged and raises only its taxable portion, while, as was indicated earlier, one consequence of higher real growth is likely to be an increase in the economic profit share itself.

Two remarks are in order. First, these estimates assume that the higher rate of inflation is generated domestically. If, by contrast, the higher rate of inflation were to be transmitted from abroad, through higher prices of imported goods and services, there would be much less of an increase in U.S. taxable income and, consequently, much more modest revenue gain, in particular from individual income taxes. Second, the reported low sensitivity of individual income tax to inflation is a very recent phenomenon. It is entirely accounted for by cuts in marginal tax rates phased in during 1981–1984 and by the indexing of the tax brackets, the zero bracket amount, and personal exemption beginning in 1985.

Federal Spending

In the years since World War II, federal government spending has shown a continuing tendency to rise in relation to GNP. Under current budgetary policies, this tendency continues over the next five years. The sources of federal spending growth, however, have varied over the years, as shown in figure 2–6 and table 2–9.

Trends in Spending. The only major component of spending that has shown a continuing tendency to rise is social security and Medicare. Absorbing only 0.3 percent of GNP in 1950, these two social insurance programs grew at a fairly steady clip and amounted to 6.6 percent of

FIGURE 2–6

FEDERAL SPENDING AS PERCENTAGE OF GNP, FISCAL YEARS 1950–1989

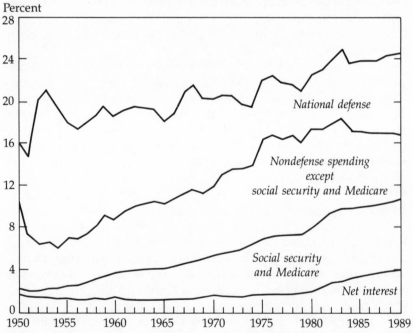

SOURCE: Congressional Budget Office.

TABLE 2-9
COMPOSITION OF BUDGET OUTLAYS, FISCAL YEARS 1950–1984

	1950	1960	1970	1980	1984
	In billions of dollars				
National defense	13.7	48.1	81.7	134.0	227.5
Social security and					
Medicare	0.8	11.6	37.4	153.6	235.8
Other nondefense spending					
Payments to individuals	12.9	12.7	28.7	129.5	160.3
Grants to state and local					
governments	1.0	4.5	15.0	57.2	50.9
Other government					
operations	11.2	13.1	27.2	69.8	88.3
Undistributed offsetting					
receipts	-1.8	-4.8	-8.6	-19.9	-32.0
Subtotal	23.3	25.5	62.3	236.6	267.5
Net interest	4.8	6.9	14.4	52.5	111.1
Total outlays	42.6	92.2	195.7	576.7	841.8
	As percentage of total outlays				
National defense	32.2	52.2	41.7	23.2	27.0
Social Security and					
Medicare[a]	1.9	12.6	18.7	26.1	28.0
Other nondefense spending	54.7	27.7	32.2	41.5	31.8
Net interest	11.3	7.5	7.4	9.1	13.2
Total outlays	100.0	100.0	100.0	100.0	100.0
	As percentage of GNP				
National defense	5.2	9.7	8.4	5.2	6.4
Social security and					
Medicare	0.3	2.3	3.9	6.0	6.6
Other nondefense spending					
Payments to individuals	4.9	2.6	3.0	5.0	4.5
Grants to state and local					
governments	0.4	0.9	1.5	2.2	1.4
Other government					
operations	4.2	2.6	2.8	2.7	2.5
Undistributed offsetting					
receipts	-0.7	-1.0	-0.9	-0.8	-0.9
Subtotal	8.8	5.1	6.4	9.2	7.5
Net interest	1.8	1.4	1.5	2.0	3.1
Total outlays	16.1	18.5	20.2	22.4	23.5

NOTE: Detail may not add to totals because of rounding.
a. Includes Medicare premiums and collections.
SOURCE: Congressional Budget Office.

GNP in 1984. Net interest spending was virtually constant at about 1.5 percent of GNP between 1950 and 1973. From then on, however, as deficits became larger and interest rates rose, net interest spending began to climb. It grew slowly at first, reaching 1.8 percent of GNP by 1979, but then took off, surging to 2.8 percent of GNP in 1982 and 3.1 percent in 1984. If deficits of about $200 billion continue, net interest outlays will continue to spiral.

The most variable component of federal spending has been national defense. Immediately after World War II, defense spending averaged only about 5 percent of GNP. In the next three years, however, the ratio of defense spending to GNP tripled, reaching 15 percent at the peak of the Korean War in 1953. From then until 1965, the ratio of defense spending to GNP declined, falling to 7.7 percent of GNP. At the height of the Vietnam conflict in 1968, defense spending reached 9.9 percent of GNP, but it thereafter resumed its decline. The low point was reached in FY1979, when defense spending absorbed 4.9 percent of the nation's output—about the same portion as it had in the 1947–1950 period. By 1984, after Carter and Reagan administration efforts to increase defense spending, the share of defense spending in GNP was 6.4 percent and rising.

Spending for nondefense programs other than social security and Medicare has been the mirror image of defense spending. Together these two categories have represented a relatively constant 14–16 percent of GNP. As defense declined from 11 percent of GNP in 1955 to 5 percent in 1979, nondefense, non-social security spending grew from 4 percent to 9 percent of GNP. Landmarks along the way included the creation of the Interstate Highway System in the Eisenhower administration, the Alliance for Progress and the manned space flight effort during the Kennedy administration, and the expansion of means-tested entitlement programs in the late 1960s and early 1970s.

Looking back over the 1950–1984 period as a whole, one sees spending increase from 16.1 percent to 23.5 percent of GNP—an increase of 7.4 percentage points. This is virtually equal to the increase in social security, Medicare, and net interest over those years, as shown in figure 2–6.

Spending Projections. In the baseline budget projections, which assume an extension of spending policies in place, the tendency of federal spending to rise faster than GNP continues over the next five years (see table 2–10). The share of outlays for national defense and net interest each rise by about 1 percent of GNP, while other spending falls.

Baseline budget outlays grow from $842 billion in 1984 to $1,305 billion in 1989—an increase of $463 billion. Defense spending accounts for $179 billion or 39 percent of the projected increase in total outlays. Social security and Medicare contribute 27 percent of the projected growth, and rising net interest costs account for another 22 percent. Other nondefense programs account for only 12 percent of the overall increase in outlays.

The baseline projections for defense assume 5 percent annual real growth in budget authority as an approximation of current policy; this is roughly the amount of increase provided in the two most recent congressional budget resolutions. About $70 billion of the $179 billion increase in defense outlays between 1984 and 1989 results from assuming a 5 percent annual real increase rather than no real growth, as CBO assumes for nondefense programs. Another $66 billion of the

TABLE 2–10
PROJECTED COMPOSITION OF BUDGET OUTLAYS,
FISCAL YEARS 1985–1989

	1985	1986	1987	1988	1989
In billions of dollars					
National defense	261.5	292.7	327.1	365.5	406.4
Social security and Medicare	253.8	273.3	296.8	324.1	353.0
Other nondefense spending					
Payments to individuals	170.0	179.6	188.3	199.1	209.5
Grants to state and local governments	55.6	57.5	60.1	62.0	64.1
Other government operations	87.6	90.4	94.8	100.0	103.6
Undistributed offsetting receipts	−33.0	−37.1	−39.0	−41.9	−45.7
Subtotal	280.2	290.4	304.2	319.2	331.5
Net interest	133.5	149.6	168.6	194.1	213.9
Total outlays	928.9	1,006.0	1,096.7	1,202.8	1,304.8
As percentage of total outlays					
National defense	28.2	29.1	29.8	30.4	31.1
Social security and Medicare[a]	27.3	27.2	27.1	26.9	27.1
Other nondefense spending	30.2	28.9	27.7	26.5	25.4
Net interest	14.4	14.9	15.4	16.1	16.4
Total outlays	100.0	100.0	100.0	100.0	100.0

(Table continues)

TABLE 2–10 (Continued)

	1985	1986	1987	1988	1989
	As percentage of GNP				
National defense	6.7	6.9	7.1	7.4	7.6
Social security and Medicare[a]	6.5	6.4	6.5	6.5	6.6
Other nondefense spending					
Payments to individuals	4.3	4.2	4.1	4.0	3.9
Grants to state and local governments	1.4	1.4	1.3	1.2	1.2
Other government operations	2.2	2.1	2.1	2.0	1.9
Undistributed offsetting receipts	−0.8	−0.9	−0.8	−0.8	−0.9
Subtotal	7.1	6.8	6.6	6.4	6.2
Net interest	3.4	3.5	3.7	3.9	4.0
Total outlays	23.7	23.7	23.9	24.2	24.3

NOTE: Detail may not add to totals because of rounding.
a. Includes Medicare premiums and collections.
SOURCE: Congressional Budget Office.

increase in defense spending consists of the dollars necessary simply to maintain the real value of budget authority in the face of higher prices. Finally, defense spending would increase by $43 billion between now and 1989 even if budget authority were frozen at the 1984 dollar level because outlays do not yet fully reflect the increases in budget authority provided in recent years.

About half of the projected growth in social security and Medicare results from price increases. Social security cost-of-living adjustments account for $40 billion out of the $117 billion growth projected over the next five years; and another $23 billion is due to medical price increases, which push up Medicare costs. A quarter of the growth is due to increases in the number of people eligible for benefits. The remaining growth results from increases in the utilization of medical care services by Medicare beneficiaries and from other factors.

The increases in net interest outlays result from the growing baseline deficits and the assumed continuation of high real interest rates. These interest costs, which threaten to consume an ever-increasing share of the budget, can be reduced only by cutting other spending or raising taxes.

Sensitivity of Spending to Economic Assumptions. The rapid increase in the federal debt, resulting from large and growing deficits, has made the budget increasingly sensitive to interest rates. As mentioned earlier and shown in table 2–4, a one-percentage-point increase in all interest rates would increase the 1989 baseline deficit by $26 billion, or 0.5 percent of GNP. This estimate is more than three times the comparable estimate made by CBO in 1981, when the debt was lower and balanced budgets were envisioned.

Most of the effect of higher interest rates on the deficit is attributable to higher net interest outlays. Higher interest rates directly increase interest costs on new borrowing and on refinanced debt. New borrowing in FY1985 is assumed to be $189 billion in the base case, ($191 billion in on- and off-budget deficits, offset by $2 billion in cash reduction and other means of financing). In addition, about $500 billion of marketable debt is scheduled for refinancing at least once during the fiscal year. If all interest rates were one percentage point higher, additional interest costs on this new and refinanced debt would amount to $4.2 billion in 1985. The direct effects of higher interest rates on spending and revenues add to the deficit and lead to additional borrowing, thus raising interest outlays indirectly by another $0.2 billion in 1985.

The direct and indirect effects of higher interest rates cumulate dramatically, given the large and growing deficits in the baseline projections. In fiscal years 1985–1989 about $1,158 billion in new debt is added while about $900 billion of the pre-1985 marketable debt is refinanced. When applied to such a large volume of financing, the direct effect of higher interest rates grows to $19.5 billion by 1989, while the indirect effect—reflecting cumulatively higher borrowing—is $7.0 billion.

Over a five-year horizon, net interest is also the component of federal spending most sensitive to differences in the rate of real economic growth even though in the short-run is the spending program most sensitive to differences in the real growth rate is unemployment compensation. (CBO's rule of thumb assumes that a 1.0 percentage point increase in real output is associated with 0.4 percentage point drop in the unemployment rate. By 1989, five years of higher economic growth drives down the unemployment rate by about two percentage points.) The number of low-income persons eligible for Medicaid, food stamps, and assistance payments also shrinks as unemployment falls. After a couple of years of faster growth, however, most of the change in outlays results from interest. Because higher real growth increases revenues and decreases noninterest spending, the federal debt is lower than it would otherwise be, and debt-service costs are correspondingly reduced. Of the $28 billion in lower outlays in 1989 resulting from 1 percent per year more growth, $5.2 billion is for unemployment compensation, $1.4 billion for other unemployment-sensitive programs, and $21.3 billion for net interest.

In preparing its baseline budget projections, which are designed to represent current budgetary policies, CBO assumes that virtually all spending is either explicitly or implicitly adjusted for inflation. About 30 percent of outlays are directly indexed to changes in the Consumer Price Index or similar indexes. Some other outlays, while not explicitly indexed, tend to respond more or less automatically to changes in the inflation rate. These outlays are generally those associated with programs in which the federal government is paying for the cost of services provided to eligible families and individuals, notably Medicare and Medicaid. The baseline budget projections also assume that discretionary appropriations are adjusted to keep pace with inflation (or, in the case of defense, to produce a particular real growth rate). These adjustments, however, require legislation and are not automatic, as are the increases in the directly and indirectly indexed programs. Finally, in computing the sensitivity of spending to inflation, CBO assumes that nominal interest rates will rise by one percentage point with a one-percentage-point increase in inflation.

Under these assumptions, growth in noninterest spending is—with some slight lags—essentially proportional to changes in the price level. Interest costs, however, rise more than proportionately because assumed higher nominal interest rates magnify the costs of servicing the growing national debt. Higher inflation, therefore, increases the share of federal spending devoted to interest payments.

Notes

1. In addition, there is considerable uncertainty pertaining to technical budget factors, such as spend-out rates and the response of taxpayers to previously enacted tax law changes.

2. All future changes in tax law that are currently on the books are assumed to be implemented on schedule.

3

The State and Local Government Sector and the Federal Deficit

John C. Weicher

Summary

State and local governments have been running a surplus that provides a partial offset to the federal deficit. This surplus is primarily caused by the growth of state and local government pension funds. Contributions to the funds by the governments and earnings on assets held by the funds have increased much more rapidly than benefits paid to retired employees. The pension fund surplus now is in the range of $40 billion annually and is expected to continue.

The surplus of the state and local government sector also increased sharply during 1983 and 1984 as a result of the general economic recovery. In the first year after the trough of the 1981–1982 recession, the surplus of the sector increased by over $15 billion, excluding social insurance funds. This surplus effectively offset more than one-third of the increase in the federal government deficit during the same year, mitigating the effects of the deficit on capital markets and the economy. The increase in the surplus was unusually large by historical standards, probably because state and local governments have increasingly relied more heavily on income and sales taxes as revenue sources, taxes that are more cyclically sensitive than the traditional revenue source, the property tax.

The cyclical component of the state and local surplus has diminished in the last half of 1984 and may well soon disappear altogether. The sector ran a similar surplus in 1977 and 1978, years of economic growth. But that surplus had vanished by the end of 1982, primarily as a result of tax cuts during 1978 to 1980 (the "tax revolt" that was spearheaded by Proposition 13 in Califor-

I would like to thank Karen Sukin for research assistance and David J. Levin and Hugh Knox of the Bureau of Economic Analysis for information on the BEA's state and local government modeling.

59

nia), followed by the recessions between the beginning of 1980 and the end of 1982. In the near future, expenditure increases substantially in excess of revenue growth are likely, and some tax cuts are also probable. The federal budget deficit is unlikely to decline as rapidly as the state and local surplus, given current policy and the economic outlook. The government sector as a whole will probably run a larger deficit than it did in 1983 and 1984.

Introduction

While the federal government has been running large and increasing deficits, state and local governments have been running large and increasing surpluses. For calendar year 1983, as the federal deficit increased by $30.4 billion over calendar year 1982, the state and local surplus rose by $11.2 billion. The behavior of the state and local sector has thus served to mitigate the economic effects of the federal deficit. It is not likely, however, that such behavior on the part of state and local governments will continue over the next few years. A decline in their surplus appears probable.

There are two reasons for the state and local surpluses: one cyclical, the other secular. The sector is very sensitive to economic conditions; it tends to run deficits during downturns and surpluses during recoveries. During the recession of 1981–1982, for example, the deficit of the sector, as measured in the National Income and Product Accounts, increased by $9.7 billion, at a seasonally adjusted annual rate: from a surplus of $6.0 billion in the third quarter of 1981 to a deficit of $3.7 billion in the fourth quarter of 1982. But by the fourth quarter of 1983, after a year of strong economic recovery, the sector had a surplus of $12.0 billion.

These figures exclude the social insurance funds—predominantly, the pension funds—of state and local governments. Particularly since 1974, the sector has continually run a large surplus in these funds, as assets have been built up to pay future liabilities to state and local government employees. In 1982 the surplus of the social insurance funds amounted to $33.7 billion, in 1983 to $37.5 billion. Further growth is in store.

The overall surplus of the sector in 1983 was $44.1 billion, almost exactly one quarter as large as the federal deficit of $178.6 billion. Thus a substantial part of the federal deficit was offset by the state and local surplus. The surplus is not heavily invested in federal government securities, but it does generate a demand for additional securities, both private and government, and tends to restrain interest rates in the capital markets.

Cyclical Changes in the Fiscal Position of State and Local Government

In the aggregate state and local governments have consistently behaved countercyclically. Excluding their social insurance funds, they ran deficits during each of the eight postwar recessions, helping to offset the decline in private demand. Then, during the recoveries, they built up surpluses.[1] Figure 3-1 depicts this pattern quarterly over the past twenty years, showing the sharp declines in the surplus during the 1973-1975 and 1980-1982 recessions.[2] The early stages of postwar recoveries have normally been marked by immediate, often abrupt improvements in the state and local fiscal position. Table 3-1 shows the change in the surplus during each cyclical contraction since 1958 and also during the first year of each subsequent recovery. The left side shows the changes in the fiscal position of the sector in the downturns. In each the sector's deficit increased, often quite substantially. Moreover, the increases themselves tended to increase over time; the sector has become more cyclically sensitive. The 1960-1961 deficit increase of $1.0 billion, for example, was about 0.20 percent of gross national product at the trough of the recession; the 1981-1982 increase of $7.3 billion was about 0.49 percent, or more than twice as large.

The right side shows the reduction in the deficit during the first year of each recovery. Again, the increasing cyclical sensitivity of the sector is apparent. The deficit reduction was only $300 million in 1958-1959 but $15.7 billion in 1982-1983.

Through at least 1977, the fiscal behavior of state and local governments can be explained reasonably well as a response to changing macroeconomic conditions and to relative prices for public and private goods.[3] The 1982-1983 experience seems to indicate much greater cyclical sensitivity.

Several structural changes in the tax systems of state and local governments have probably contributed to increasing their cyclical sensitivity. Individual income and sales taxes have been used more and more by the sector throughout the postwar period, while the property tax—the main source of revenue since the 1930s—has declined in importance. In 1951, for example, property taxes accounted for over 40 percent of state and local tax revenues, sales taxes for about one-third, and individual income taxes for about 5 percent. By 1981 property taxes had declined to less than one-third of tax revenue while income taxes had risen to almost 20 percent; sales tax revenue remained about the same in importance. During these three decades,

62

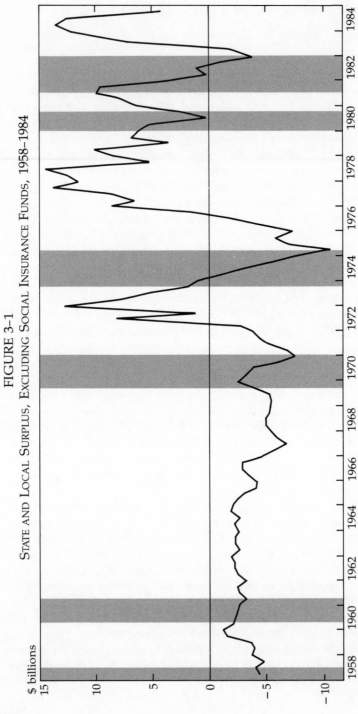

FIGURE 3-1

STATE AND LOCAL SURPLUS, EXCLUDING SOCIAL INSURANCE FUNDS, 1958–1984

NOTE: Seasonally adjusted annual rate. Shaded areas are recessions.

SOURCES: U.S. Department of Commerce, *The National Income and Product Accounts of the United States*, and *Survey of Current Business*, various issues.

TABLE 3-1

CYCLICAL CHANGES IN THE STATE AND LOCAL GOVERNMENT
SURPLUS, EXCLUDING SOCIAL INSURANCE, 1957–1983
(billions of dollars)

Recession (peak to trough)		*Recovery (during first year)*	
Date	Swing	Date	Swing
1957:3 to 1958:2	n.a.	1958:2 to 1959:2	0.3
1960:2 to 1961:1	− 1.0	1961:1 to 1962:1	0.7
1969:4 to 1970:4	− 2.7	1970:4 to 1971:4	5.3
1973:4 to 1975:1	− 9.4	1975:1 to 1976:1	7.0
1980:1 to 1980:3	− 2.9	1980:3 to 1981:3	3.7
1981:3 to 1982:4	− 9.7	1982:4 to 1983:4	15.7

n.a. = not available.

SOURCES: U.S. Department of Commerce, *The National Income and Product Accounts of the United States; Survey of Current Business,* various issues.

also, state and local corporate income taxes increased from less than 5 percent to about 7 percent of the total. In 1984 forty states had individual income taxes, and forty-five had general sales taxes, compared with nineteen and twenty-four, respectively, at the end of World War II. Only Alaska and New Hampshire had neither. This shift was greeted with favor by many economic analysts, because income and sales taxes are more elastic than the property tax. Particularly during the long economic expansion of the 1960s, state and local revenues from their own sources (taxes and service charges) grew faster than the overall economy, partly as a consequence of the gradual change in the tax bases. But this also meant that in recessions revenue declined more, or rose less, as happened in both 1974–1975 and 1980–1982.

The ability of the sector to run deficits and the meaning of reported deficits deserve discussion. All states except Vermont and all local governments are required by their constitutions or their laws to balance their budgets, usually annually. Should a deficit inadvertently occur, it can only be remedied by reducing expenditures, raising taxes, or borrowing; state and local governments cannot print money. Reducing expenditures and raising taxes on short notice are quite difficult; borrowing to meet current obligations (as opposed to capital projects) is usually forbidden. To avoid unexpected difficulties, state and local governments gradually accumulate surpluses during prosperous years, which can be spent if need be during years of unexpected recession. A common rule of thumb is that an accumulated balance of 5 percent of projected expenditures is desirable.[4] During most postwar recessions, such a level would have been adequate to cover the deficits in current general revenues and expenditures that were actually experienced.

State and Local Government Pension Funds

The proper analytical treatment of state and local pension funds has been a vexing question, and as a result relatively little attention has been given to their fiscal significance. Some economists have pointed out that state and local pension funds are much more like private pension funds than they are like other government pensions, notably social security; but they are included with social security in the National Income and Product Accounts. Economists question whether this is a reasonable distinction. They also point out that the "surplus" in these funds is merely a positive cash flow; it does not imply that the funds are actuarially sound or even that their actuarial position has improved.[5] It can also be argued that, under slightly different institutional arrangements, the pension surplus would not show up in the state and local sector at all; the states might simply hire private firms to operate their funds, and the surplus would then be recorded as an expenditure by the sector.

Although these issues are important for a full understanding of state and local pension funds, they go beyond the scope of this paper. For analyzing the relation between the state and local sector and the federal deficit, what is important is that the sector regularly generates a supply of loanable funds in the capital markets. That supply would still exist under alternative operating procedures, and its relation to the federal deficit would be unchanged.

State and local government pension funds have been growing rapidly since at least 1957 (when systematic data first became available in the census of governments) and probably throughout the postwar period. Table 3-2 shows the total receipts, payments, and surpluses of these funds since 1960. As mentioned in the previous section, the funds have continually run surpluses, in recessions as well as in periods of economic growth. Indeed, the annual surplus has increased each year since at least 1961. It is likely to continue to do so for many years to come. Data Resources, Inc. (DRI) and the Urban Institute project that employees' and employers' contributions and earnings on investments will continue to grow faster than benefit payments to the end of the century, and the Urban Institute further projects that they will do so for the next forty years.[6] DRI forecasts annual social insurance fund surpluses rising gradually from $41 billion in 1984 to $63

TABLE 3-2
STATE AND LOCAL GOVERNMENT PENSION FUNDS, 1961–1982
(billions of dollars)

Fiscal Year	Receipts	Payments	Surplus	Employee Contributions	Government Contributions	Earnings on Investments
1961	3.393	1.300	2.093	1.140	1.652	0.601
1962	3.724	1.412	2.312	1.201	1.806	0.717
1963	3.997	1.589	2.408	1.288	1.883	0.826
1964	4.787	1.844	2.943	1.466	2.256	1.065
1965	5.260	2.008	3.252	1.626	2.418	1.216
1966	5.771	2.219	3.552	1.771	2.630	1.370
1967	6.580	2.684	3.896	1.960	3.055	1.565
1968	7.578	2.829	4.749	2.194	3.590	1.793
1969	8.570	3.220	5.350	2.452	3.976	2.142
1970	9.848	3.638	6.210	2.788	4.600	2.460
1971	11.310	4.155	7.155	3.159	5.241	2.912
1972	12.620	4.920	7.700	3.400	5.750	3.471
1973	14.878	5.812	9.066	4.166	6.649	4.064
1974	16.527	6.639	9.888	4.207	7.821	4.500
1975	18.898	7.490	11.408	4.488	9.116	5.294
1976	21.848	8.422	13.426	4.869	10.652	6.327
1977	25.347	9.767	15.580	5.233	12.369	7.744
1978	28.032	10.782	17.250	5.691	13.660	8.681
1979	31.959	12.273	19.686	6.072	15.339	10.548
1980	37.313	14.008	23.305	6.466	17.532	13.315
1981	43.441	15.625	27.816	7.289	20.020	16.133
1982	48.961	18.267	30.694	8.123	21.808	19.030

NOTE: Data are for fiscal years ending during the calendar year (usually June 30).
SOURCE: U.S. Bureau of the Census, *Census of Governments, Employee Retirement Systems*, various issues.

billion by 1989 and $108 billion by the year 2000. In 1981 the Urban Institute estimated that assets would increase by $140 billion from 1980 to 1985, $150 billion from 1985 to 1990, $600 billion in the 1990s, and about $4 trillion in the first quarter of the twenty-first century. These projections are increasingly uncertain as they are carried further out into the future and depend on assumptions about future economic conditions, particularly interest rates, inflation, and salaries; but any plausible set of assumptions implies continued increases in the surplus for the 1985–1989 period and well beyond. As it happens, the Urban Institute projections have probably been slightly conservative so far in the 1980s.

In the ten years from 1971–1972 to 1981–1982, according to the census of governments, the number of beneficiaries increased almost as much (1.4 million) as the number of contributors (1.7 million); but average monthly contributions per employee nearly tripled (from $90 to $250) while average benefits doubled (from $220 to $440).

Earnings on investments have grown particularly rapidly, more than quintupling in the past decade, and now account for about 40 percent of annual receipts, up from about 25 percent in 1971. They are projected to continue rising, to almost half of total receipts by 1989 and to more than half by 1999.

The reason for the continued growth in the social insurance fund surplus is that most state and local pension funds are not fully funded. They must continue to build their assets to meet or come reasonably close to the asset targets they have set. Some ten years ago J. Richard Aronson devised the concept of the "mature trust fund," which is the hypothetical maximum value that a pension fund attains when it is adequate to cover all outstanding liabilities owed to workers in the pension plan.[7] Under various assumptions about interest rates and pension plan provisions, the unfunded balance for all state and local pension funds combined was well over half of a mature trust fund in 1971, and substantial additional contributions would be needed to achieve maturity by the year 2000. To some extent these contributions have been forthcoming from state and local governments; in 1980 it was estimated that the unfunded balance had declined both absolutely and as a share of the mature trust fund.[8]

The contributions needed to build pension funds to any given amount depend very largely on the interest rate earned on the assets of the fund. In the 1980s interest rates have been unusually high, in part at least because of the federal deficit.[9] One of the relatively minor consequences of the high rates has been that state and local governments have been able to accumulate assets in their pension funds somewhat more rapidly than they probably anticipated. This may enable them to lower their contributions to the funds and to adopt slightly lower tax rates. A greater-than-expected surplus as a result of high interest rates at present may lead to a lower surplus in the future. Conversely, a decline in interest rates, if the federal deficit is brought under control, may impel state and local governments to increase their contributions to pension funds, raising the social insurance fund surplus. The empirical significance of current high interest rates cannot be estimated very well and is probably small in any case, since rates have been high for only a few years, a short period in the timetable of pension funds. But they could be increasingly important.

Pension fund investments in 1981–1982 totaled $245 billion, almost double the $124 billion of 1976–1977. About 22 percent of this amount in 1981–1982 ($55 billion) was invested in federal government securities, $84 billion in corporate bonds, and $54 billion in corporate stocks. In the past five years, however, the net additional investment was much more concentrated in federal securities ($43 billion, or 35 percent) than in either bonds or stocks (both about $27 billion, or 22 percent). This pattern of investment indicates that the pension funds are not directly buying a large share of the additional federal debt; but their purchases of bonds, stock, and mortgages helps to raise the prices of these securities and induce other investors to shift into federal government issues.[10]

Recent Trends in the Sector and Implications for the Future

The large surplus in the "other funds" accounts of the state and local sector is not likely to persist. The experience of the past six years offers a guide to what is likely to happen. In 1977 the sector had a $19 billion surplus, excluding social insurance funds; revenue was $315 billion, expenditure $296 billion. In 1978 the surplus was still almost $16 billion.

There were several reasons for the surplus. State and local government revenues from their own sources had been growing, as a result of both inflation and real economic growth. Federal grants-in-aid had also been increasing; by 1978 they were more than double the amount of 1972 ($70 billion versus $31 billion). In addition, capital outlays, which are part of general expenditures, had flattened out after 1974, perhaps in response to the New York City fiscal crisis; capital outlays were $44.8 billion in both 1975 and 1978.

During the next five years, however, the surplus disappeared, as changes occurred in many of the factors that had given rise to it. Table

3-3 shows the quarterly changes in the surplus, at a seasonally adjusted annual rate. The remainder of this section discusses the reasons for the sector's shift from surplus to deficit.

TABLE 3-3

STATE AND LOCAL GOVERNMENT SURPLUS LESS SOCIAL INSURANCE
SURPLUS, QUARTERLY, 1977-1984
(billions of dollars)

Date		Budget Surplus	Social Insurance Surplus	Surplus Net of Social Insurance
1977:	1	23.7	17.1	6.6
	2	26.1	17.7	8.4
	3	32.0	18.3	13.7
	4	30.4	18.8	11.6
1978:	1	31.6	19.2	12.4
	2	34.0	19.7	14.3
	3	25.7	20.6	5.1
	4	29.8	21.6	8.2
1979:	1	32.3	22.4	9.9
	2	26.8	23.3	3.5
	3	30.9	24.2	6.7
	4	31.6	25.2	6.4
1980:	1	30.9	25.7	5.2
	2	26.2	25.9	0.3
	3	30.0	27.7	2.3
	4	35.1	28.8	6.3
1981:	1	35.3	29.8	5.5
	2	36.7	30.6	6.1
	3	37.3	31.3	6.0
	4	32.0	31.9	0.1
1982:	1	28.8	32.3	-3.5
	2	32.0	32.9	-0.9
	3	31.3	33.5	-2.2
	4	31.5	35.2	-3.7
1983:	1	34.1	36.0	-1.9
	2	43.9	36.9	7.0
	3	47.4	38.0	9.5
	4	51.2	39.1	12.0
1984:	1	53.9	40.5	13.4
	2	54.5	41.9	12.6
	3	45.8	43.3	2.5

SOURCES: Same as table 3-1.

1978–1980: The Tax Revolt. The growth of the sector was abruptly slowed, if not halted, by the "tax revolt" that began with the passage of Proposition 13 by the voters of California in June 1978 and continued until 1980. Proposition 13 sharply reduced property taxes in California and placed stringent limits on future increases. In the next two years, there were twenty-seven reductions or limitations in state personal income taxes, twenty-three state-imposed property tax limitations, one reduction in sales tax rates, and twenty-three contractions in the sales tax base (exemptions or rate reductions for food or drugs). Nine states indexed their income taxes as part of these reductions. Many localities also cut property tax rates at the same time.[11] These cuts reduced total state tax revenues by about $4 billion annually.[12] For the sector as a whole, annual tax reductions over the three fiscal years 1978 through 1980 accumulated to about $13.6 billion.[13] This figure is about 6 percent of total state and local taxes in fiscal year 1980. The change is perhaps less than the widespread publicity given to the tax revolt might lead one to expect. But the tax revolt clearly affected the behavior of the sector; as table 3–4 shows, state and local tax revenue in real dollars peaked in 1977–1978 and did not exceed that level again until 1982–1983. The sector has continued to grow, however, as both total general revenues and general expenditures have increased in real terms.

During the period of the tax revolt, the state and local surplus declined from $14.3 billion during the second quarter of 1978 to $6.4 billion during the fourth quarter of 1979, at a seasonally adjusted annual rate.

Recession, 1980–1982. The three years 1980 to 1982 saw two recessions, extending over eight of the twelve quarters, with a short recovery in between. The state and local fiscal situation responded quickly and sharply to each of these economic changes. During the first recession the surplus declined almost to zero by the end of fiscal year 1980. Then it rose during the 1980–1981 recovery back to its 1979 level, remaining about $6 billion for the four quarters ending in September 1981. But during the second recession the surplus again vanished quickly, and the sector ran a deficit throughout calendar year 1982.

To meet the fiscal problems of these three years, a number of states drew down their accumulated balances during the recessions and did not build them back up during the intervening recovery. At the end of fiscal year 1981, four states had deficits in their general fund balances, and twelve others had balances equal to less than 1 percent of projected 1982 outlays.[14] The second recession was particu-

TABLE 3–4

REAL STATE AND LOCAL REVENUES AND EXPENDITURES, 1962–1983
(billions of 1972 dollars)

Fiscal Year	Total General Revenue	Total Taxes	Total General Expenditures
1962	77.2	55.5	86.0
1963	87.5	61.9	89.9
1964	94.8	66.2	96.0
1965	100.7	69.7	101.4
1966	110.1	75.1	109.8
1967	117.1	78.3	119.9
1968	125.5	83.8	126.9
1969	135.5	90.8	138.2
1970	146.5	97.2	147.1
1971	154.6	101.3	160.8
1972	169.7	111.0	170.2
1973	185.8	118.3	177.0
1974	189.0	118.9	181.1
1975	188.8	117.0	190.6
1976	198.2	121.3	198.6
1977	210.3	129.4	201.9
1978	218.6	133.9	205.4
1979	218.7	130.9	208.7
1980	224.4	131.1	216.6
1981	226.5	130.8	218.0
1982	225.9	131.9	215.6
1983	230.4	134.6	220.7

SOURCE: U.S. Bureau of the Census, *Government Finances,* various issues.

larly difficult for state and local governments, because they formulated their budgets for fiscal year 1983 on the expectation that the recession would end by the middle of 1982. In fact, it continued until the end of the year. As a result, by the end of fiscal year 1983, eight states, including California, New York, and Pennsylvania, had deficits, and fourteen had accumulated balances less than 1 percent of outlays. For all states combined, accumulated balances were 1.3 percent of projected 1984 expenditures.[15] For the first time in many years, state and local government employment declined: from 1980 to 1982, full-time-equivalent employment in the sector fell by 2 percent, a decline that was concentrated in local government (about 2.5 percent).

To meet the fiscal problems of these years, many state and local governments reversed direction and raised taxes. The Tax Foundation estimates that state taxes alone were raised by about $16 billion annually during the three calendar years 1981 to 1983—about $4 billion in each of the first two years and $8 billion in the last.[16] For the sector as a whole, tax increases have been estimated at $18 billion for the two and one-half years from the beginning of 1981 to the end of fiscal year 1983.[17] The increase was slightly larger than the reduction during the years of tax revolt, both in dollars and as a share of total state and local taxes.

At first state and local governments tried to avoid raising the taxes that they had just lowered. During 1981 and 1982, ten states raised their general sales taxes, and five raised their personal income taxes. Gasoline and other excise tax increases were much more common. But in 1983, as the recession unexpectedly continued and worsened, fourteen states raised their sales taxes, and twelve raised their income taxes. Local governments, which had reduced their property taxes during 1978–1980, generally raised income or sales taxes or user fees.

These tax increases were not enough to enable the sector to balance its general account budget during the recession, but they certainly contributed to the large surpluses that quickly developed during the recovery that began in 1983.

Federal Grants-in-Aid since 1977. Federal grants to state and local governments had been growing rapidly in both nominal and real terms during the three years leading up to 1977–1978. As table 3–5 shows, this was part of a long-term trend dating back to the Kennedy administration and indeed to the Great Depression. Much of the increase during the mid-1970s occurred for specific programs in social services and health care (Medicaid).

But the year 1978, has so far turned out to be virtually the high-water mark of federal grants, at least in real terms. Over the next three years grants increased only about in line with inflation. A 50 percent increase in welfare payments and a doubling of federal aid for housing and urban renewal (in the Section 8 housing program and Urban Development Action Grants) were offset by stability in general revenue sharing and slow growth in aid to education.

The 1980s have seen a decline in both nominal and real grants. In 1980 Congress abolished the state component of general revenue sharing, reducing grants by $2.2 billion beginning in fiscal year 1981. The Reagan administration came into office with proposals to reduce federal domestic spending, including several of the major grant pro-

71

grams. It persuaded Congress to eliminate the public service employment component of the Comprehensive Employment and Training
Act (CETA), amounting to about $4 billion annually. Aid to elementary
and secondary education was cut by about $600 million in fiscal year
1981 and by over $1 billion in 1982. These and similar cuts were large
enough to offset the automatic increases in welfare benefits resulting
from the recession during 1981 and 1982. As table 3–5 shows, nominal
outlays were about the same in 1981 and 1983 while real outlays fell by
about 12 percent.

TABLE 3–5

NOMINAL AND REAL FEDERAL GRANTS-IN-AID, 1962–1983
(billions of dollars)

Fiscal Year	Nominal Dollars	1972 Dollars[a]
1962	7.1	10.1
1963	8.7	12.2
1964	10.0	13.9
1965	11.0	15.0
1966	13.2	17.5
1967	15.4	19.8
1968	17.2	21.3
1969	19.1	22.6
1970	21.9	24.5
1971	26.1	27.8
1972	31.3	31.9
1973	39.3	38.4
1974	41.8	38.0
1975	47.0	38.9
1976	55.6	43.0
1977	62.6	46.1
1978	69.6	48.1
1979	75.2	47.9
1980	83.0	48.7
1981	90.3	48.3
1982	86.9	43.1
1983	90.0	42.6

a. 1972 dollar figures refer to the calendar year rather than to the fiscal year;
therefore "nominal" and "1972 dollars" figures for 1972 differ slightly.
SOURCES: Same as tables 3–1 and 3–4.

Capital Outlays. The decade of the 1970s was one of stable and even declining state and local capital expenditures, in real terms. By 1977–1978 real outlays were over $6 billion (in 1972 dollars), or 16 percent, below the 1974–1975 peak. This was in sharp contrast to the 1960s, when real outlays rose by over 50 percent. Table 3–6 shows the trends of the past two decades. The most important factor contributing to the decline was a reduction in highway construction, amounting to about 50 percent during the 1970s. Another was the decline in the birthrate,

TABLE 3–6

NOMINAL AND REAL STATE AND LOCAL GOVERNMENT
CAPITAL OUTLAYS, 1962–1983
(billions of dollars)

Fiscal Year	Nominal Dollars	1972 Dollars[a]
1962	16.1	23.0
1963	17.6	24.7
1964	19.1	26.5
1965	20.5	27.9
1966	22.3	29.6
1967	24.2	31.1
1968	25.7	31.9
1969	28.2	33.4
1970	29.6	33.2
1971	33.1	35.3
1972	34.2	34.9
1973	35.3	34.5
1974	38.1	34.7
1975	44.8	37.1
1976	46.5	36.0
1977	44.9	33.0
1978	44.8	31.0
1979	53.2	33.9
1980	62.9	36.9
1981	67.6	36.2
1982	66.4	32.9
1983	68.0	32.2

a. 1972 dollar figures refer to the calendar year rather than to the fiscal year; therefore "nominal" and "1972 dollars" figures for 1972 differ slightly.
SOURCE: Same as table 3–4.

which began in the late 1950s and continued until the late 1970s. This decline has reduced the demand for additional public school construction; indeed, many school districts have closed schools and sold some buildings to private school systems or private enterprises. Some buildings have been converted for the use of other state and local government agencies, reducing the demand for additional government buildings.

In the late 1970s real outlays began rising again. Their growth has been halted at least temporarily, however, by the tax revolt and the recession. By 1982–1983 real outlays were down about 13 percent from 1979–1980, though still slightly above 1977–1978.

Accounting conventions governing the treatment of the capital projects of state and local governments complicate the interpretation of the sector's fiscal position as reported in the National Income and Product Accounts. Outlays are treated as expenditures, but the funds borrowed to finance the projects are not treated as revenue. Instead, the taxes raised to pay off the bonds are revenue. This means that the sector can show a deficit even if it is balancing its current accounts and is paying the principal and interest on its bonds as they become due. Thus the changes in capital outlays described in this section should not necessarily be regarded as implying corresponding changes in the surplus of the sector. But they do constitute a reduction in the demand for capital by state and local governments, and the reduction in real capital outlays during the 1970s probably did contribute to the strong fiscal position of the sector by 1977.

The Outlook for the Sector

By the end of fiscal year 1984, the fiscal situation of state and local governments had improved considerably. Only two states still had deficits in their general funds, compared with eight a year earlier; eighteen had surpluses of at least 5 percent. Accumulated balances totaled $5.3 billion, or 2.9 percent of projected expenditures, both more than double the previous year's figures.[18] But the developments of the past few years—since the last time that the state and local government sector had a large surplus—indicate why it is improbable that the present large surplus will persist. Tax cuts and expenditure increases are both likely to occur as direct responses to the surplus. For fiscal year 1985 expenditures are projected to grow faster than revenues in thirty-five states. Federal grants will probably not decline further, but a significant real rise is also not to be expected. The acute cyclical sensitivity of the sector has been vividly illustrated by the marked reduction in the surplus during the third quarter of calendar year 1984 (the first quarter of fiscal year 1985 for most states), as the rate of economic growth slowed; the surplus net of social insurance funds declined by $10 billion at a seasonally adjusted annual rate. Thus the sector's fiscal position seems likely to be worse than it is now by the time the next recession begins.

The Tax Outlook. The growth in taxes slowed dramatically in 1984, and cuts are likely if the economy continues to improve. State taxes in 1984 were raised by a net of just under $1 billion: $2.8 billion of tax increases, partly offset by $1.9 billion in reductions. Most of the reductions occurred as temporary increases enacted during the recession expired and were not renewed. Of ten such income tax increases, three were terminated ahead of their original expiration date, and two were allowed to end on schedule; only two were extended. (In November 1984 three states had taken no action on temporary increases scheduled to expire at the end of 1984 or during 1985.) Only two of the six temporary sales tax increases were permitted to expire, however; three were extended, and a fourth was extended at a lower rate.

Although some reduction of state and local tax rates seems likely, there is no evidence that it will be as abrupt or extensive as the 1978–1980 tax revolt. Public pressure for tax cuts appears to be much less. All five state tax limitation measures on the 1984 ballot were rejected by the voters.

One factor that may limit tax reductions, at least temporarily, during the current recovery is the desire of many states to build up their accumulated balances. By the end of 1984, twenty-three states had established stabilization, or "rainy day," funds. These funds are intended as a cushion against unexpected revenue shortfalls. Only five states, however, have established procedures for automatically depositing funds in these accounts. In six others, funds are to be provided by appropriation. In the remaining states, the surplus (if any) is to be deposited in the stabilization fund, often with a ceiling of 2 to 5 percent of revenues or expenditures. During the recovery, balances in these funds increased rapidly, from $700 million at the end of fiscal year 1983 to $1.9 billion a year later. Four states had no money in their funds, however, and three more had sums amounting to less than 1 percent of their general fund expenditures.[19]

The Outlook for Capital Expenditures. Although many state and local taxes are likely to be cut in the near future, expenditures are likely to increase. In particular, capital outlays are likely to rise. In recent years there has been increasing public concern over deterioration of public infrastructure, meaning the transportation, water, and sewer systems in particular. This concern has already resulted in a federal tax increase; in 1982 the Congress enacted an increase of six cents per gallon in the federal gasoline tax, to be used for highway and mass transit construction. This action will cause total government capital outlays to increase, although its effect on the state and local government sector is uncertain. The Congressional Budget Office (CBO) has estimated that total government capital outlays will have to rise by $17 billion per year (in 1982 dollars) between 1983 and 1990 to meet infrastructure "needs," as defined by the federal agencies that have some responsibility for providing the facilities (such as the Federal Highway Administration). "Need" is, of course, an inherently imprecise concept, and it might well be possible to maintain the existing infrastructure and meet demand for growth at a lesser cost. At the same time, the CBO calculations omit schools, hospitals, and other public capital investments. CBO does not specifically estimate the state and local share of the additional infrastructure outlays, but it appears to be between half and three-quarters of the total, that is, between $8 and $13 billion annually.[20] That sum would raise state and local capital outlays by 10 to 20 percent. Any substantial part of the increase will cause state and local capital outlays to begin rising again in real terms.

The Outlook for Federal Grants. Federal grants-in-aid are not likely to continue the downward trend of the early 1980s. The budget cuts achieved by the Reagan administration in its first year in office have not been repeated. In education, for example, the cuts in elementary and secondary aid programs of 1981 and 1982 have been succeeded by nominal increases sufficient to maintain the 1982 real level of spending in 1983 and 1984. Further, the administration's 1985 budget proposal is one-sixth larger than its 1984 proposal. This does not automatically imply an increase, however, because the 1985 request is only slightly larger than the amount actually approved by Congress in 1984, but it seems to mark a significant shift in the administration's policy, which may well result in some increase in federal grants. The state-local fiscal situation may improve if federal policy really does change, but the improvement is likely to be small.

The Overall Outlook. When these various factors are put together, it seems likely that the state and local surplus will dwindle in the near future, even if the economy remains strong, as it did in 1978 and 1979. Taxes are likely to rise more slowly or be cut, reducing the growth rate (though not the amount) of state and local revenue; and expenditures are likely to rise more rapidly during the recovery. Both DRI and the Bureau of Economic Analysis (BEA) project a decline in the surplus. DRI expects the surplus net of social insurance funds to decline from $7.6 billion in 1984 to $0.8 billion in 1985; including the insurance funds, it expects a decline from $50 to $48 billion.[21] The latest BEA forecast (September 1984) shows a much sharper decline: from a surplus of $13.4 billion, excluding social insurance funds, in the first quarter of 1984, to a deficit of $3.9 billion by the second quarter of 1985, with continuing deficits through 1986. Even including the social insurance funds, BEA foresees a decline in the surplus by $9 billion from mid-1984 to the end of 1986.[22] It should be emphasized that neither forecast anticipates a recession during the forecast period, although both project a much slower rate of growth than the economy has recently experienced. Both are also based on a decline in the growth of revenues and an increase in the growth of expenditures.

Either or both of these forecasts may well turn out to be wrong in detail, but the general trends that they show are consistent with the recent and the more distant past. Over the next few years, growth in the federal deficit is not likely to be offset by growth in the state and local surplus—certainly not to the extent that it was in 1983. The total deficit of the government sector will therefore require a larger share of the funds available in the U.S. capital market unless the federal deficit is significantly reduced.

Notes

1. The terminology of the state and local fisc is unsatisfactory. The National Income and Product Accounts (NIPA) and the census of governments divide the total surplus or deficit into two categories: social insurance funds and "other." The latter is by far the larger. It includes both current and capital outlays for goods and services and transfer payments to individuals on the expenditure side and taxes, nontax receipts, and federal grants-in-aid on the revenue side. In the aggregate, these categories are commonly termed "general expenditures" and "general revenues" in the census of governments and related Census Bureau data on the sector. But the difference is not usually described as the "general account surplus." The "other" surplus, as reported in the NIPA, also includes the net surplus of state and local government enterprises, such as public utilities and liquor stores. Between 1980 and 1983 the surplus of government enterprises gradually increased from about $6 billion to $8 billion, at a seasonally adjusted annual rate. Thus the "other surplus" was higher than the "general account surplus"; however, the cyclical

changes were very similar. It would be possible to subtract the surplus of government enterprises to arrive at an NIPA version of the "general account surplus," but the NIPA does not use the "general account" terminology. There are also conceptual differences between the NIPA and the census of governments' treatment of the sector, which will be discussed subsequently. I have therefore chosen to use the standard categories and terminology, despite the awkwardness of having to describe the budget category of most interest for this paper as "other" or "excluding social insurance."

2. The data are for fiscal years ending during the calendar year. For nearly all state and local governments, fiscal years end in June.

3. Edward M. Gramlich, "State and Local Budgets the Day after It Rained: Why Is the Surplus So High?" *Brookings Papers in Economic Activity* (1978), no. 1.

4. Peter D. Skaperdas, "State and Local Governments: An Assessment of Their Financial Position and Fiscal Policies," *Federal Reserve Bank of New York Quarterly Review*, vol. 8, no. 4 (Winter 1983–1984), pp. 9–10.

5. See, for example, Gramlich, "State and Local Budgets," pp. 192–194.

6. Data Resources, Inc., "The Long-Term Outlook," December 1983 and Urban Institute et al., *The Future of State and Local Pensions*, Final Report (Washington, D.C.: Urban Institute, April 1981), esp. pp. 18-20–18-26. This report lists three organizations and one individual as authors on the title page. The introduction states that it was primarily written by Hal Hovey, but he is not listed as one of the authors.

7. J. Richard Aronson, "Projections of State and Local Trust Fund Financing," in David J. Ott et al., *State-Local Finances in the Last Half of the 1970s* (Washington, D.C.: American Enterprise Institute, 1975), esp. pp. 69–80.

8. These data have been provided to me by Professor Aronson. They are not strictly comparable to the earlier data, but the differences do not invalidate the general pattern of change.

9. The relation between the federal deficit and interest rates lies outside the scope of this paper. It is discussed by Phillip Cagan in chapter 8 of this volume.

10. From a broader point of view, it is likely that not all of the state and local pension fund growth constitutes a net increase in saving throughout the economy. Contributors are likely to reduce their private saving for retirement because of their membership in the pension fund. There is an extensive research literature on this substitution. On the basis of her review of the literature, Munnell estimates that workers reduce saving by sixty-five cents for each dollar saved in their pension plans (Alicia H. Munnell, *The Economics of Private Pensions* [Washington, D.C.: Brookings Institution, 1982]). The Urban Institute estimated that in 1980 larger state and local pension plans had an unfunded liability equal to 44 percent of their asset targets, or total liability, but that the increase in the unfunded liability would be only about 15 percent of the increase in total liabilities during the 1980s (Urban Institute et al., *Future of State and Local Pensions*, pp. 18-24). On the assumption that Munnell's estimates apply to public sector pensions and that the Urban Institute projections prove accurate, then it appears that the net increase in saving (state-local

government and private combined) is about 20 percent of the annual state-local pension fund surplus during the 1980s. (Pension fund assets increase by eighty-five cents for each dollar of future liabilities, while private saving by employees falls by sixty-five cents for each dollar.) This does not affect the analysis in the text.

11. George E. Peterson, "The State and Local Sector," in John L. Palmer and Isabel V. Sawhill, eds., *The Reagan Experiment* (Washington, D.C.: Urban Institute Press, 1982).

12. Tax Foundation, "State Tax Action in 1979," *Tax Foundation's Tax Review*, vol. 40, no. 10 (November–December 1979); and idem, "State Tax Action in 1980," vol. 41, no. 9 (October 1980).

13. Skaperdas, "State and Local Governments," p. 9.

14. National Conference of State Legislatures, "State Fiscal Conditions as States Entered 1982" (Denver, 1982), p. 6.

15. National Governors Association and National Association of State Budget Officers, *Fiscal Survey of the States 1984* (Washington, D.C., 1984), table A-2.

16. Tax Foundation, "State Tax Prospects, 1984" *Tax Foundation's Tax Review*, vol. 45, no. 1 (April 1984).

17. Skaperdas, "State and Local Governments," p. 10.

18. Data on the states' fiscal situation at the end of their 1984 fiscal years is taken from Steven D. Gold and Corina L. Ecki, "State Budget Actions in 1984" (Denver: National Conference of State Legislatures, 1984).

19. For a discussion of "rainy day" funds, see Steven D. Gold, "Preparing for the Next Recession: Rainy Day Funds and Other Tools for States" (Denver: National Conference of State Legislatures, 1983). Three states have created funds since this paper was written.

20. Congressional Budget Office, *Public Works Infrastructure: Policy Considerations for the 1980s* (Washington, D.C., April 1983).

21. Sara Johnson, "State and Local Government," *Data Resources U.S. Review* (December 1984), pp. 77–81. It should be noted that DRI projects renewed growth in the surplus, including social insurance funds, by about $10 billion annually in 1986 and 1987. This could offset a significant fraction of the expected increase in the federal deficit in those years.

22. This projection is taken from the September 28, 1984, forecast of the BEA quarterly econometric model, the latest forecast to be decontrolled for public use at the time of writing. Unpublished memorandum, U.S. Department of Commerce, Bureau of Economic Analysis, provided by George Green. This forecast incorporates the sharp decline in economic growth that occurred during the third quarter of 1984, but not the moderate improvement during the fourth quarter. It may therefore be too pessimistic.

4

The Deficit Experience in Industrial Countries

Vito Tanzi

Summary

This chapter focuses on the industrial counties as a group rather than on any individual country. It is divided into three sections. The first reviews the difficulties encountered in comparing the fiscal balances of different countries. It discusses issues related to the comprehensiveness of the measure of fiscal balance used; the timing of expenditure and revenue; the effect of changes in economic activity; the effect of changes in the price level; and effects of temporary policies. Taking these issues into account, it presents various concepts of fiscal deficit, some of which try to neutralize the effect of changes in economic activity and of changes in prices. The conclusion reached is that conventional measures of fiscal deficits are unsatisfactory but that the alternatives proposed (structural deficit, inflation-adjusted conventional deficit, or inflation-adjusted structural deficit) raise even more questions. In any case, it is argued, in considering the effect of the fiscal deficit on financial markets under current conditions, the conventional measure is preferable. Other concepts may at times be more useful in connection with other objectives of economic policy.

The second section presents basic fiscal statistics for the industrial countries and shows the degree of fiscal deterioration that has occurred over the past decade. Statistics related to conventionally measured deficits, to structural deficits, and to inflation-adjusted deficits for eighteen countries are presented and briefly discussed.

The third section raises, as a working hypothesis, the possibility that financial markets have become so well integrated that a country-by-country look at the fiscal deficit and its consequences may not be very helpful in understanding the effects of deficits on the international economic scene. It treats the industrial countries as parts of one economy, therefore, and aggre-

I would like to thank Phillip Cagan, Luigi Spaventa, Sir Alan Walters, and Peter Heller for valuable comments and Ziba Farhadian for statistical assistance. Views expressed in this paper are strictly personal. They do not necessarily reflect official positions of the International Monetary Fund.

gates their fiscal deficits, their gross national products, and their savings. The concept of "world deficit" is developed, and the relations between the world deficit and the aggregated measures of savings and GNPs are estimated. The ratio of aggregated fiscal deficits particularly to aggregated saving rose sharply after 1979 and almost doubled for the major industrial countries from 1981 to 1983. This was the period when the real rate of interest also rose in all the countries considered. The recession in Europe and the attempts of some large countries to reduce their fiscal deficits helped to contain the rise in long-term real interest rates.

It is argued that, should the recovery in economic activity spread to other countries while the fiscal balances remain in deficit, a further increase in interest rates seems probable. A slowdown of economic activity in the United States, however, could put downward pressures on real rates even if the fiscal deficit remained at its present percentage of GNP. We have to look at all the elements, both domestic and foreign, that contribute to pressures on financial markets. Isolating the fiscal deficit, or even more isolating the fiscal deficit of one country, is not likely to provide a satisfactory understanding of the effects of the deficit on real interest rates.

This chapter has three sections. The first discusses the difficulties of comparing the fiscal balances of different countries. The second presents, for several countries and for a time span of about a decade, some essential fiscal statistics. The third, considering the major industrial countries as parts of one economy, aggregates their fiscal deficits, GNPs, savings, and so on, and estimates relevant ratios for the aggregates.

Conceptual Issues and Definitions

Fiscal deficits are conventionally defined as the difference between budgetary government expenditure and revenue. They are often related to the gross national product to obtain a ratio that can presumably be used to make intertemporal or intercountry comparisons. The casual reader of the financial press may feel that such a measure is objective and not controversial. Unfortunately, many complex problems arise in attempting to use that measure to compare the fiscal stance of different countries or to compare the measure for different years in the same country. Only the major issues are discussed briefly here. These issues play a large role in generating alternative measures of fiscal deficits and consequently in explaining why different observers often reach different conclusions about the stance of fiscal policy that countries are following or should follow.

Comprehensiveness of Measure. The issue of comprehensiveness has several dimensions. The measure of the fiscal deficit should be a good reflection of a country's fiscal policy. But what, exactly, does this mean? How widely in space and time does one cast the net? Let us consider this question. Almost all countries have fiscal activities that are outside the scope of the central government budget. These may be extrabudgetary activities of the central government (including lending operations) or activities of public bodies—state and local governments, social security institutions and other pension funds, public enterprises, and so on—that are often outside the national budget. In different countries these activities may constitute a large or a small part of the total. Furthermore, their fiscal balance may have a different sign from that of the central government. As John Weicher shows in chapter 3, in recent years state and local governments in the United States have shown substantial surpluses, which in part have neutralized the large deficits of the central government. At the same time, federal credit programs have expanded enormously.[1] These programs raised "the ratio of Federal and federally assisted *lending* to all funds advanced by nonfinancial sectors in the U.S. credit market . . . [to] 17 percent in 1983" and "the ratio of Federal and federally assisted *borrowing* to all funds raised by nonfinancial sectors in U.S. credit markets to 56 percent in 1983."[2] Unfortunately, since comparative information on these lending and borrowing activities of governments is not available for different countries, their relative effects on credit markets cannot be assessed.[3]

Another issue is directly related to the scope of public sector activity in the economy. Suppose, for example, that in country A electricity is provided by public corporations while in country B it is provided by private corporations. Suppose also that total outlays of these corporations (including investment spending) exceed total revenues (excluding borrowing). Then in country A the (public) corporations' deficit will contribute to the public sector fiscal deficit while in country B the (private) corporations' deficit will not. But the pressure on the credit market will be the same. Thus, a bias may be introduced in the comparisons if one considers a broader definition of the government sector when the role of the public sector is different in different countries.[4]

Another important issue has been raised by several writers.[5] They have pointed out that the conventional definition of the deficit, even when extended to cover the whole public sector, ignores expected future commitments by the government, ignores government capital gains and losses during the budget year, and ignores the fact that some public expenditure results in the accumulation of valuable real assets, such as buildings and roads.[6] Assume that under current legislation the present value of future social security contributions is less than the present value of future social security benefits. The net position of the public sector is then worse than implied by the fiscal deficit.[7]

Or suppose that the government owns mineral resources and that the prices of these minerals rise. Then the net wealth of the public sector rises, and the increase, it is argued, should be taken into account in estimating the deficit. Similar results would be obtained if the government accumulated assets over time by, for example, buying buildings.[8] In effect, it is argued, the permanent income of the country has increased, so that a higher consumption (including public consumption) can be sustained even though the current (measured) income may not have changed.

As this brief discussion shows, there are great difficulties in determining what is the best measure of the fiscal deficit. Although many of the points made by critics of the conventional measure undoubtedly have some validity and some of the alternative measures may be useful in particular circumstances, the conventional measure remains the most useful in an analysis of financial markets. Furthermore, this measure is more easily calculated when the analysis relates to different countries.

Timing of Expenditures and Revenues. The question here is, Should the fiscal deficit reflect cash or accrual concepts? At the beginning of the Vietnam War in the mid-1960s, a broad consensus developed among American fiscal experts that the accrual concept was preferable for appraising the appropriateness of fiscal policy. The reason was that, as additional orders for defense items were received by the defense industry and before any cash payments had been made, employment and incomes had already been affected. Similarly, before tax payments are made, individuals and corporations have already taken into account those liabilities and have reduced their spending accordingly. That consensus reflected the Keynesian view then prevalent of how fiscal policy affects the economy. In today's world, where the importance of the deficit may be assessed more by its pressure on financial markets than by its direct effect on goods and labor markets, the cash concept may be preferable.[9] Data of the Organization for Economic Cooperation and Development (OECD) are consistently on a national accounts (or accrual) basis; data of the International Monetary Fund (IMF) published in the *World Economic Outlook* are mostly on a cash basis when they refer to the central government and on a national accounts basis when they refer to the general government, which includes state and local governments.[10] The fiscal deficit for the United States commonly reported in the press is on a cash basis for the fiscal year.

Effect of Changes in Economic Activity. At least since the 1950s it has been realized that the fiscal deficit not only affects the level of economic activity but also is affected by it.[11] On both the revenue and the expenditure sides of the budget there are dynamic elements, endogenous to the system, that are beyond the control of the policy makers. The responsiveness of tax revenue to economic activity (the built-in flexibility) implies that, in the absence of discretionary measures, the deficit is likely to increase automatically in recessions and to fall in booms. Therefore, in the face of changing economic activity, the uncritical comparison of fiscal deficits over different years for a given country, or over different countries for a given year, may lead to wrong conclusions. Suppose, for example, that country X is going through a strong expansion in economic activity while country Y is in the middle of a recession; one could not conclude from the observance of similar fiscal deficits that the two countries are pursuing comparable fiscal policies. The same argument obviously applies when the fiscal policy of the same country is compared for two different periods.

It has recently become fashionable to think in terms of a structural and a cyclical component of the fiscal deficit. The concept of the structural deficit has been formulated and measured.[12] This concept is analytically related to the full-employment budget surplus (FEBS) that played such a large role in the New Economic Policy pursued in the United States by the Kennedy and Johnson administrations. The main differences between the structural deficit and the FEBS are two: First, the structural deficit no longer has the strong normative connotation of the FEBS. In other words, it no longer necessarily guides fiscal policy but is for many, though not all, observers just a statistic. Second, although the FEBS was related to a relatively well-defined rate of unemployment or capacity utilization (that is, to potential output), the structural deficit is at times defined in relation to a "normal" or "trend" level of output. Because different observers are unlikely to agree on what constitutes a normal or trend level of output and because it has become progressively more doubtful that there is any objective measure of potential output, the estimated measures of structural deficit are inevitably open to ambiguity.[13] In fact, that is the main problem with structural deficits. As shown in the following section, widely divergent estimates are produced by different assumptions about output. There is simply no objectivity to this measure of fiscal policy.

Effect of Changes in the Price Level. Comparisons over time for the same country or between countries for the same year can also be affected by different rates of inflation. The issues are complex, and only the most basic points are made here.[14] The argument made by economists who would adjust the fiscal deficit for the effect of inflation is that inflation brings with it a higher nominal rate of interest and reduces the real value of the outstanding public debt. In a simple Fisherian world, such a higher rate of interest is approximately equal to the rate that would prevail without inflation plus an inflationary component equal to the expected rate of inflation.[15] This inflationary component broadly compensates the lender for the erosion in the real value of the principal.[16] Traditional accounting, however, treats the whole interest payment (real plus inflationary component) as a current cost rather than partly as a repayment of principal. The result is that expected inflation raises the interest component of the budget and the size of the deficit as traditionally measured. There is thus a direct relation between the rate of inflation that a country experiences and the conventionally measured deficit.[17]

The proponents of adjustments to that deficit argue that those who receive the interest payments will not consider as income (and thus will not spend) the part that is necessary to compensate them for the erosion of their principal.[18] In the absence of monetary or fiscal illusions, they will maintain unchanged the *real* value of their financial assets and will be willing to use that part to buy additional (government) bonds. Thus this inflation adjustment should be considered neither an income by the holders of the public debt nor a current expense in the public budget.[19] It is amortization, and amortization payments should not be included in the deficit.

The inflation-adjusted measures of the fiscal deficit attempt to make this correction either by estimating the net reduction in the real value of the public debt held by the public (that is, by multiplying the nominal value of the debt by the rate of inflation) or by assuming that all interest payment above some (more or less arbitrary) real interest rate (say, 3 percent) is amortization.[20] Once the fiscal deficit has been corrected for inflation, its size falls, the ranking of countries by the size of their deficits changes, and, more important, fiscal policy appears less expansionary than would have been assumed from the traditional measure.[21]

A full discussion of inflation-corrected fiscal accounts would require far more space than can be used here, but a few comments are necessary. First, the implicit assumption that individuals do not suffer from fiscal or monetary illusions (that is, that they distinguish between real interest incomes and monetary corrections) may not be realistic.[22]

Second, the corrections that are made are partial: they look at the effect of inflation on the real value of the debt but not at the effect of inflation on government expenditure and revenue. In industrial countries inflation generally has a more positive effect on revenue than on expenditure, and this reduces the deficit.[23] Thus, if an inflation adjustment is made to the interest expense (or to the real value of the debt), it should also be made to the tax revenue. A lower inflation would reduce the interest payment but would also reduce tax revenue. The net effect of inflation on the conventionally measured deficit depends on which of these two influences is stronger.[24]

Third, the implicit assumption that, regardless of the rate of inflation, individuals would wish to maintain their real demand for government bonds unchanged *at a given real rate of interest* does not seem realistic. A constant real demand for bonds might require an increasing real rate of interest, so that an adjustment that assumes a constant real rate may not be realistic.[25] If bond buyers become convinced that at some point the central bank will expand the money supply, they will demand higher nominal rates on long-term bonds than would seem warranted by the current expected rate of inflation.

Fourth, inflation does not affect the wealth of the bondholders in the straightforward manner implied by the Fisher effect. Nominal interest rates may not adjust for inflation à la Fisher, for example, but may increase by more or less than the rate of inflation. Furthermore, even if interest rates have adjusted fully for inflation at the time the securities are issued, later increases in inflation that had not been anticipated at that time will produce unanticipated capital losses. It is unlikely that in such cases individuals would use other income to maintain constant their real demand for public securities.[26]

Fifth—and somewhat related to the previous point—inflation affects individuals and income classes in their roles as consumers, taxpayers, wage earners, savers, asset holders, lenders, borrowers, and so on. Because of this multiplicity of influences, it is difficult and perhaps not meaningful to single out the effect associated with the holding of public bonds on effective demand. If an individual is suffering capital losses in his holdings other than government securities, is it realistic to assume that his real demand for government bonds will not be affected by inflation? In this connection, it is also important that when nominal interest rates increase because of inflation, the progressivity of the tax system may cause the increases to overcompensate some lenders (those subject to low marginal tax rates) but undercompensate others (those with high marginal tax rates). These differential effects will inevitably influence the real demand for bonds.[27]

Finally, inflation-adjusted fiscal deficits look backward at fiscal policy rather than forward in an ex ante manner. Yet, under particular circumstances, a fiscal policy that, adjusted for inflation, appears restrictive ex post may have been expansionary ex ante and may in fact have been a cause of inflation. Assume, for example, that a fiscal deficit is financed immediately by a stimulative policy of monetary expansion, and assume also that the existing debt was held mostly in bonds of long maturity. Then assessing the fiscal policy ex post may lead to a mistaken conclusion that the fiscal policy has been restrictive (because the government has gained substantially through the inflationary depreciation of outstanding debt). Clearly, inflation complicates the comparison of fiscal deficits both through time and across countries.[28]

Effects of Temporary Policies. Comparisons can also be affected by policy actions that reduce the deficit of a country for a particular year but do not reduce the underlying, or core, deficit.[29] Suppose, for example, that in a particular year a country (1) sells some of its public corporations to the private sector, as is being done in the United Kingdom and other countries, (2) sells an unusually high number of exploration rights, as was done in the United States about 1982, (3) declares a tax amnesty that induces taxpayers to pay unpaid tax liabilities, as was done in Italy, (4) sells zero coupon bonds or bonds at a discount and does not impute an interest charge, as is being proposed in several countries, (5) postpones inevitable wage increases for public employees to the beginning of the next fiscal year, or (6) imposes a temporary surtax, as was done in the United States in the late 1960s and has been done in France several times.[30] All these measures reduce the current year's fiscal deficit without reducing the country's longer-run or core deficit, except for the decrease in future interest payments associated with the lower public debt due to the reduced deficit for the current year. They make the fiscal situation of the country for that particular year look better than it really is.

The various issues discussed in this section should be seen as red flags on the way to reaching strong conclusions, from the use of comparative statistics, about the relative fiscal policies of countries. They indicate that all the measures of fiscal deficits are unsatisfactory. I believe that, in spite of the obvious shortcomings of the conventional measure, it is still preferable for assessing the effects of fiscal deficits on financial markets now being discussed under the general economic conditions that have prevailed in the industrial countries in recent years. It is the one that is used in the third section. In the following section comparative statistics are provided on the conventional deficit, the structural deficit, the inflation-adjusted conventional fiscal deficit, and even the inflation-adjusted structural deficit. The last adjusts the conventional deficit for both cyclical factors and inflation. No statistics are provided on the core deficit.

Basic Fiscal Statistics

Table 4–1 shows, for the seven largest industrial countries (commonly referred to as the G-7 countries), four alternative measures of the fiscal deficit of the *central* government. The four measures are the conventionally measured deficit, the structural deficit, the inflation-adjusted conventional deficit, and the inflation-adjusted structural deficit. The conventional measure is the one published in the *World Economic Outlook* of the International Monetary Fund.[31] The others have been calculated on the basis of particular assumptions. The structural deficit is the one that would have prevailed if, *ceteris paribus*, economic activity had remained at some "potential" level. In other words, it is the deficit that cannot be attributed to the influence of a cyclical slowdown. The inflation adjustment is made by taking the public debt at midyear and multiplying it by the year's rate of inflation. This gives a measure of the "inflation tax," which is then added to government revenue to recalculate the fiscal deficit. This adjustment can be made either to the conventional deficit, to obtain the inflation-adjusted conventional deficit, or to the structural deficit, to obtain the inflation-adjusted structural deficit.

As one moves from the conventional deficit to the inflation-adjusted structural deficit, a progressive shrinkage of the deficit is observed. This shrinkage is a direct function of the gap between the actual and the assumed "potential" level of economic activity and of the rate of inflation. It is easy to see from table 4–1 why different observers often reach different conclusions about the degree of restrictiveness of fiscal policy. Consider, for example, the United States in 1982. The conventional deficit expressed as a share of GNP was 4.3 percent while the inflation-adjusted structural deficit was only 0.6 percent. In the 1979–1981 period the latter is shown to have been in surplus.[32] Italy provides an even more extreme example. In 1982 the conventional deficit was 15.1 percent of GNP while the inflation-adjusted structural deficit was only 2.9 percent.

By the conventional measure, Germany and the United Kingdom have been most successful in reducing the deficit while the fiscal

TABLE 4-1
ALTERNATIVE MEASURES OF CENTRAL GOVERNMENT FISCAL DEFICITS, G-7 COUNTRIES, 1975–1984
(percentage of GNP)

		1975	1976	1977	1978	1979	1980	1981	1982	1983	1984[a]
Canada	A	2.3	1.8	3.5	4.6	3.5	3.5	2.2	5.3	6.2	6.6
	B	2.2	2.2	3.5	4.5	3.8	3.6	2.5	3.3	4.1	4.7
	C	—	0.3	2.2	3.2	1.2	0.9	-0.3	2.5	4.5	5.1
	D	—	0.7	2.2	3.1	1.6	1.1	—	0.8	2.5	3.3
France	A	2.6	1.2	1.0	1.6	1.5	1.1	2.6	2.8	3.3	3.3
	B	2.1	1.1	0.7	1.6	1.7	1.1	2.0	2.1	2.2	1.9
	C	—	-0.2	-0.3	0.3	0.1	-0.6	0.8	0.7	1.4	1.6
	D	—	-0.3	-0.5	0.3	0.3	-0.6	0.3	0.1	0.4	0.3
Germany	A	3.6	2.8	2.2	2.1	1.8	1.7	2.2	1.9	2.0	1.4
	B	2.1	2.4	2.0	2.1	2.3	1.9	1.1	-0.5	-0.6	-0.8
	C	—	2.4	1.8	1.6	1.3	1.1	1.6	1.1	1.4	0.9
	D	—	2.0	1.6	1.6	1.7	1.2	0.4	-1.3	-1.2	-1.3

Italy	A	10.7	9.1	9.0	13.1	10.8	10.8	12.8	15.1	16.5	16.9
	B	10.7	10.0	9.3	13.1	11.3	11.5	12.1	12.8	12.4	12.6
	C	—	1.3	0.5	6.0	2.5	0.3	2.9	4.6	6.5	8.2
	D	—	2.0	0.7	6.0	2.9	0.8	2.4	2.9	3.4	4.8
Japan	A	4.3	5.0	5.1	5.3	6.2	6.1	5.9	5.5	5.5	4.7
	B	4.3	4.9	5.1	5.3	6.3	6.3	6.1	5.5	5.3	4.7
	C	—	4.2	4.2	4.3	5.5	5.2	4.9	4.8	5.3	4.4
	D	—	4.1	4.1	4.3	5.6	5.4	5.1	4.8	5.0	4.4
United Kingdom	A	7.9	5.5	3.1	5.0	5.3	4.8	4.2	2.9	4.9	3.5
	B	7.1	4.7	2.4	5.0	5.7	3.3	1.3	0.2	2.5	1.5
	C	—	1.3	-1.3	1.4	0.9	-1.1	0.4	0.3	3.0	1.7
	D	—	0.5	-1.9	1.4	1.2	-2.4	-2.2	-2.2	0.7	-0.3
United States	A	4.9	3.3	2.7	2.0	1.2	2.4	2.5	4.3	5.8	4.8
	B	2.7	1.9	2.0	2.0	1.2	1.6	1.8	2.2	3.8	4.0
	C	—	1.9	1.1	0.1	-1.0	—	0.1	2.6	4.4	3.5
	D	—	0.6	0.5	0.1	-1.0	-0.7	-0.5	0.6	2.5	2.7

NOTE: A = conventional deficit; B = structural deficit; C = inflation-adjusted conventional deficit; D = inflation-adjusted structural deficit.
a. Estimated.

SOURCE: Based on data published in International Monetary Fund, *World Economic Outlook.*

situation seems to have deteriorated in Canada, France, Italy, and the United States. Some improvement has also been registered by Japan since the late 1970s. When the effect of the cycle is taken out by using the structural deficit, the relative results do not change much, although the deficits get smaller for all the countries. Structural fiscal deficits have grown in Canada, France (after 1980), and the United States; they have fallen considerably in Germany and the United Kingdom and, in the past couple of years, somewhat less in Japan. The situation as described by the inflation-adjusted measures, which are much lower than the other measures, can be seen in table 4–1.

Tables 4–2, 4–3, and 4–4 rely on data prepared by the staff of the Monetary and Fiscal Policy Division, Economics and Statistics Department, OECD. These tables cover a larger group of countries and a longer period. Unlike table 4–1, which relates to the central government and uses a cash concept of accounting, they relate to the general government and use an accrual (that is, national income account) concept. Table 4–2 shows the conventional fiscal balance, table 4–3 the structural fiscal balance, and table 4–4 the inflation-adjusted fiscal balance. The tables also show aggregated data for the seven major countries, the smaller countries, and the eighteen countries combined. The data have been aggregated by relative size of GNPs, using 1982 GNP weights and exchange rates.

Table 4–2 points to a considerable deterioriation of the fiscal situation since 1970. The period can be divided into three subperiods. The first, from 1970 to 1975, shows a dramatic and sudden increase in fiscal deficits in 1975, although in some countries (the United Kingdom, Italy, Belgium, Ireland) the deterioration had started before the oil shock of 1973 and the sharp recession of 1975.[33] During the second period, from 1975 to 1979, the fiscal situation improved in many countries, mostly because of the strong economic recovery and the high rate of inflation that swelled revenues. Because the tax systems in the major countries were generally not indexed for inflation, the countries benefited from substantial fiscal dividends associated with the high rates of inflation. The very low real rates of interest in this period also helped to keep spending down. For the seven major countries the general government conventional fiscal deficit fell from 4.3 percent of GNP in 1975 to 1.7 percent in 1979. For the whole group the improvement was less dramatic because the fiscal deficit of the smaller countries continued to grow through this period.

The post-1979 period was again one of deterioration, at least until 1983, when the recovery in the United States and, to a lesser extent, in other G-7 countries started to reduce the deficit. The effect on revenue of the slowdown in economic activity was compounded by the fall in the rate of inflation since it is nominal income growth rather than real income growth that determines the size of the "fiscal dividend." An economic recovery accompanied by high real rates of interest and low inflation would not bring an improvement in the fiscal situation of these countries equivalent to that in the 1975–1979 period. Between 1979 and 1983 the combined deficit of the G-7 countries rose from 1.7 percent of GNP to 4.1 percent while that of the whole group rose from 1.8 percent to 4.3 percent. In this period the deterioration of the U.S. fiscal situation (from a surplus of 0.6 percent in 1979 to a deficit of 3.9 percent in 1983) was highly significant; in the other countries the overall deterioration was from a deficit of 3.5 percent of GNP in 1979 to one of 4.5 percent in 1983.[34]

Table 4–3 gives estimates of structural fiscal deficits. For each country two series are shown. The top one estimates the deficit in connection with a "potential output" defined as a "trend output measured from peak to peak."[35] One problem with this measure is that economies are generally not at peak levels. Between one peak and the next economies operate at lower levels of economic activity and thus generate less tax revenue and, perhaps because of unemployment, more public expenditure. In other words, the higher fiscal deficits in the nonpeak years lead to an accumulation of nominal public debt that must be financed. In recognition of this, the lower series shows structural deficits calculated at an average level of economic activity or, more precisely, at the level of economic activity that prevails at midcycle.

Table 4–3 highlights a few messages. First, it shows how sensitive the fiscal deficit is to cyclical fluctuations.[36] As widely recognized, the fiscal deficit influences economic activity and is in turn influenced by it. Table 4–3 shows the results obtained by playing the counterfactual game of assuming away the cycle in a *ceteris paribus* situation.[37] The differences between the results shown in table 4–3 and those shown in table 4–2 presumably reflect the effect of the cycle on the fiscal deficit.

Second, a comparison of the two estimates of structural deficit for each country in table 4–3 shows how sensitive those estimates are to the assumptions made. In many cases the two series are widely different, raising the obvious question whether one or the other or either can be relied upon to guide economic policy.[38]

Third, even when the fiscal deficits are corrected for cyclical effects, large differences among countries remain. Some, such as Italy, Belgium, Denmark, Greece, and Ireland, have very high structural deficits; in others the problem appears far less serious.

Finally, the aggregation of the structural deficits of all the coun-

TABLE 4-2
GENERAL GOVERNMENT CONVENTIONAL FISCAL DEFICITS, 1970–1984
(percentage of GNP)

	1970	1971	1972	1973	1974	1975	1976	1977	1978	1979	1980	1981	1982	1983	1984[a]
Australia	-2.9	-2.4	-2.2	0.2	-2.4	0.6	3.0	0.7	2.2	1.5	0.6	-0.5	-0.4	4.0	3.7
Austria	-1.0	-1.5	-2.0	-1.3	-1.3	2.5	3.7	2.4	2.8	2.4	1.3	1.2	2.6	3.3	2.3
Belgium	2.0	3.0	4.0	3.5	2.6	4.7	5.4	5.5	6.0	7.0	8.2	12.1	11.0	11.1	10.3
Canada	-0.9	-0.1	-0.1	-1.0	-1.9	2.4	1.7	2.4	3.1	1.8	2.5	1.1	5.3	5.9	5.3
Denmark	-3.2	-3.9	-3.9	-5.2	-3.1	1.4	0.3	0.6	0.3	1.9	3.3	6.7	9.4	7.8	6.0
Finland	-4.4	-4.6	-3.9	-5.8	-4.7	-2.7	-5.0	-3.2	-1.4	-0.5	-0.5	-1.5	0.5	1.4	0.7
France	-0.9	-0.7	-0.8	-0.9	-0.6	2.2	0.5	0.8	1.9	0.7	-0.2	1.8	2.6	3.2	3.5
Germany	-0.2	0.2	0.5	-1.2	1.3	5.7	3.4	2.4	2.5	2.7	3.1	3.8	3.5	2.7	1.4
Greece	0.1	0.9	0.3	1.4	2.2	3.4	2.6	2.1	1.7	1.9	5.1	12.6	9.9	9.9	9.8
Ireland	3.7	3.5	3.2	4.2	7.0	11.3	7.5	6.9	8.8	10.7	11.6	13.9	16.1	13.6	12.3
Italy	5.0	7.1	9.2	8.5	8.1	11.7	9.0	8.0	9.7	9.5	8.0	11.9	12.7	11.8	12.4

Japan	−1.9	−1.4	−0.4	−0.5	−0.4	2.7	3.7	3.8	5.5	4.8	4.5	4.0	3.4	3.1	2.3
Netherlands	0.8	0.5	0.6	−0.6	0.4	3.0	2.9	2.1	3.1	4.0	4.1	5.4	7.4	6.6	5.9
Norway	−3.2	−4.3	−4.5	−5.7	−4.7	−3.8	−3.1	−1.7	−0.6	−1.8	−5.0	−5.4	−4.9	−5.4	−2.4
Spain	−0.7	0.6	−0.3	−1.1	−0.2	—	0.3	0.6	1.8	1.7	2.0	3.0	5.8	6.0	5.7
Sweden	−4.4	−5.2	−4.4	−4.1	−2.0	−2.8	−4.5	−1.7	0.5	3.0	3.6	4.7	6.2	5.0	3.5
United Kingdom	−3.0	−1.5	1.2	2.6	3.7	4.5	4.9	3.1	4.2	3.2	3.5	2.8	2.1	3.7	2.8
United States	1.1	1.5	0.3	−0.6	0.3	4.2	2.1	0.9	−0.2	−0.6	1.2	0.9	3.8	3.9	3.1
Total major seven[b]	0.1	0.9	0.6	—	0.8	4.3	2.9	2.2	2.2	1.7	2.4	2.5	4.0	4.1	3.4
Total smaller countries[b]	1.4	1.2	1.2	1.3	0.9	0.9	1.1	1.0	2.1	2.5	2.6	3.7	4.9	5.4	4.9
Total of countries above[b]	0.1	0.6	0.4	0.1	0.6	3.9	2.7	2.0	2.2	1.8	2.4	2.7	4.1	4.3	3.6

a. Estimated.
b. Aggregated by relative size of GNP, using 1982 weights and exchange rates.
SOURCE: Organization for Economic Cooperation and Development.

TABLE 4-3
GENERAL GOVERNMENT STRUCTURAL FISCAL DEFICITS, 1970–1984
(percentage of GNP)

	1970	1971	1972	1973	1974	1975	1976	1977	1978	1979	1980	1981	1982	1983	1984[a]
Australia	-2.9	-1.9	-1.9	1.1	-2.0	0.1	2.7	-1.0	0.3	-0.2	-1.4	-1.2	-2.1	1.6	2.9
	-2.2	-1.2	-1.2	1.8	-1.3	0.8	3.3	-0.3	1.0	0.5	-0.7	-0.6	-1.4	2.3	3.6
Austria	-2.1	-2.4	-2.3	-1.3	-1.2	0.5	2.7	2.1	1.5	2.4	1.6	0.2	1.3	2.2	1.6
	-1.6	-1.9	-1.8	-0.8	-0.7	1.0	3.2	2.7	2.0	2.9	2.1	0.7	1.8	2.7	2.1
Belgium	2.0	2.3	4.0	4.8	4.4	3.9	5.9	4.1	4.3	5.1	7.4	9.1	7.7	7.0	6.2
	3.6	3.9	5.7	6.4	6.0	5.5	7.5	5.8	5.9	6.8	9.1	10.7	9.3	8.6	7.8
Canada	-1.4	-0.1	0.2	-0.2	-1.1	2.4	2.0	2.2	2.9	1.6	1.7	0.5	1.2	1.9	2.1
	-0.3	1.0	1.3	0.9	—	3.5	3.1	3.3	4.0	2.7	2.8	1.6	2.3	3.0	3.2
Denmark	-3.2	-4.4	-3.2	-3.9	-3.9	-1.7	-0.1	0.1	-0.7	1.9	1.6	2.7	6.6	5.5	4.4
	-2.4	-3.6	-2.3	-3.1	-3.1	-0.8	0.7	0.9	0.2	2.7	2.4	3.5	7.5	6.4	5.3
Finland	-5.4	-6.6	-4.8	-5.8	-4.7	-3.6	-7.0	-6.2	-4.6	-1.7	-0.5	-2.1	-0.2	0.9	1.2
	-4.8	-6.0	-4.2	-5.2	-4.0	-2.9	-6.3	-5.6	-4.0	-1.1	0.2	-1.4	0.4	1.5	1.8
France	-0.9	-0.7	-0.4	-0.4	-0.7	0.4	-0.2	0.2	1.7	0.8	-0.8	0.2	0.6	0.7	0.1
	0.4	0.6	0.9	0.9	0.6	1.7	1.1	1.5	3.1	2.1	0.5	1.5	1.9	2.0	1.4

96

Germany	0.1	0.2	—	-1.3	0.5	3.4	2.2	1.3	1.7	2.3	2.5	2.4	0.9	-0.5	-1.7
	1.5	1.6	1.4	0.1	1.9	4.8	3.6	2.7	3.1	3.7	3.9	3.8	2.3	0.9	-0.3
Greece	-1.5	-0.6	-0.4	1.4	—	1.4	0.8	-0.1	—	0.3	3.0	9.3	5.7	5.1	4.9
	0.9	1.9	2.1	3.8	2.4	3.8	3.3	2.4	2.4	2.7	5.4	11.7	8.2	7.5	7.3
Ireland	2.5	2.0	2.7	4.0	6.8	10.3	5.7	6.5	9.2	10.7	11.7	13.3	14.3	10.6	9.1
	4.0	3.5	4.2	5.5	8.3	11.8	7.1	8.0	11.7	12.2	13.2	14.8	15.8	12.0	10.6
Italy	5.2	6.7	8.4	8.3	8.1	10.1	8.4	7.3	9.1	9.7	8.6	12.0	12.0	9.7	9.4
	6.0	7.5	9.2	9.1	8.9	10.9	9.2	8.1	9.9	10.5	9.4	12.9	12.8	10.5	10.2
Japan	-1.9	-1.7	-0.6	-0.3	-0.7	1.9	2.9	3.1	4.9	4.3	4.1	3.5	2.8	2.2	1.3
	-1.3	-1.2	—	0.3	-0.2	2.4	3.4	3.7	5.5	4.8	4.7	4.1	3.4	2.8	1.9
Netherlands	0.8	0.5	0.4	0.1	1.1	0.9	1.9	0.4	0.8	1.3	1.5	1.7	1.9	1.1	0.8
	3.5	3.2	3.1	2.8	3.8	3.6	4.6	3.1	3.5	4.0	4.2	4.4	4.6	3.8	3.5
Norway	-3.2	-4.5	-4.8	-6.4	-5.2	-4.7	-3.3	-2.5	-1.8	-2.3	-4.3	-5.4	-5.4	-5.4	-2.5
	-3.0	-4.2	-4.5	-6.1	-5.0	-4.5	-3.0	-2.2	-1.5	-2.0	-4.0	-5.1	-5.2	-5.1	-2.2
Spain	-0.7	0.3	-0.1	-0.4	0.6	—	0.3	0.8	1.7	1.1	1.0	1.3	3.5	3.7	3.2
	0.3	1.3	0.9	0.5	1.6	1.0	1.3	1.8	2.7	2.1	2.0	2.3	4.5	4.7	4.2
Sweden	-4.4	-5.9	-5.2	-4.0	-0.8	-1.6	-3.9	-3.7	-2.2	1.7	2.6	2.1	2.6	1.6	1.1
	-3.3	-4.7	-4.0	-2.9	0.4	-0.4	-2.8	-2.5	-1.0	2.9	3.7	3.2	3.8	2.8	2.3

(Table continues)

97

TABLE 4-3 (Continued)

	1970	1971	1972	1973	1974	1975	1976	1977	1978	1979	1980	1981	1982	1983	1984ᵃ
United Kingdom	-3.0	-1.6	0.8	3.6	3.7	3.2	3.4	1.7	3.8	3.2	1.1	-1.8	-3.3	-1.6	-2.0
	-0.7	0.7	3.1	5.9	6.0	5.5	5.7	4.0	6.1	5.5	3.5	0.5	-1.0	0.7	0.4
United States	—	0.5	—	0.2	-0.7	0.9	-0.4	-0.6	-0.9	-1.2	-0.7	-1.6	-0.3	0.2	0.5
	1.8	2.3	1.8	2.0	1.1	2.6	1.4	1.2	0.9	0.6	1.1	0.2	1.4	2.0	2.2
Total major seventh[b]	-0.4	0.2	0.4	0.6	0.2	2.0	1.3	1.0	1.6	1.3	1.2	0.6	0.9	1.0	0.7
	1.1	1.6	1.9	2.0	1.7	3.5	2.8	2.5	3.0	2.7	2.6	2.1	2.4	2.4	2.2
Total smaller countries[b]	-1.6	-1.6	-1.3	-0.7	-0.5	0.1	-0.7	0.1	0.5	1.3	1.4	1.7	2.2	2.6	2.6
	-0.4	-0.4	-0.1	0.5	0.7	1.3	1.9	1.1	1.8	2.5	2.6	2.9	3.4	3.8	3.8
Total of countries above[b]	-0.5	-0.1	0.2	0.4	0.1	1.7	1.2	0.9	1.5	1.3	1.2	0.7	1.1	1.2	1.0
	0.9	1.4	1.6	1.9	1.5	3.2	2.6	2.3	2.9	2.7	2.6	2.2	2.5	2.6	2.4

NOTE: The top series for each country estimates the deficit in connection with a "potential output," the lower series at the level of economic activity prevailing at midcycle.

a. Estimated.

b. Aggregated by relative size of GNP, using 1982 weights and exchange rates.

SOURCE: Organization for Economic Cooperation and Development.

tries shown in the table may lead to the rather surprising and unwarranted conclusion that there is no major fiscal problem in an international sense. As is shown in the third section of this chapter, this is not the case. Aggregated structural deficits rose until 1975 but since then have shown little trend and have ranged between 2 and 3 percent of GNP.[39] This average hides the fact that they rose in the United States and fell in Germany, Japan, and the United Kingdom. Even at these levels they lead to debt accumulation and to growing expenditures on interest payments.

The concept of the structural deficit, and perhaps even more that of the inflation-adjusted structural deficit, is particularly attractive to Keynesian economists, who believe that fiscal policy works mainly through its direct effect on aggregate demand and has little to do with inflation. To them, a fiscal deficit that is the consequence of a recession helps to sustain demand during the downswing but is not a vehicle for returning to full employment. They argue that a fiscal policy aimed at promoting full employment and a high level of economic activity may require substantial structural deficits during a period of inadequate demand, depending on the behavior of the private sector. In their view crowding out of private activity by the fiscal deficit does not occur as long as monetary policy is accommodative and the economy is not operating at full capacity.

This line of reasoning can be misleading for the effect on capital markets. It is conventional fiscal deficits that must be financed, not structural or even inflation-adjusted fiscal deficits. The net sale of bonds in nominal values in a given year, either to citizens or to foreigners, is determined by the size of conventional fiscal deficits and not by theoretical concepts. To the extent that it is the sale of bonds that creates pressures on capital markets or on exchange rates, the traditional measure of the deficit cannot be ignored. Of course, the sale of government bonds may generate less pressure on the financial market when there is little private demand for credit (that is, during a downswing) than during a boom.[40] That is one reason why it is so difficult to find statistical relations between deficits and interest rates.

Table 4–4 indicates the extent to which adjusting for both the cycle and the rate of inflation gets away from reality. If taken seriously, the results in that table would indicate—as some economists have actually argued—that fiscal policy has been excessively restrictive even in countries such as Italy, where public expenditure as a share of GNP has grown by as much as twenty percentage points over the period shown in the table.[41]

TABLE 4-4
GENERAL GOVERNMENT INFLATION-ADJUSTED STRUCTURAL FISCAL DEFICITS, 1971–1984
(percentage of GNP)

	1971	1972	1973	1974	1975	1976	1977	1978	1979	1980	1981	1982	1983	1984[a]
Australia	-3.4	-3.3	-1.2	-5.6	-3.2	-0.2	-3.4	-1.1	-1.7	-3.0	-2.6	-3.5	0.5	2.4
Austria	-2.7	-2.8	-2.0	-2.2	-0.5	1.7	1.3	1.0	1.9	0.2	-1.3	0.1	1.6	0.2
Belgium	1.3	2.3	2.2	-1.1	-1.4	2.5	1.7	3.3	4.0	4.8	5.6	2.9	2.5	2.3
Canada	0.9	1.2	0.9	0.1	3.7	3.3	3.5	4.0	2.5	2.6	1.3	1.8	2.4	2.6
Denmark	-3.1	-1.5	-1.6	-0.4	0.7	2.0	2.6	1.5	3.8	3.4	3.8	7.0	5.7	4.4
Finland	-5.0	-3.1	-3.4	-1.3	-0.3	-3.8	-3.0	-2.2	0.6	2.7	1.0	2.2	3.0	3.0
France	—	0.3	0.3	-0.5	0.6	0.1	0.6	2.1	1.0	-0.7	0.3	0.7	0.8	0.2
Germany	2.0	1.8	0.6	2.3	5.0	3.5	2.5	2.9	3.3	3.2	3.0	1.6	0.4	-0.8
Greece	1.4	1.3	1.3	-1.5	1.9	1.2	0.3	-0.3	-1.6	0.2	6.4	3.2	2.2	1.7
Ireland	0.8	1.7	2.4	3.6	5.6	1.8	3.8	7.8	6.4	4.8	6.2	8.3	6.8	5.7
Italy	5.3	6.5	3.8	-0.7	2.0	-0.3	-2.4	2.6	1.2	-3.4	1.4	2.0	—	2.3

Japan	-0.7	0.3	1.1	1.2	2.9	3.4	3.4	5.1	4.4	3.3	3.1	2.7	2.3	1.3
Netherlands	-0.7	-0.7	-0.7	-0.1	-0.4	1.2	0.6	1.9	2.3	1.4	1.3	1.7	2.4	1.5
Norway	-4.0	-4.3	-5.7	-4.4	-3.8	-2.5	-1.9	-1.3	-2.0	-4.1	-5.3	-5.4	-5.3	-2.3
Spain	1.1	0.8	0.3	1.3	0.7	1.0	1.6	2.3	1.5	1.2	1.2	2.9	2.9	2.4
Sweden	-2.8	-2.3	-0.8	3.5	2.5	0.3	1.0	1.9	4.8	6.9	5.4	4.8	3.3	2.4
United Kingdom	-5.1	-1.0	0.9	-1.6	-5.3	-2.3	-3.6	2.1	-0.6	-4.0	-4.4	-4.5	-1.5	-1.8
United States	1.2	1.0	0.6	-1.1	0.8	0.2	-0.1	-0.5	-1.3	-1.1	-1.4	0.4	1.2	1.4
Total major seven[b]	0.6	1.1	0.9	-0.3	1.3	1.0	0.5	1.5	0.7	-0.1	—	0.7	1.1	0.9
Total smaller countries[b]	-1.4	-1.2	-0.8	-1.0	-0.4	0.6	0.1	1.1	1.5	1.3	1.3	1.5	2.1	2.0
Total of countries above[b]	0.4	0.8	0.7	-0.4	1.1	0.9	0.5	1.5	0.8	0.1	0.1	0.8	1.2	1.0

a. Estimated.
b. Aggregated by relative size of GNP, using 1982 weights and exchange rates.
SOURCE: Organization for Economic Cooperation and Development.

Fiscal Deficits and the International Credit Market

International Character of Capital Market. The previous section presented estimates of fiscal deficits for many industrial countries. One who believed that a relation exists between the fiscal deficit of a country and that country's real rate of interest might be tempted to use those estimates to test such a relation for each country. This country-by-country approach, however, is unlikely to capture the relation between the fiscal situation and the behavior of real interest rates for one important reason: countries are not isolated but are all parts of a credit market that is becoming progressively more international. Therefore, there may be valid reasons to concentrate on an aggregated picture of fiscal developments in industrial countries.

In recent years long-term real interest rates increased not just in countries such as the United States, where the size of the fiscal deficit was increasing but also in countries such as Germany and the United Kingdom, where the size of the fiscal deficit was falling.[42] One could, of course, argue that these synchronous increases in real interest rates were caused by common external factors, such as the increase in the price of oil or the policies of monetary restraint, that affected all the countries. But one could also argue that they were due to the growth in aggregated deficits as proportions of aggregated savings.[43] Such an approach would give substance to a criticism of U.S. fiscal policy frequently made in Europe: that, given the size of the American economy, regardless of what fiscal action European countries took, they would still face high real interest rates as long as the fiscal deficit in the United States remained high. In other words, it would take a very large reduction in the deficits of other countries to make a dent in the aggregate deficit as long as the U.S. deficit was large and growing.

A discussion of, say, the labor or the housing market, would focus on national or regional factors because the price of labor or houses is likely to be determined by national or even regional supply and demand schedules. Houses and, to a lesser extent, workers do not cross national frontiers. Their prices are thus only marginally affected, at least in the short run, by factors beyond the national border. Some prices, however, are set in broader markets. The price of oil or gold, for example, is not determined by national demand and supply schedules. The same is true for many other commodities that are internationally traded and that, apart from distortions created by import duties and subsidies, respond to the law of one price. The price of gold is basically the same in New York, Hong Kong, Milan, and London.

The market for money—the credit market—is much closer in character to the gold or oil market than to the housing or labor market. Helped by the recent technological revolution in the information and communication fields, financial managers are now able to follow closely what happens in the money markets of different countries.[44] This revolution has made it possible for managers to have rapid access to much of the relevant information about domestic and foreign credit markets and to give instructions that can move enormous sums of money within minutes from one financial center to another. As someone has put it: "There is only one real money in the world [today] and that's balances at the Federal Reserve."[45] Those balances can be changed within seconds. Some governments attempt to prevent these movements through regulations and capital controls, which can temporarily insulate a national financial market from the rest of the world. Over the longer run (which may not be very long), the attempts generally fail unless government control is so extensive as to leave little scope for private initiative.

A strong argument can be made that the market for money is now an international market in which the price of money or credit—the interest rate—is determined by the intersection of truly international supply and demand schedules. The annual flow of international lending (bank lending and bond issues) runs in the hundreds of billions of U.S. dollars.[46] The size of the Eurocurrency market, 80 percent of which is in Eurodollars, in 1983 exceeded US$2 trillion, or more than ten times the amount of U.S. private savings.[47]

The international character of the credit market has been implicitly understood by those international finance economists who have developed the theoretical concept of interest rate parity. This concept has carried to the credit market the law of one price that had been developed for traded goods. Interest rate parity means that interest rates, adjusted for differential rates of taxation and inflation, for different maturities and default risks, and for expected changes in the exchange rates, cannot diverge for very long across countries.[48] When they do diverge, money moves out of the countries with interest rates lower than the equilibrium rate and into the countries with rates higher than the equilibrium rate. These capital movements continue as long as national interest rates diverge from the internationally determined equilibrium rate.[49]

If the concept of interest rate parity is empirically valid (and if national credit markets are as integrated as described above), it has powerful implications for an interpretation of the effects of fiscal deficits on capital markets and, consequently, on interest rates. Fiscal pressures on interest rates within one country, for example, cannot be assessed by relating the demand for credit to the supply of credit within that country. This may be so even when the country is as large as the United States. It makes little sense to relate the U.S. fiscal deficit to the supply of U.S. savings, as has been done in many empirical attempts and in many discussions that have tried to find a connection, or have argued that one exists, between the U.S. fiscal deficit and the U.S. real rate of interest.[50]

The U.S. demand for credit, whether originating in the public or in the business sector, can be met by the U.S. supply of credit *as well as* by the rest of the world's supply of credit. But, obviously, the U.S. demand for credit must compete against the rest of the world's demand for credit. If the U.S. demand rises because of a higher fiscal deficit at a time when the rest of the world's demand falls, interest rates need not rise. *Mutatis mutandis,* given the U.S. demand for credit, an increase in net investment or in fiscal deficits in Europe or Japan is likely to cause U.S. as well as foreign interest rates to rise.

Figure 4–1 offers a graphical view of interest rate determination in an international setting for a given output. G represents the govern-

FIGURE 4–1

INTERNATIONAL DEMAND FOR AND SUPPLY OF LOANABLE FUNDS

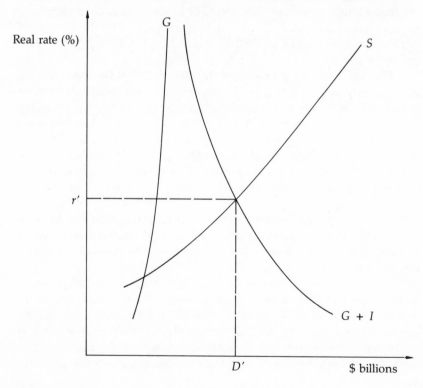

ments' net demand for funds, which is assumed to be identical with the combined fiscal deficits of the countries. This schedule is shown to be mildly positive-sloping to capture the fact that a higher real interest rate (shown on the vertical axis) is likely to be accompanied by a higher fiscal deficit (*ceteris paribus*). $G + I$ represents the total demand for credit, where I can represent either gross or net investment, depending on whether the supply schedule, S, represents gross or net private saving. The equilibrium real rate is shown by r' and the level of credit at which demand and supply are in equilibrium by D'.[51]

Since the U.S. credit market is the most efficient, the largest, and the least regulated, the U.S. interest rate is arguably the best indicator of the international real rate.[52] It is, in a broad sense, the best measure of the opportunity cost of investing money anywhere else. The differences between the U.S. rate and those of other countries can be attributed to the various factors mentioned above.

Let us now consider one by one the elements behind the schedules that make up figure 4–1, concentrating particularly on G, which represents the combined fiscal deficits of the countries and thus reflects the governments' demand for loanable funds. Our discussion argues in favor of aggregating the fiscal deficits of all countries, not just the industrial countries, to assess the total effect of governments' credit demands. Taken literally, this would require the aggregation of more than a hundred countries. This is hardly feasible and not really necessary since the economies of the largest countries are so large that concentration on them captures a sizable share of the total. In 1983, for example, the G-7 countries (the United States, Japan, Germany, France, the United Kingdom, Italy, and Canada) accounted for at least 70 percent of the nonsocialist world's GNP. The G-7 countries are so large compared with the other OECD countries that the basic proportions hardly change when the group of industrial countries is extended beyond the G-7 countries.[53] Since far more data are available for this smaller group and little is gained by extending it, the analysis below is limited to G-7 countries.[54]

Fiscal Deficit of G-7 Countries. Table 4–5 provides some basic data for the G-7 countries combined. Columns (1) and (2) show the ratio of the combined fiscal deficits to the combined GNPs. Column (1) refers to central governments and column (2) to general governments, that is, to a broader group, which includes local governments and some other public institutions. These data show only minor differences from those in tables 4–1 and 4–2. The ratio of fiscal deficit to GNP was very low until 1975, when it grew sharply because of large increases in current public expenditure and a slowdown in economic activity.[55]

TABLE 4–5
BASIC DATA ON AGGREGATED FISCAL DEFICITS AND SAVINGS
OF G-7 COUNTRIES, 1972–1983
(percent)

	Percentage of G-7 GNP				Percentage of G-7 GPS		Percentage of G-7 NPS	
	CGD (1)	GGD (2)	GPS (3)	NPS (4)	CGD (5)	GGD (6)	CGD (7)	GGD (8)
1972	n.a.	0.7	19.8	10.3	n.a.	3.4	n.a.	6.6
1973	n.a.	—	20.9	11.3	n.a.	—	n.a.	—
1974	n.a.	0.8	19.9	9.7	n.a.	4.0	n.a.	8.2
1975	4.8	4.3	20.7	10.2	23.3	20.8	47.4	42.3
1976	3.6	2.8	20.3	9.8	17.9	14.0	37.1	29.2
1977	3.2	2.1	20.2	9.6	16.0	10.6	33.6	22.3
1978	3.5	2.4	21.4	10.7	16.3	11.1	32.6	22.2
1979	3.1	1.8	20.7	9.9	15.0	8.9	31.4	18.7
1980	3.5	2.5	20.2	9.0	17.6	12.4	39.2	27.6
1981	3.7	2.6	20.3	8.9	18.4	12.8	42.1	29.4
1982	4.6	4.0	19.8	8.1	23.4	20.3	57.1	49.4
1983	5.7	4.1	19.6	7.9	28.9	20.9	71.6	51.7

n.a. = not available.

NOTE: CGD = central government deficit; GGD = general government deficit; GPS = gross private savings; and NPS = net private savings. All the national figures were converted to dollars using the average exchange rates for each year. The dollar figures were then aggregated, using GNPs as weights, and divided as required. Because this table was calculated independently from table 4–2, there are some minor differences in the figures shown in column 2 from those in table 4–2.

SOURCE: Table 4–1 and data made available by OECD.

Between 1975 and 1979 the ratio of fiscal deficit to GNP fell considerably because of a slowdown in the relative growth of public expenditure and a sustained economic recovery that, in conjunction with high rates of inflation and progressive tax systems, raised the amount of taxes collected. From the lower point reached in 1979 the combined deficit rose sharply, reaching very high levels by 1982–1983. These trends apply both to the central government only (column 1) and to general government (column 2). As a consequence, the demand for credit on the part of the governments of these countries grew enormously.[56]

Was this increase in fiscal deficits accompanied by increasing private sector savings, as some recent popular versions of Ricardo's equivalence theorem argue?[57] Columns 3 and 4 cast some light on this question and provide information on the supply schedule of figure 4–1. For either gross private savings (column 3) or net private savings (column 4), the conclusion is the same: there is no evidence of a relation of a Ricardian type between fiscal deficits (or debt accumulation) and the saving behavior of the private sector. In fact, both net and gross private savings fell significantly in the 1979–1983 period, which was exactly the period when fiscal deficits were growing fastest.[58] Between 1979 and 1983 the ratio of gross private savings to GNP fell by 1.1 percentage points, and the ratio of net private savings to GNP fell by 2.0 percentage points.

Columns 5, 6, 7, and 8 also provide evidence on the degree to which government borrowing was absorbing the supply of gross private savings (columns 5 and 6) or of net private savings (columns 7 and 8). In my view, the relevant relation is the one with net private savings. The reason is that, although in theory depreciation allowances could be used by enterprises to buy government bonds, in practice they are generally used by the enterprises themselves to replace depreciated investment or to make new investment.[59] Columns 7 and 8 show that in 1982 and 1983 a very large share of all net private savings was absorbed by the governments' need to finance their fiscal deficits. Starting in 1979, the ratio of fiscal deficit to net private savings rose sharply, reaching very high levels in 1982 and 1983 and thus putting sharp pressure on the capital markets.

While the governments were absorbing progressively larger shares of the G-7 net private savings, what was happening to the other component of the total net demand-for-credit schedule, namely, investment? For the G-7 group gross private domestic investment as a share of GNP fell from 18–19 percent in the 1977–1979 period to 17 percent in 1980–1981 and to 15 percent in 1982–1983. As a proportion of gross private savings, it fell from about 90 percent in 1976–1979 to about 85 percent in 1980–1981 and to about 75 percent in 1982–1983.

Table 4–6 shows the funds raised by the private sectors of the seven largest countries in the 1980–1983 period. The basic conclusion is the same as that derived from the data on fixed investment cited above. In 1982 the private sectors of all the countries except the United Kingdom reduced the quantity of funds raised; in some, the reduction was dramatic. In 1983 the U.S. private sector's demand for funds rose significantly, but that of the other countries, including the United Kingdom, did not. Thus, to some extent, *the public sectors' higher financing needs were compensated for by the private sectors' lower needs.*

This implicit accommodation of the private sector to the government's sharply higher financing demands did not prevent long-term

TABLE 4–6
FUNDS RAISED BY PRIVATE SECTOR, G-7 COUNTRIES, 1980–1983
(percentage of GNP)

	1980	1981	1982	1983[a]
Canada	14.1	14.4	3.3	3.5
France	13.6	13.1	11.8	10.8
Germany	10.9	10.6	8.3	8.8
Italy	12.0	12.5	9.0	9.1
Japan	12.2	12.2	12.1	11.8
United Kingdom	9.0	9.5	10.5	9.4
United States	9.7	9.1	6.8	9.5

a. Preliminary.

SOURCE: Bank for International Settlements, *Fifty-fourth Annual Report*, Basel, June 18, 1984, p. 45.

real interest rates from rising sharply in 1981 and even more in 1982 and 1983, although in the absence of that accommodation they would probably have increased even more. For the G-7 countries combined, long-term real interest rates rose from about 1 percent in 1976–1979 to 1.9 percent in 1980, 4.2 percent in 1981, 5.4 percent in 1982, and 6.0 percent in 1983.[60] This increase continued into 1984 because of a rising demand for credit by the private sector in the United States as well as in some European countries. This increase in private demand has been partly compensated for by the lower public demand associated with lower deficits.[61]

Share of the United States in the G-7 Totals. The previous section treated the G-7 countries as a unit and showed that the combined fiscal deficit grew sharply in recent years in relation to the combined GNPs and the total pool of savings. By 1982–1983 these deficits were absorbing very large proportions of G-7 net private savings. This factor inevitably put strong pressures on credit markets and contributed to significant increases in real interest rates even though the public sector's higher demand for credit was in part neutralized by a lower private demand for credit as a consequence of the severe recession, which in Europe continued well into 1983. In this section the role of the U.S. fiscal deficit in the totals is shown.

Table 4–7 presents the relevant information. In 1983 the United States contributed 42.8 percent of total G-7 gross private savings and 35.5 percent of total G-7 net private saving (columns 1 and 2). These percentages were sharply higher than those in 1979 but close to those in 1972. The main reason for these changes was the appreciation of the exchange rate: as the dollar grew stronger, the share of U.S. saving in the total also grew. Between 1979 and 1983 the share of the U.S. fiscal deficit in the total grew sharply, from 15.9 percent for central government and − 13.3 percent for general government to 49.5 percent and 46.7 percent, respectively (columns 3 and 4). Similar proportions had been experienced briefly in 1975, but they had fallen dramatically by 1979. By 1983 the U.S. fiscal deficit was absorbing sharply higher shares of G-7 net private savings than in previous years. The U.S. central government fiscal deficit's share of G-7 net private savings, for example, rose from 5.0 percent in 1979 to 11 percent in 1980, 12.6 percent in 1981, 25.1 percent in 1982, and 35.5 percent in 1983.

TABLE 4–7

SHARE OF UNITED STATES IN AGGREGATED G-7 TOTALS, 1972–1983

(percent)

	U.S. GPS as Percentage of G-7 GPS (1)	U.S. NPS as Percentage of G-7 NPS (2)	U.S. Fiscal Deficit as Percentage of G-7 Fiscal Deficit		U.S. Fiscal Deficit as Percentage of G-7 GPS		U.S. Fiscal Deficit as Percentage of G-7 NPS	
			CG (3)	GG (4)	CG (5)	GG (6)	CG (7)	GG (8)
1972	41.2	34.7	n.a.	20.8	3.7	0.7	7.2	1.4
1973	39.2	35.5	n.a.	—	2.5	− 1.3	4.6	− 2.5
1974	38.8	33.3	n.a.	19.7	0.3	0.8	0.5	1.6
1975	40.2	35.7	46.0	44.2	10.7	9.2	21.8	18.7
1976	39.3	33.2	41.9	34.5	7.5	4.8	15.6	10.1
1977	38.7	32.8	37.7	20.1	6.0	2.1	12.7	4.5
1978	34.7	28.0	24.9	− 3.3	4.1	− 0.4	8.1	− 0.7
1979	34.3	26.7	15.9	− 13.3	2.4	− 1.2	5.0	− 2.5
1980	34.0	24.7	28.0	19.6	4.9	2.4	11.0	5.4
1981	38.7	31.2	29.9	15.9	5.5	2.0	12.6	4.7
1982	40.8	31.0	43.9	44.8	10.3	9.1	25.1	22.1
1983	42.8	35.5	49.5	46.7	14.3	9.8	35.5	24.2

n.a. = not available.

NOTE: GPS = gross private savings; NPS = net private savings; CG = central government; and GG = general government. All the national figures were converted to dollars using the average exchange rates for each year. The dollar figures were then aggregated and divided as required.

SOURCE: Based on data made available by OECD.

That is, in 1983 the deficit of the U.S. central government was absorbing more than a third of the total net private savings of the G-7 countries. The percentages for the general government are only marginally less dramatic.[62]

Between 1979 and 1983 the U.S. central government fiscal deficit rose from 1.2 percent to 5.8 percent of U.S. GNP (see table 4–1); the central government fiscal deficit of the other six countries of the G-7 group rose from 4.6 percent to 5.6 percent of the GNP of those countries. The percentages for the general government's fiscal deficits are as follows: for the United States, 0.6 percent in 1979 and 3.9 percent in 1983; for the other six countries, 3.7 percent in 1979 and 4.3 percent in 1983.[63] In either case, the U.S. deficit has put pressures on the credit market of the G-7 countries. The downswing in economic activity experienced by the G-7 countries is likely to have prevented a greater rise in real interest rates. Should the fiscal deficits of the G-7 countries remain as high as in recent years while the U.S. recovery spreads to the other countries, higher real rates would be expected. Should the United States experience a slowdown, the public sector's higher demand for credit (associated with a fiscal deficit made higher by the cycle) could very well be neutralized by the private sector's lower demand for credit. Which of these two effects would be predominant is difficult to tell. What happened in the rest of the world would also play a substantial role.

Concluding Remarks

This paper has surveyed the fiscal experience of the industrial countries with particular emphasis on the major countries. In spite of obvious difficulties in assessing the fiscal situation of individual countries, and even more in comparing the fiscal situation of different countries, the statistical information available supports the conclusions that (1) over the past decade there has been a gradual and fairly general deterioration of the fiscal situation of the OECD countries and (2) in more recent years, and in relative terms, the U.S. fiscal situation has deteriorated more than that of other countries.

It is, however, important to realize that, even though the fiscal deficit has grown considerably in the United States, its magnitude, expressed as a share of gross national product, is not unusually high: it is still lower than those of several European countries and is of the same order of magnitude as that of Japan, a country not usually thought to be in a serious fiscal situation. Given the size of the U.S. economy, however, what happens to it has important implications for other countries. Thus the large absorption of the pool of savings of the industrial countries by the growing U.S. deficit after 1979 may have been an important factor in bringing about higher real interest rates.

Notes

1. The Office of Management and Budget reports that "in absolute terms, annual Federal and federally assisted net lending . . . increased 239 percent, from $25.5 billion in 1974 to $86.5 billion in 1983. . . . In 1983, Federal and federally assisted borrowing totaled $281 billion, up from an average of $32 billion a year during the first half of the 1970s." See OMB, *Special Analyses, Budget of the United States Government, FY 1985,* 1984, pp. F-1–F-2.

2. Ibid. (italics added).

3. Without detailed knowledge about the subsidy content of these programs, it is difficult to assess their effect on the aggregate demand for, and supply of, credit.

4. I owe this point to Alexandre Kafka. This discussion assumes that the borrowing requirements would be the same. The assumption becomes unrealistic when additional spending by the public corporations is brought about by political pressures or when the fact that public corporations cannot go bankrupt induces larger borrowing by them.

5. Michael Boskin, "Federal Government Deficits: Some Myths and Realities," *American Economic Review, Papers and Proceedings,* vol. 72, no. 2 (May 1982), pp. 296–303; John Bossons, "Measuring the Viability of Implicit Intergenerational Social Contracts" (Paper presented to the Fortieth Congress of the International Institute of Public Finance, Innsbruck, Austria, August 28–September 1, 1984; Willem H. Buiter, "Measurements of the Public Sector Deficit and Its Implications for Policy Evaluation and Design," *IMF Staff Papers,* vol. 30, no. 2 (June 1983), pp. 306–49; and Laurence J. Kotlikoff, "The Economic Impact of Deficit Finance," *IMF Staff Papers,* vol. 31, no. 2 (September 1984).

6. A point that has often been ignored is that some public expenditures result in expected future liabilities. Thus the "assets" associated with loss-making railroads, subways, airlines, atomic energy plants, and public steel mills bring about a stream of future liabilities.

7. That is, the measure of the public debt should include the discounted net difference between future expenditure and revenue. The assumption that there will not be any change in the law in future years seems unrealistic, however.

8. Robert Eisner and Paul J. Pieper, "A New View of the Federal Debt and Budget Deficits," *American Economic Review* (March 1984), pp. 11–29.

9. This is the concept recommended by the International Monetary Fund, *Draft Manual on Government Finance Statistics* (Washington, D.C.: IMF, 1974).

10. International Monetary Fund, *World Economic Outlook,* Occasional Paper 27 (Washington, D.C.: IMF, 1984).

11. See E. Cary Brown, "Fiscal Policies in the Thirties: A Reappraisal," *American Economic Review,* vol. 46, no. 5 (December 1957), pp. 857–79; and

David Lusher, "The Stabilizing Effectiveness of Budget Flexibility," *Policies to Combat Depression* (New York: NBER, 1956), pp. 77–90. Some economists of the rational expectations school today believe that fiscal policy may have no effect on economic activity since individuals may fully anticipate policy actions by the government. Furthermore, they believe that how public expenditure is financed, whether by taxes or by borrowing, may also have no effect on economic activity.

12. Estimates of structural fiscal deficits in industrial countries are provided in the second section of this paper.

13. For example, what is the potential output of a country that runs into balance-of-payment bottlenecks well before its productive capacity is fully utilized?

14. The interested reader should look at Buiter, "Measurements of the Public Sector Deficit"; Eisner and Pieper, "A New View of the Federal Debt"; and at the papers presented at the international conference on "Economic Policy and National Accounting in Inflationary Conditions" held at Dorga, Italy, January 25–28, 1984. Two conference volumes, edited by Giorgio Szëgo, will be published by North-Holland.

15. The literature on the "Fisher effect" is enormous. See, for example, the studies included in Vito Tanzi, ed., *Taxation, Inflation, and Interest Rates* (Washington, D.C.: IMF, 1984).

16. Taxes on interest based on nominal values may complicate these conclusions. See ibid.

17. This relation depends on the relative size of the public debt (its share of GNP) and its maturity. The higher the share of the debt in GNP and the shorter its maturity, the greater will be the sensitivity of the conventionally measured fiscal deficit to changes in expected inflation.

18. Thus this part will not contribute to total demand.

19. Logically it should not be taxed.

20. It has been argued that the long-term real rate of interest is 3 percent, so that the real deficit must be measured in relation to this value. See Bossons, "Measuring the Viability."

21. See, for the United States, Eisner and Pieper, "A New View of the Federal Debt"; for Canada, John Bossons and D. Peter Dungan, "The Government Deficit: Too High or Too Low?" *Canadian Tax Journal*, vol. 31 (January–February 1983), pp. 1–29; for the United Kingdom, Buiter, "Measurements of the Public Sector Deficit," and Marcus Miller and Simon Babbs, "The True Cost of Debt Service and the Public Sector Financial Deficit" (mimeographed, April 1983); for other European countries, Alex Cukierman and Jorgen Mortensen, "Monetary Assets and Inflation-induced Distortions of the National Accounts—Conceptual Issues and Correction of Sectoral Income Flows in 5 EEC Countries" (mimeographed, June 1983). It is no accident that most of the authors who have argued along these lines can be classified as Keynesians.

22. I have argued elsewhere that the very low after-tax real rates of interest experienced during much of the 1970s were at least in part the result of fiscal illusions. See Vito Tanzi, "Inflationary Expectations, Economic Activity, Taxes, and Interest Rates," *American Economic Review*, vol. 70, no. 1 (March 1980),

pp. 12–21.

23. This positive effect on revenue is due to bracket creep, which affects all incomes, and to the distortion of taxable capital incomes (capital gains, profits, and interest rates) due to inflation. For a detailed discussion of these effects of inflation on tax revenue, see Vito Tanzi, *Inflation and the Personal Income Tax, An International Perspective* (Cambridge: Cambridge University Press, 1980).

24. It is necessary to recognize, however, that these two effects of inflation are different in principle. The rise in revenues as inflation increases happens whether the public recognizes it or not, and taxpayers are unable to do anything about it except put pressure on policy makers to cut taxes. The reinvestment of interest receipts viewed as repayment of principal depends on the public's recognition of part of interest as repayment of principal and on bondholders' decisions to maintain their wealth in the face of this depreciation of real value.

25. This comment applies also to methods of adjustment, such as those of Miller and Babbs ("The True Cost of Debt Service") and of Bossons ("Measuring the Viability"), that remove from the deficit all the excess in interest payment above a constant real rate of interest.

26. See the article by Phillip Cagan, *The AEI Economist*, November 1981.

27. For a discussion of this point, see Vito Tanzi, *Inflation and the Personal Income Tax*, chaps. 10, 11.

28. Estimates of inflation-adjusted fiscal deficits are provided in the second section of this paper.

29. The core deficit can be defined as the fiscal balance that would exist if the economy were on its trend and no temporary measures had distorted taxes and expenditures. See, on this definition, Vito Tanzi and Mario Blejer, "Fiscal Deficits and Balance of Payments Disequilibrium in IMF Adjustment Programs," in Joaquin Muns, ed., *Adjustment, Conditionality, and International Financing* (Washington, D.C.: IMF, 1984), pp. 117–36.

30. The imposition of a once-for-all (*una tantum*) tax on wealth to reduce the fiscal deficit, now being discussed in Italy, would be another example of these temporary policies.

31. It is on a cash basis except for Canada, which is on a national income accounts basis.

32. In 1983–1984, because of the sharp fall in the rate of inflation and the pickup in economic activity, the differences among these measures were much reduced.

33. In 1975 the countries tried to maintain real incomes by sharply increasing public expenditure.

34. This discussion relates to general, not central, government.

35. See Patrice Muller and Robert W. R. Price, "Structural Budget Deficits and Fiscal Stance," OECD, Economics and Statistics Department, *Working Papers*, July 1984, p. 4. This source should be consulted for more detail on the methods used to estimate these structural deficits.

36. The effect of the cycle will be magnified if prices rise during booms and fall (or at least increase more slowly) during recessions.

37. In the process, price changes, changes in interest rates, and changes in expectations are assumed away.

38. Compared with the structural deficit, the full-employment budget surplus of the New Economics appeared at the time to be much more objectively defined and measured.

39. In a recent interesting paper R. Glenn Hubbard has analyzed the behavior of structural deficits over the past two decades. His conclusions are "(1) the declines in potential income [in OECD countries in the second half of the 1970s] had the immediate effect of raising budget deficits; (2) the higher budget deficits persisted because of the slow adjustment of government spending; (3) the responses of fiscal systems to changes in potential income, anticipated deficits, and cyclical disturbances did not change after 1973" (see "Structural Government Budget Deficits: Reappraisal and Implications" [Paper presented to the 40th Congress of the International Institute of Public Finance, Innsbruck, Austria, August 28–September 1, 1984], pp. 12–13).

40. Those who defend the use of inflation-adjusted fiscal deficits generally argue that inflation is not caused by fiscal deficits and that the real demand for bonds is not affected by inflation, so that the nominal demand for bonds grows in line with inflation and the financing of the deficit does not become more expensive because the real rate of interest is not affected. They also often argue that a less restrictive monetary policy will keep real rates low.

41. For two such examples, see Cukierman and Mortensen, "Monetary Assets and Inflation-induced Distortions"; and Olivier J. Blanchard and Lawrence H. Summers, "Perspectives on High World Real Interest Rates" (Paper presented at the Brookings Panel on Economic Activity, September 13–14, 1984).

42. See IMF, *World Economic Outlook,* Occasional Paper 27, table 2–7, p. 121.

43. The rise in real interest rates continued after the effects of the two factors mentioned should have disappeared. As tables 4–1 and 4–2 show, there was a sharp growth in the ratio of fiscal deficit to GNP in a majority of industrial countries. When concepts such as inflation-adjusted structural deficits are used, the increase is not visible.

44. See Martin Mayer, *The Money Bazaars: Understanding the Banking Revolution around Us* (New York: E. P. Dutton, 1984).

45. Ibid., p. 75.

46. Net international bank lending was $215 billion in 1982 and $185 billion in 1983 (estimate by the Bureau of Statistics of the IMF). For those two years, international net bond issues were $58.5 billion and $59 billion, respectively (estimate by the Bank for International Settlements).

47. Mayer (*The Money Bazaars,* p. 96) reports that foreign exchange trading accounts for "probably $100 billion a day."

48. These needed adjustments make the empirical testing of this theory difficult.

49. There is an ongoing academic debate on just how perfect the international capital market is. Various papers have debated the issue. See Martin Feldstein and C. Harioka, "Domestic Savings and International Capital Flows," *Economic Journal* (London), vol. 90 (June 1980), pp. 314–29; Martin

Feldstein, "Domestic Saving and International Capital Movements in the Long Run and the Short Run," *European Economic Review* (Amsterdam), vol. 21 (March/April 1983), pp. 129–51; Jeffrey D. Sachs, "The Current Account and Macroeconomic Adjustment in the 1970s," *Brookings Papers on Economic Activity* (1981), no. 1, pp. 201–68; Jeffrey D. Sachs, "Aspects of the Current Account Behavior of OECD Economies," in E. Claassen and P. Salin, eds., *Recent Issues in the Theory of Flexible Exchange Rates* (Amsterdam: North-Holland, 1983), pp. 101–28; Arnold C. Harberger, "Vignettes on the World Capital Market," *American Economic Review, Papers and Proceedings of the Ninety-second Annual Meeting of the American Economic Association* (Nashville), vol. 70 (May 1980), pp. 331–37; James Tobin, "Comments on 'Domestic Saving and International Capital Movements in the Long Run and the Short Run' by M. Feldstein," *European Economic Review* (Amsterdam), vol. 21 (March/April 1983), pp. 153–56; and Alessandro Penati and Michael Dooley, "Current Account Imbalances and Capital Formation in Industrial Countries, 1949–81," *IMF Staff Papers*, vol. 31, no. 1 (March 1984), pp. 1–24.

At the center of the debate has been a correlation of average saving rates of individual countries with those countries' investment rates. It is argued that the less perfect the capital market, the higher the correlation, since in isolation countries would need to finance their investment with their own saving. In a world with an integrated capital market, of course, a country's investment can be financed by foreign saving (by capital inflows) as long as the rate of return to that investment is higher than the rate abroad. As often happens in academic debates, this issue is far from being settled.

50. See, for example, the studies cited in James R. Barth, George Iden, and Frank S. Russek, "Do Federal Deficits Really Matter?" *Contemporary Policy Issues*, vol. 3, no. 1 (Fall 1984–85), pp. 79–94.

51. One could argue that figure 4–1 should also take into account money creation, which can also satisfy the demand for credit on the part of the government or the private sector. If this were done and if money expansion did not affect nominal value, one would want to shift the supply schedule, *S*, to the right by the amount of money creation. This movement would reduce the rate of interest. When money changes are anticipated, however, they do affect nominal values, and the changes in nominal values may totally neutralize the interest-reducing effect (the liquidity effect) of the monetary expansion. If money creation brings about higher nominal interest rates, for example, this would affect the size of the conventionally measured deficit and thus the demand for credit by the government. Some recent papers have presented evidence that the liquidity effect has largely disappeared in the United States. The change in monetary policy that occurred in several countries about 1979 when inflationary expectations were high, however, is likely to have contributed at the time to increases in real rates.

52. An alternative would be to average the rates of the various countries. But, as pointed out earlier, this would imply averaging different risks, tax effects, and so on.

53. See table 4–2.

54. Up to 1982 there was a large net demand for credit from some of the

largest developing countries, such as Brazil, Mexico, and Argentina. In 1983 these countries contributed much less to the international demand for credit. OPEC's surplus also disappeared. OPEC surpluses do not enter any of the tables.

55. Current disbursements of government as a percentage of gross domestic product rose from 29.5 percent in 1973 to 31.4 percent in 1974 and to 34.4 percent in 1975. The growth of real GDP at market prices was 0.2 percent in 1974 and −0.4 percent in 1975.

56. Over the period shown in the table, the ratio of general government debt to GNP rose by about fourteen percentage points, nine of them during the 1979–1983 period.

57. See discussion in chapter 7.

58. For the G-7 countries combined, the real recession (fall in real GDP) did not come until 1982. The evidence on household sector saving is more ambiguous. It declined in some countries and rose in others.

59. The fact that the managers of corporations are often not their owners implies that they will prefer to reinvest available funds rather than pay them out to the shareholders and thus allow them to buy government bonds. There is evidence, however, that corporations have in recent years bought some public bonds.

60. See IMF, *World Economic Outlook*, Occasional Paper 27, p. 121. These composites are averages of individual country rates, weighted for each year in proportion to the U.S. dollar values of the respective GNPs in the preceding three years. In the United States long-term real interest rates fell from 2.3 in 1976 to 0.7 in 1979. They rose to 2.1 in 1980, 4.2 in 1981, 6.6 in 1982, and 6.7 in 1983. The real interest rates are derived by using the annual change in the average GNP deflators to adjust the corresponding nominal rates.

61. The combined deficit of the G-7 countries, expressed as a share of GNP, is expected to fall from 4.1 to 3.4 percent between 1983 and 1984 (see table 4–2).

62. Again it must be repeated that as the dollar appreciates, it takes a larger share of non-U.S. savings to finance a given percentage of the U.S. deficit. If the U.S. central government deficit is added to the U.S. gross private domestic investment and this total is taken as a share of G-7 total gross private saving, that share rises from about 50 percent in 1979–1980 to 65 percent in 1983. For the general government, that share rises from about 47 percent in 1979–1980 to 60 percent in 1983.

63. Calculated from data in table 4–2.

Bibliography

Barro, Robert J. "Are Government Bonds Net Wealth?" *Journal of Political Economy*, 82 (November–December 1974): 1095–117.

Barth, James R., George Iden, and Frank S. Russek. "Do Federal Deficits Really Matter?" Paper presented to the Western Economic Association meeting, Las Vegas, Nevada, June 1984.

Blanchard, Olivier J., and Lawrence Summers. "Perspectives on High World Real Interest Rates." Paper presented at the Brookings Panel on Economic Activity, September 13–14, 1984.

Boskin, Michael. "Federal Government Deficits: Some Myths and Realities." *American Economic Review, Papers and Proceedings* 72, no. 2 (May 1982): 296–303.

Bossons, John. "Measuring the Viability of Implicit Intergenerational Social Contracts." Paper presented to the 40th Congress of the International Institute of Public Finance, Innsbruck, Austria, August 28–September 1, 1984.

Bossons, John, and D. Peter Dungan. "The Government Deficit: Too High or Too Low?" *Canadian Tax Journal* 31 (January–February 1983): 1–29.

Brown, E. Cary. "Fiscal Policies in the Thirties: A Reappraisal." *American Economic Review* 46, no. 5 (December 1957): 857–79.

Buiter, Willem H. "Measurements of the Public Sector Deficit and Its Implications for Policy Evaluation and Design." *IMF Staff Papers* 30, no. 2 (June 1983): 306–49.

Cukierman, Alex, and Jorgen Mortensen. "Monetary Assets and Inflation-induced Distortions of the National Accounts— Conceptual Issues and Correction of Sectoral Income Flows in 5 EEC Countries." Mimeographed. June 1983.

De Leeuw, Frank, and Thomas M. Holloway. "The High-Employment Budget: Revised Estimates and Automatic Effects." *Survey of Current Business* 62, no. 4 (April 1982).

Eisner, Robert, and Paul J. Pieper. "A New View of the Federal Debt and Budget Deficits." *American Economic Review* (March 1984): 11–29.

Feldstein, Martin. "Domestic Saving and International Capital Movements in the Long Run and the Short Run." *European Economic Review* (Amsterdam) 21 (March/April 1983): 129–51.

Feldstein, Martin, and C. Horioka. "Domestic Savings and International Capital Flows." *Economic Journal* (London) 90 (June 1980): 314–29.

Frankel Jacob A., and Assaf Razin. "Budget Deficits and Rates of Interest in the World Economy." National Bureau of Economic Research, Working Paper no. 1354 (May 1984).

Gerelli, Emilio, and Alberto Majocchi. *Il deficit pubblico: Origini e problemi* [The public deficit: origins and problems]. Milan: Franco Angeli, 1984.

Harberger, Arnold C. "Vignettes on the World Capital Market." *American Economic Review, Papers and Proceedings of the Ninety-second Annual Meeting of the American Economic Association* (Nashville) 70 (May 1980): 331–37.

Hubbard, R. Glenn. "Structural Government Budget Deficits: Reappraisal and Implications." Paper presented to the 40th Congress of the International Institute of Public Finance, Innsbruck, Austria, August 28–September 1, 1984.

International Monetary Fund. *Draft Manual on Government Finance Statistics.* Washington, D.C.: IMF, 1974.

———. *World Economic Outlook.* Occasional Paper 27. Washington, D.C.: IMF, 1984.

Kotlikoff, Lawrence J. "The Economic Impact of Deficit Finance." *IMF Staff Papers* 31, no. 2 (September 1984).

Lusher, David. "The Stabilizing Effectiveness of Budget Flexibility." In *Policies to Combat Depression.* New York: N.B.E.R., Inc., 1956: 77–90.

Mayer, Martin. *The Money Bazaars: Understanding the Banking Revolution around Us.* New York: E. P. Dutton, 1984.

Miller, Marcus. "Inflation-adjusting the Public Sector Financed Deficit." In *The 1982 Budget,* edited by J. Kay. London: Basil Blackwell, 1983: 48–74.

Miller, Marcus, and Simon Babbs. "The True Cost of Debt Service and the Public Sector Financial Deficit." Mimeographed. April 1983.

Muller, Patrice, and Robert W. R. Price. "Structural Budget Deficits and Fiscal Stance," OECD. Economics and Statistics Department, *Working Papers,* July 1984.

Office of Management and Budget. *Special Analyses, Budget of the United States Government, FY 1985,* 1984.

Penati, Alessandro, and Michael Dooley. "Current Account Imbalances and Capital Formation in Industrial Countries, 1949–81." *IMF Staff Papers* 31, no. 1, March 1984: 1–24.

Price, Robert W. R., and Jean-Claude Chouraqui. "Public Sector Deficits: Problems and Policy Implications." *OECD Studies* (June 1983): 13–44.

Sachs, Jeffrey D. "Aspects of the Current Account Behavior of OECD Economies." In *Recent Issues in the Theory of Flexible Exchange Rates,* edited by E. Claassen and P. Salin. Amsterdam: North-Holland, 1983: 101–28.

———. "The Current Account and Macroeconomic Adjustment in the 1970s." *Brookings Papers on Economic Activity* (1981), no. 1: 201–68.

Spaventa, Luigi. "The Growth of Public Debt in Italy: Past Experience,

Perspectives, and Policy Problems." *Banca Nazionale del Lavoro Quarterly Review*, no. 149 (June 1984): 119–49.

Tanzi, Vito. *Inflation and the Personal Income Tax, An International Perspective*. Cambridge: Cambridge University Press, 1980.

———. "Inflationary Expectations, Economic Activity, Taxes, and Interest Rates." *American Economic Review* 70, no. 1 (March 1980): 12–21.

Tanzi, Vito, ed. *Taxation, Inflation, and Interest Rates*. Washington, D.C.: IMF, 1984.

Tanzi, Vito, and Mario Blejer. "Fiscal Deficits and Balance of Payments Disequilibrium in IMF Adjustment Programs." In *Adjustment, Conditionality, and International Financing*, edited by Joaquin Muns. Washington, D.C.: IMF, 1984: 117–36.

Tobin, James. "Comments on 'Domestic Saving and International Capital Movements in the Long Run and the Short Run' by M. Feldstein." *European Economic Review* (Amsterdam) 21 (March/April 1983): 153–56.

U.S. Treasury Department. "The Effect of Deficits on Prices of Financial Assets: Theory and Evidence." Washington, D.C., March 1984.

5

International Issues Raised by Criticisms of the U.S. Budget Deficits

Gottfried Haberler

Summary

Large U.S. budget deficits have come under severe criticism abroad, in developed industrial countries as well as in less-developed countries (LDCs). U.S. budget deficits, it is said, have raised interest rates, which have attracted capital from abroad, causing a sharp rise of the dollar in the foreign exchange markets and huge trade deficits. The strong dollar puts other countries under inflationary pressure and increases the burden of the huge debt of LDCs.

Before considering the merits of this criticism. I discuss in the first section whether it is true that budget deficits raise interest rates. There is a strong theoretical presumption that this is indeed true: If the government borrows in the market—in other words, sells bonds—the price of bonds declines, implying a rise in the interest rate. Those who deny this have to show that the increased supply of bonds will be matched by increased demand. Several reasons are discussed why the increased supply of bonds may be matched by increased demand so that government borrowing does not drive up interest rates.

Supply-siders argue that if the budget deficit is due to lower taxes, the tax cut will stimulate savings, which constitutes additional demand for bonds so that interest rates will not rise. There is a tiny kernel of truth in this argument, but I believe that most experts will agree that only a small fraction of the additional supply of bonds will be matched by additional demand. A better case can be made, however, for the proposition that tax cuts stimulate investment. In that case interest rates will rise.

It has been argued that capital inflows from abroad will provide the matching demand for bonds, so that interest rates can remain unchanged. This has indeed happened on a large scale—and will be examined later in this chapter. The capital inflow requires, however, higher interest rates. Hence, this argument does not change the conclusion that government deficits drive up interest rates.

The Ricardian equivalence theorem is a sophisticated argument for the proposition that government borrowing does not raise interest rates because additional supply of bonds is automatically matched by additional demand. The theorem, put forward by members of the rational expectations school, states that rational individuals will realize that heavy government borrowing will lead to higher taxes in the future. To provide for larger future tax liabilities, individuals will save more, thus providing the matching demand for bonds. To counter a possible objection that the tax burden may fall on future generations, an "intergenerational" model has been developed; this model assumes that rational individuals care about posterity and save enough to lighten the tax burden on their children and grandchildren.

I reject the theorem on the ground that people simply do not know what their future tax liabilities will be, let alone that of their children and grandchildren. It seems to be rational expectations gone wild. The theorem is called "Ricardian" because David Ricardo supposedly developed it more than 100 years ago. It is true that Ricardo stated the theorem, but he then rejected it on the ground that it was unrealistic.

In the second section the "Keynesian" position is discussed. It is argued that in a Keynesian world characterized by mass unemployment and stable or declining wages and prices, government deficit spending would call forth additional output and not lead to higher interest rates. This was approximately the situation in the early 1930s when Keynes wrote The General Theory, but this surely is not the situation now. We have not lived in a Keynesian world since World War II. We do not have full employment either. It is a question of judgment whether we are closer to the Keynesian extreme or to the classical one. My guess is that we are closer to the latter.

The overall conclusion is that what might be called the common sense view—that government deficits do raise interest rates—is correct. That conclusion does not, however, answer the question whether the U.S. budget deficits in recent years have pushed interest rates so much as to justify foreign criticism.

The third section deals with the European criticism of U.S. macropolicies and of large budget deficits in particular. The criticism has been blunted, though not stopped, because the United States has been experiencing an unexpectedly vigorous and sustained recovery with low inflation, despite high interest rates and large budget and trade deficits.

In sharp contrast to earlier recoveries from world recessions, the current one has been much less vigorous in Europe than in the United States. This is due to structural handicaps of European economies: elaborate and overgenerous welfare measures have made wages more rigid, and wage push by labor unions stronger, than in the United States. The United States is blessed by a large domestic free trade area, while the European economies suffer from fragmentation. The European Common Market is supposed to establish free *trade among its members. Actually, the Common Market falls far short of complete economic integration. Moreover, the United States has the great advantage of competitive private enterprise in transportation, communications, and electric power. In Europe those vital services are provided by bureaucratic, often inefficient, public monopolies (national airlines, railroads, and so forth.), which are impervious to foreign competition.*

The theory put forward by some Keynesians that the contrast between Europe and the United States is due to "Keynesian" policies in the United States (large budget deficits) while European countries have much smaller budget deficits, is rejected. Socialist France has followed Keynesian policies and as a consequence has suffered large trade deficits. France was forced to devalue the franc several times and to maintain tight exchange control reminiscent of the notorious Schachtian policy during the Nazi period in Germany.

The fourth section, in a short digression, calls attention to a remarkable report of the General Agreement on Tariffs and Trade (GATT) and the vision of future trade policy it presents. It is not a negotiated document trying to accommodate different viewpoints; it is a staff report presenting a consistent liberal stance—liberal in the classical sense of laissez faire. The vision for trade policy that it presents is a reaffirmation of the liberal American policy of free, nondiscriminatory trade, which served the world so well in the early post–World War II period. The development of this policy since World War I is briefly sketched, and a recent decision of the Reagan administration—the imposition of "voluntary" export restrictions on foreign exporters of steel to the United States—is critically analyzed to highlight the importance of rethinking and reconfirming the adherence to the liberal tradition.

In the 1970s the United States was criticized by Europe for not playing the role of a locomotive to pull the rest of the world out of the recession. In the sixth section, I show that during the past two years, the U.S. locomotive has pulled very hard, but the response of the European economies has been very weak.

The power of the U.S. economic locomotive is measured by the size of the U.S. trade deficits. U.S. interest rates are high partly because of high investment demand, which in turn is due to tax incentives and the strong expansion. Thus the trade deficit, high interest rates, and the strong dollar are part and parcel of the pull of the locomotive, for which the Europeans asked. Nonetheless, these factors are the prime target of European criticism of U.S. policy.

I conclude that the Europeans got what they wanted. They should not blame the United States but should try to remove their structural handicaps, which are the real reason for their poor performance.

I discuss briefly the alleged danger that the dollar may plunge from its present height with disastrous consequences for the United States and the world economy. Capital has been pouring into the United States, but at some point "the nerves of the foreign investors will crack," and there will be a stampede out of the dollar. This theory is a bit melodramatic, though the possibility of a sharp reversal of the recent rise of the dollar cannot be entirely excluded. It is inconceivable, however, that the Federal Reserve, the International Monetary Fund, and other leading central banks would stand idly by and let the dollar slump. The markets do understand this, though the doom-sayers of the dollar seem to be unaware. It is, therefore, most unlikely that such an irrational stampede out of the dollar will occur.

In the last section I discuss the criticism of U.S. policies by the LDCs. The LDCs have been the principal beneficiaries of the U.S. locomotive. Their exports to the United States have increased by leaps and bounds, yet the LDCs are among the sharpest critics of U.S. policies.

The third world is a very heterogeneous group. Some countries, Taiwan, South Korea, and Malaysia among them, have been doing very well despite high interest rates and protectionist policies in the industrial countries. Some oil-rich countries, like Nigeria, have squandered their new riches through gross mismanagement. There are also the really poor and backward countries, mainly in Africa, and the advanced LDCs, mainly in Latin America. I briefly discuss Argentina, an extreme but not entirely atypical example of a less-developed country. Argentina is potentially a very rich country with excellent human and material resources and has no business being less developed. I include a brief sketch of the mismanagement by successive regimes, starting with the first Peron government, which has led to Argentina's present plight.

Introduction

The U.S. budget deficits have become a matter of international concern. The United States is being criticized abroad both in industrial countries and in the less-developed countries, largely on the same grounds. This is, I believe, a new phenomenon. I do not recall any earlier occasion when the fiscal policy of a country became a major concern abroad.

The general line of criticism is well known. U.S. budget deficits, it is said, have driven up U.S. interest rates, nominal as well as real. This has attracted capital from abroad, which in turn has pushed up the exchange value of the dollar, causing huge U.S. trade deficits. Interest rates abroad, too, have been pushed up, and foreign countries are put under inflationary pressure by the depreciation of their currencies and are forced to retrench. Before considering the details and merits of the criticism, I should clarify my position on some basic issues and clear up some misconceptions.

It has been said that the overvalued, strong dollar and the resulting trade deficits are the consequence of floating exchange rates. Under fixed rates, it is said, there could be no overvalued dollar.

That this is fallacious becomes clear when we reflect what would have happened under fixed exchanges. Given the large U.S. budget deficits and high interest rates, under fixed exchanges much more foreign capital would have been attracted to the United States than under floating because the foreign investor in dollars would know that the dollar could only go up. Under floating there is always the risk that the dollar has already appreciated too much. Thus foreign countries could suffer large losses of international reserves and would be put under intense deflationary pressure. If the pressure could not be relieved by floating, it is very likely that countries would be driven to impose import restrictions and exchange controls. This is exactly what happened in the 1930s, with catastrophic results for world trade. It happened again, though in a much milder form, when Bretton Woods broke down in the early 1970s, and yet again, in mild form, in recent years in France.

The conclusion is that floating is here to stay.[1]

Do Budget Deficits Raise Interest Rates?
The Ricardian Equivalence Theorem

In the United States, supply-siders and many monetarists, especially in Treasury circles, are arguing that budget deficits do not raise interest rates. This statement seems to defy the basic economic law of demand and supply, specifically that an increase of supply depresses the price: if the government increases the supply of government bonds by running large budget deficits and printing bonds, the price of bonds will decline, that is to say, interest rates will go up.

Those who deny that deficits raise interest rates have to show that an increase in the supply of government bonds will be matched by an increase in demand. (Before going into that question, I should point out that putting the problem in terms of demand and supply of bonds does not imply the adoption of what is now often called, disparagingly, a "flow" rather than a "stock" analysis of the budget deficit and its effect on interest rates.) It is indeed possible to think of circumstances in which this will be the case. It has been argued, for example, that if a tax cut has caused the deficit, it is possible that the tax cut will stimulate savings and thus increase demand for bonds. Supply-siders are fond of this argument. It is most unlikely, however, that this will happen on a sufficient scale to obviate a substantial rise in interest rates.

An obvious possibility of additional demand for bonds to match

125

the increased supply is capital inflows from abroad. This has indeed happened on a considerable scale. The projected U.S. budget deficits are so large, however, it is most unlikely that capital inflows from abroad will be large enough for interest rates to remain unchanged. It would at any rate require high interest rates to induce such large capital imports.

A sophisticated argument purporting to show that deficits in general do not raise interest rates and do not crowd out private investment is the so-called Ricardo equivalence theorem, which David Ricardo supposedly put forward. This theorem, which has become popular among members of the rational expectations school in recent years, states that under certain reasonable assumptions, it makes no difference whether the government finances its deficit by taxing or by borrowing.

This surprising theory has been spelled out by Robert J. Barro in a widely quoted article "Are Government Bonds Net Wealth?"[2] Barro supposes that, with government expenditures unchanged, taxes are reduced, and the resulting deficit is financed by issuing bonds. The unsophisticated analyst would argue that the public will react to the tax cut by spending the larger part of the windfall on consumption and saving only a small portion. Only part of the increased supply of bonds will, therefore, be matched by additional demand; and the price of bonds will decline, that is to say, interest rates will rise.

No, say the sophisticated rational expectations theorists. People will realize that the increased public debt will have to be serviced. This means that future tax liabilities will increase, and the discounted present value of the additional future tax liabilities must be equal to the additional debt. It follows that consumption will not increase. In other words, the increase in disposable income will be saved; thus the additional supply of bonds will be fully matched by additional demand.

The unsophisticated analyst would perhaps reply that the additional taxes to service the debt may not fall on the present generation of tax payers, but on posterity. To counter this argument Barro has developed an intergenerational model showing that the present generation will save exactly enough to make sure that future generations will not suffer from the profligacy of the present.

I must confess that this theory strikes me as rational expectations gone wild, carried to extremes, if not to say *ad absurdum*. People just do not think that way. Nobody knows what his or her share, if any, in future tax liabilities will be, let alone that of their children and grandchildren, and it would not be rational to spend scarce time and brainpower trying to figure it out.

What is very likely to happen, however, is that many people will assume, rightly or wrongly but not irrationally, that large budget deficits will lead to inflation. The development of inflationary expectations will make shambles of any equivalence of taxes and borrowing.

In an important paper James M. Buchanan criticized Barro for not mentioning that the equivalence theorem had been put forward by David Ricardo in his *Principles* more than 100 years ago.[3] As Gerald P. O'Driscoll pointed out a year after Buchanan's article was published, Ricardo finally rejected the equivalence theorem as unrealistic. O'Driscoll states, "It was precisely because Ricardo perceived taxation and debt issuance as nonequivalent that he was of the opinion that 'preference should be given to the first.'"[4] Ricardo puts it as follows: "In point of the economy" there is no real difference "between financing the war by taxes or by debt."[5] "For twenty million in one year, one million per annum for ever, or 1,200,000 L for 41 years are precisely of the same value; but the people who pay the taxes" never see it that way. "The war taxes are more economical; for when they are paid an effort is made to save the amount of the whole expenditure of the war, leaving the national capital undiminished." If the war is financed by debt, people "would have some vague idea that [the interest on the debt] will be paid by posterity." There would be little saving, and "therefore the national capital is diminished."[6]

We may conclude that Ricardo was more realistic than his modern, unwitting followers.

Walter Salant drew my attention to the fact that James Tobin and Richard Goode have subjected the Ricardian theorem as restated by Barro to a searching criticism.[7] Tobin patiently and convincingly demonstrates why Barro's equivalence theorem, especially the intergenerational part of it, does not work. Tobin's detailed analysis fully confirms the view expressed above that it is hopelessly unrealistic to assume that the discounted future tax liabilities govern people's behavior in such a way that the increased supply of bonds resulting from government borrowing is fully matched by additional saving, so that interest rates remain unchanged.[8]

The Keynesian Position

While supply-siders and rational expectations theorists deny that large budget deficits boost interest rates, and supply-siders claim credit for the good recovery of the U.S. economy in 1983–1984 (a claim that in my opinion is unjustified), Keynesians reject the conclusions of both schools and regard the good performance of the U.S. economy as the result of Keynesian policy of deficit spending, unwittingly pursued by the Reagan administration. Some of them feel that there has been too much of a good thing, that the budget deficits have become too large and should be trimmed by raising taxes.

To deal with inflationary pressures Keynesians recommend incomes policy. I shall not discuss in this essay the problem of incomes policy, but I should like very briefly to make clear my position, which I have discussed in contributions to earlier volumes of *Contemporary Economic Problems* and elsewhere.

I reject incomes policy in the sense of wage and price controls, including tax-oriented incomes policy. These policies have never worked. I think that the proponents of incomes policy are right, however, when they say that the short-run trade-off between unemployment and inflation can be improved; or, as I prefer to say, the pains of disinflation in the form of transitory unemployment and lost output can be and should be reduced (though not entirely eliminated) by appropriate measures. The appropriate measures are not controls but rather decontrols, measures designed to make the economy more flexible and competitive by reducing the monopoly power of business and labor, by deregulating industry, and the like. Free trade would be the most effective and efficient antimonopoly policy. A policy along these lines (which on an earlier occasion I have called "Incomes Policy II," as distinguished from "Incomes Policy I" consisting of wage and price control) is sometimes referred to, especially in Europe, as "supply oriented policy." This policy has nothing to do with the policy recommended by supply-siders in the United States.

After this digression on incomes policy, I return to the main theme.

Government borrowing does not crowd out private investment or drive up interest rates in another economic situation. I have in mind what may be described as a "classical" Keynesian world, that is, a state of the economy with mass unemployment, stable or falling prices, constant marginal cost, and a Keynesian liquidity trap. This was approximately the state of the economy during the Great Depression in the early 1930s when Keynes wrote *The General Theory*. There is widespread agreement that if the government in such a world engages in deficit spending financed by borrowing from the banking system, output and employment would expand at stable prices, and interest rates would not rise. Private investment would not be crowded out; on the contrary, rising output would stimulate private investment.

The trouble is that we no longer live in a Keynesian world. True, we are not in a classical full-employment situation either. We are somewhere between the two extremes, the Keynesian of perfectly elastic supply and the classical of totally inelastic supply.[9] There is a good deal of unemployment and slack now, and there is some elasticity of aggregate output with respect to an expansion in effective demand. Inflationary expectations have been sensitized by a long period of inflationary abuse, and numerous bottlenecks exist. Hence, inflation would quickly accelerate when aggregate demand expands.[10]

What are the implications for the problems of the budget and its effect on interest rates?

First, a word on what would be the situation under classical full employment. If full employment is taken literally as implying totally inelastic supply, government deficit spending and borrowing would crowd out private investment, and interest rates both nominal and real would rise, accompanied by more or less inflation, depending on monetary factors.

What about the intermediate positions? Are we close enough to full employment so that government borrowing will drive up interest rates? This is a matter of judgment. My own guess is that we are indeed much closer to full employment than to the Keynesian extreme. In other words, the bulk of unemployment is not Keynesian but classical.

The general conclusion of our analysis so far is that what might be called the common sense view is correct: government deficits do raise interest rates. This does not, of course, answer the question whether government borrowing was the major cause of high interest rates in recent years, so as to justify European criticism of U.S. fiscal policy. This question will be discussed further in the last section of this chapter.

Criticism of U.S. Fiscal Policy in Other Industrial Countries

To begin with, the criticism of the U.S. budget deficits has been blunted by the unexpectedly vigorous recovery of the U.S. economy despite high interest rates, large trade deficits, and a strong dollar. The cyclical recovery since 1982 has been not only the most vigorous but also the least inflationary since 1960.

Furthermore, part of the trade deficit is due to a cyclical discrepancy, the U.S economy expanding fast while the rest of the world, developed as well as less developed, lags behind. To the extent to which this is true, the U.S. trade deficit is a natural and beneficial phenomenon because it means that the United States is performing the highly desirable function of a locomotive pulling the world economy out of the recession. Moreover, the criticism one often hears that the richest country in the world should not import capital from poor countries is beside the point, and the process is self-correcting; the

U.S. trade deficit will decline when the rest of the world catches up with the U.S. recovery.

In sharp contrast to earlier recoveries from world recession, the current one has been much less vigorous in Europe than in the United States. Some of the reasons of the poor performance of Western Europe have been authoritatively stated by Stephen Marris, the former chief economist of the Organization for Economic Cooperation and Development. I quote some salient facts noted by Marris:

> European economies are in important respects less flexible than the American economy. . . . European workers are generally better protected against economic misfortune than their American counterparts. Collective agreements and government regulations give them more job security. But this makes it more difficult and expensive for European employers to lay off workers when demand weakens. And, they are more reluctant to take on new workers when demand picks up, preferring instead to work overtime. Provisions for unemployment are also more generous in Europe. Laid-off workers have more time to look around for a new job. But, by the same token, this slows down the movement of labor from declining to expanding industries.
>
> Labor mobility is also inhibited in Europe by the greater rigidity of the *relative* wage structure between industries, occupations, and regions. It is more difficult for employers in expanding industries to bid up wages to attract labor, or for laid-off workers in declining industries to bid down wages to get their jobs back.
>
> . . . The main culprit is the downward rigidity of real wages, coupled with the high taxes. . . . Between 1960 and 1983 the ratio of general government expenditures to gross national product (GNP) in the European Community rose from 32 percent to 52 percent.
>
> . . . In America the overall burden of taxation is lower, and real incomes seem to have adjusted more flexibly to the shocks of the 1970s. 20 million new jobs have been created in America since 1973. . . . Against this, there was a net *loss* of around 2.5 million jobs in the European Community over the same period. Compared with Europeans, Americans coming into the labor force have been more willing to accept whatever level of real wages was necessary to induce employers to hire them; in other words, to "price themselves" into jobs.[11]

The contrast between Europe and the United States was highlighted in 1983 by the crippling strikes in the United Kingdom and West Germany. In Britain the coal miners' strike (which is still not settled at this writing, November 1984) is threatening the recovery after the recession. In Germany the strike of metal workers for a thirty-five-hour week at the same pay as the forty-hour week was settled by a costly compromise. In the United States, however, wage settlements have been surprisingly moderate in the recovery, so far at least.

To Marris's list of handicaps of the European economies compared with that of the United States, I would add the following: The U.S. economy enjoys the tremendous advantage of a large free trade area and of private competitive enterprise in transportation, communications, and electric power, which is partly due to the large size of the market.[12]

Over the years the importance of a large internal free trade area has increased and is likely to increase further because of the rapid technological advances that have occurred and are still occurring in transportation and communications.

True, the European Common market was supposed to establish free trade among the members of the European Community (EC). Tariffs and quotas have indeed largely been abolished on trade between the members of the EC, but many impediments to the free movement of commodities still exist. Some member countries tend to substitute more or less subtle administrative restrictions for tariffs and quotas, and the Common Market hardly applies to the growing trade in services.[13] Furthermore, some members, particularly France, have tight exchange control, which is a major obstacle to free trade, though its ostensible purpose is "merely" to restrict capital flows. Exchange control makes it impossible to integrate financial markets—a very serious handicap. Customs formalities and inspection at the borders between the members are still in place, and controllers and customs officials are very active to justify their existence.

Equally important, the European countries, unlike the United States, are burdened by the existence of national public monopolies in transportation, communications, and electric power. These public monopolies suffer from bureaucratic inefficiencies and are impervious to international competition. In addition, numerous nationalized industries suffer from the same handicaps. Unlike private industries, state enterprises are under strong pressure to buy their inputs (raw materials, intermediate goods, machinery, etc.) from domestic sources, even if the cost is much higher than imports would be.

Marris is not satisfied with the structural explanation of the contrast between Europe and the United States. He insists that a basic

131

difference between European and American macropolicies is at least equally responsible. While the United States is running huge budget deficits, Europe's recovery is being held back by low structural deficits. In other words, European policies are not sufficiently expansionary ("Keynesian").

I find this conclusion entirely unconvincing for two reasons. First, European macropolicies have not been uniform. There is, for example, a sharp contrast between the two largest economies—those of France and West Germany.

France, on the one hand, under the socialist government of François Mitterrand, has pursued Keynesian policy as recommended by Marris, running large budget deficits and, as a consequence, has experienced huge trade deficits and high inflation. Last year France was forced to switch course toward an "austerity" program. How far it will go remains to be seen. The rate of growth has declined, and unemployment has increased. France still bears the albatross of nationalized banks and industries.

West Germany, on the other hand, has pursued a much more cautious policy. The German economy has staged an export-led cyclical recovery. Although quite modest compared with the recent U.S. recovery and with earlier German ones, it was remarkable in that the inflation rate has been brought down to below 2 percent at this writing (November 1984). Unemployment, however, is still high, about 10 percent, and the metal workers' strike of summer 1984 has slowed the recovery. I will discuss further the nature and causes of high unemployment later in the chapter.

The second reason why Marris's theory is unconvincing is that, given the structural rigidities and immobility of labor he describes, an expansionary (Keynesian) macropolicy would quickly reignite inflation as exemplified by France. Helmut Schlesinger made this point. He made it clear that the Bundesbank would stick to its cautious policy, because accelerated inflation would soon be followed by recession.

I have stressed the long-run structural advantages of the U.S. economy compared with European economies as the main reason for the great strength of the dollar. It will be well to look back and to ask why fewer than ten years ago the dollar was so weak it had to be devalued sharply against other major currencies, especially the German mark, the Swiss franc, and the Japanese yen.

The answer is that in the short run the favorable effect of the long-run structural factors can be swamped by exogenous inflationary shocks or by cyclical factors.[14] About 1964, for reasons that need not be further discussed here, the United States entered an inflationary period. The crucial fact was that the U.S. inflation rate was much higher than that of Germany, Switzerland, and Japan. These countries refused to accept the inflation that they would have had to endure if they had maintained a fixed exchange rate with the dollar. The dollar therefore came under pressure and in the end had to be sharply devalued. Even after its spectacular rise in the past two years, the dollar is still below its value vis-à-vis the three strong currency countries of the 1970s.[15]

The GATT Report: A Digression on Trade Policy

After the other sections of this essay were written, the first chapter of the annual report of GATT, *International Trade 1983/84*, became available in fall 1984. As usual, it stands out among reports of international institutions, because it is not a negotiated document, trying to accommodate different, often divergent, viewpoints. The GATT document is a staff report that develops a consistent liberal stance—liberal in the classical sense of laissez faire, *laissez-passer*, not in the perverted modern sense.[16]

The report dwells upon the superior performance of the U.S. economy compared with that of the Western European economies in the current cyclical recovery. It points out that this contrast did not exist in other recoveries since 1960. The report described this change by saying that "the U.S. locomotive no longer pulls," making reference to the "locomotive" theory that was popular in the 1970s. The United States was then admonished by European critics to play its role of locomotive, that is to say, to expand fast to pull the rest of the Western world out of the recession.

Actually, the U.S. locomotive pulled much harder in the current recovery; specifically U.S. imports rose twice as much as in earlier recoveries. The European economies, however, did not respond as in earlier recoveries. Why? The GATT report mentions roughly the same structural impediments and inflexibilities to adjustment that are more pronounced in Europe than in the United States, which were mentioned above. Rigid and excessively high wages, overgenerous welfare measures, and intra-European fragmentation of markets despite the existence of a "Common Market" are the principal trouble spots.

In contrast to Marris and to other Keynesians, the authors of the GATT report do not think that the way to speed up growth in the European economies is through government deficit spending and concerted reflation. They believe that recurrent stimulations of economies, whether or not they work in the short run, are likely to increase fluctuations in the long run. In other words, a policy of fine tuning

133

minor recessions would be counterproductive. The authors suggest that modest upswings and downswings are a natural and probably beneficial feature of market systems.

The last four pages of the first chapter sketch GATT's vision of what the future trade policy should be. It is in effect a call for a return to the liberal policies pursued by the United States in the postwar years, which have served the Western world so well.

I will briefly recall the origin and development of this policy. An early move occurred in 1922 when the United States abandoned its previous adherence to the conditional most-favored-nation principle (MFN) and accepted the classical unconditional MFN clause. The liberal U.S. policy was taken up by Cordell Hull, Roosevelt's secretary of state. Hull started the policy of the reciprocal trade agreement in 1934 and nurtured it through the dark period of the depression, the Second World War, and the sharp decline of liberalism in the period immediately after World War II. The policy came into full bloom in the late 1940s and 1950s, after Hull's departure when GATT was set up. In numerous multilateral conferences, tariffs of the United States and other countries were sharply reduced. Quantitative, nontariff measures such as quotas were banned. Nondiscriminatory tariffs were ensured by the unconditional MFN clause.

A recent move by the Reagan administration, which prides itself on being the champion of free enterprise and free trade, highlights the importance of rethinking, and rededication to, the traditional U.S. liberal, nondiscriminatory trade policy. The administration has adopted what must be described as the worst possible method to protect the steel industry from foreign competition—the pressuring of foreign steel exporters to cut steel exports by "voluntary" action. William Brock, the trade representative, tried to sell this policy as a "liberal" policy on the ground that it avoids the overt use of import quotas.

Quotas are bad enough. On the microeconomic level they stifle competition in the industries where they are applied. On the macroeconomic level, when widely used, they tend to disturb the delicate balance of the payment adjustment mechanism. Quotas are much worse than tariffs, but they are better than the proposed system of pressuring foreign exporters to restrict exports "voluntarily." The reason is that in principle it would be possible to administer quotas in a nondiscriminatory way by selling import licenses in free auction markets. (Unfortunately, little use is being made of this possibility.)

The proposed system has all the disadvantages of quotas and will involve the U.S. government in obnoxious discriminatory dealing with exporting countries. Instead of letting market forces decide from where steel is imported, thus ensuring that it will come from the cheapest sources, the new system lets bureaucrats decide. The policy has been described as a brilliant political move, even by critical commentators, because it has been praised by the steel industry, which got its protection, and by steel importers, on the ground that it avoids quotas. This demonstrates the degree of ignorance of the interested public in trade policy.

In view of this situation, some further comments are in order. The basic trouble of the U.S. steel industry is that wages are much too high. They are not only much higher than wages in competitive foreign countries, but also about 75 percent higher than wages in the U.S. non-farm business sector, and some 50 percent higher than in U.S. manufacturing industries. Wages in the automobile industry are also too high. The recent contract between General Motors and the Union of Automobile Workers (UAW) seems to have further increased the disparity.

Every import restriction, tariff or nontariff, raises the domestic price and thus is a burden on the consumer, driving a wedge between the price inside and the price outside the country. Under a tariff the difference in prices is collected by the U.S. Treasury as a duty. Under quantitative restrictions, if the import licenses go to the foreign exporter, the difference in prices is pocketed by the foreign exporter. Under the tariff the terms of trade improve; under quantitative restrictions they deteriorate. It has been estimated that the Japanese automobile firms receive an annual subsidy of at least $2 billion a year from the United States because the price of Japanese cars has increased. The total "cost to the [American] consumer in 1983 was $4.3 billion plus additional losses in consumer welfare due to the constraint on the choice of cars. The cost per job saved [in the U.S. automobile industry] therefore was at least $160,000 per year."[17] Crandall adds: "Employment creation at this cost is surely not worth the candle."[18] The cost to the U.S. economy of the steel protection has not yet been determined.

This outrageous policy has received very little attention in the media. What has caught attention is the increase in the bonuses of the executives of the automobile firms, though these constitute merely a drop in the bucket.

The policy is, of course, very popular among the foreign exporters; they become accomplices of the protectionists in the United States (such as the UAW), and they lose every incentive to fight for free trade. Free trade thus loses one of its most important allies.

The U.S. Locomotive Pulls

The U.S. locomotive has pulled hard in the current recovery. *The*

Economist has taken up this theme and, in an article titled "The Mighty Borrower," says, "Other countries have had reason to thank the American boom. In 1982 they all urgently needed an economic recovery, and they all wanted theirs to be export-led. . . . America has pump-primed the world out of the 1980–82 recession."[19]

The response of the European economies has, however, been weak. This is not the fault of the United States. The Europeans have to blame themselves for their structural handicaps. It should be kept in mind, first, that the strength of the pull of the U.S. locomotive is measured by the size of the U.S. trade deficit and, second, that the U.S. trade deficit has a cyclical component. When the European economies respond, U.S. exports will increase, and the trade deficit will shrink.

High interest rates, large capital imports, the overvalued, strong dollar, and the large U.S. budget and trade deficits are the targets of European criticism.

High U.S. interest rates are due partly to heavy government borrowing, partly to strong investment demands. It is difficult to estimate the comparative strength of the two factors, but it is certain that in the current U.S. recovery, private investment has gone up much more sharply than is generally recognized.[20] The strong investment demand for funds is due to tax incentives and the rapid expansion of the economy.

The strong dollar is due not only to high U.S. interest rates but also to the fact that the United States has again become the safe haven for foreign investors from Europe and elsewhere because of unsettled economic and political conditions abroad. This is not the fault of the United States.

High interest rates, large capital imports, the strong dollar, and the trade deficits are part and parcel of the pull of the U.S. locomotive that the Europeans wanted.

The critics of U.S. policies cannot have it both ways. They cannot have a rapid U.S. expansion and at the same time stable, low interest rates. They cannot have a strong pull of the U.S. locomotive and low trade deficits. They cannot have U.S. trade deficits and no capital flowing into the United States. The dollar cannot come down without the foreign countries putting their house in order to stop capital flight.

Instead of blaming the United States for all their troubles, the Europeans should put their own house in order. That would take care of most of their problems.

This view is now gaining support in Europe. Otmar Emminger, the former president of the German Bundesbank, has cautiously endorsed this view in an important paper, saying that the European complaints of the high U.S. interest rates overlook the fact that the high rates are "the unavoidable consequence of the U.S. expansion." He expressed the view that "up to now the effect of the U.S. expansion on the rest of the world has been predominately positive."[21] In a later paper Emminger reiterated his opinion "that if one weighs the positive and negative elements [of the strong dollar and the huge U.S. trade deficits] against each other, the balance for most other countries, and for the world economy in general, is positive—at least in the short run."[22]

Professor Herbert Giersch has argued for some time that high unemployment in Germany and elsewhere in Europe is not Keynesian but structural; it is specifically a result of wages being rigid and too high in two senses. First, the overall wage level is too high, and profits are too low. Second, relative wages between regions and sectors of the economy are rigid and out of line. The policy conclusions are straightforward. What is required is not a more expansive monetary and fiscal policy (reflation), but structural reforms.

Giersch has recently restated his views in an impressive paper, "Perspective for the World Economy"[23] He concluded that for Germany and other European countries to catch up with the United States, they must reduce taxes substantially, improve depreciation allowances, abolish regulations in many areas, and make wages more flexible. In other words, what holds back German investment and growth is not a tight or expensive supply of investible funds due to high U.S. interest rates, but slacked demand for investment funds due to structural weaknesses, institutional rigidities, and faulty policies.

France, as so often in the past, has been a special case. As Herbert Lüthy has said, "French clocks show a different time."[24] France has bucked the liberal trend—liberal in the classical sense of laissez faire. It has gone Socialist. The Keynesian policies and wholesale nationalization of the Mitterrand government have triggered massive capital flight. To stem the outflow of funds, France has established tight exchange control with searches at the border and censorship of the mail, reminiscent of the Schachtian system under the Nazi regime.[25] Members of Mitterrand's cabinet have, nonetheless, been in the forefront of criticism of U.S. fiscal policy.

Before discussing the complaints of the LDCs, I will mention one more problem that concerns the industrial countries.

The Foreign Exchange Value of the Dollar

There is again much talk about the alleged danger that the dollar may plunge from its present height with disastrous consequences for the

United States and for the rest of the world. This theme has been on and off in the media since Stephen Marris raised the specter of the "collapsing" dollar in an article "Crisis Ahead for the Dollar" in *Fortune* magazine. The argument is familiar: Foreign capital is pouring into the United States "to help finance the U.S. budget deficits." At some point, however, "the nerves of the foreign investor will crack," and there will be a stampede out of the dollar.[26]

To speak of the "collapse" of the dollar is, in my opinion, a bit melodramatic, though a sharp reversal of the recent trend of the dollar can perhaps not be entirely excluded.[27] Even if the worst happens, it is inconceivable that the Federal Reserve, the International Monetary Fund (IMF), and other leading central banks would stand idly by and let the dollar slump. They would organize a rescue operation for the dollar as they did in 1978. The markets will probably realize this, though the doomsayers of the dollar do not. There is, therefore, a good chance that there will be no collapse of the dollar; in other words, that there will be a soft landing, rather than a crash landing.[28]

This is not the end of the story, however. Suppose huge budget deficits continue, capital imports and the trade deficit shrink, and the dollar declines in a more or less orderly fashion. In that case U.S. interest rates would go up and government borrowing would crowd out private investment. The consequence would be either a recession if the Federal Reserve stands firm or, if monetary policy is lax, inflation followed later by an even more serious recession.

It is, therefore, of the utmost importance that the budget deficits be gradually reduced. That would make more savings available for productive private investment, offsetting the decline of capital inflow from abroad. Thus a smooth transition is conceivable. Of course, in practice things may not work out so smoothly even if the macroeconomic levers, budget deficits, and monetary policy seem to be set correctly. We cannot assume completely successful fine tuning. After all, the business cycle is still alive, I would argue, however, that a mild recession is not a calamity.

Needless to add, some exogenous shocks may upset the best laid plans. Some political or economic disturbances abroad would revive the demand for dollars. Or some trouble at home—a flare-up of inflation or a mass default of LDCs threatening major U.S. banks—would have the opposite effect.

Criticism of U.S. Fiscal Policies in the Less-Developed Countries

The third world countries are the chief beneficiaries of the U.S. recovery and of the strong dollar. Nonetheless, they are among the sharpest critics of U.S. policies in general and of the U.S. budget deficits in particular. This should not surprise us, for the less-developed countries have been habitual complainers. Their representatives in the United Nations and other international organizations have been blaming the industrial countries in general and the United States in particular for all their economic troubles. It is said, for example, that the strong dollar has put a heavy burden on them because prices of many commodities, such as crude oil, are usually expressed in terms of dollars and thus automatically increase when the dollar goes up in the foreign exchange market. This argument, which is also used in industrial countries, overlooks the fact that the prices of these commodities are determined in competitive markets. Even the price of crude oil has *not* gone up with the strong dollar. On the contrary, it has sharply dropped in terms of dollars, despite the Organization of Petroleum Exporting Countries (OPEC).

There is, however, some truth in the contention that the burden of their huge foreign debt is increased by the appreciation of the dollar, though this charge refers only to the structural component of the rise in interest rates, not to the cyclical part.

The less-developed countries do have legitimate grievances about the protectionist policies of the industrial countries. Unfortunately, most less-developed countries make things much worse through highly protectionist measures of their own. They should understand that a further reduction in the volume of trade caused by their protectionist measures will not alleviate the loss caused by protection in the industrial countries. On the contrary, it means a further deterioration of their economic welfare.

The LDCs of the third world are a very heterogeneous group, much more so than the industrial countries. In Southeast Asia, Taiwan, South Korea, Malaysia, Singapore, Thailand, and Hong Kong are doing very well despite high interest rates and protectionist policies in the industrial countries. The countries on the Arabian peninsula, Saudi Arabia, Kuwait, the United Arab Emirates—the core of OPEC—float on nearly half of the free world's oil reserve. Other oil-rich countries, like Nigeria, have squandered their newly discovered riches by gross mismanagement. There are the really poor and backward countries, the "fourth world," mainly in Africa.

There are, finally, some potentially very rich countries with excellent human and material resources, which have no business being less developed. Argentina is the outstanding example. Although its situation is extreme, it is by no means entirely atypical.

In the past Argentina has often been compared with Australia. Years ago Colin Clark, in his celebrated pioneering study *Conditions of*

Economic Progress, predicted confidently that Argentina's real per capita GNP would soon approach that of the United States and Canada.[29] This was not an unreasonable prediction, but it did not work out that way. Why? A brief description is in order.[30]

The source of Argentina's plight is uncontrolled and wasteful spending by the government, especially by a great variety of state enterprises. This spending started under the first Peron regime, which forced industrialization and coddled trade unions—all at the expense of agriculture, the natural backbone of the Argentine economy. The successive military governments that followed the ouster of Peron failed to bring about a radical change in policy. On the contrary, the state enterprises, many of them run by top officers of the armed forces, continued their inefficient, wasteful projects and pushed ahead with often grotesquely ill-considered projects. Road bridges were built with no traffic to cross them; nuclear power plants were built when the capacity for generating electricity already exceeded demand, and petrochemical plants were completed long before there was any use for their products. Military expenditures skyrocketed. The result was huge government deficits and galloping inflation. Thus Argentina's economy languished when countries like Mexico and Brazil had respectable growth. When the world recession struck, Argentina tried to keep its economy going by borrowing abroad and by printing money at home.

Unfortunately, the democratic government of President Alfonsin, which came to power in 1983, has not brought about a radical reversal of past policies. In some respects it has made things even worse. A populist regime is not in a good position to resist excessive wage demands and protectionist pressures.

Countries like Argentina should restore their creditworthiness by accepting and carrying out the austerity program recommended by the IMF. They should restrain monetary growth to curb inflation and establish a realistic exchange rate by floating. The "classical medicine" (to use Keynes's expression) will not work, however, unless the major structural impediments are removed. Specifically, public spending, which has skyrocketed in the past ten years, should be sharply cut; and government budget deficits, including those of public enterprises, must be sharply trimmed. As many of the state enterprises as possible should be denationalized and turned over to private hands. For that, help of foreign corporations would be indispensable. Foreign direct investment should, therefore, be encouraged. A similar point has been made by Anne Krueger, vice-president of the World Bank. In a wide-ranging speech she argued for a shift from "debt financing" to "equity financing."[31] Equity financing, direct investment from abroad, provides not only capital but also entrepreneurship and management know-how. Furthermore, it will be necessary to phase out the very expensive policy pursued in many of these countries of keeping down food prices by high subsidies.[32] These policies, along with excessive indexation of wages, are the driving force of inflation. With these cost trends unchanged, monetary-fiscal disinflation would bring the economy to a grinding halt. A policy of pure monetarism, relying exclusively on monetary-fiscal restraint, makes no sense.

Without a drastic change in policies a default on the outstanding debt will be unavoidable. To postpone the default by new credits would be throwing away good money after bad and would make the final adjustment even more difficult. Reform along the lines indicated would, after a painful transition, start a beneficial circle and restore creditworthiness.

Notes

1. These problems have been discussed in some detail in my contribution, "The International Monetary System in the World Recession" in William Fellner, ed., *Essays in Contemporary Economic Problems: Disinflation*, 1983–1984 (Washington, D.C.: American Enterprise Institute, 1984), pp. 87–129.

2. Robert J. Barro, "Are Government Bonds Net Wealth?" *Journal of Political Economy*, vol. 82 (November/December 1974), pp. 1095–117. See also Robert J. Barro, *Macroeconomics* (New York: Wiley, 1984), pp. 380–93.

3. James M. Buchanan, "Barro on the Ricardo Equivalence Theorem," *Journal of Political Economy*, vol. 84 (April 1976), pp. 337–41. Buchanan had discussed the equivalence theorem in his *Public Principles of Public Debt*, 1958. Barrow acknowledged that he was unaware of Ricardo's theory.

4. Gerald P. O'Driscoll, "The Ricardian Nonequivalence Theorem," *Journal of Political Economy*, vol. 85 (February 1977), pp. 207–10.

Vito Tanzi drew my attention to the fact that Vilfredo Pareto referred to the Ricardian equivalence thorem. According to Tanzi, "While not contesting the Ricardian argument of the equivalence . . . Pareto observed that no taxpayer makes the Ricardian calculations." He concluded that "deficit financing is one way of inducing the citizens to accept what they would not accept with taxes. For example, if during the war the governments had tried to collect through taxes as much as they collected through loans, it is very likely that they would not have succeeded." (Letter written by Pareto to Benvenuto Griziotti. Cited in Griziotti's "Fatti e teorie delle finanze in Vilfredo Pareto," *Rivista di Scienza delle Finanze* [1944], pp. 136–40. The citation is on p. 137.)

Tanzi points out that the Ricardian theorem is an example of "fiscal illusion." Another example is a theorem put forward by John Stuart Mill that people in general resent paying direct taxes but "let themselves be fleeced" by indirect taxes (ibid.).

5. The phrase "in point of the economy" is puzzling; "ideally" is perhaps the right word.

6. The quotations come from Ricardo's paper "Funding System," which was written after the *Principles*, but the gist of the theory can be found already in the *Principles*. See *The Works and Correspondence of David Ricardo*, Piero Sraffa, ed. (Cambridge: Cambridge University Press, 1951), vol. 1, *The Principles*, pp. 244–49, and vol. 4, "Funding System," pp. 186–88. The problem of budget deficits and interest rates, including Ricardo's equivalence or rather nonequivalence theorem, was thoroughly discussed by William Fellner in his paper "Monetary and Fiscal Policy in a Disinflationary Process: Justified and Unjustified Misgivings about Budget Deficits," in *Essays in Contemporary Economic Problems: Disinflation*, p. 70.

7. See James Tobin, *Asset Accumulation and Economic Activity: Reflections on Contemporary Macroeconomic Theory*, Yrjö Jahnnson Lectures (Chicago: University of Chicago Press, 1980), pp. 31, 50, 54–57; and Richard Goode, *Government Finance in Developing Countries* (Washington, D.C.: Brookings Institution, 1984).

8. Richard Goode, too, takes a dim view of the equivalence theory, which he says is put forward by "adherents to an extreme version of rationalistic theory. . . . On the face the theory seems implausible. It implies that people can predict the future tax system, economic conditions and their own position" (Goode, *Government Finance*, p. 196).

9. Strictly speaking, even the depressed period of the early 1930s did not quite correspond to the Keynesian model. Keynes himself was fully aware of this. There were some bottlenecks, and prices rose after the cyclical turning point in 1933 with expanding demand. In fact, the U.S. prices rose at what was then regarded as an alarming rate, although unemployment was still very high—an early case of stagflation. Those price increases were due, however, to deliberate price- and cost-boosting measures of the New Deal.

10. Keynesians have been slow to recognize the changed world. Keynes, himself, however, recognized the changed economic climate already in 1937, one year after the appearance of *The General Theory*; and in three famous articles in the *Times*, he urged a shift in policy to curb inflation, although at that time inflation in Britain was not very high by postwar standards and unemployment was still about 10 percent. We have to distinguish between Keynesian economics and the economics of Keynes. Keynes's articles are reprinted in T. W. Hutchison, *Keynes versus the 'Keynesians' . . .? An Essay in the Thinking of J. M. Keynes and the Accuracy of Its Interpretation by His Followers*, Hobart Paperback No. 11 (London: Institute of Economic Affairs, 1977). See also *The Collected Writings of John Maynard Keynes*, vol. 21 (Cambridge: Cambridge University Press, 1982), pp. 384–95.

11. Stephen Marris, "Why Europe's Recovery Is Lagging Behind: With an Unconventional View of What Should Be Done about It," *Europe, Magazine of the European Community*, March/April 1984.

Since this was written an important, wide-ranging paper by Ambassador Arthur F. Burns, "The Economic Sluggishness of Western Europe" (delivered at the Dunlap Distinguished American Lecture, University of Dubuque, Iowa,

September 5, 1984, to be published), has become available. Burns presents a thorough analysis of the structural handicaps of Europe as compared with the United States and vividly describes the excesses of the welfare state and the oppressive regulatory climate in many European countries.

12. Since this was written, *The Economist* of London has taken up the subject (issue of November 24, 1984, "Why Europe Has Failed," p. 13, and "Europe's Technology Gap," pp. 93–98). The articles describe in considerable detail the enormous benefits the United States derives from the fact that its economy is a real free trade area of continental size with no restrictions or formalities at the state borders; that public utilities, airlines, railroads, and so on are in private hands, which ensures efficient competitive large-scale production; and that safety, health, and other regulations are uniform throughout the country.

In stark contrast, Europe is sorely handicapped because the "common market" has failed dismally to establish real free trade; public utilities, airlines, and so on are in public hands, which means that levels of output are way below the optimum; and safety, health, and other regulations vary from country to country. The article points out that these impediments explain why Europe lags badly behind the United States and Japan in the development of high-technology industries. Thus Europe has been prevented from fully participating in "the biggest market-driven wave of economic development [the world] has known, detonated by an explosion of knowledge. By one estimate, nine times as much scientific knowledge has been generated since the Second World War as mankind was able to produce in all its previous history. The amount of information in the world now doubles every eight years. Prosperity goes to countries that have a mechanism to put it to use." ("How Europe Has Failed," *The Economist*, London, November 24, 1984, p. 13).

13. For details see *The Economist*, London, June 23, 1984, p. 29.

14. These two factors are not always separable. Both the OECD and the EC routinely publish cyclically adjusted budget deficits for their members.

15. For details, see my contribution in *Essays in Contemporary Economic Problems: Disinflation*.

16. The GATT report has received hardly any attention in the media. A notable exception is an excellent article by Samuel Brittan, "The U.S. Loco No Longer Pulls," *Financial Times*, September 13, 1984. Mr. Brittan pays high tribute to the principal author of the report, Jan Tumlir, executive director of GATT. I wish to associate myself with that tribute.

17. Robert W. Crandall, "Import Quotas and the Automobile Industry: The Costs of Protectionism," *The Brookings Review* (Washington, D.C.: Brookings Institution, Summer 1984), p. 16.

After this was written, the excellent, comprehensive study *Exports of Manufactures from Developing Countries—Performance and Prospects for Market Access* (Washington, D.C.: Brookings Institution, 1984) by William R. Cline came to my attention. Cline's conclusions are similar to mine. He estimates that about one-third of U.S. imports of manufactures are now under "voluntary" import restriction. (See also his article "Protectionism: An Ill Trade Wind Rises," *Wall Street Journal*, November 6, 1984.)

18. Crandall, "Import Quotas."

19. "The Mighty Borrower," *The Economist*, London, September 22, 1984, p. 15.

20. On this point see the testimony of William A. Niskanen before U.S. Congress, Joint Economic Committee, August 8, 1984, in Council of Economic Advisers, *The Midyear Economic Outlook*.

21. See Otmar Emminger, "Der Währungspolitik stehen unruhige Zeiten bevor. Trendwende des Dollars/Rückkehr zur Normalität oder neue Turbulenzen?" in Deutsche Bundesbank, *Auszüge aus Presseartikeln*, Frankfurt am Main, April 6, 1984.

22. Otmar Emminger, "Adjustments in World Payments: An Evaluation," draft of a paper for the conference sponsored by the Federal Reserve Bank of Boston, May 20–21, 1984.

23. "Perspektiven der Weltwirtschaft" [Perspective for the World Economy], preliminary version, Kiel, 1984 (mimeographed).

After this was written, I learned through an article in the *Wall Street Journal* (November 19, 1984, front page) under the title "Machines Blamed for Europe's Joblessness," that Professor Giersch's theory about wages being too high has recently been confirmed by an expert report to the European Commission (EC) in Brussels. The report finds that European industries have invested too much in labor-saving machines. In fact, "the EC countries spent some 20 percent of their gross domestic product on fixed investment in the past 10 years, compared with 16 percent in the United States. But the EC managed to increase GDP by only 1.7 percent a year compared with 2.3 percent in the United States." The report concludes "that prosperity might be better served by employing human beings even if there is a machine that can do the same job [more cheaply]. Europe has actually gotten a poor return from heavy capital spending over the past decade."

According to the report, the main reason is that wages are too high and too rigid. I would add that interest rates are too low. High wages and low interest rates induce excessive substitution of capital for labor and high unemployment. I further conclude that there was after all some merit in the much maligned U.S. high-interest policy. It is needless to add that U.S. interest rates will have to come down when the economy slows down or goes into recession, as it will sooner or later.

(The quotations come from the article in the *Wall Street Journal*. The title of the report is "Some Aspects of Industrial Productive Performance in the European Community: An Appraisal," in *European Economy*, no. 20, Commission of the European Communities, Belgium, July 1984.)

The assertion that in some European countries real wages are too high has received its most thorough econometric test in an article by Jacques R. Artus, "The Disequilibrium Real Wage Rate Hypothesis: An Empirical Evaluation" (International Monetary Fund *Staff Papers*, vol. 31, no. 2, June 1984, pp. 249–302). The author concludes:

As far as the manufacturing sector is concerned, there are indeed strong reasons to believe that in France, the Federal Republic of Germany, and the United Kingdom the real wage rate is too high, in the sense of being incompatible with high employment. In particular, in these three countries we did not find any evidence that a large part of the actual increase in the share of labor costs in value added is warranted by long-run changes in production techniques, in the price of energy, or in the relative availability of labor and capital.

24. *Frankreich's Uhren gehen anders* [French clocks show a different time] is the title of a famous book by the Swiss historian Herbert Lüthy.

25. *The Economist*, London, May 13, 1984, reported from Switzerland that French customs officers have increased their "harassment" of people heading for Switzerland, giving "unjustified rough treatment to aged travellers." Things became so bad that the Swiss ambassador to France warned that if it did not stop "the relations between the two countries would be damaged."

26. Stephen Marris, "Crisis Ahead for the Dollar," *Fortune*, December 1983.

27. "The Slowdown of the World Economy and the Problem of Stagflation: Some Alternative Explanations and Policy Implications," background paper for the *World Development Report*, 1984 (Washington, D.C.: World Bank, forthcoming).

28. This conclusion has been greatly strengthened by recent events. The Bundesbank has strongly intervened in the foreign exchange market by selling dollars to bolster the deutsche mark and to dampen the rise of the dollar. It is safe to conclude that the bank would intervene at least as energetically to prevent an excessive slide of the dollar.

29. Colin Clark, *Conditions of Economic Progress* (London, 1951).

30. The following analysis is partly based on a very interesting article: "Flag Day for Argentina," *The Economist*, London, April 1984, pp. 11–12. *The Economist* lays its finger on the right spot, but it goes too far in blaming all the trouble on the successive military regimes. The trouble started earlier with the Peron regime (1946 to 1953).

Since this essay was written, Argentina has reached an agreement with the IMF (December 28, 1984; see IMF Press Release No. 84/43) that provides a stand-by credit of SDRs 1,694 that "may be drawn over the next 15 months." The money is to support an austerity program that is supposed to bring down the rate of inflation from 700 percent in1984 to "approximately 150 percent during the last quarter of 1985" and reduce "the public sector deficit from 10 percent in 1984 to 5 percent in 1985." It remains to be seen how this will work out.

31. Anne Krueger, "Aspects of Capital Flows between Developing and Developed Countries" (paper presented at the Pinhas Sapir Conference on Development, Tel Aviv, Israel, May 28–31, 1984, mimeographed).

32. In agricultural exporting countries, like Argentina, the food subsidies take the form of restrictions on exports of agricultural products to keep food prices down. The results are huge losses of output and lower tax revenues.

6

Deficits in the United Kingdom

Alan Walters

Summary

Substantial financial deficits of the public sector have been a problem in the United Kingdom for at least two decades. Governments, of all political hues, have attempted to boost the real economy by increasing public expenditures or reducing tax rates. During the 1970s, deficits in the United Kingdom rose beyond levels that, in relative terms, were expected in the United States during the 1980s, causing continuous problems of funding and capital flight. Pressure on the reserves and on the exchange rate, together with sharply rising interest rates, has been associated with inflationary expectations of monetary expansion.

Recent British governments have concluded that this is no way to run an economy. Ultimately, markets have forced the government to introduce monetary-fiscal austerity measures. In 1980 Britain inaugurated the Medium-Term Financial Strategy to control public spending, deficits, and monetary growth. Only when these are seen to be under control can there be any hope of long-term stability in finance prices and interest rates. The evidence suggests that, after a hesitant start, this strategy has been broadly successful.

What lessons can the United States learn from the experience of the United Kingdom? The main one is that persistent deficits are bound to cause some financial problems, including high interest rates generated by expected increases in the rate of inflation and the accompanying uncertainties. Although the United States as the custodian of the world's money has much longer lines of credit than the United Kingdom, these must eventually end. Credit, like time, must have a stop.

Introduction

For most private entities or institutions, deficits are temporary phenomena. A deficit implies that one must borrow in order to finance it, and ever-increasing indebtedness is not even an admissible, let alone desirable, policy for any firm or family. Even for government, the need

147

to borrow to pay debts presents a serious constraint on the budgetary policy. Somebody must provide the money to pay the government's bills.

The deficit of the public sector must therefore be counterbalanced by surpluses elsewhere. There are only two possibilities: the government must borrow either from the domestic private sector or from foreigners. The government sells financial assets to the private sector and to foreigners in order to get the cash to pay its bills. The private sector and foreigners, jointly considered, must have a surplus just sufficient to pay for the financial assets supplied by the government (see table 6–1). Expressed as a simple accounting rule:

Financial deficit	=	Financial surplus +	Financial surplus
of government		of private sector	of foreigners

or as a change in the ownership of financial assets:

Net sales of		Net acquisition of		Net acquisition of
financial assets	=	financial assets	+	financial assets
by government		by private sector		by foreigners

The net acquisition of U.K. financial assets by foreigners is, of course, the financing of the current account of the balance-of-payments deficit. If one assumes that the private sector has the same financial surplus year after year (and many distinguished economists have ventured such a proposition), then an increase in the government deficit is associated with *equal* increase in the deficit on the current balance of payments.[1]

This may take the form of "crowding out" the U.K. export indus-

---

TABLE 6–1
FINANCIAL BALANCES OF THE UNITED KINGDOM, 1982–1983
(£ billions)

Sector	1982	1983
Public deficit	−7.7	−10.8
Private surplus	14.5	13.0
Foreign deficit	−5.9	−2.0
(Residual error)	(−0.9)	(−0.2)
Total	0.0	0.0

NOTE: Detail may not add to totals because of rounding.
SOURCE: *Bank of England Quarterly Bulletin*, vol. 24, no. 2 (June 1984), pp. 216–17.

tries or "crowding in" imports to meet the additional absorption of resources created by the deficit. Foreigners are induced to invest in— or at least extend credit to—the United Kingdom. Alternatively, one may suppose that the appetite of foreigners for additional U.K. financial assets is very limited, so that variations in the government's deficit must be reflected in an increase in private sector saving or a reduction in their investment, so that they have a larger financial surplus. The private sector is "crowded out."

From the late 1960s until 1972, the private financial surplus of the United Kingdom was fixed at about £800 to £1,000 million.[2] Any increase in the public sector deficit would appear in a deteriorating current balance of payments—in other words, the United Kingdom would borrow from foreigners to finance the increased government deficits. The exhaustion of stocks of foreign exchange and liquid financial assets, combined with the reluctance of foreigners to lend (except on the most onerous terms), forced a discipline on the budget.

When during this period the United Kingdom exhausted its lines of credit and had to approach both the International Monetary Fund and friends (then flush) such as the United States, they insisted each time on a reduction in the deficit. Most political leaders thought it unsatisfactory, if not quite disgraceful, to sink to such depths of financial mismanagement that creditors dictated the broad outlines of our fiscal and monetary policy.

Deficits and the Public Sector Borrowing Requirement

In the United Kingdom there has long been for many purposes a more useful aggregate than the financial deficit; it is the public sector borrowing requirement (PSBR).[3]

The PSBR records the cash that the public sector has to borrow in order to pay its bills and measures the financial needs of the public sector. To obtain the PSBR, one must add to the financial deficit other expenditures that need financing (see table 6-2). These include mainly the government borrowing required to finance onlending (primarily to nationalized industries) and the money to finance the lags in the cash receipts from tax liabilities. This PSBR is, of course, far broader than the budget deficit—or in the case of the United States the federal deficit—of all the countries in the Organization for Economic Cooperation and Development. Not only does it include items that would be clearly considered "off-budget," such as the financing of the investment program of the nationalized telecommunications corporations, it also embraces the accounts of local authorities and other public agencies. The borrowing requirement then tells us the total

TABLE 6-2

THE FINANCIAL DEFICIT AND THE BORROWING REQUIREMENT
OF THE PUBLIC SECTOR, 1979-1983

(£ billions)

	1979	1980	1981	1982	1983
Public saving	+3.3	+2.7	+3.7	+6.1	+4.8
Capital transfers	−0.3	−0.4	−0.2	−0.6	−1.2
Capital expenditures	−11.4	−13.0	−12.1	−12.8	−14.3
Total financial deficit	−8.4	−10.6	−8.6	−7.3	−10.8
Onlending	+1.4	−0.5	+0.6	+1.4	−0.8
Accruals adjustment	−2.8	+0.8	+1.6	−1.9	+0.7
Miscellaneous transactions (including liquid assets)	−0.6	+0.0	−0.3	−0.5	+0.5
Financial transactions requiring financing	+3.6	+0.4	+1.9	−1.0	+0.4
Unidentified PSBR	+0.7	+0.8	+0.1	−1.4	+0.4
Total PSBR	−12.7	−11.8	−10.6	−5.0	−11.6
PSBR as percentage of GDP at market price	6.5	5.2	4.2	1.8	3.9

NOTE: Detail may not add to totals because of rounding.

SOURCE: *Financial Statistics*, HMSO, London, 1984, and *Bank of England Quarterly Bulletin*, vol. 24, no. 2 (June 1984).

demand for new financing or the total cash requirements of the public sector.[4]

The underlying criterion for inclusion in the PSBR is the Treasury guarantee. If the obligations of any institution are ultimately the liability of the Treasury, then all such expenditures, whether capital or current, are included in the PSBR. There is no escape into off-budget categories of spending as there is in the United States. It is supposed that the Treasury guarantee insulates such expenditures from market tests and so preempts funds that would otherwise be spent by the private sector.

To understand better the statistics in table 6-2 and to compare them with the U.S. government deficit, use the financial deficit of the public sector instead of the PSBR. The financial deficit in 1981 and 1982 was about £2 billion less than the PSBR, that is, about 1 percent less as a fraction of gross domestic product (GDP).

The Medium-Term Financial Strategy

Since the mid-1970s it has been widely accepted policy in the United Kingdom that some control of the PSBR at low values is needed to produce stable financial conditions. The experience with high values of the borrowing requirement—and for this purpose we can consider high above 5 percent of GDP—has been unfortunate, even bitter. The Labour party, for example, which gained power in 1974, embarked on a program of expansionary public spending as soon as it assumed office. The borrowing requirement, already at 7.6 percent of GDP in 1974, rose to 10 percent in 1975.[5] This was widely thought to be justified by the fact that the economy was in the sharpest contraction of the postwar period. Nevertheless, the large increase in the borrowing requirement gave rise to almost continuous crises in financial markets. Interest rates soared. Yet there was great difficulty in selling sufficient debt to the nonbank private sector, as market operators anticipated even further declines in the prices of gilt-edge securities, accompanied by a tumbling exchange rate for sterling.

To finance the current account deficit on the balance of payments, the British government resorted to substantial foreign borrowing. The stocks of foreign assets (particularly foreign exchange) were depleted. The expansionary budget drew in imports and kept potential exports in the home market. The increased public sector deficit spilled over substantially into a current account deficit.[6]

The first priority of the Conservative government, which came into office in May 1979, was to reduce the rate of inflation and to provide a sound and stable financial framework. This policy involved steadily reducing the rate of growth of the money supply and reducing the PSBR as a fraction of GDP. The government saw monetary policy and fiscal policy not as alternatives but rather as complementary policies for financial stability. If there were likely to be burgeoning deficits of the public sector, it would be difficult, perhaps impossible, to institute a policy of restraining monetary growth such that inflation could be reduced (eventually to zero). Indeed no one would believe the policy, and credibility was everything.

In an effort to secure a credible policy, the government developed the Medium-Term Financial Strategy (MTFS). For four or five years into the future, this set out planned rates of growth of the money supply and the desired path of the PSBR as a percentage of GDP. The target for the money supply was sterling M3, an aggregate that interpreted money supply broadly to encompass time deposits, large certificates of deposit, and so forth. In fact, about two-thirds of the total of sterling M3 consisted of interest-bearing deposit liabilities of the banking system.[7]

The choice of such a wide measure of the money supply can be explained first by its close relationship to the methods of credit rationing, which has a long history in the United Kingdom, and second by the ease of associating the increase in sterling M3 with the PSBR.

Increase in sterling M3	= PSBR	− Sales of public debt to nonbank private sector	+ Bank lending in sterling to private sector	+ External and foreign currency items

In figure 6-1 the paths of these elements show that there is no close correlation year to year in the growth of sterling M3 and the PSBR. Sales of debt, private lending, and foreign currency changes vary considerably. But it was correctly thought that a *persistently* high PSBR would be bound to be reflected ultimately in a high rate of growth in sterling M3 and therefore, in the rate of inflation. Indeed it has been suggested that the main purpose of controlling sterling M3 was to provide "an overriding constraint" on the deficit and other aspects of policy.[8] Many thought that the sterling M3 targets were useful primarily because they restrict the PSBR, and only secondarily because they directly influence the rate of inflation.

The MTFS proposed plans for government spending and taxation that, with the PSBR, were consistent with the proposed growth rate of sterling M3. This implied, among other things, a forecast in the amount of bank lending to the private sector. The MTFS envisioned a policy that must not crowd out private credit markets; room must be left for industry to finance its program of expansion and modernization.

Table 6-3 shows PSBR targets as percentages of GDP. Two features are central. First, the program did not allow for the usual cyclical oscillation in receipts and expenditures. There was no formal embrace of the concept of the full employment budget deficit, and with good reason. The concept of full employment was numerically elusive. Pursuing chimerical targets of full employment had brought Britain into the league of high inflators. The four- to -five-year period of the MTFS would almost certainly embrace most if not all phases of trade cycles, with some adjustments to reflect the effects of the level of trade activity on the percentages. The MTFS figures themselves were relevant to the prevailing level of activity in 1979, which, in retrospect, turned out to be the upper turning point in the cycle.

Second, although the start date of 1979 was an upper turning point of the cycle, there was also a very large structural deficit. The

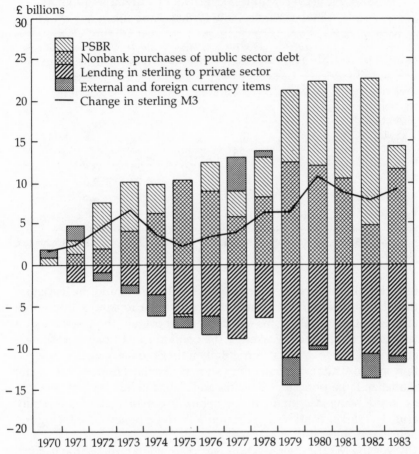

FIGURE 6–1
COUNTERPARTS TO MONETARY GROWTH, 1970–1983

£ billions

PSBR
Nonbank purchases of public sector debt
Lending in sterling to private sector
External and foreign currency items
— Change in sterling M3

SOURCES: *Bank of England Quarterly Bulletin*, vol. 23, no. 2 (June 1983), p. 203. The data for 1982 and 1983 have been added from *Bank of England Quarterly Bulletin*, vol. 24, no. 2 (June 1984).

actual deficit in 1979 was of the order of 5 percent of GDP, while at the top of a boom one would have expected to have achieved a surplus (a feat last achieved a decade before). Nor can one claim that 1979 was an accidental year. Even the average deficit from the peak of 1973 to the peak of 1979 was about 6 percent of GDP. The 1979 structural deficit was at least more than 6 percent and perhaps even larger than 10 percent of GDP. So it was clear that there was a deep and persistent underlying structural deficit.

It was also widely recognized, in the more responsible elements

153

TABLE 6–3
PSBRs, Projected and Realized, as Percentages of GDP,
Fiscal Years 1980–1981 to 1985–1986

PSBR		1980–1981	1981–1982	1982–1983	1983–1984	1984–1985	1985–1986
Projected (by date of projection)							
March	1980	3.75	3.0	2.25	1.5	—	—
	1981	—	4.25	3.25	2.0	—	—
	1982	—	—	3.50	2.75	2.0	—
	1983	—	—	—	2.75	2.5	2.0
November	1983	—	—	—	3.25	2.5	—
Realized		5.6	3.4	3.25			

SOURCES: PSBRs and November Statement 1983 by the Chancellor of the Exchequer, HMSO, London.

of both political parties and by officials in the Bank and the Treasury, that this structural deficit made it very difficult to control the monetary aggregates or the rates of inflation. Above all, the presence of a large structural deficit weakened the confidence of holders and dealers of debt. Large deficits, particularly if they persist, cause consternation in the City. Experience has shown that governments normally monetize large persistent deficits, and debt holders become anxious to avoid being caught in a collapsing bond market and liquidity crunch. Market confidence required a credible policy of reducing the deficit and the PSBR.

For the MTFS, the reduction was planned in terms of the *nominal* PSBR. This is important primarily because it has become fashionable to argue that the appropriate measure of fiscal policy is not the nominal but the *real* PSBR—that is, the PSBR adjusted for inflation.[9] One should count as current real expenditure only the real rate of return on public debt (say 2 to 3 percent); the yield over and above this figure is simply analogous to a repayment of the principal that would occur in an inflation-free system. It is not a current cost of government borrowing. Thus the deficit, or PSBR, so adjusted for inflation, is thought to be a better measure of budgetary conditions than the unadjusted PSBR.

Whether the inflation-adjusted PSBR is a better measure of budgetary conditions may be debated, but there is little doubt that it is much inferior to the nominal PSBR as a target for financial policy.[10] To control inflation it was necessary to impose a discipline on the *nominal* PSBR. As Minford has shown, the main reason for choosing a nominal PSBR is that it provides a much smoother adjustment path than any inflation-adjusted deficit.

A central criticism of using the PSBR in any form to control inflation is that it takes into account changes in obligations or assets for a particular year and not those likely or even bound to occur in future years. It does not measure the discounted present value of the receivables and payables in the future. And it may be argued that it is this wealth that measures the effect of the public sector.

Although one might admit these criticisms of the use of the current deficit or PSBR, no one could conceivably draw up a balance sheet for the public sector that could carry the least bit of conviction. Yet it is important that decisions that spill over into future years (such as delaying an investment) be taken into account in budgetary planning. The MTFS managed to make some adjustment for such shifting obligations by the fact that four out of five years were planned consistently. Spillovers were accounted for. True, the adjustment is a crude one, but it is about the best that can be done.

Targeting the PSBR

Two major problems with targeting the PSBR arise, first, from the large seasonal component and, second, from the inevitable, though unsystematic, error in the outcome. Because the tax-paying season occurs primarily in the fall and winter months, the borrowing requirement for the financial year (beginning in April) tends to occur almost entirely in the late spring and summer months. Unfortunately this seasonal influence cannot be predicted accurately because of frequent administrative changes and amendments to the tax system. These are compounded by progressive attempts to control public expenditures. The net result is that it is difficult to know how the budgetary conditions are developing during the year; even after the year closes it is some time before the accounts are complete. Monthly or even quarterly borrowing figures give only vague clues as to the eventual condition of the budget.

Furthermore, since the PSBR is the difference between two very large numbers, the error in it is always likely to be large. The total expenditure of the public sector amounts to about £125 billion, so it is not surprising that the Treasury found that the average error (ignoring sign) between forecast and outcome was about £3 billion, or about 1 to 1½ percent of GDP.

It might appear that the progressive decline in the PSBR, targeted in the MTFS at about 1 to $1\frac{1}{2}$ percent a year, was far too refined and could easily be swamped by the ordinary errors of outcome. This is true. But it does not follow that it is unwise to take accurate aim at a PSBR target because, on average, one is bound to miss by a mile, just as it does not follow that because a marksman hits the bull's-eye only rarely, he is unwise to aim at the center of the target. The purpose of the PSBR target is to give guidance on expenditure programs and tax rates. It is therefore just as essential to have a precise target as it is for the marksman to aim at the bull's-eye. But one should have a sense of proportion and purpose in judging the achievements ex post.

The Achievements of the MTFS

With all the caveats discussed above, I think it is reasonable to claim that the outcome of the MTFS was successful in many ways. Clearly the PSBRs did decline consistently over the 1980–1984 period. Sometimes the decline was much more precipitous than anticipated, as from 1980–1981 to 1981–1982, but sometimes it was much less, as in the following year (see table 6–3). In view of the errors to be expected, this was not out of court.

The other singular feature was that the percentages both planned and achieved, after the original MTFS formulation in March 1980, were all rather higher than the first formulations. This was primarily because of the recession into which Britain descended during 1979–1980. The actual realized PSBR, as a percentage of GDP, tended to be about one to one and one-half percentage points (even two percentage points in 1980–1981) above the original planned figures. The deviation represents an allowance for the built-in stabilizers. The majority of those in the economics profession in the United Kingdom of course thought that to be far too little and even thought the government had been perverse in offsetting the normal automatic stabilizers.[11]

As with all these calculations, it depends upon one's view of the desiderata. The government's argument in the MTFS was that in 1979 the structural PSBR was far too large and quite unsustainable in an environment of low inflation. The case of the critics was that, irrespective of the size of the structural PSBR in 1979, the rapid and steep decline in the level of activity and employment called for an increase, not a decrease, in the level of the PSBR. In other words, the critics did not accept one or other of the government's propositions. It was argued, for example, that by adjusting for inflation and the level of activity the deficit was really a surplus (and had been for a decade) and that it was entirely tenable and would in any case improve with the higher level of activity that fiscal expansion would surely bring about.[12] Generally the critics thought that at tolerable levels of unemployment, inflation would be contained only by income and price controls.[13] Granted the government's case, then the realized PSBRs were near enough to the target path, as adjusted for the level of activity, to pronounce the program a considerable success, at least as far as these intermediate targets were concerned.[14]

As for the ultimate objective of reducing the rate of inflation in the medium term, the government could claim that the MTFS had well served its purpose. Inflation fell from an underlying rate of more than 15 percent in 1980 (it peaked at 22 percent in May 1980) to about 5 percent by the end of 1982. Although most economists and commentators (the most notable exception being Patrick Minford) thought there would be a resurgence of inflation, particularly after the election of June 1983, the rate of increase of retail prices stayed at the 5 percent level for the next two years until November 1984. The Treasury continues to forecast a gently declining rate of inflation over the next two years, whereas the outside forecasters have revised their estimates to show only a very modest increase.[15]

One cannot readily claim that the success in bringing down the rate of inflation was solely or even largely due to the decline in the deficit. There are many other factors. Among British economists I suspect that the most popular proximate explanation is the increase in and persistence of high unemployment. For many monetarists the debate turns on whether there has been a substantial monetary squeeze from 1979. Whatever the explanation, the main transmission mechanism was thought to be the exchange rate; thus the real appreciation of sterling from 1977 to the end of 1980 (a 35 to 40 percent appreciation) was the harbinger of the recession as well as the reduction in the rate of inflation through the low increases or reductions in prices of traded goods.

A substantial school of thought also argues that the real appreciation of sterling was the main cause of the recession and the disinflation. Sterling rose, however, because North Sea oil was replacing manufactured exports, and the real value of oil production increased with the price rise of 1979. This "Dutch disease" version of events suggests that neither a substantial fiscal nor monetary squeeze was evident and that the pressure was largely structural.[16]

It is not possible to review the arguments and the evidence here to determine which explanation is consistent with the facts. That task must be left as unfinished business. But we can review two of the achievements of the fiscal targets of the MTFS—financial stability and lower rates of interest. First, there is little doubt that the budgetary side of the MTFS did secure more stable financial conditions than had been experienced for perhaps as long as two decades.[17] Since 1981 there has been no suggestion of any prolonged "funding strike"; that is, the authorities have had little difficulty in selling sufficient gilt-edged securities to finance the funding targets. Indeed the authorities overfunded the PSBR in order to contain the growth of sterling M3 by selling more gilt-edged securities than were needed to finance the PSBR. The gilt-edged market entered a prolonged period of bullish sentiment.

The other characteristic of stable financial conditions was the absence of a run on sterling. Indeed the balance of payments on current account and the stocks of foreign currencies reached an all-time high in 1981 during the operation of the MTFS.[18] The United Kingdom began to accumulate a substantial nest-egg of foreign investment, accounting for some 50 percent of the transitory oil revenues. Net external assets grew from 2 percent of national income in 1977 to 25 percent in 1983 (£55.6 billion) and 32 percent in 1984.[19]

The second characteristic of the period is more contentious. The chancellor, in introducing his budgets, has clearly argued that smaller deficits and PSBRs as well as containment of the money supply will help to keep interest rates lower than they would otherwise be. To avoid misunderstanding, it is necessary to emphasize that no one claimed deficits to be the *only* factor determining interest rates, but the clear implication was that the government viewed the deficit and PSBR as important influences on interest rates. The precise way in which the PSBR affects interest rates and the term structure is much disputed. There is, however, some degree of agreement that *persistently* high deficits cause fears of monetary expansion and thus of higher inflation rates. The inflationary premium will be included in credit contracts in the form of higher nominal rates. Yet this argument applies primarily to long-term debt and expectations about interest rates on future short-term credit instruments. For short-term interest rates, an important determinant is current monetary policy. In the United Kingdom, at least after mid-1980, monetary policy has been characterized as a gentle but persistent disinflationary pressure. There has been no evidence of sharp and persistent tightening nor of considerable laxity.[20] Over these years the yield curve was almost flat but with a very slight upward slope. This suggests that the market expected interest rates to remain the same or to decline slightly over the long run.

A useful indicator of the effect of fiscal deficits on interest rates can be obtained by comparing the history of U.K. and U.S. interest rates with the history of their deficits. The statistics in figure 6–2 show

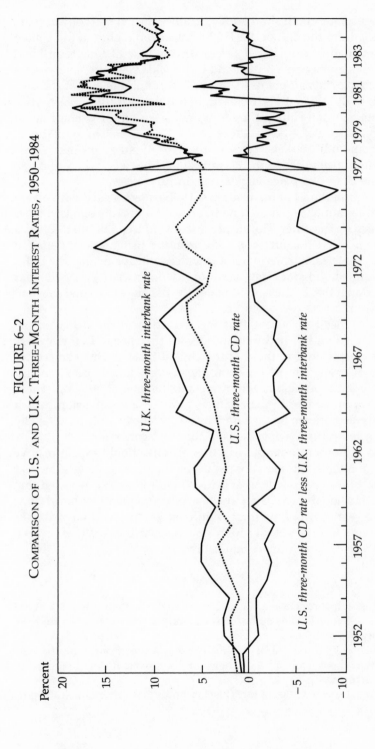

FIGURE 6-2

COMPARISON OF U.S. AND U.K. THREE-MONTH INTEREST RATES, 1950–1984

Percent

U.K. three-month interbank rate

U.S. three-month CD rate

U.S. three-month CD rate less U.K. three-month interbank rate

NOTE: Annual data, 1950–1976; monthly average data, January 1977–June 1984. Rates at close on July 6: U.K., 10.3; U.S., 11.8.

SOURCE: Her Majesty's Treasury.

that interest rates, both short and long, since the general convertibility of sterling from the end of the 1950s, have been higher in the United Kingdom than in the United States. In the case of long-term bond yields, the gap between British and U.S. yields was very wide—some five or six percentage points—from 1974 through the end of the decade. But in the 1980s the gap closed; in the last year (July 1983 to June 1984) yields in the United Kingdom have been on the average about one percentage point below those of the United States. Similarly, in the three-month markets, rates in the United Kingdom have fallen significantly below those in the Eurodollar markets, where the gap was more than two percentage points in June 1984.

This turnaround in interest rates has been associated with a very different fiscal policy, on the one hand, and a broadly similar monetary policy on the other. The steady downward trend of the PSBR as a percentage of GDP contrasts starkly with the rising federal deficit in the United States. Furthermore, it is widely anticipated that the PSBR of the United Kingdom will continue its downward path, whereas there is doubt that in the United States the deficit will decline substantially over the next two years.

It is difficult to believe that the reduction in the deficit of the United Kingdom has had little to do with the change in the level of interest rates relative to those of the United States.[21] One conjectures that the difference in the long-run rates is very largely due to markedly different expectations with respect to the rates of inflation. These in turn are influenced by expectations of monetary expansion, which are partly determined by the forecast future deficits, duly modified by the expected future savings rates of the two economies.

It is important to emphasize that no one should expect relative long-term interest rates to vary month by month or even year by year with the PSBR or the federal deficit. When it is clearly expected that the deficit, though high, is a transitory phenomenon that may last as long as a year or two, then there is little reason to expect interest rates to respond. It is *persistently* high deficits that eventually dominate expectations and thus affect interest rates.[22]

Notes

1. This simple conclusion was urged on a reluctant government by Lord Kaldor and Wynne Godley of the "new Cambridge school," luminaries of the University of Cambridge.

2. This was formulated as a principle of macroeconomics by the new Cambridge school. From 1973 on, however, the private financial surplus increased dramatically.

3. Indeed, many critics of the Thatcher policy have alleged that the gov-

ernment has made a fetish of the PSBR. Willem Buiter, *The Times*, November 23, 1983.

4. The PSBR does *not* include cash required to finance maturing debt.

5. PSBR calculated as a percentage of GDP at market prices. *Central Statistical Office, Annual Abstract of Statistics*, London, 1979, tables 14.1 and 17.11; and *Central Statistical Office, Economic Trends*, 367, London, May 1984, p. 6.

6. It is also worth noting, however, that there was a substantial financial increase in the surplus of the private sector over this period, partly because of increased personal saving.

7. Another view defines sterling M3 as the residual currency and deposit liability of the banking sector (including the Bank of England) of the United Kingdom, after consolidation to cancel intersectoral assets and liabilities.

8. See John Fforde, "Setting Monetary Objectives," *Bank of England Quarterly Bulletin*, vol. 23, no. 2 (June 1983), p. 203.

9. It is particularly important to examine the use of the real PSBR critically, since it seems to be accepted as a guiding star by such conservatives as Milton Friedman and such liberals as James Tobin.

10. This has been argued in detail by Patrick Minford, "The Development of Monetary Strategy," in John Kay, ed., *The 1982 Budget* (Oxford: Basil Blackwell, 1982).

11. It is not clear that this is the case. The realized PSBR, for example, was almost two percentage points above the planned PSBR in 1980–1981. The average estimate of the fall in GDP from 1979 to 1981 was about 5 percent. With a multiplier of about 2 (I am here taking the value advocated by Blinder and Solow, not the one calculated by the Cambridge economists, Feathersone and Godley, of 3.75), the adjustment is somewhere near the zone that would be advocated. If one follows the Cambridge findings, the government overdid it.

12. The best-developed case along these lines is by Willem Buiter and Marcus Miller in "Changing the Rules: Economic Consequences of the Thatcher Regime," *Brookings Papers on Economic Activity*, no. 2 (1983), pp. 305–79.

13. See, for example, James Meade, "A New Keynesian Approach to Full Employment," *Lloyds Bank Review*, October 1983, pp. 1–18.

14. According to Buiter and Miller, "Overall the designers of MTFS could be satisfied with the results ('Changing the Rules,' p. 324)."

15. In June 1984 estimates of the retail price index by the Treasury and the leading outside forecasters were as follows:

	Treasury	Consensus	Range
1984 4th qtr.	4.0	5.2	3.7 to 6.0
1985 4th qtr. (2d for Treasury)	4.0	5.9	2.1 to 6.0

(Consensus is the unweighted average of leading forecasters.)

16. See, for example, K. Alec Christal, "Dutch Disease or Monetarist Medicine? The British Economy under Mrs. Thatcher," *Review of the Federal Reserve Bank of St. Louis* (May 1984), pp. 27–37.

17. This takes us back to the first Labour government of the 1960s.

18. The surpluses on current account (billions of pounds, seasonally adjusted) were: 1980—3.6; 1981—7.3; 1982—5.8; 1983—2.9; 1984 (1st qtr.)—0.8. *Bank of England Quarterly Bulletin*, vol. 24, no. 2 (June 1984), p. 165.

19. Ibid., p. 221. Oil Revenues now are at a peak 3 percent of GDP.

20. It might be argued that the last quarter of 1981 is an exception. The tightening was only brief, however, and does not affect the general thrust of policy during the four-year period. Similarly, the much more modest tightening during 1982–1983, under the cloud of electoral uncertainties, can be construed as a small adjustment.

21. The movements of relative interest rates also affect the relative deficits since interest costs are a substantial component of the deficits in both countries.

22. This view is contested by Martin J. Bailey, Paul G. Balabanis, George Tuvlas, and Michael Ulan, "U.S. Deficits and Interest Rates," Department of State, Washington, D.C., May 1984. They argue that there is no evidence that large deficits are associated with high interest rates.

7

The Effect of Government
Deficits on Capital Formation

John H. Makin

Summary

This paper investigates the effect on private capital formation that may be expected to arise from an increase in actual and prospective government deficits, while controlling for other determinants of the desired capital stock. It begins by presenting some background on the magnitude of actual and prospective federal deficits in the 1980s and their implications for the federal debt burden.

Also examined is the standard crowding-out view and conditions under which crowding out may not occur. These include the low interest-elasticity of investment expenditure, the high interest-elasticity of saving, and the Ricardo-Barro proposition that financing government expenditure by shifting from tax to bond finance produces no net effect on aggregate demand. Conditions sufficient to preclude any concern over crowding out are found to be quite stringent and unlikely to be fulfilled.

Pursuing a less traditional line of investigation, the paper also studies the effect on investment of uncertainty about policy regimes. It examines penalties to capital formation implicit in nonindexed portions of the tax code in which large actual and prospective deficits raise the likelihood of higher inflation. Responses after the fact to such inflationary distortions in the nonindexed corporate sector of the tax code are considered primarily responsible for the enactment of irregular tax reform measures such as ACRS and ITC. The paper concludes with a presentation of a neoclassical model of business investment designed to estimate the effect of deficits on private capital formation. Estimates of the shadow price of capital are then employed to calculate the change in the present value of consumption benefits associated with the estimated effect of deficits on private capital formation. Results suggest that the 1980–1989 actual and prospective U.S. deficits imply a consumption loss equivalent to between $800 billion and $1 trillion, or roughly 2–3 percent of each year's GNP between 1980 and 1989.

Introduction

There is no consensus on the effect of government deficits on capital formation. Given our current ability to understand the formation of expectations and to measure the responsiveness of private saving and investment to changes in real after-tax interest rates, a decisive answer to the question of whether a neutral (with no effect on relative prices) tax cut replaced by the sale of government bonds to finance the deficit reduces private capital formation is impossible.

This essay takes the view that the effects of deficits large enough to produce the recent sharp increases in the ratio of federal debt and total debt to gross national product deserve careful scrutiny. Between 1982 and 1984 federal deficits totaled about $490 billion. That sum, roughly equal to the cumulative total of federal deficits from the Revolutionary War to the end of the Vietnam War, was sufficient to boost sharply the ratio of federal debt to GNP from about 35 percent to about 43 percent.[1] The outlook as of late 1984 was for the ratio to continue rising and to reach over 50 percent by the end of the decade. If, as capital theorists have suggested, larger stocks of debt relative to income imply higher real interest rates, the negative effect on capital formation could be both considerable and not readily reversible. The irreversibility arises because, even if 1984–1989 deficits were cut by the $100 billion per year necessary to stabilize outyear federal debt-to-GNP ratios, the result would be only to stabilize real interest rates, not to lower them, as some who link high real rates with large flow deficits would suggest. Viewed in this way, drastic action to reduce deficits will be sufficient only to contain past and prospective damage to capital formation. Actual enhancement of capital formation will have to await the longer-run goal of gradually lowering the ratio of overall debt to GNP by sharply curtailing the contribution made to the ratio by rapid increases in federal debt.

Before examining further these and other issues, I want to clarify what is meant in this essay by government deficits. Here a dollar rise in the government deficit will mean a dollar rise in government spending or a dollar cut in tax revenue not entirely offset by some other government unit. In addition, the deficits to be discussed are not those that would be offset by the negative effect on the stock of outstanding government debt arising from inflation or higher interest rates or by the movement of economic activity to some arbitrary full-employment level. Nor will I pay attention to the important issue of unfunded government liabilities. In short, this essay bypasses the many intriguing questions about "when is a deficit really a deficit?" raised by L. J. Kotlikoff, R. Eisner and P. J. Pieper, and others.[2]

The question under investigation here can be put succinctly. Has U.S. capital formation been depressed by the decision to fund a large and prospectively rising share of government spending by borrowing instead of taxing? Since 1982 the gap between federal government spending and revenues has risen sharply and is projected to remain high for the balance of the 1980s. This statement is true for actual, measured federal deficits, high employment deficits, and high employment deficits adjusted for price and interest effects. While state and local surpluses have reduced overall government deficits, they have not yet eliminated them and very likely will not eliminate them in the foreseeable future.

Deficits have in part arisen from tax cuts designed to enhance capital formation. Measures such as accelerated depreciation schedules or investment tax credits designed to lower the user cost of capital inputs have historically produced a sharp—if temporary—positive impact on capital formation. Since such measures are a major part of 1981 and 1982 tax legislation, their effect will be considered when I examine recent data on capital formation.

Capital formation is not sought for its own sake. A larger capital stock enhances overall capacity to produce goods and services while increasing productivity and real wages of labor. Steady and rising capital formation also increases the likelihood that the capital stock will embody a large and rising share of the ongoing qualitative improvements in capital equipment (technological progress) that are so important to sustained economic growth. While only about 15 percent of U.S. growth comes from capital accumulation, according to classic studies by R. M. Solow and E. Denison,[3] almost one-half of the growth comes from technological progress, which enhances factor productivity. Technological progress captures that share of growth because of qualitative improvements in human and physical capital that result from ongoing capital formation and production of new vintages of capital equipment.

A more direct approach to assessing the value of steady capital accumulation is suggested by R. C. Lind's calculation of the "shadow price of capital," which is the present value of the future stream of consumption benefits associated with one dollar's worth of investment.[4] Allowing for the 7–10 percent difference between the marginal product of capital and the rate at which the public discounts future increases in output arising from more current investment, Lind has estimated the shadow price of capital to be $3.80. This figure, largely the result of a tax code that keeps the marginal return on private investment well above the social rate of time preference, will be useful when translating possible effects of deficits on investment into consumption gains or losses measured in current dollars.

With the foregoing considerations in mind, I proceed to investigate the question of what effect, if any, on private capital formation may be expected from a rise in actual and prospective government deficits while controlling for other determinants of the desired capital stock.

Deficits in the 1980s and the Burden of Debt

Tax cuts enacted in 1981 and 1982 reduced the fiscal 1984 share of tax revenue in GNP to less than 20 percent, while military spending and indexed entitlements were largely responsible for pushing federal spending to 24 percent of GNP. One result of these changes, together with the projected path of the economy over the rest of the decade, has been prospective deficits in the range of $200 billion to $300 billion annually.

The ratio of debt to GNP linked to the real interest rate, accompanied by tax treatment of capital purchases, determines the user cost of capital, an important factor in determining investment spending. Therefore it is important to understand the relation between deficits and the debt-to-GNP ratio. The growth of the debt-to-GNP ratio is determined by the sum of two (percentage) components: the ratio of the primary deficit (government spending on all but interest, minus tax revenues) to the national debt, plus the difference between the interest rate on the debt and the growth of GNP. I call the first the *primary revenue gap* and the second the *interest-growth gap*. Both can take on positive or negative values, but the prospects for a negative primary revenue gap seem remote at present.

The rate of growth of the debt-to-GNP ratio in terms of the two gaps is derived as follows: the deficit or change in federal debt is written as the sum of interest payments on the national debt plus the primary deficit, or

$$\Delta D = iD + G - tY \qquad (1)$$

where D = national debt; i = nominal interest rate on debt; G = federal government expenditure; t = average tax rate; and Y = GNP. Dividing (1) by D and subtracting the rate of growth of GNP, $(\Delta Y/Y)$ gives ratio of the rate of growth of the debt to GNP expressed in terms of the primary revenue gap and the interest-growth gap:

$$(\Delta/D) - (\Delta Y/Y) = \frac{G - tY}{D} + i - (\Delta Y/Y) \qquad (2)$$

$$\text{(primary} \qquad \text{(interest-}$$
$$\text{revenue} \qquad \text{growth}$$
$$\text{gap)} \qquad \text{gap)}$$

TABLE 7-1

PROXIMATE DETERMINANTS OF THE RATIO OF U.S. FEDERAL DEBT
TO GNP, 1980-1989

| | Primary Revenue Gap | Interest-Growth Gap | Debt/GNP | |
			H[a]	A[b]
1980	0.7	2.7	34.7	34.7
1981	− 1.0	1.8	35.0	34.0
1982	2.2	6.7	38.0	37.4
1983	8.4	0.9	41.6	41.8
1984	4.5	− 1.5	42.9	43.4
1985[c]	3.2	1.0	44.7	
1986	2.8	0.8	46.3	
1987	2.6	0.6	47.8	
1988	2.2	0.9	49.3	
1989	2.0	1.0	50.7	

a. Hypothetical ratios calculated from the two gaps using equation 2. Differences from actual ratios are due largely to fiscal-year versus calendar-year measures.
b. Debt figures are gross federal debt including debt held by the public and by government accounts. This avoids the need to forecast divisions between the two in arriving at projections of future values.
c. Future values calculated from Congressional Budget Office projections.

Table 7-1 presents actual projected values for the primary revenue gap and the interest-growth gap in the United States during the 1980s, with implied ratios of debt to GNP. Between 1980 and 1984, the contribution of each of the two gaps to growth of the debt-to-GNP ratio varied considerably, with the biggest increases coming from the 6.7 percent interest-growth gap in 1982 and the 8.4 percent primary revenue gap in 1983. During 1984 relatively rapid growth coupled with some easing of interest rates was largely responsible for the slowing in the growth of debt to GNP.

The projections by the Congressional Budget Office used to calculate future gaps and therefrom to calculate future debt-to-GNP ratios suggest a stabilization of both gaps to a mean sum of 3.4 percent over the 1985-1989 period. The result is a debt-to-GNP ratio of 50.7 percent in 1989. Were the sum of the gaps to change by one percentage point on either side of 3.4 percent, implied 1989 debt-to-GNP values would range from a low of 48.3 percent to a high of 53.2 percent. As I shall show later on, a five percentage point move in the debt-to-GNP ratio can have significant implications for investment and implied consumption gains or losses.

Consider the history of U.S. federal debt-to-GNP ratios since World War II. From a post–World War II level of 107 percent, the ratio fell steadily to a low of about 25 percent in 1974, after almost three decades during which real growth exceeded real interest rates by a healthy margin. Slower real growth during the mid-to-late 1970s and sharply higher real interest rates since 1980, together with higher spending levels and lower tax rates, pushed the debt-to-GNP ratio to nearly 43 percent by 1984, with projected deficits implying a ratio of more than 50 percent by 1989. While there may be no optimal debt-to-GNP ratio, levels over 50 percent imply severely constrained government spending simply by virtue of the implied interest burden. At 50 percent of GNP, debt service alone takes 6.0 percent of GNP if average interest on the debt is 12.0 percent. (August 1984 CBO projections, more optimistic about interest rates, put 1989 debt service cost at 4.1 percent of GNP.) Non-interest budget outlays for 1989 are currently projected at 20.8 percent of GNP. With an interest burden at 6.2 percent of GNP, the 20.8 percent outlay puts total spending at 27 percent of GNP compared with CBO projected 1989 revenues of 18.9 percent of GNP, a gap of 8.1 percent.

The 8.1 percent gap between the ratio of expenditure to GNP and the ratio of revenue to GNP is troublesome for private capital formation when viewed in flow terms. Net private saving amounts to just over 5 percent of GNP (5.1 percent in 1983). If federal deficits consume more than net private saving, then private capital formation must be financed by either business, saving surpluses of local and state governments, or capital inflows from abroad. This last source, while necessarily implying large trade-balance deficits, would probably also require high real U.S. interest rates and a strong dollar, all characteristics of the American economy in deficit during the 1982–1984 period. That configuration is not likely to enhance capital formation in America's export sector.

The outlook for the burden of interest on the debt in the longer run calls for reducing the gaps of the early 1980s. Were the sum of the primary revenue gap and the interest-growth gap to stay at the 1980–1983 mean of 4.5 percent, the ratio of federal debt to GNP would reach 87 percent by 1999. That ratio would mean that at 12 percent, interest on the debt would absorb more than 10 percent of GNP, more than three times the 1984 share of 3.1 percent.

Beyond upward pressure on real interest rates, a rising debt-to-GNP ratio threatens to create a dangerous self-reinforcing growth of deficits. Deficits by definition add to debt, and larger debt adds to deficits because more debt means a larger interest bill for government. The only way to break the link between debt and deficits is either to raise tax rates or to broaden the tax base whenever debt increases. In short, the usual commitment of governments to maintain expenditure while resisting tax increases translates into a self-reinforcing feedback mechanism: deficits raise debt; higher debt means even higher deficits, which in turn create even higher debt; and so on.

The increase in the share of interest payments on debt in total government spending implied by a period of a rising debt-to-GNP ratio is already apparent. Net interest payments on government debt were 8.0 percent of government spending in 1974, 10.4 percent in 1981, and 12.7 percent in 1984. CBO projects that they will reach 16.3 percent in 1989. The absorption of tax revenues into debt service requirements constitutes one of the costs of large deficits, as painful choices between cutting spending on established government programs or raising taxes are either made or postponed in favor of more debt accumulation. If marginal tax rates are increased, incentives to invest are reduced, especially if the debate over growing deficits results in political pressure for corporations to pay their share.

Beyond such indirect penalties to investment, deficits that are sufficiently large to raise debt-to-GNP ratios may imply a direct reduction of investment. O. J. Blanchard identifies a direct, positive relationship between real interest rates and the ratio of debt to GNP. Higher real interest rates raise the user cost of capital, which in turn lowers investment by reducing the desired capital stock.[5]

The Standard Argument: Crowding Out

The basic crowding-out argument relies on three key elements, each of which is widely disputed among economists both on empirical and on theoretical grounds: the responsiveness of investment to expected, real after-tax returns; the elasticity of private saving with respect to real after-tax returns; and the net wealth component of government securities. The effect on resource allocation of the way in which spending or taxes change, with the uncertainty about the outlook for inflation and relative prices engendered by large fiscal deficits, raise further questions about the effect of deficits on capital formation. These questions are far from resolved, either on the theoretical or on the empirical level.

A close look at the standard crowding-out argument helps delineate theoretical and empirical questions concerning the effect of government deficits on real interest rates and private capital formation. Figure 7-1 is a standard representation of saving and investment schedules in relation to after-tax real interest (r). Investment (I) measures the real increase in the capital stock net of depreciation. Each

FIGURE 7-1
STANDARD VIEW OF CROWDING OUT

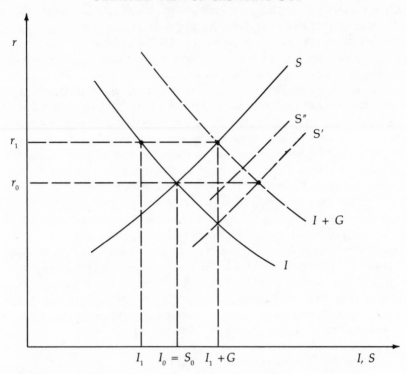

schedule is drawn for a given tax code. Saving (S) measures real private saving. The initial equilibrium is at r_0 with real private investment equal to real private saving. I and S schedules may also be viewed as demand for borrowed funds and supply of loanable funds schedules.

Crowding out arises when the investment schedule is shifted to $I + G$ by a real increase in the government deficit financed by the sale of bonds. The new schedule, $I + G$, is parallel to the original schedule since the government's demand for funds is totally interest inelastic. Given $I + G$ and S schedules, the new equilibrium after-tax real interest rate is r_1. The implied level of private real net investment is I_1 and crowding out is given by $(I_0 - I_1)$.

If, as some have argued, openness of world capital markets means that the S schedule is infinitely elastic at r_0, increased government borrowing is accommodated at r_0 and no crowding out occurs, at least domestically. Alternatively, crowding out is reduced as the interest elasticity of real net private capital formation with respect to the real after-tax rate of interest declines, assuming the economy has slack and is able to produce more. Introducing the role of expectations as suggested by R. J. Barro and others further modifies the analysis of crowding out.[6] I will suppose that the government deficit reflected in the $I + G$ schedule in figure 7-1 arises because of a neutral tax cut matched by an increase in the sale of government bonds. Under the Ricardo-Barro equivalence theorem, rational savers will increase saving by an amount sufficient to meet interest payments on the debt and ultimately to pay off the principal. Since the present value of such interest payments and principal repayment will equal the value of bonds sold, the savings schedule shifts to S', just enough to keep r at r_0. No crowding out occurs because government bonds, under the extreme-rationality view, represent zero net wealth for private households. With no net effect of government bonds on aggregate demand, the equilibrium after-tax real interest rate is unaffected. This result holds irrespective of the shapes of the I or S schedules.

The extreme-rationality view of the effect on net wealth of a larger supply of government bonds holds only if households place equal weight on the welfare of future generations as they do on their own, a concern known as the intergenerational transfer motive. If, alternatively, households place less—or no—weight on the welfare of future generations, issuance of long-term government bonds on which future generations will make payments for principal and interest means that the present value of such liabilities to current households will be less than the face value of the bonds. As a result, net wealth of households will be increased, albeit by less than the full value of government bond issues. The saving schedule will shift by less, say to S'', and some crowding out will result given the shapes of investment and saving schedules in figure 7-1.

Crowding out may also be reduced by a non-neutral change in the tax code. Suppose that a larger deficit financed by an increased sale of government bonds results from tax cuts in the form of accelerated depreciation allowances or investment tax credits, such as were enacted in 1981 and numerous times before. The result shown in figure 7-2 would be a shift in the private net real investment schedule to I' and a reduction (shown) or elimination of crowding out depending on the degree of the shift and the interest elasticity of private investment and saving. (Crowding out is reduced to $I_0 - I'$ in figure 7-2 given the shift of the I schedule to I'.) In sum, a nonneutral tax cut may result in zero or even negative net crowding out of private capital formation even though the equilibrium real after-tax interest rate is increased.

The view that "deficits don't matter," at least not for net private

FIGURE 7-2
Change in Tax Code Reducing Crowding Out

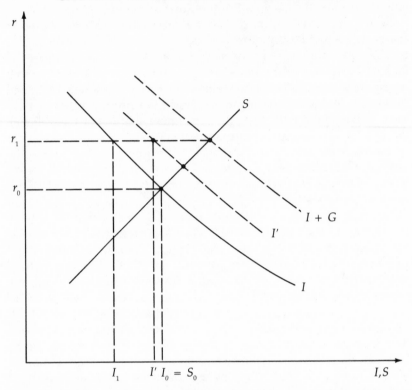

capital formation, requires either one of the following three conditions or some combination of them: interest inelasticity of private investment; infinitely elastic supply of funds from domestic saving or capital inflow; or the view on the part of households that government bonds are merely offsets for future tax liabilities.

While inhomogeneity of the capital stock and many volatile exogenous factors (including the tax code) that affect investment behavior make difficult any estimation of the interest elasticity of investment, the theoretical case for a positive response of investment to a lower real interest rate, or lower rental value of a unit of capital, is well established. Results of empirical investigation by R. E. Hall and D. W. Jorgenson and others of the effects of tax policy on investment are consistent with a positive response of real investment to lower real interest rates.[7] Overall, the notion that net private investment is unresponsive to changes in real, after-tax interest rates is very likely the weakest basis for the notion that deficits don't matter. Rejection of the interest-inelasticity argument, however, leaves two more difficult issues to resolve: the shape of the saving function and the question of whether government bonds are viewed by households as net wealth. Both are ultimately empirical questions since economic theory does not decisively determine either.

Theoretical analysis of saving is complex because of heterogeneity among savers, considerations of the life cycle, the role of intergenerational transfer motives, and opposite income and substitution effects of changes in the after-tax real interest rate. A widely cited estimate by M. J. Boskin put the elasticity at a positive 0.4,[8] but many regard that estimate as too high. These issues are concisely discussed by L. H. Summers, who argues for a higher interest-elasticity of saving based on direct estimation of utility function parameters.[9] The stability of the private saving rate during the 1980s, given volatile and rising after-tax real rates, continues to suggest to some that the elasticity is low. For others with opposite assumptions, it suggests that private saving is poorly measured by standard flow data or that other determinants of saving have changed sharply. The openness of world capital markets has been offered, without the support of overwhelming empirical evidence, as reason to expect a high interest-elasticity of saving. Considerable responsiveness of capital inflows to high U.S. interest rates (the mirror image of large trade balance deficits) is consistent with this view, but the rise during part of 1984 of U.S. real interest rates indicates, *ceteris paribus*, that the elasticity of the world saving supply schedule is less than infinite.

The cacaphony of opposing views on the interest elasticity of saving leads me, with some trepidation, to suggest that the elasticity is likely positive and perhaps, by virtue of openness consideration, larger than Boskin's 0.4. At the same time there is no compelling empirical evidence that it approaches infinity or any level sufficiently high to dispel, by itself, concern that crowding out may be a problem.

The most fashionable disputed element of the crowding-out view is whether households see government bonds as net wealth or simply as reminders of future tax liabilities. On one hand, some find intuitively unappealing the strong rational notion that intergenerational altruism is sufficient to motivate, say, a seventy-year-old purchaser of a thirty-year bond to add to savings enough for his children or grandchildren to service and retire the government debt he buys. On the other hand, it seems naive to suppose that investors in government securities and taxpayers generally are totally unaware of just who will provide the means at least to service, if not to retire, a larger stock of government debt.

Empirical investigations, predictably, have not resolved the question of whether households view government bonds as net wealth. Some investigators, including J. E. Tanner, L. Kochin, and R. C. Kormendi, have tested the hypothesis that aggregate consumption or saving is unaffected by measures of government debt and did not reject it.[10] Others, like W. Buiter and J. Tobin and M. S. Feldstein, obtain results consistent with the notion that changes in government spending or taxes can have a substantial impact on aggregate demand.[11] C. I. Plosser, by examining responses of asset markets to changes in fiscal policy, finds no evidence of crowding out in response to a substitution of debt for tax financing.[12] He does find, however, that unanticipated increases in government spending may raise real rates of return and thereby induce temporarily higher output through the Barro-Hall intertemporal labor substitution argument.[13] On balance, the mixed empirical evidence concerning the relation between deficits and aggregate demand leaves a cautious analyst unwilling to conclude that the threat of crowding out is fully eliminated by an obliging outward shift in the private saving function.

A middle-of-the-road reading of the theory and empirical evidence overall suggests a view of the world not unlike that represented in figure 7-1. Interest elasticity of investment is not zero, and the interest elasticity of saving is not infinity. A shift from tax to bond financing of government spending probably causes some outward shift in the private saving function but not enough to leave after-tax real interest rates unchanged.

Recent Behavior of U.S. Investment

In view of the considerable uncertainty underlying the theoretical and empirical foundations for the crowding-out phenomenon, a look at actual recent investment behavior in relation to what would have been predicted is worthwhile.

The behavior since 1970 of net U.S. private investment (GNET) based on 1972 measurement is shown in figure 7-3.[14] The annual rate of change of GNET is plotted using quarterly data in figure 7-4 (superimposed on comparable data for gross private investment to display the close relation between annual growth rates of the two series.)

Figure 7-3 shows that real net capital formation in mid-1983 stood about where it had in 1970 during a brief recession. Over that same period real GNP rose by about 50 percent, while real capital consumption (a rough measure of total depreciation) rose by 88 percent. In short, while the U.S. net real capital stock was increasing at a faster rate during 1983 than at any time in the previous decade, it was doing so from a very low base.

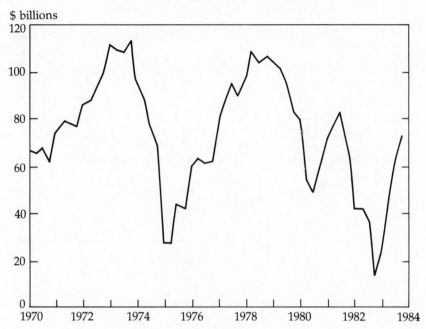

FIGURE 7-3
NET PRIVATE INVESTMENT, 1970–1984

$ billions

SOURCE: Citibase data tape, third quarter 1984.

Three major cycles of real net investment began during the 1970–1983 period. Two were completed, and the third is underway. The first came after the expansionary 1971–1972 period when (in 1972) accelerated depreciation and an investment tax credit, which had been removed in 1970, were reinstated. The first oil crisis and the ensuing sharp recession in 1974–1975 terminated that episode of capital formation. An end to the recession in 1975, coupled with an increase to 10 percent (from 7 percent) of the investment tax credit, initiated a second rise in investment that largely paralleled the path of the overall expansion in 1975–1980, a period when real interest rates frequently were negative. A brief resurgence of real net capital formation during late 1980 and early 1981 collapsed in the last half of 1981 with the onset of recession after the shortest recovery in postwar history. Real investment began its third sharp recovery since 1970 during mid-1982, slightly before the November 1982 cyclical trough, stimulated no doubt by the provisions of the Economic Recovery Tax Act (ERTA) of 1981 and the Tax Equity and Fiscal Responsibility Act (TEFRA) of 1982. The latter, while mitigating somewhat the effective tax reductions for

175

FIGURE 7–4
CHANGES IN NET PRIVATE INVESTMENT AND
GROSS PRIVATE INVESTMENT, 1970–1984

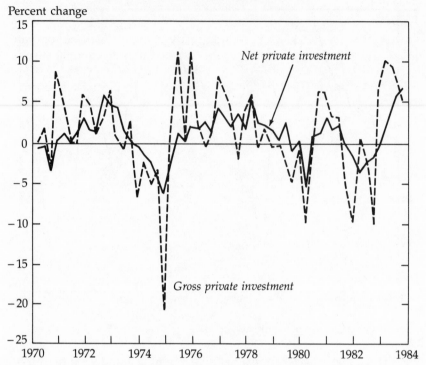

SOURCE: Citibase data tape, third quarter 1984.

corporations under ERTA, left intact some notable acceleration of depreciation. Largely as a result of ERTA and TEFRA, the effective average corporate tax rate fell to 36.5 percent, well below rates of 41.6
percent in 1981 and 46.6 percent in 1980, levels representative of rates
during the 1970s.

The behavior of real net capital formation since 1980, on the sur-
face at least, appears to have been an example of the ability of changes
in the tax code to overcome the depressing effect of high real interest
rates. Such episodic tax reform in the face of declining investment that
produces a bunching-up of expenditures on capital equipment, likely
associated with increased cyclicity of overall economic activity and
employment, is typical of U.S. policy since 1954. There have been no
fewer than fourteen major corporate tax reforms since 1954, and their
frequency has increased, no doubt accounting in part for an increase
in overall uncertainty that has tended to lead to a concentration of

investment on shorter-term projects with a relatively short pay-back period.

The relation during the 1980s between deficits and capital formation suggested by the discussion so far is as follows. There were sharp increases in actual and prospective deficits during 1981 and 1982. Such deficits, in the absence of a perfectly interest-elastic supply of saving and less-than-perfect foresight or total intergenerational altruism on the part of households, caused after-tax real interest rates to rise. The negative effect of the high real rates on capital formation appears to have been overcome by changes in tax policy (ERTA-TEFRA) that have lowered the rental cost of capital inputs. Viewed in this way one might say that, to the extent that higher deficits measure ERTA-TEFRA–reduced tax revenues from corporations, they are the cause of higher capital formation.

There are two serious caveats to this flippant view of deficits and capital formation. First, one must consider the typical response pattern of investment to corporate tax reform (reductions). Second, one must consider how investment has behaved since 1981 in relation to what would have been predicted based on its overall postwar behavior. In other words, given a combination of high after-tax real interest rates and tax breaks since 1981, has real net investment behaved normally by postwar standards, or has some new set of factors been at work?

A change in tax policy, such as accelerated depreciation or enhanced investment tax credits, operates on investment by lowering the cost of services of capital. The result is a finite increase in the desired stock of capital. Net investment increases to bring capital stock up to the desired level. Once that higher stock is achieved, net investment drops back to the level that prevailed before the change in tax policy. The only ongoing effect of the change in tax policy is a positive effect on gross investment arising from replacement of a larger capital stock. Further, if the initial change in tax policy is rescinded, the resulting drop in the desired stock of capital accentuates the swing of real net investment, as during 1970 when the investment tax credit and other incentives to capital formation were rescinded.

Empirical investigation of the effects of tax policy changes on investment behavior by Hall and Jorgenson suggests that the response of investment to such policy changes peaks after two to three years and then falls off rapidly, largely disappearing after five years.[15] This lag pattern suggests that the response of real net investment to 1981–1982 tax policy changes ought to peak during 1984. The lagged response of investment to the ERTA-TEFRA corporate tax reform package may well have been partly responsible for the unexpected strength of the economy during 1984.

The typical response pattern of investment to changes in tax policy coupled with possible persistence of large deficits and attendant high real interest rates for the rest of the 1980s suggests that a sharp slowdown in investment during 1985 or 1986 is likely unless real interest rates fall sharply. Lower real interest rates appear unlikely in view of high levels of the debt-to-GNP ratio. Tax policy changes very favorable to capital formation have temporarily shielded investment from the depressing effect of high after-tax real interest rates. But ERTA-TEFRA provides only a temporary antidote to high real rates. If that antidote wears off while real rates remain high, the negative effect on capital formation could be devastating. Needless to say, if post-1984 tax reform were to include further repeal of ERTA provisions, the drop in investment would be sharper still. The basic point to remember is that changes in tax policy change net investment only temporarily.

Before attempting some empirical analysis of investment behavior, it is useful to consider the effect of uncertainty and other indirect consequences of deficits on investment behavior. Under the view that investment really represents a commitment to a given outlook for relative prices, increased uncertainty about that outlook arising from large deficits will be harmful.

Indirect Effects of Deficits on Capital Formation

Historically, large deficits have been associated with or have resulted in higher inflation. M. S. Feldstein has argued convincingly that a larger real deficit in a fully employed economy must raise the inflation rate, lower capital intensity, or both.[16] Empirical investigations undertaken during the 1970s have shown that higher inflation has meant more volatility of inflation and of relative prices. These phenomena have been found to be associated with slower economic growth due in turn to their likely negative effect on capital formation. Distortions arising largely from an unindexed tax system like that of the United States have also resulted in a negative effect of inflation on capital formation. This section considers indirect negative effects of deficit-induced inflation on capital formation arising from absolute and relative price level uncertainty and from an unindexed tax code.

The effect of deficits on uncertainty about the outlook both for inflation and for relative prices, along with its attendant depressing effect on capital formation, comes from two sources. First is the straightforward link from larger deficits to higher inflation and from higher inflation to more uncertainty about inflation and relative prices. A second link runs from large deficits to uncertainty about how they will be financed. Large deficits financed by bond sales, if we are to believe formulations like figure 7-1, place upward pressure on interest rates both nominal and real. Considerable uncertainty attaches to the question of when and how much the Federal Reserve will employ monetary expansion in an attempt to cushion the upward pressure of heavy bond sales on interest rates. Further, in the short run it is difficult to predict the effect of accelerated money growth on real and nominal interest rates. Initially a "surprise" acceleration of money growth may lower real and nominal rates, particularly short-term rates due to liquidity effects. But if surprise growth of money puts the money supply above the Federal Reserve's prestated target range, expectations of a reversal of the higher money growth may push rates up in the forward-looking credit market. If money growth remains high, higher anticipated inflation will push up nominal rates. Overall the existence of large deficits clouds the outlook for monetary policy, which adds to uncertainty about inflation and relative prices that in turn depresses capital formation.

The work of Martin Feldstein, Lawrence Summers, and others, well represented in *Inflation, Tax Rules and Capital Formation,* a collection of papers on the interaction of inflation with the largely unindexed U.S. tax code, strongly suggests another channel for a negative effect of inflation on capital formation. Feldstein's introductory overview to the 1983 collection of his papers introduces the major strands of this literature:

> Inflation distorts the measurement of profits, of interest payments, and of capital gains. The resulting mismeasurement of capital income has caused a substantial increase in the effective tax rate on the real income from the capital employed in the nonfinancial corporate sector. At the same time, the deductibility of nominal interest expenses has encouraged the expansion of consumer debt and stimulated the demand for owner-occupied housing. The net result has been a substantial reduction in the accumulation of capital in nonfinancial corporations.
>
> The rate of business fixed investment in the United States has fallen quite sharply since the mid-1960s. The share of gross national product devoted to net nonresidential fixed investment fell by more than one-third between the last half of the 1960s and the decade of the 1970s. The ratio of net fixed nonresidential investment to GNP averaged 0.042 from 1965 through 1969, but only 0.030 from 1970 through 1979.

The corresponding rate of growth of the nonresidential capital stock declined by an even greater percentage: between 1965 and 1969, the annual rate of growth of the fixed nonresidential capital stock averaged 5.7 percent; in the 1970s, this average dropped to 3.8 percent. By the second half of the 1970s, the capital stock was growing no faster than the labor force, thereby eliminating the increase in capital per worker as a source of productivity growth.[17]

The *ex post* penalty imposed by inflation on saving in the United States, especially during the 1970s, suggests reasons for the low level of the U.S. saving rate. Taxes are levied on nominal interest earnings and nominal capital gains. The effect on after-tax real returns has been devastating. M. S. Feldstein and J. Slemrod investigated the experience of a hypothetical investor who bought and held a Standard and Poors' 500 portfolio between 1957 and 1977.[18] Both the portfolio and the consumer price level more than doubled during that time, so the investor had no real gain while the tax law treated him as having made a 100 percent gain on which a capital gains tax was levied. After-tax real returns were roughly *minus* the capital gains tax rate of about 30 to 35 percent depending on the status of the investor. Even though reductions in capital gains tax rates have been enacted since 1977, the effect is merely to reduce the negative rate of return on nominal returns that only keep up with inflation.

M. S. Feldstein and L. Summers find that the greatest effect inflation has on tax burdens comes from the overstatement of corporate profits resulting from tax-accounting rules tied to nominal magnitudes.[19] Evaluation of depreciation allowances and inventory-replacement costs based on historical values results in understatement of capital maintenance requirements that rise as inflation rises and cause historical cost estimates to understate current replacement costs. The result is overstated profit, which is taxed. Feldstein and Summers estimated that such mismeasurement of depreciation and inventories raised the 1977 tax burden of nonfinancial corporations by $32 billion, a 50 percent increase in the total tax paid on income from corporate sources.

Independent corroboration of the "Feldstein-Summers effect" is reported by J. H. Makin and V. Tanzi in a study of interest-rate behavior.[20] They report on tests of the effects on nominal interest rates of anticipated inflation and other variables employing a structural model formulated in after-tax real terms. Normally such models imply that the nominal rate rises by more than the rise in anticipated inflation. The reason is, once again, the tax code, which taxes nominal interest earnings as ordinary income. If inflation rises by 1.0 percent, maintenance of a constant after-tax real rate requires a 1.5 percent rise in the nominal interest rate given a tax rate of one-third. Most empirical investigations, however, resulted in an estimated effect on nominal interest rates equal to only about 75 percent of the increase in anticipated inflation.[21] The implication appeared to be that investors failed or were unable to take account of the negative effect on after-tax real returns arising from taxation of purely nominal increases in interest rates.

A structural model including an investment equation that captured the Feldstein-Summers effect resolved the apparent mystery. If a rise in anticipated inflation means for investors a forseeable increase in the tax burden due to mismeasurement of depreciation and inventories, anticipated inflation shifts the investment schedule downward. The result is a drop in the equilibrium after-tax real interest rate and resultant negative pressure on the nominal rate at the same time that the rise in anticipated inflation is pushing up the nominal rate. The net effect of these and other reactions considered by Makin and Tanzi is a theoretical response coefficient of nominal interest to changes in anticipated inflation well below unity and in line with most empirical estimates.

The foreseeable overstatement of corporate profits given unindexed costing of capital equipment and inventories creates a direct negative link between anticipated inflation and capital formation. The negative effect of deficits on capital formation is, in this context, directly proportional to the effect of deficits on anticipated inflation.

Large deficits, the tax code, and attendant phenomena may produce yet another negative effect on capital formation. When deficits are large enough to be unsustainable, they result in widespread speculation about drastic changes in government expenditure and revenue policies with alterations in the tax code. Such prospective changes, widely discussed since early 1984, raise the possibility of sharp changes in equilibrium relative prices, which in turn have a powerful effect on investment decisions. Prospective sharp cuts in military spending obviously affect the investment outlook in aerospace industries. Possible elimination or reduction of deductibility of household interest payments would sharply affect the investment outlook in real estate, not to mention the value of the existing stock of housing. Deficits that grow large enough to result in a consensus that something will have to be done put investment plans on hold until the exact nature of major deficit reduction measures or tax reforms, if indeed any are ever enacted, becomes clear.

Many of the uncertainty factors discussed here are difficult to quantify and therefore are difficult to test empirically. The relation between uncertainty about inflation and uncertainty about relative prices and their effect on economic activity is, however, empirically testable using Livingston survey data on inflationary expectations.[22] A proxy measure for uncertainty about relative prices is included with more standard explanatory variables in the investment equations estimated in the following discussion.

A Framework for Analysis of Investment: Estimation of Effects of Deficits on Capital Formation

The familiar neoclassical theory of investment as articulated by Hall and Jorgenson[23] sets the rental value of capital services at

$$c = q (r + \delta) \Phi \tag{3}$$

where c = after-tax rental value of capital services; r = the expected real return on capital; δ = the rate of depreciation; and Φ = a combination of statutory tax rates on profits, accelerated depreciation provisions, and investment tax credits.

Rewriting the marginal product of capital as the output capital ratio y/k times η_{yk}, the elasticity of output with respect to capital input or capital's share of output in a neoclassical Cobb Douglas production function:

$$MP_k = \eta_{yk} \, y/k \tag{4}$$

where k = capital stock and y = real output.

Transposing (3) and substituting from (4) for MP_k gives an expression for the price of a unit of capital:

$$q = \frac{y/k \; \eta_{yk}}{(r+\delta)\Phi} \tag{5}$$

Multiplying both sides by K^*, the capital stock at which (3) is satisfied, and rearranging terms gives:

$$K^* = \eta_{yk} \, (y/c) \tag{6}$$

Investment (I) follows from a change in the desired capital stock. Therefore

$$I = \Delta K^* = \eta_{yk} \, y/c \, [\hat{y} - \hat{c}] \tag{7}$$

where ^ over a variable designates percent rate of change. Equation 7 links investment positively to the growth of output and negatively to the rate of change of the user cost of capital.

Investment is expenditure undertaken by forward-looking decision makers. Equation 6 expressing the desired capital stock in terms of the *levels* of output and the user cost of capital, conditional on the productivity of capital, η_{yk}, is appropriate in a static environment. But a change in the desired capital stock will depend on current *and prospective* changes in y and c over the life of the capital equipment the purchase of which is contemplated. Therefore, (7) is rewritten as

$$I = \eta_{yk} \, y/c \, [\hat{y}^* - \hat{c}^*] \tag{8}$$

where * designates current actual and expected future changes in output and the user cost of capital.

Expectations about future changes in output and user cost are unobservable variables, so empirical analysis of investment is, in this view, frustrated by speculative attempts to represent the collective expectations of investors regarding these variables. This consideration becomes particularly important in regard to expectations about *changes* in the user cost of capital. User cost, described by equation 3, depends on expected real interest rates, depreciation rates, and tax policy toward investment. Such tax policy includes, in effect, statutory rates on corporate income and any investment tax credits (ITC) or accelerated cost recovery schedules (ACRS).

ITC or ACRS provisions are unique. When enacted they describe ensured, prospective reductions in user cost (ignoring the TEFRA rescission of ERTA provisions), elevate the desired capital stock, and in turn cause a once-and-for-all increase in investment. If, as is likely, the move toward the desired capital stock is spread over time, a distributed lag effect may occur on investment arising from changes in user cost. Hall and Jorgenson discovered just such an effect.[24] A distributed lag effect may also occur as a response of investment to changes in real income.

Direct measures of user cost are available. An annual series running back to the early 1960s has been prepared by the Congressional Budget Office. A series also appears in Charles Hulten and James Robertson.[25] These series display relatively little year-to-year change in user cost. Interpolation of the annual data to a quarterly format for use in estimation with quarterly data on investment and other variables produces largely indecisive results, due probably to the low information content of essentially annual data in a quarterly format and the relative smoothness of the series which makes estimating limits difficult.

The investment equation requires a variable along with income growth to serve as a proxy for both current and expected values of real interest rates and taxes on income from capital. The ratio of federal debt to GNP or its change is hypothesized to serve this role. A higher ratio increases the likelihood of higher future statutory tax rates on both capital and labor income and raises the likelihood of future re-scissions of ACRS or ITC. Also as O. J. Blanchard shows, the ratio of total debt to GNP determines the real interest rate; so to the extent that the ratio of federal debt to GNP tracks that ratio, it serves as a proxy for the level of the real interest rate.[26] Now, if the capital stock adjusts only partially toward its equilibrium value during an interval of a quarter or a year, a drop in the real interest rate that elevates the desired stock of capital will result in more investment. Specifically, if

$$I_t = K_t - K_{t-1} = \lambda[K^*_t - K_{t-1}] \tag{9}$$

then from (6)

$$I_t = \lambda \, \eta_{yk} \, (y/c) - \lambda K_{t-1} \tag{10}$$

A rise in the level of the real interest rate or effective marginal tax rate on capital will raise the user cost (c) and reduce investment. To the extent that a rise in debt to GNP serves as a proxy for a rise in current and prospective values of both tax rates and real interest rates, it will reduce investment.

The most straightforward formulation ties investment behavior, as a flow representing a change in the capital stock toward its equilib-rium value, to current and prospective *changes* in real income and user cost. The implication is that changes (or percent changes) in income and user cost, or their proxies, ought to enter the investment equa-tion. Results of empirical investigation confirm that growth of real income has a robust positive effect on investment as suggested by equation 8. Direct measures of levels and level changes of user cost have a statistically weak negative impact.[27] Both a federal-debt-to-GNP-ratio proxy for user cost and the changes thereof have a robust negative effect on investment.

First I shall examine results describing investment in terms of output growth and the level of debt to GNP; next I consider as explan-atory variables for investment, output growth, and the change in debt to GNP. Inflation uncertainty and a direct measure of user cost are also tested for explanatory power. The latter, it will be seen, produces results more consistent with observable investment behavior.

Table 7-2 reports results of estimating an equation, describing real U.S. net investment using quarterly data for the period from 1960:I through 1982:III. The equation in table 7-2 regresses real net investment on real GNP growth, the level of federal debt to GNP, a measure of inflation uncertainty, σ_t, and CBO's direct measure of user cost for equipment. GNP growth rates follow directly from equation 8. Debt/GNP is a proxy for prospective levels of or changes in user cost, while user cost captures the current actual level of that variable (cur-

TABLE 7-2

ESTIMATION OF $(GNET)_t = \beta_0 + \beta_{10}\hat{y}_t + \beta_{11}\hat{y}_{t-1}$
$$- \beta_2 \left(\frac{Debt}{GNP}\right)_t - \beta_3\ user_{t-4} - \beta_4\sigma_t$$

Sample Period	β_0	β_{10}	β_{11}	β_2	β_3	β_4	$\bar{R}_2$	F
1960:I to	404.3	0.72	0.41	-673.3	-544.2	-6.21	0.91	114.1
1982:III	(4.14)	(3.88)	(2.55)	(4.13)	(2.00)	(1.21)		

NOTES: Estimated simultaneously with an ARMA (1–1) residual noise model. Includes dummy variable for 1975–1. t-statistics in parentheses.

rent and lagged percent changes in actual user cost were insignificant).[28] The measure of inflation uncertainty, σ_t, is taken from the dispersion in the Livingston survey data and serves as a proxy for prospective uncertainty about relative prices, which, as discussed previously, ought to have a negative effect on investment.

All variables have anticipated signs. Current and lagged growth elevate investment while the ratio of federal debt to GNP, actual user cost, and inflation uncertainty reduce it. The statistical significance of the latter two variables is marginal. The user-cost real interest proxy, the ratio of federal debt to GNP, produces a robust negative impact on investment. Based on the estimate of β_2 reported in table 7–2, a one percentage point increase in the ratio of federal debt to GNP reduces net investment by about $15 billion in 1984 dollars. The implication of this result is either that the level of federal debt to GNP is serving as a good proxy for current and prospective changes in user cost or that a partial adjustment of the capital stock to its equilibrium value during the quarter is resulting in an apparent link between investment and levels of user cost.

Table 7–2 results suggest a specific link between deficits and capital formation. Deficits large enough to raise the ratio of federal debt to GNP, termed "imprudent deficits" by D. D. Purvis and N. Bruce,[29] imply less private capital formation. Viewed in this manner, the "imprudent" characterization by Bruce and Purvis is appropriate. More specifically, the primary revenue gap and the interest-growth gap (recall table 7–1 and discussion) must add up to a positive number for deficits to be associated with lower investment. This is a common-sense result. If the capacity of governments to service debt and the capacity of households and businesses to hold it are proportional to GNP, then the deficits to be concerned about are those that make government debt grow more quickly than GNP.

Table 7-3 reports results of employing a distributed lag on changes in the debt-to-GNP ratio as a proxy for current and prospective changes in user cost. Results suggest that contemporaneous and four lagged values of the change in debt to GNP all produce a significant negative impact on investment (see second equation in table 7-3). This result is consistent with a negative relationship between the level of user cost and the desired capital stock or a negative relationship between the change in user cost and the flow of investment. A larger positive change in user cost produces a fall in investment, which in turn results in a steady state reduction in the stock of capital.

The first equation in table 7-3 suggests that in the presence of a direct measure of marginal user-cost lagged four quarters, the change in debt to GNP lagged four quarters becomes insignificant while lags zero through three remain significant. Inflation uncertainty remains only a marginally significant depressant of investment.

Implications for the path of investment of results reported in tables 7-2 and 7-3 are quite different in terms of its volatility over time, although implications of level and change results for cumulative investment changes are similar. Table 7-4 shows the path of investment under each result attributable to hypothetical changes in debt to GNP over five years. The portrayed movements of changes in the debt-to-GNP ratio are similar to actual movements represented in table 7-1. The figures for investment are based on an estimate of an investment drop of $15 billion in 1984 dollars in response to a one percentage point rise in debt to GNP shown in table 7-2 (hereafter the "level result") and an estimated drop of $75 billion in 1984 dollars in response to a one percentage point rise in the *change* of debt to GNP shown in table 7-3 (hereafter the "change result").

Although the total investment loss over five years under both level and change results is similar (neglecting discounting), the change result reveals a far more volatile path of investment than the level result, which in fact corresponds much more closely to the actual path of investment. The change result implies that stabilization of the debt-to-GNP ratio is all that is required to produce a temporary rise in investment, which in turn helps eliminate losses accumulated during periods when the rise in debt to GNP is accelerated. The level result means that for every percentage-point rise in debt to GNP investment is permanently lower.

The actual path of investment, as represented in figure 7-3, is far more like the path implied by the change result. That result implies that stabilizing the debt-to-GNP ratio would contain the damage done by a series of accelerating increases. A steady, continued rise in debt to GNP, however, would mean no reversal of accumulated negative

TABLE 7-3

ESTIMATION OF $(GNET)_t = \beta_0 + \beta_{10} \hat{y}_t + \beta_{11} \hat{y}_{t-1} - \sum_{j=0}^{4} \beta_{2j} (\Delta Debt/GNP)_{t-j} - \beta_3\, user_{t-4} - \beta_4 \sigma_t$

(Sample period: 1960:I–1982:III)

Equation	β_0	β_{10}	β_{11}	β_{20}	β_{21}	β_{22}	β_{23}	β_{24}	β_3	β_4	R^2
1	277.7	0.69	0.50	−841.8	−894.4	−920.7	−654.9	−16.2	−975.6	−7.58	0.94 $F\,(13,71) =$
	(5.33)	(3.92)	(2.85)	(5.90)	(5.08)	(5.23)	(4.09)	(0.12)	(4.12)	(1.62)	98.9
2	61.85	0.82	0.68	−716.9	−729.2	−915.6	−570.7	−287.1			0.93 $F\,(11,73) =$
	(7.34)	(4.67)	(3.88)	(4.99)	(4.20)	(5.11)	(3.72)	(2.34)			98.55

NOTES: Estimated simultaneously with an ARMA (1–2) residual noise model. Includes dummy variable for 1975:I. t-statistics in parentheses.

TABLE 7–4

ALTERNATIVE INVESTMENT CHANGES

(billions of 1984 dollars)

Year	Debt/ GNP (%)	Percentage Point Change in Debt/GNP	Investment Relation to Debt/GNP	
			Level (table 7–2)	Change (table 7–3)
0	35.0	0	0	0
1	36.0	1.0	– 15.0	– 75.0
2	39.5	3.5	– 52.5	– 187.5
3	42.5	3.0	– 45.0	37.5
4	43.5	1.0	– 15.0	150.0
5	45.5	2.0	– 30.0	– 75.0
Total			– 157.5	– 150.0

SOURCE: Calculated from equation in table 7–3.

pressure on investment, while continued acceleration in the rise of the ratio would mean a continued fall in investment.

Interestingly, the level and change results imply similar total cumulative investment losses over an extended period. The cumulative total investment loss over five years of about $150 billion (shown in table 7–4) for the change result is roughly equivalent to losses implied by the level result from a five-year rise of debt to GNP by ten percentage points, at a stable rate of two percentage points per year such as actually occurred between 1980 and 1985 (see table 7–1).

The cost of less investment, in terms of forgone aggregate consumption, is difficult to estimate; but an attempt at such measurement provides a clearer idea of the implications of the excessively rapid growth of federal debt that is linked to large deficits. The procedure, as developed by R. C. Lind,[30] involves some fairly complicated calculations, but the concept behind it is simple. The U.S. tax code results in a sizable wedge being driven between the marginal rate of return on private sector investment and the social rate of time preference. Compounding at the former rate, set at around 13 percent with the marginal propensity to save at 0.2, while discounting at the latter rate set at around 6 percent results in a shadow price of capital of about 3.8. This is the estimate obtained by Lind.

The Lind estimate implies that a rise in the debt-to-GNP ratio of about ten percentage points spread over five years results in a cumulative loss in terms of present value of consumption benefits of $570 billion ($150 × 3.8). Looking ahead, one can see that the present value equivalent of such losses in 1984, at a rate of $114 billion per year for the 1985–1989 period, would be $443 billion in 1984 dollars, or about 12 percent of 1984 GNP.

Table 7–5 compares the outlook for 1985–1989 investment, assuming stabilization of debt to GNP in 1986, with the outlook under the currently projected debt to GNP path (table 7–1). The present value of the investment gain from such stabilization, relative to the outcome given the projected growth of debt to GNP, is about $82 billion in 1984 dollars. That figure represents a consumption gain equivalent to $312 billion, about 8.5 percent of 1984 GNP.

Conclusion

Tax cuts and net increases in federal spending since 1981 have driven a deficit wedge between expenditures and receipts equal to more than 5 percent of GNP. Tax and spending policies effective during 1984, together with economic projections, suggest that deficits of this magnitude will continue for the balance of the decade. For the given path of expenditures the result is replacement of $1.2 trillion in actual tax revenues with additional sales of $1.2 trillion in government bonds that will by 1989 raise the ratio of federal debt to GNP to more than 50 percent, or to a level of debt close to $3 trillion. This essay has explored the question of whether this development will reduce private net capital formation.

I find that private capital formation has and will continue to be reduced by the direct and indirect effects of large actual and prospective federal deficits. I hasten to add that such a conclusion can and will be disputed, both on theoretical and empirical grounds. Disagreement is hardly surprising in view of the difficulties involved in identifying an economically meaningful measure of government deficits and in assessing its possible effect on net private capital formation.

The conditions necessary for an absence of direct effects of deficits on capital formation are stringent; but, if any one of them is met, then in theory capital formation is immune from direct damage by deficits. The theory that investment has total interest inelasticity is most easily dismissed as being without theoretical or empirical support. Infinite interest elasticity of private saving, especially in an open economy with open capital markets, would also leave after-tax real interest rates and private investment unaffected by increased demands placed on credit markets by deficit financing. Empirical evidence, however, suggests that the interest elasticity of U.S. saving is finite. The U.S. economy is too large to face infinitely elastic supply

189

TABLE 7-5

ALTERNATIVE INVESTMENT PATHS, 1983–1989
(billions of 1984 dollars)

Year	Stable Debt/GNP in 1986				Debt/GNP Rise along Projected Path			
	D/G	ΔD/G	Δ(ΔD/G)	I	D/G	ΔD/G	Δ(ΔD/G)	I
1983	41.6							
1984	42.9	1.3						
1985	44.7	1.8	0.5	− 37.5				− 37.5
1986	46.3	1.6	−0.2	+ 15.0				+ 15.0
1987	46.3	0	−1.6	+120.0	47.8	1.5	−0.1	+ 7.5
1988	46.3	0	0	0	49.3	1.5	0	0
1989	46.3	0	0	0	50.7	1.4	−0.1	+ 7.5
Total investment increase 1985–1989				97.5				− 7.5
(PV discounted at 9 percent)				(70.9)				(−11.1)

NOTES: PV = present value. D/G = ratio of debt to GNP. I = investment.

SOURCE: Calculated from equation in table 7–3.

schedules in world markets for almost anything, and credit markets are no exception.

The extensive theoretical debate on whether government bonds are net wealth is very important to analysis of the question of deficits and private net capital formation. If the extreme, ultrarational view embodying full intergenerational altruism holds, then government bonds are viewed as no more than the discounted present value of future taxes. As a result, the switch from tax to bond financing leaves aggregate demand unaffected; and, irrespective of the shapes of investment or saving schedules, there is no effect on private capital formation. Empirical evidence, difficult to obtain, is mixed on this essentially empirical issue. My reading of the evidence together with my doubts about the extreme intergenerational altruism required to view government bonds as zero net wealth—Would society on balance be indifferent if all government debts were repudiated tomorrow?—lead me to doubt the extreme rational view.

Because of the theory and evidence bearing on these matters, I am unwilling to accept any of the extreme views necessary to dismiss the possibility that increases in deficits sufficiently large to raise the ratio of government debt to GNP will depress private capital formation. The depressive effect may be mitigated temporarily by tax cuts that lower the rental price of capital and increase the desired capital stock, like accelerated depreciation or investment tax credits enacted in ERTA-TEFRA. If, however, deficits remain large enough to accelerate the rise in debt-to-GNP ratio and real interest rates remain high, after cessation of the temporary, stimulative effect of such measures, my findings suggest that capital formation will fall.

Coupled with direct negative effects of deficits on capital formation are indirect negative effects. Larger deficits increase the probability of higher inflation and contribute to attendant increased uncertainty about future price levels and relative prices. Empirical evidence suggests that these phenomena depress investment. In addition, a largely unindexed U.S. tax code carries heavy penalties for investment in an inflationary environment in the form of inflated, taxable profits, resulting from understatement of replacement costs for inventories and capital equipment. Such investment penalties have been documented empirically and have been found to be substantial.

Concerning deficits and capital formation, an important difference exists between the situations before and after the 1981–1982 period. Before then, actual and prospective deficits—especially structural deficits—were tiny or nonexistent in relation to actual and projected deficits after that time. Consequently, thorough empirical analysis necessary to measure the effect of actual and prospective deficits above 5 percent of GNP has not been possible. Attempts to measure the effect of deficits on interest rates have therefore been thwarted, whereas the countercyclicity of deficits and the procyclicity of interest rates would leave a casual analyst of postwar data with the impression that larger deficits ought to *lower* interest rates. The lack of sufficient data to measure the full economic effect of unusually large deficits does not justify a presumption, based only on a theoretical possibility, that sustained large deficits will not depress net private capital formation.

Estimates reported in this essay suggest that 1980–1989 actual and prospective deficits will continue to raise the ratio of federal debt to GNP, pushing it from about 34 percent in 1980 to more than 50 percent by 1989. Expressed in 1984 dollars, the 1979–1984 investment losses associated with the rise in debt to GNP over that period imply a consumption loss equivalent to $570 billion based on Lind's estimation of the shadow price of capital. Prospective losses for the 1985–1989 period similarly measured and adjusted to 1984 present values amount to $312 billion. These losses total 24 percent of 1984 GNP, or roughly 2.4 percent of each year's GNP between 1979 and 1989.

Notes

1. The figures measure the ratio of gross federal debt to GNP, which includes both debt held by the public and debt held by government accounts. Since the mix between these two components changes over time (a rise in the share of government-held debt is projected by the Congressional Budget Office for 1985–1989), the gross debt figure is desirable for comparisons over time.

2. L. J. Kotlikoff, "The Economic Effects of Government Expenditures," NBER Working Paper No. 964 (August 1982); and R. Eisner and P. J. Pieper, "A New View of the Federal Debt and Budget Deficits," *The American Economic Review* (March 1984), pp. 11–29.

3. R. M. Solow, "Technological Change and the Aggregate Production Function," *Review of Economics and Statistics* (August 1957); and E. Denison, *Accounting for United States Economic Growth 1929–69* (Washington, D.C.: Brookings Institution, 1974).

4. R. C. Lind, "A Primer on the Major Issues Relating to the Discount Rate for Evaluating National Energy Options," in R. C. Lind et al., *Discounting for Time and Risk in Energy Policy* (Washington, D.C.: Resources for the Future, 1982), pp. 21–94.

5. O. J. Blanchard, "Current and Anticipated Deficits, Interest Rates and Economic Activity," *European Economic Review* (June 1984), pp. 7–28.

6. R. J. Barro, "Are Government Bonds Net Wealth?" *Journal of Political Economy* (November/December 1974), pp. 1095–1117.

7. R. E. Hall and D. W. Jorgenson, "Tax Policy and Investment Behavior,"

The American Economic Review (June 1967), pp. 391–414. More recent "q theory" studies of investment are discussed by Abel and Blanchard (1938). Such investigations that relate investment to changes in the valuation of an additional unit of capital relative to its cost still leave unexplained a large fraction of investment, but they do not contradict the notion of investment responsiveness to real interest rates.

8. Michael J. Boskin, "Taxation, Saving and the Rate of Interest," *Journal of Political Economy* (April 1978), part 2, pp. 23–27.

9. L. H. Summers, "The After-Tax Rate of Return Affects Private Savings," NBER Working Paper No. 1351 (May 1984).

10. J. E. Tanner, "Empirical Evidence on the Short-Run Real Balance Effect in Canada," *Journal of Money, Credit and Banking* (November 1970), pp. 473–85; L. Kochin, "Are Future Taxes Anticipated by Consumers?" *Journal of Money, Credit and Banking* (August 1974), pp. 385–94; and R. C. Kormendi, "Government Debt, Government Spending and Private Sector Behavior," manuscript (Chicago: University of Chicago Press, 1978).

11. W. Buiter and J. Tobin, "Debt Neutrality: A Brief Review of Doctrine and Evidence," unpublished manuscript; and M. S. Feldstein, "Government Deficits and Aggregate Demand," *Journal of Monetary Economics* (January 1982), pp. 1–20.

12. C. I. Plosser, "Government Financing Decisions and Asset Returns," *Journal of Monetary Economics* (May 1982), pp. 352–72.

13. R. J. Barro, "Output Effects of Government Purchases," *Journal of Political Economy* (December 1981), pp. 1086–1121; and R. E. Hall, "Labor Supply and Aggregate Fluctuations," in K. Brunner and A. Meltzer, eds., *Carnegie Rochester Conference Series in Public Policy*, vol. 12 (Amsterdam, 1980).

14. GNET equals gross private investment (GPI) less a stable trend allowance for capital consumption. As a result, GNET and GPI move in tandem (see figures and appendix), separated largely by a capital consumption allowance.

15. R. E. Hall and D. W. Jorgenson, "Tax Policy and Investment Behavior," *The American Economic Review* (June 1967), pp. 391–414.

16. M. S. Feldstein, "Fiscal Policies, Inflation and Capital Formation," *The American Economic Review* (September 1980), pp. 636–50.

17. M. S. Feldstein, *Inflation, Tax Rules and Capital Formation* (Chicago: University of Chicago Press, 1983), p. 1.

18. M. S. Feldstein and J. Slemrod, "Inflation and the Excess Taxation of Capital Gains on Corporate Stock," *National Tax Journal* (June 1980), pp. 107–118.

19. M. S. Feldstein and L. Summers, "Inflation, Tax Rules and Long-Term Interest Rates," *Brookings Papers on Economic Activity* (Washington, D.C.: Brookings Institution, 1978), pp. 61–69.

20. J. H. Makin and V. Tanzi, "The Level and Volatility of Interest Rates in the United States" and "The Role of Expected Inflation, Real Rates and Taxes," forthcoming in *International Monetary Fund Volume* (1984).

21. Mismeasurement of anticipated inflation would bias downward its estimated effect on nominal interest rates. This explanation is not adequate for

estimates in the 0.75 range. That result has been obtained with many alternative measures of anticipated inflation, most of which have been found to be unbiased predictors of actual inflation.

22. J. H. Makin, "Anticipated Money, Inflation Uncertainty and Real Economic Activity," *The Review of Economics and Statistics*, vol. 64, no. 1 (February 1982), pp. 126–34.

23. Hall and Jorgenson, "Tax Policy and Investment Behavior."

24. Ibid.

25. C. Hulten and J. Robertson, "Taxation of High Technology Industries," *National Tax Journal* (September 1984), pp. 327–45.

26. Blanchard, "Current and Anticipated Deficits."

27. The time series on user cost for structures displayed insufficient movement to enable identification of an estimate of its impact on investment.

28. The ratio of overall public and private debt to GNP may be a more comprehensive measure of pressure on user cost. That series moves with federal debts to GNP. A rise in overall debt to GNP also produces a robust negative effect on investment. Since our interest is primarily in the effect of federal deficits on capital formation, it is useful to employ the federal-debt-to-GNP ratio as a proxy for overall debt pressure.

29. D. D. Purvis and N. Bruce, *Evaluating the Deficit: The Case for Budget Cuts* (Toronto: C. B. Howe Institute, 1984).

30. Lind, "A Primer on the Major Issues."

8

Financing the Deficit, Interest Rates, and Monetary Policy

Phillip Cagan

Summary

Federal deficits are traditionally viewed as a stimulus to aggregate demand and a depressant of private investment. When U.S. deficits increased sharply in the second half of 1982, the economy was in a deep recession, and the stimulus was welcome. Continued large deficits as the economy recovered in 1983, however, brought unwelcome prospects of a crowding out of private investment and of pressures to ease the strain on financial markets through monetary expansion, which could prove inflationary. Yet, through 1984 at least, the rise in investment was strong, and inflationary pressures remained dormant. This chapter describes how the financial accommodation of the deficits was achieved.

The confounding of the expected traditional outcome reflected mainly two developments. First, the reduction of taxes in 1981, which produced the large deficits, substantially raised the after-tax rate of return on business investment. The resulting increase in business cash flows funded much of the rise in investment, which the Treasury deficit could thus be viewed as financing. The remaining investment was financed by business borrowing in competition with the Treasury, and interest rates were held high. Second, without much crowding out of investment, the additional funds needed to finance the large deficit came mainly from the attraction of high U.S. interest rates to international capital flows. The usual U.S. capital outflow turned into a net inflow in 1982, which by 1984 accounted for a major part of the financing of the deficit increase. Although a state and local government budget surplus also contributed, a rise in household saving encouraged by certain tax reductions in the 1981 act was inconsequential.

The increase in demand for U.S. assets appreciated the foreign exchange rate of the dollar, which depressed exports and stimulated imports. A large

I am indebted to Maryam Homayouni for statistical assistance.

capital inflow ensued, for which the counterpart in the balance of payments was a deficit in the foreign trade account. Thus the crowding out of the deficit bypassed private investment and fell on export and import-competing industries.

The role of large deficits in raising interest rates was not immediately clear because rates had been high since the late 1970s. It was especially unclear for high short-term rates, which would not have risen earlier in anticipation of large deficits to come later. The rise in interest rates initially can be attributed instead to the escalating inflation. Upward adjustments of interest rates to inflation came during the 1970s and lasted into the early 1980s. Monetary restriction at the beginning of the 1980s also raised interest rates. Downward adjustments of rates to the ensuing disinflation came slowly. Even though an easing of monetary policy precipitated a sharp fall in interest rates in mid-1982, the rates in real terms remained historically high. These high real rates in 1983 were widely attributed to the accompanying large deficit.

Economists held two opposing views of the effect of the deficit on interest rates: on the one hand, that it would be very large, on the assumption that the demand and supply for credit are extremely interest inelastic; on the other hand, that it would be minimal, on the assumption that Treasury debt is highly substitutable for other capital. The outcome was contrary to both views: the supply of credit, particularly capital inflows, responded to the rise in interest rates, but a substantial rise in rates was nevertheless necessary.

How long the sizable capital inflow would last was unclear. Considerable uncertainty over the future effect of deficits and inflation on interest rates was indicated in 1984 by their term structure, in which long-term rates remained usually far above short-term rates. Monetary policy nevertheless pursued a course during 1984 that did not force interest rates up much further and so far has kept inflation in abeyance.

The "burden" of deficits on the private economy is traditionally attributable to a crowding out of private investment and reduced future productive capacity. Since little of either of these occurred in 1983 and 1984, the principal burden was the adjustment to the foreign trade deficit and the growing federal debt, which will require distortionary taxes to raise revenues to cover the interest payments. The magnitude of this burden depends on real interest rates. Indeed, given projections of continued large deficits if no budgetary changes are enacted, interest rates could eventually rise further if private credit demands expand or credit supplies contract.

As the prospect of large federal deficits materialized in the 1980s, their consequences for the economy became national issues. The government's need to borrow large sums in credit markets created the prospect of crowding out private borrowing and investment. The accompanying upward pressure on interest rates, it was said, would endanger the business recovery. And any steps by the Federal Reserve to alleviate the financial tightness could undermine its anti-inflation policy. This chapter examines these issues under four headings: the method of financing the deficits and the crowding out of other expenditures, the behavior of interest rates, the inflationary depreciation of outstanding government debt, and the effect on monetary policy.

Financing the Deficit

The Sources of Financing. Figure 8-1 graphs the components of saving and investment in the national income accounts (NIA) quarterly from 1978 to 1984 in current dollars; the two parts of the figure show the uses of funds for investment and the federal deficit and the sources of these funds from saving. The major sources are grouped into households, businesses (covering retained earnings and depreciation allowances), state and local government (when in surplus), and foreigners (when net lenders rather than borrowers). The state and local government budgets and the international capital flows can at times be net users of funds, but in recent years they have been net suppliers to U.S. credit markets. The total of this gross saving finances the federal deficit and gross domestic investment, the latter subdivided in figure 8-2 into residential construction, business fixed plant and equipment, and inventory accumulation. Because of the way the data are collected, measured gross saving and investment differ by a small statistical discrepancy ignored here.

The NIA federal deficit, which was less than $25 billion at an annual rate as recently as 1979, ranged between $50 and $75 billion during most of 1980–1981 and then rose sharply during 1982 to *add* over $100 billion to its annual rate. In 1983 and 1984 the annual rate fluctuated between $160 and $180 billion.[1] As gross investment declined and absorbed less saving during the recession of 1981–1982, the rise in the deficit in those years was financed without much increase in total saving. When business activity recovered in 1983–1984, however, gross investment expanded vigorously while the deficit remained high. The sources of funds show how this increase in total demand for credit was supplied.

All four major components of saving helped finance the deficit increase, but not equally. As shown in figure 8-1, personal saving declined during 1982 and in the 1983 cyclical recovery but in the first half of 1984 rose above its 1982–1983 average rate. The state and local government surplus increased in 1983. (This development is discussed in chapter 3.) By the first half of 1984 personal saving and the

FIGURE 8-1
Sources and Uses of Funds for Investment and Government Deficit, Quarterly, 1978–1984

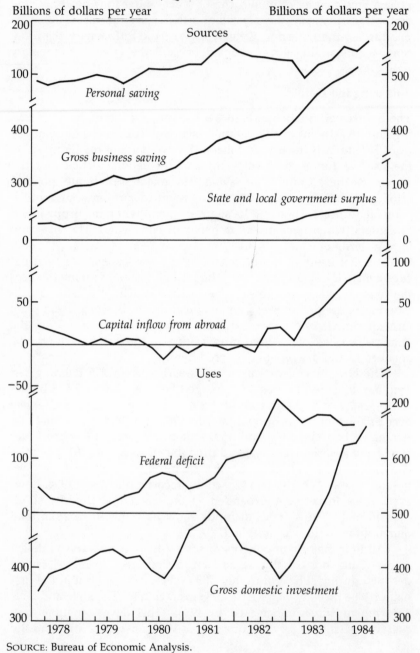

Billions of dollars per year

Billions of dollars per year

SOURCE: Bureau of Economic Analysis.

FIGURE 8-2
COMPONENTS OF GROSS DOMESTIC INVESTMENT, QUARTERLY, 1978–1984

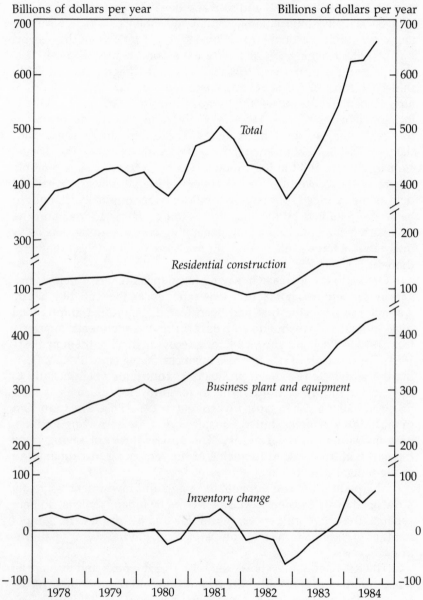

SOURCE: Bureau of Economic Analysis.

state and local government surplus together had added $34 billion more than in 1982 to national saving. Gross business saving increased over $90 billion during 1983, which was almost triple its annual growth from 1980 to 1982, and rose another $30 billion in the first half of 1984. Finally, international capital movements, which normally show net U.S. investing abroad, turned to net inflows in the second half of 1982, reaching $80 billion by the second quarter of 1984. This financed all the increase in the deficit from the beginning of 1982 to mid-1984. Most of the net change reflected a decline in bank lending abroad; banks reduced lending to most countries, not mainly to those facing a debt crisis. Bank deposits are the funnel for the major part of foreign lending to the United States. These deposits grew substantially in 1982 but only moderately in 1983 and 1984. (See the discussion in chapter 9.) Capital inflows had been viewed as a possible source of funds even before the anticipated large increase in federal deficits materialized, but large net inflows were originally thought to be severely limited by the inability of the economy to maintain the necessary payments balance by generating corresponding deficits in international trade. This turned out to be less of a limitation than was thought.

Owing to the increase in saving to finance the larger deficit, private investment had not by mid-1984 experienced the crowding out by a scarcity of financing that had been feared. Figure 8-2 graphs total gross domestic investment and its principal components quarterly from 1978 to 1984 and shows a strong recovery in all of them in 1983–1984. The more rapid rise in gross business saving since 1980, reflecting the sizable reduction in profit taxes, contributed significantly to the greater supply of funds. The increase in gross business saving financed half the rise in gross investment in 1983–1984. The reduction in profit taxes in effect shifted a major part of the borrowing for business investment to the Treasury. The other sources of saving came forward with the needed financing of the remaining investment and of the federal deficit.

The path of the components of saving and investment is greatly influenced by the business cycle as well as by federal deficits. To help separate these two influences, figures 8-3 and 8-4 display the components as cyclical patterns and compare them with the average patterns in past cycles.

The left-hand panel shows the series for the peak and five subsequent quarters of the 1981–1982 contraction and of an average of the series in five past business contractions between 1953 and 1975. The atypical 1980 contraction and first postwar cycle, 1948–1949, are excluded. To allow for differences in price movements among the cycles,

FIGURE 8-3

Sources and Uses of Funds for Investment and Government Deficit, 1981–1984, Compared with Averages for Past Business Cycle Phases, 1953–1975

(percentage of GNP)

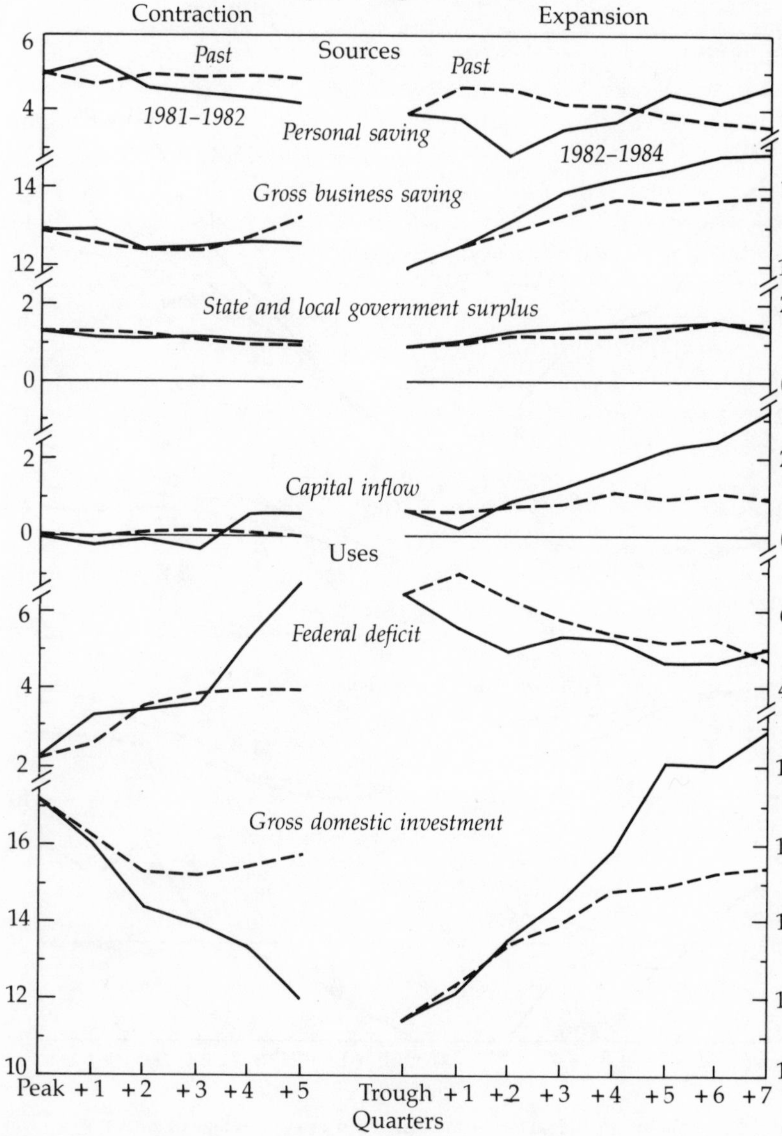

NOTE: Components are in real terms and expressed as a percentage of an average of real GNP for all quarters in the cycle phase. The average of past cycles is for the five cycles 1953–1975, indexed to the peak and trough levels of the 1981–1982 cycle.
SOURCE: Bureau of Economic Analysis.

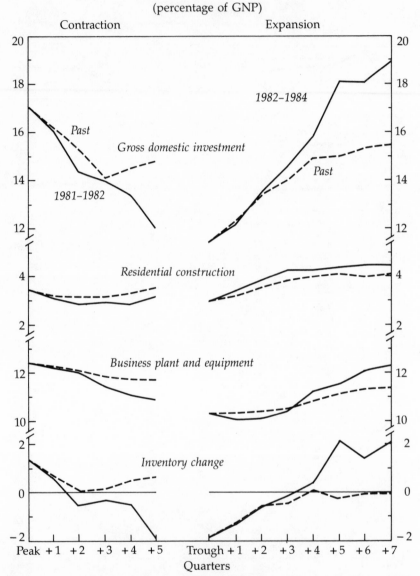

FIGURE 8-4
COMPONENTS OF GROSS INVESTMENT, 1981–1984,
COMPARED WITH AVERAGES FOR PAST BUSINESS CYCLE PHASES,
1953–1975
(percentage of GNP)

NOTE: Components are in real terms and expressed as a percentage of an average of real GNP for all quarters in the cycle phase. The average of past cycles is for the five cycles 1953–1975, indexed to the peak and trough levels of the 1981–1982 cycle.
SOURCE: Bureau of Economic Analysis.

the series are measured in real terms and as percentages of an average of real GNP for the six quarters of each contraction. (Dividing every figure by the same average GNP avoids the distortion of quarterly fluctuations in GNP.) For ease of comparison, the average past cyclical pattern for each component is raised or lowered so that it starts in the peak quarter at the same level as the pattern for 1981–1982. Hence, the compared patterns in figures 8-3 and 8-4 are comparable in their movements but *not* in their levels.

The right-hand panel makes the same comparison for the trough and subsequent seven quarters of 1982–1984 and of an average of the five past business recoveries. Again, the average pattern for each component has been adjusted to the level of the 1982 trough, so that only movements in the patterns are comparable.

The exceptional behavior of the current federal deficit stands out in this comparison. Typically in contractions the deficit had leveled off. In the business contraction of 1981–1982, however, the deficit at first rose in line with previous cyclical movements but in the third quarter of 1982 jumped up by $1\frac{1}{2}$ percent of average GNP and in the fourth quarter did so again for a total rise of 3 percent. In the business recovery of 1982–1984 the deficit declined in line with past cycles but still retained most of its initial rise to 5 percent or more of GNP.

In the 1981–1982 contraction, personal and gross business saving declined in relation to the pattern of past cycles, while the state and local government surplus was about the same. The aggregate of these three declined only slightly in relation to past cycles. Consequently, the sharp rise in the deficit at the end of the 1981–1982 contraction was accommodated by a capital inflow and a decline in gross investment relative to the pattern of past cycles. In figure 8-4, which shows the cyclical patterns of gross investment and its three major components, the relative decline of the total in the recession can be attributed mainly to business investment in capital and inventories.[2]

For the business recovery shown in the right-hand panel of figure 8-3, all the sources of saving except the state and local surplus expanded in 1982–1984 in relation to past cycles. Aggregate saving was nevertheless relatively low in the first stages because of a weak recovery in the personal component. By the fifth quarter of the recovery, however, all these sources of saving, including personal saving, had expanded in relation to past cycles. Their expansion financed the large deficit, as well as a normal pattern of recovery in gross investment for the first four quarters and its abnormal increase thereafter, mainly attributable to inventory investment.

The Crowding Out Issue. These cyclical patterns give scant indication of the feared crowding out of investment. A possible crowding out occurred during the business contraction, mainly through inventory investment in the trough quarter, but that probably owed as much to the severity of the business contraction as to high interest rates. The cyclical decline in investment, which was somewhat greater than normal, not improbably reflected unusually high real interest rates attributable to the deficits. But interest rates were also forced to be high in real terms in part because their effect in curtailing investment had been blunted. First, housing demand used to be curtailed by a drying up of mortgage funds, reflecting a flight of deposits from thrift institutions when market interest rates rose above deposit-rate ceilings. Now those ceilings had been removed. Moreover, the conventional fixed rates on mortgages were giving way to variable rates, which are more manageable to home buyers because initial payments are lower. Second, business investment had been buoyed by the tax cut of the Economic Recovery Act of 1981, which, after the partial reversal by the 1982 act, cut the tax on the return from new corporate investment by half, from 30 to 15.8 percent.[3] Despite high interest rates, by the sixth quarter of the business recovery the three components of investment were as high in relation to the cycle peak as in past cycles or higher.

The absence of any overall crowding out of investment in 1984 can be attributed to the expansion in the sources of funds. A major source of funds to finance the deficit, as noted, has been capital inflows. Crowding out still occurred, but the capital inflows shifted it to foreign trade through a corresponding current account deficit. The appreciation of the dollar is the mechanism by which capital inflows attracted by high interest rates reduce exports and stimulate imports, thus transferring the crowding out of the deficit from domestic capital goods to industries competing for exports and against imports. In 1983 the current account deficit reached $34 billion, and for all of 1984 it was expected to be $80 billion. The deficit in goods alone, excluding services, was much greater, $60.6 billion in 1983 and running well over a $100 billion rate in 1984.

The Economic Recovery Act of 1981 as amended, which was intended to induce greater personal saving but in that respect was largely ineffective, had some of the desired effect on credit supply in unexpected ways. By 1983 the reduction in business taxes had produced an increase in business saving, and the rise in interest rates due to the federal deficit had turned an international capital outflow into an inflow. In this way a crowding out of capital investment was largely avoided, but the tax cut did not produce a cyclical expansion in capital investment greater than usual as it was intended to do. To be sure, economic growth was greater as productivity improved. Output per hour of labor in the nonfarm business sector rose 3.5 percent in 1983 and continued to rise at an annual rate of 3.1 percent in the first half of 1984. But this improvement was spurred by vigorous cost cutting in the face of disinflation and import competition. These increases, though not unusual by the standards of earlier cyclical recoveries, suggest that the decade-long slowing of productivity growth may have ended.

Measurement Error in the Capital Inflow. The size of the capital inflow may be somewhat overstated, though not enough to question its importance in deficit financing. The data can be questioned because of the large statistical discrepancy in foreign trade accounts. The NIA capital inflow is equated to the deficit in the current trade and services account, since these two subgroups cover the total of international payments and must balance. But in the international transactions reported by the Department of Commerce, where capital flows are measured for disaggregated components, the discrepancy between the latter and the NIA figure for total net foreign investment has become quite large since 1978.[4] In general the discrepancy can be attributed to an underreporting of capital inflows, which makes the measured net U.S. investment abroad far larger than the NIA current account deficit or surplus. The NIA figure is therefore to be preferred.

There is reason to believe, however, that the discrepancy also reflects some error in the recorded current account. For all countries in the world the current account deficits and surpluses sum not to zero, as they would if recorded accurately, but to a sizable aggregate deficit, which was $74 billion in 1983.[5] The United States undoubtedly contributes to the measurement discrepancy to some extent, mainly through an underreporting of service receipts.[6] Thus the U.S. current account *deficit* and NIA capital *in*flow are correspondingly *over*stated, and similarly a current account *surplus* and capital *out*flow are *under*stated. This can be true even when the statistical discrepancy is zero, if an underreporting of capital outflows is sufficient to offset the underreporting of service receipts. Yet, although the measured amount of the capital inflow may conceivably be overstated by $5–10 billion, the *increase* in the measured capital inflow in 1982 and 1983 is certainly not greatly overstated.

The Rise in Interest Rates

The Accommodation of Large Deficits—Opposing Views. The market mechanism for accommodating sources and uses of funds to an increase in federal deficits is a rise in interest rates. The rise stimulates saving and discourages investment expenditures. Given a federal deficit that has to be financed, the only question is how far interest rates must rise to produce the accommodation. Economic writings provide two opposing views of the outcome: one is that the increase will be extremely high, the other that, on the contrary, it will be minimal.

The first view is based on the belief that the supply and demand for credit are very inelastic to changes in interest rates, so that achievement of a given expansion of demand or reduction in supply requires a very large increase in interest rates. Belief in such interest inelasticity of saving and investment began in the 1930s and continued with the early econometric models of the 1940s and 1950s, which found little or no response of saving or investment (other than housing) to changes in interest rates. Although subsequent studies report some response, they generally find it to be slow and weak. An argument sometimes made that the investment response has even declined in recent years is based on the gradual disappearance of credit rationing. Credit in the past was artificially curtailed by deposit-rate ceilings at times of monetary restriction and by other regulations of depository institutions. Those dependent on depository institutions for loans—mainly farmers, small businesses, and home buyers—were forced to borrow less. Under deregulation the allocation of a given volume of credit among insistent borrowers is accomplished less by credit rationing and more by sharp increases in interest rates until the market is cleared of excess demand.[7]

The opposite view that an increase in the deficit has a minimal effect on interest rates is based on the proposition that the rate of return on capital largely determines interest rates. Although the rate of return is not directly affected by government deficits, it was increased by the accompanying reduction in business taxes in 1981, which would raise interest rates. (As discussed in chapter 7, this increase could have been partly offset if the increase in government debt had raised expectations of future increases in taxes that would reduce the expected after-tax rate of return.) To conclude from this view that the size of the deficit does not matter assumes that increased funds to finance a larger deficit can be attracted without raising interest rates. For a given level of GNP such an increase in financing can only occur, however, to the extent that taxpayers see the deficit as a postponement of taxation and augment current saving to cover future levies[8] or to the extent that there are capital inflows from abroad. If the supply of funds is not infinitely elastic, higher interest rates will be needed to finance larger deficits.

The actual increase in interest rates in 1983–1984 proved to be neither minimal nor extremely high. Figure 8-5 shows for 1978–1984 a long- and a short-term rate on U.S. securities, the differential between

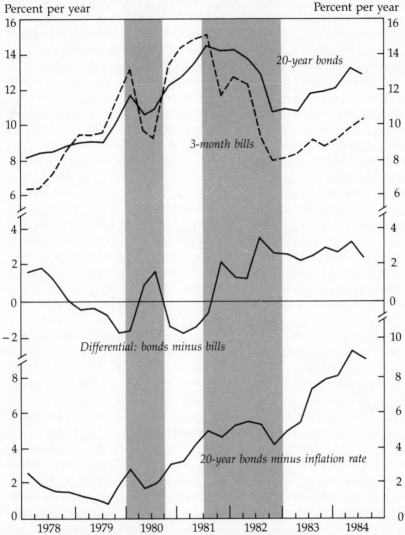

FIGURE 8–5
YIELDS ON TREASURY SECURITIES, QUARTERLY, 1978–1984

NOTE: Quarterly yields are averages of monthly data. Inflation rate is GNP deflator over eight quarters ending concurrently. Shaded areas are National Bureau of Economic Research business contractions.
SOURCE: Federal Reserve Board and Bureau of Economic Analysis.

the two, and the "real" long-term rate (measured by the nominal rate minus the rate of inflation for the previous two years). The shaded areas denote business recessions. The real rate of interest was rising steadily in the 1980s as inflation subsided. At the end of 1983 it was almost 8 percent, well above a normal real long-term rate of 3 to 4 percent. It appears neither that supply and demand were totally interest inelastic nor that substitutions among assets were perfect.

The increase in the real rate was the incentive required to attract the expanded supply of financing. The expanded financing occurred, domestically, through a rechanneling of income from consumption to saving and, internationally, through a rechanneling of world saving into dollar assets. Part of this expansion is related to the business cycle and hence will change with the cycle, while the noncyclical remainder will eventually be limited by the public's willingness to absorb government debt. The sustainability of the capital inflow in particular is thus widely questioned. As dollar assets become a larger and larger fraction of world portfolios, the desire to acquire more should eventually slacken.[9] It would then take a further rise in U.S. interest rates to continue attracting world saving. Should the capital inflow decline, there would be downward pressure on the exchange rate and upward pressure on domestic interest rates that would moderate but not reverse the decline. Forecasts of declines in the capital inflow and the high dollar exchange rate had proved mistaken for 1983 and 1984, casting doubt on the near-term importance of limits on dollar holdings, but the possibility of a decline in the dollar exchange rate nevertheless kept financial markets on edge.

Concern was also expressed in 1983 that high interest rates resulting from large deficits could not only crowd out investment but also abort the business recovery. But far from being aborted, the recovery was considerably stronger through 1983 and early 1984 than most forecasts of it. Consistently with traditional theory and in contrast to the feared effects of high interest rates, the large deficit clearly served as a short-run economic stimulus. The mistaken belief that the accompanying high interest rates could abort the recovery failed to distinguish between supply restrictions and demand pressures on credit markets. High interest rates can precipitate a business downturn when they reflect a curtailment of investment demand resulting from a restriction in the supply of credit, such as from contractionary monetary conditions. When an expansion in demand for credit raises interest rates, some borrowers are temporarily forced out of the market, but aggregate borrowing and aggregate demand are not reduced; the high interest rates are indicative of expanding rather than contracting business activity. As it turned out, crowding out of private investment did not occur in 1983, because of the increase in saving and capital inflow. But even if considerable but incomplete crowding out had occurred, the deficit added to aggregate demand in the short run and would not have aborted the recovery.

Interest Rates before the Large Deficits Began in 1982. The unusually high interest rates beginning in the late 1970s could not initially be attributed to deficits. Indeed, interest rates *fell* in mid-1982 just as the deficits started to rise sharply. To isolate the effect of deficits on interest rates after 1982, we need to clarify the timing of the various influences on them during the preceding several years. Two important influences were lagged adjustments to inflation and monetary tightening.

During the 1970s, as inflation escalated, the rise in interest rates barely kept up. When adjusted for depreciation in the purchasing power of money owing to inflation, rates of interest remained low; the real rate was generally zero or negative for Treasury bills and unusually low for bonds. Since interest is taxed as income, after-tax real rates were even lower. Nominal interest rates rose to compensate for higher inflation, but the adjustment lagged behind the escalating inflation during most of the 1970s. Interest rates rose until mid-1981 (figure 8-5) except for the dip and recovery in the first half of 1980 during the credit controls imposed from March to May and the concurrent short business recession. That rates continued to rise in 1981 even though the inflation rate peaked in early 1980 and declined fairly steadily thereafter can be ascribed partly to a catching up to the previous increase in inflation and partly to restrictive monetary conditions that tightened financial markets.

Monetary policy is more difficult to interpret than usual during these years because of changes in the financial environment affecting the behavior of the various monetary aggregates. Nevertheless, it seems fairly clear that the growth of transactions money balances, defined to include the new instruments, generally ranged between 7 and 9 percent per year from 1977 to mid-1981 except for the first half of 1980.[10] Despite this fairly unchanged monetary growth, a tightening of financial markets was initially produced by a rise in the inflation rate after the oil price increases of late 1979, which substantially reduced real money balances. From the end of 1978 to the second quarter of 1981, M1 balances deflated by the consumer price index contracted 10 percent. The consequent monetary tightening, as well as the decline in net exports due to the appreciation of the dollar on foreign exchange markets, held business activity stagnant in the second and third quarters of 1981. During the third quarter M1 growth began a sharp decline, and real money balances contracted further, which led to a drop in economic activity in the fourth quarter (although, with the plateau in activity, the cycle peak is dated July 1981).

Despite some decline in short-term interest rates in the fourth quarter of 1981, both long- and short-term rates remained fairly high until mid-1982. Such persistence of high rates after two years of declining inflation and particularly during a business recession was unusual. The persistence of high rates reflected a heavy business demand for credit[11] and continued tightness by the Federal Reserve, which was anxious to dampen inflationary expectations and was concerned that easing would be viewed by the market as a reversal of the anti-inflationary policy. When business failed to recover in mid 1982, however, monetary policy eased, and interest rates fell sharply.

The rise that occurred in real rates of interest after 1980 can be viewed, therefore, as part of a long process of bringing down the inflation rate. Although the decline in inflation justified a reduction in the premium that expectations of inflation added to nominal interest rates, such an adjustment takes time. Most declines in the inflation rate are initially seen as temporary. Long-term rates do not adjust until the decline in inflation is expected to last. Although temporary dips in inflation can be relevant to short-term interest rates, the adjustment of those rates to inflation requires shifts in demands and supplies for funds that are not likely to be made on a temporary basis. Of course, if expectations of inflation simultaneously and uniformly declined across the market, interest rates could drop immediately without any trading, but such uniformity of expectations is undoubtedly rare. Just as nominal interest rates were slow to adjust upward and were low in real terms when inflation escalated during the 1970s, so the inflation premium in rates has given way slowly to the disinflation after 1980.

In addition to the slow decline in the inflation premium, interest rates were held up for a while by the monetary restriction. Monetary growth declined more than inflation did from mid-1981 to mid-1982 to contract real money balances, as noted above, and this restriction combined with a heavy business demand for credit to keep rates unusually high despite the declining inflation. When monetary policy turned to stimulus in mid-1982, interest rates dropped sharply, although they were still high in real terms. The three-month bill rate sank to a low of 8 percent in the fourth quarter of 1982 and then rose slowly, reaching 10 percent in mid-1984. Given an inflation rate of around $4\frac{1}{2}$ percent for most of 1983, the real bill rate fell to $3\frac{1}{2}$ percent and was higher thereafter. Historically even $3\frac{1}{2}$ percent is a high real rate for a short-term Treasury bill.

High Interest Rates and Large Deficits, 1982 and Later. There are two popular explanations of why real rates remained unusually high after the easing of monetary policy in mid-1982: inflationary expectations remained high to keep up nominal rates, and large deficits arrived in the second half of 1982 to keep real and nominal rates high. As inflation continued low and short-term rates rose during 1983 and 1984, it became increasingly clear that by then the deficits were mainly responsible for the high real rates. This explanation also appears to be consistent with world government deficits, as discussed in chapter 4.

Although expectations are not directly observable, their important role in interpreting these movements can be inferred from the term structure of interest rates. The term structure is the relation between interest rates on securities of the same risk and their length of time to maturity. Normally interest rates rise for longer maturities, reflecting a premium to compensate for the risk of larger capital losses on the longer maturities. The relation is therefore affected by expectations of future changes in interest rates. A permanent rise in rates, for example, would produce a capital loss on outstanding securities that would increase for longer maturities, the expectation of which would add extra compensation to their risk premium. An expected fall in rates would subtract from their risk premium. Similarly, an expected rise in deficits or in inflation would be expected to raise future interest rates and so would add to the premium. Although a tightening of monetary policy first raises interest rates, it does so only for a limited period, so that future rates are expected to be lower; consequently, the tightening raises short-term above long-term rates.

The term structure is represented by the differential between the twenty-year bond and the three-month bill rates in figure 8-5. Although the bond rate is ordinarily higher than the bill rate to compensate for the risks of holding the longer maturity, the bill rate temporarily went higher in 1979–1980 owing to bursts of high inflation that reduced real money balances and again in 1981 owing to monetary restriction. Forecasts of rising deficits in 1981 and early 1982, before they materialized, could have contributed to high bond yields but not at that time to high short-term rates, since only the actual deficit within the maturity period of the security is relevant.

High long-term interest rates after 1982 could reflect continued high inflationary expectations for the years ahead. But these expectations for a period only three to six months ahead, relevant for short-term rates, could not have remained high in view of the substantial disinflation from 1980 to 1983. Therefore, although the inflation premium may often adjust slowly, by 1983 its influence on the bill rate must have abated. That points to the importance of the deficits. By the second half of 1982, the large deficits materialized. They can explain why short-term rates remained high when monetary policy had eased and why thereafter both short- and long-term *real* rates have remained high.

The recession of 1981–1982 brought short-term rates down well below bond rates. During the business recovery, however, the differential of long-term over short-term rates steadily widened from 150 basis points in the fourth quarter of 1982 to 350 points in the second quarter of 1984. This widening, which was contrary to the usual narrowing in recoveries, suggests that investors expected much higher future short-term interest rates. Conceivably the expectation was of an escalation of inflation. An alternative, not incompatible, interpretation of the higher differential was that investors also expected interest rates to rise as expanding credit demands of the private sector clashed with the large federal deficit. There has been much publicity about an impending clash and little solid indication in 1983–1984 that the deficit would be sufficiently reduced in the near future to head off a clash. Given that the outcome of such developments is highly uncertain, the long-short differential can be equivalently viewed as a higher-than-normal risk premium in long-term rates rather than an expectation of a specific increase in future rates. An important effect of this high differential is to shift borrowing toward short-term loans, with a consequent shortening of the life of capital investments undertaken.

It has been proposed that greater variability in the economy after 1979, reflecting the disruptive effects of disinflation and the Federal Reserve's change in operating procedure in October 1979, increased risk and so the general level of interest rates.[12] Greater risk cannot explain the increase in both long- and short-term rates, however, unless it reduced total saving or except temporarily if it increased the demand for money balances. Despite the increase in variability, gross saving plus net capital inflow expanded in relation to GNP as noted from 1981 to 1983; this expansion argues against explaining high short-term rates by greater risk.

In 1984 the market's expectation of rising interest rates, as indicated by the term structure, contrasted sharply with the forecast of the president and the secretary of the Treasury that interest rates would soon come down. Their forecast supposed a continuing decline in the inflation premium and ignored any effect of the deficit on interest rates.[13] The justification for ignoring the deficit was presented in a Treasury report, which surveyed the literature and reported that many empirical studies of the past two decades or so could find no effect of U.S. deficits on interest rates.[14] A similar survey by the Congressional

Budget Office reported that, although many such studies found no effect, a fair number did claim to find an effect.[15] Whatever the claims, it is questionable whether most of these empirical studies can be relied on. The problem of allowing for both the stock and the flow effects of deficits on interest rates is difficult to handle.[16] And the problem of the adequacy of the evidence presented is serious. In most peacetime years before 1983 the deficit was not large, and therefore any effect was relatively small and difficult to detect. Given the problems of empirical verification, the best argument that deficits raise interest rates is simply the longstanding proposition that increases in demand raise prices, applied in this case to credit demand and the price of borrowing.

Measuring the Deficit in Real Terms

An argument sometimes presented for downgrading the importance of recent deficits is that they are not large when properly adjusted for inflation. The adjustment proposed is to deduct the decline in real value of the outstanding Treasury debt or, equivalently, to measure the deficit as the change in real value of federal debt outstanding. The combination of the large federal debt and recent high rates of inflation produces considerable "real capital gains" for the government (its liability for debt, allowing for depreciation in real terms from inflation, is reduced) and, of course, equal capital losses for holders of the outstanding debt. These declines in real value of the outstanding debt have been attenuated by the disinflation, but they are still sizable. If other "real capital gains" of the government are also taken into account, such as increases in the market value of the Treasury's gold stock and other assets, the deficit shrinks further, and the budget measured as the change in the government's real net worth can be turned into a surplus.[17]

The relevance of inflationary depreciation in real value of the outstanding debt is that nominal interest rates become higher to compensate for the expected amount of depreciation. Thus, budget interest payments are higher, and part of them can be viewed as a repayment of the real principal lost through inflationary depreciation. Repayment of principal should be treated in a capital account, not as current expenditure. If it is taken out of the current account budget, the deficit is reduced.

The alternative definitions of the government budget call for clarification of what it is supposed to measure. One can define the budget in a variety of ways to meet different criteria. If we are mainly concerned with the effect on interest rates, the relevance of any "real capital gains" to the government depends on their effect on the demand and supply for credit. While capital gains of the government do not change its current borrowing needs, corresponding real capital losses of the public may influence national saving. If the public suffers capital losses, it may seek to restore the loss by saving more. If the public sees higher nominal interest payments as a repayment of principal to compensate for the real capital losses of inflation, the repayment will be treated not as income but as a transfer of capital and will presumably be reinvested concurrently to keep wealth intact in real terms. Saving by the public will be that much greater and will supply that amount of the government's borrowing. (Given the taxation of all nominal interest receipts, this perceived compensation might be greater than the expected rate of inflation.)[18]

Whenever the actual real depreciation of debt is greater than expected because inflation has exceeded expectations, the holders suffer a real capital loss without any compensation. Since such losses may be offset in the long run by capital gains on other wealth holdings, it is unlikely that most people will save more immediately to compensate for net capital losses as soon as they occur. They will presumably try to compensate gradually, however, which implies that unanticipated real depreciation of debt will increase saving modestly—say by 2 to 5 percent per year of any loss, as suggested by estimates of wealth effects[19]—and anticipated depreciation, for which interest payments fully compensate, will increase saving dollar for dollar. (Whether this saving is reinvested in government securities or not is unimportant for the general effect on interest rates.) Whether government borrowing to finance a deficit has a large or a small effect on interest rates, therefore, depends on how much more the public saves to make up for real capital losses due to inflation.[20]

To the extent that the perceived interest repayment of principal is reinvested, it will add to NIA saving, chiefly personal saving of households, which includes most of the reinvestment of earnings by financial institutions to the benefit of households. Yet, as can be seen in figure 8-1, personal saving did not go higher than normal in 1978–1980 to reflect the substantial increase in inflationary depreciation of debt in those years. Indeed, personal saving as a percentage of GNP has declined in recent years; it declined more in the 1981–1982 business recession and subsequent recovery than in past cycles, as shown in figure 8-3. Households either have not treated the large inflationary premium in government interest rates as a repayment of principal to be reinvested or have reduced their saving for other reasons.[21]

The actual reported deficit has been financed largely without the increase in household saving that would reflect a reinvestment of debt repayments or that would be implied by the Ricardian equivalence theorem.[22] An expanded supply of funds has come instead from gross business saving, reflecting larger business depreciation allowances, and from capital inflows. This casts doubt on the real deficit as the appropriate measure of the effect on interest rates.

Monetary Policy and the Deficit

The Federal Reserve has repeatedly voiced concern over the deficit since large increases first became likely. The monetary authorities were not so much concerned with the initial stimulative effects of the deficit, which, coming in the recession of 1982, could be welcomed, as with the upward pressure on interest rates. High interest rates made it politically more difficult for the Federal Reserve to tighten monetary policy when the business expansion needed restraining and also when high rates threatened to disrupt the banking system and international financial markets as third world countries struggled to service their debt burdens. The third world debts appeared to be a major concern of the Federal Reserve in mid-1982 when it shifted from a tight to a strongly stimulative monetary growth to bring interest rates down from high levels. Again in early 1984, as interest rates were rising, the Federal Reserve hesitated to tighten monetary policy actively, despite the strong business expansion, because of continuing third world debt problems and election year concerns over the cost of borrowing.

Many studies have claimed to find that increased deficits have historically led to higher monetary growth, presumably because the policy of targeting interest rates led the Federal Reserve to monetize deficits partially in order to moderate the upward push on interest rates.[23] The shift toward monetary targeting during the 1970s was supposed to end such a reaction by decoupling the conduct of policy from interest-rate movements. But interest rates were never entirely ignored by the Federal Reserve, and their targeting was partially reinstated in the second half of 1982. Except for a brief period from late 1979 to mid-1982, therefore, monetary policy has been conducted with an interest-rate target in one form or another. This was often the reason why monetary growth rose in cyclical expansions.

The past evidence on deficit monetization, however, is far from clear despite the findings of numerous studies. In business expansions the budget deficit was usually declining and so did not correlate positively with the rising monetary growth and interest rates. But in business recessions countercyclical monetary policies coincided with automatic increases in the budget deficit to produce the appearance of a positive correlation between the two. Yet both may have reflected the business cycle and may not in fact have been directly related. It is not easy for econometric equations to distinguish a direct connection from common cyclical movements. Movements in recent decades are also correlated because of an upward trend in deficits (as a percentage of GNP) and monetary growth rates. But this rise in monetary growth does not reflect a decision to monetize the increasing deficits. The rise in monetary growth was an accommodation to other demand pressures.

However the past evidence is interpreted, monetary policy is often subject to political pressures to moderate rising interest rates and thus may at times be forced to allow monetary growth rates that are too high to prevent an escalation of inflation. This possibility colors market assessments of monetary policy, particularly when the deficit is large. During 1984 Federal Reserve policy could best be described as a compromise between restraining a rigorous business expansion and holding down interest rates. The strong monetary growth that began in mid-1982 ended a year later, in mid-1983. In the first half of 1984 annual monetary growth averaged 6 to 7 percent and in the second half much lower but remained in the middle of the monitoring range set as the policy objective. This growth was consistent with continuation of the prevailing inflation rate of 5 percent or so and must eventually be reduced if inflation is to come down further. There was concern, however, that lower monetary growth would add to the credit tightening that was expected as business expanded. The Federal Reserve hoped to moderate the effect of large Treasury borrowing on financial markets without losing the previous inroads against inflation.

The Federal Reserve is certainly not bound to monetize deficits in the same way it did in the 1940s when it pegged the prices of Treasury securities. It can follow an anti-inflationary policy of successive reductions in monetary growth, despite large deficits, if it is willing to let the market determine interest rates, no matter how high they may be. But that course is made difficult by the international and domestic consequences of further increases in interest rates.

Another obstacle to an anti-inflationary policy is the explosive effect of higher interest rates on the federal budget. When the interest rate on the government debt exceeds the rate of growth of GNP, interest payments can cause the deficits to grow faster than GNP.[24] Without legislative action to raise tax rates, revenues would grow more or less in proportion to GNP and would not expand fast enough to prevent an exploding deficit. Then the financing of the growing deficit would further raise interest rates and feed on itself. Even monetization of such growing deficits to hold interest rates down might not succeed if it produced expectations of higher inflation and raised nominal interest rates even further. Such an explosive path would force Congress to take action on the budget, since the explosion would otherwise produce such a large federal debt that repudiation through high inflation might become appealing as the only alternative. The sheer possibility of such an uncontrollable explosive path hangs as a dark cloud over the bond market. A reassuring property of such a dire path is that its slow acceleration in the early stages gives ample time to work out more appealing alternatives.[25]

Conclusion: The Economic Effects of the Large Deficit

The federal budget records the dollar value of economic resources used for government purposes. Total budget expenditures measure the total resources absorbed. Except to the extent that previously idle resources are put back to work, government expenditures necessarily crowd out the private use of the same resources. Which private uses are thus crowded out depends on how the budget is financed. A common view initially was that the Treasury borrowing would crowd out private borrowing and retard capital investment financed by borrowing. The future would thus be "burdened" with a smaller capital stock and productive capacity than would otherwise have been produced. But the actual crowding out in 1983 and 1984 was quite different.

The increase in demand for funds was substantially met by a greater supply, especially from abroad, providing the financing for the budget deficit as well as a cyclical expansion of business investment in line with the expansions in past cycles. A substantial reduction in business tax rates and a corresponding increase in the after-tax rate of return on new capital stimulated investment, which was stronger at the prevailing high real rates of interest than could otherwise have been expected. The reduction in business taxes increased after-tax profits and depreciation allowances, thus generating the strong rise in business saving that financed part of the investment expenditures. Since the large deficits reflected in part the reduction in business taxes, the cost of financing this investment was shifted in effect from business stockholders to the Treasury, without producing on this account a major reallocation of resources. The major reallocation resulted instead from the funds attracted from abroad and those lent to the government by domestic sectors that would otherwise have been used elsewhere. The capital inflow from abroad affected resource use by appreciating the dollar and increasing net imports; these effects crowded out the domestic industries that sell abroad or compete with imports.

Aside from the current use of resources, the large deficits also affect the claims on future resources. The traditional net indebtedness of foreigners to the United States is shifting over to a net U.S. indebtedness abroad, which represents a net claim by foreigners on future U.S. output. In addition, the increase in federal debt is an obligation to impose future taxes to cover interest payments to holders of the debt. Taxes to pay the interest on a large federal debt are only a transfer of income, to be sure; but since all taxes are distortionary, the transfer is a burden on the future economy. The magnitude of this burden of debt is not fixed, however, but varies with the interest rate. In 1983 interest payments on the federal debt were 2.9 percent of GNP and growing.[26] In 1950 they were only 2.0 percent, even though the outstanding debt was 69 percent of GNP after the large deficits of World War II and only 35 percent in 1983. The difference in interest payments reflected the interest rate, which averaged $2^{1/4}$ percent per year for federal debt in 1950 and $9^{1/2}$ percent in 1983. Interest rates are unlikely to fall to the levels of 1950, although they might decline considerably if inflationary expectations declined and the deficits were reduced. There is a Catch-22 here, in that interest rates may not decline much as long as Treasury borrowing remains high to finance large deficits.

The deficits are projected to remain large for the foreseeable future, barring new legislation, and might be larger if a recession developed. The financing and economic effects of the deficit appear highly unstable, however. It is not clear how long markets can absorb a high volume of Treasury securities without further increases in real interest rates, which would add further to the deficits. While the present accommodation to the deficits involves little or no crowding out of private investment, this could change. A decline in the capital inflow would depreciate the dollar and thus work to improve the foreign trade gap. That would bring relief to the export- and import-competing industries but force the private use of resources to be crowded out elsewhere. A crowding out of private investment, especially in housing, through further increases in interest rates would be very likely. Even apart from any reallocation of resources, a rise in interest rates would add to the cost of servicing debt and be especially burdensome to third world debtors and U.S. taxpayers. Forecasts by the administration and the CBO of the deficit over the next half-decade assume that real interest rates will not rise, but how long large deficits can be financed at current real interest rates is an open question.

Notes

1. Net borrowing requirements of the U.S. Treasury to cover financing of off-budget outlays were higher by about $12 billion. Some of this extra Treasury borrowing adds to the total demand for credit because not all of the off-budget outlays would otherwise have been made by the private sector.

2. One-third of the large inventory increase in the first quarter of 1984 was an exceptional increase in farm inventories, of which $9.8 billion, or almost one-half of the farm portion, reflected federal transfers under the payment-in-kind (PIK) program. This was the maximum size of the PIK program. It was $4.7 billion in the preceding quarter, about $3.0 billion in the succeeding quarter, and negligible in other quarters.

Since the PIK program was simply a transfer of commodities without payment, we should remove the transfer from the data in assessing the financial effects of the deficit. This increases the reported deficit and reduces reported inventory and gross investment by the amounts above.

3. In 1983 and after, assuming a before-tax real rate of return of 4 percent and 6 percent inflation. See Charles R. Hulten and James W. Robertson, "Corporate Tax Policy and Economic Growth: An Analysis of the 1981 and 1982 Tax Acts," in *Changing Domestic Priorities* (Washington, D.C.: Urban Institute, 1984).

4. The sudden appearance of a large statistical discrepancy in 1978 in the flow of funds, implying large unreported capital inflows, suggests capital flight from the Middle East and subsequently from Latin America in the late 1970s.

5. International Monetary Fund, *World Economic Outlook*, Occasional Paper 27, 1984, p. 187.

6. It is generally assumed that efforts in the other direction are smaller. These include unreported imports, such as illegal narcotics, which cause the current account deficit to be understated. Insofar as the funds produced by illegal imports are used to purchase U.S. assets, these capital inflows are usually not reported.

7. For an elaboration of the role of credit rationing in financial developments, see Albert M. Wojnilower, "The Central Role of Credit Crunches in Recent Financial History," *Brookings Papers on Economic Activity*, 1980, no. 2, pp. 277–326.

8. In this behavior the public saves out of income enough to finance expected increases in government expenditures to service the debt. The motive is to avoid undesired changes in consumption over the life cycle. If taxpayers discount all future taxes into the indefinite future, they save enough more to match the increased government borrowing, and there is no effect on interest rates. This is known as the Ricardian equivalence theorem (See Robert J. Barro, "Are Government Bonds Net Wealth?" *Journal of Political Economy*, vol. 82 [November/December 1974], pp. 1095–117). If the discounting is limited to the lifetime of each taxpayer, saving and interest rates are related to the ratio of government debt to income (see Oliver J. Blanchard, "Current and Anticipated Deficits, Interest Rates, and Economic Activity," *European Economic Re-*

view, vol. 25 [June 1984], pp. 7–27).

9. About a tenth of world saving went into dollar assets in 1983 and no doubt a somewhat higher fraction in 1984, of which perhaps half came from Latin American countries. See the discussion in chapter 9.

10. This is true for regular M1 and for M1 adjusted to include overnight repurchase agreements and Caribbean Eurodollar deposits. Although the Federal Reserve's adjustment of NOW account data for 1981 shows a sharp decline in growth beginning early in that year, it is questionable whether that adjustment is appropriate. For an analysis of monetary developments in this period, see Phillip Cagan, "Monetary Policy and Subduing Inflation," in William Fellner, ed., *Essays in Contemporary Economic Problems, 1983–1984 Edition: Disinflation* (Washington, D.C.: American Enterprise Institute, 1984), pp. 21–53.

11. Bank loans to business were unusually strong in the first year of the 1981–1982 recession (see ibid.).

12. See Eduard J. Bomhoff, *Monetary Uncertainty* (Amsterdam: North-Holland, 1983), chap. 5.

13. The *Annual Report* of the Council of Economic Advisers for 1984 presented the conventional view that the deficits have raised interest rates.

14. Office of the Assistant Secretary for Economic Policy, U.S. Treasury Department, "The Effect of Deficits on Prices of Financial Assets: Theory and Evidence," January 1984.

15. Congressional Budget Office, *The Economic Outlook,* February 1984, pp. 69–71, 99–102.

16. See discussion by John Makin in chapter 7.

17. For an exposition of this view and the data, see Robert Eisner and Paul J. Pieper, "A New View of the Federal Debt and Budget Deficits," *American Economic Review,* vol. 74 (March 1984), pp. 11–29.

18. It is unclear whether the market compensation takes account of taxes. The relatively low real interest rates during most of the 1970s suggest not. See Vito Tanzi, "Inflationary Expectations, Economic Activity, Taxes, and Interest Rates," *American Economic Review,* vol. 70 (March 1980), pp. 12–21.

19. See Thomas Mayer, *Permanent Income, Wealth, and Consumption* (Berkeley: University of California Press, 1975).

20. Increased saving to compensate for real capital losses on government debt assumes that the debt is seen as wealth. In the Ricardian equivalence theorem, however, the public discounts the future value of taxes to cover interest payments on the debt, so that the net wealth of the public—consolidating debt holders and taxpayers as one group—is zero.

21. What these other reasons might have been is not clear. Suppose that retained earnings are viewed by households that own the businesses as part of personal saving. Even including these retained earnings, the combined net saving of households and businesses did not increase in 1978–1981; *net* business saving has been essentially flat. Furthermore, capital gains of households in common stocks were minor in these years and so do not explain the decline in saving that emerges when NIA measured saving is reduced by inflationary interest receipts. Similarly, total net capital gains, which combine

stocks and all financial assets, are inadequate to explain the saving decline.

22. See note 8.

23. Gerald P. Dwyer, Jr., "Deficits and Monetary Policy," *Journal of Money, Credit and Banking,* forthcoming November 1985.

24. See Thomas Sargent and Neil Wallace, "Some Unpleasant Monetarist Arithmetic," *Quarterly Review,* Federal Reserve Bank of Minneapolis (Fall 1981).

25. The Congressional Budget Office (*The Economic Outlook,* February 1984, p. 118) found an explosive path under various circumstances. If the rate of interest paid by the government equals the rate of growth of nominal GNP and if the structural deficit (ignoring cycles) that excludes interest payments equals 3 percent of GNP, the ratio of the public debt to GNP grows without limit. But initially it grows slowly. If the ratio starts at 50 percent in the year 1990, it reaches under present tax rates and projections only 80 percent in the year 2000, 110 percent in 2010, and 140 percent in 2020.

26. Excluding Federal Reserve banks. These figures are published in *Monthly Treasury Bulletin* and *Statistical Abstract of the United States.*

9

Budget Deficits, Exchange Rates, International Capital Flows, and Trade

Eduardo Somensatto

Summary

Recent public debate over the direction and the magnitude of the likely effects of deficits has been marked by considerable disagreement, particularly over the effect of budget deficits on the external sector of the economy or, more specifically, on exchange rates, trade, and capital flows. The conventional view among economists is that higher budget deficits and developments in the external sector are closely linked: a higher budget deficit raises domestic interest rates, which attract foreign capital and lead to an appreciation of the domestic currency. The higher exchange rate makes imports less expensive at home and exports more expensive abroad, creating a trade deficit. A budget deficit, therefore, leads to a loss of international competitiveness and in time to a matching trade deficit.

A cursory review of recent evidence for the United States tends to support most of the propositions of the conventional view. Foreign capital has been transferred to the United States, the dollar has on average appreciated against all major currencies, and the trade balance has sharply deteriorated.

Nevertheless, the conventional view has recently been challenged on empirical grounds and considerably refined analytically. The empirical challenge has arisen mainly from the lack of a strong correlation between deficits and interest rates and between nominal interest rates and the exchange rate. This challenge has also given rise to alternative explanations for recent economic events in the external sector of the United States. The explanations most frequently cited are that the strength of the dollar and the inflow of foreign capital are due to the relative improvement of the political and eco-

I would like to express my sincere appreciation for the helpful assistance provided by Lawrence Bouton and Maryam Homayouni and the helpful comments and suggestions from Phillip Cagan. Naturally, all of the disclaimers apply.

nomic environment in the United States and that deterioration of the trade balance can be attributed to the better performance of the U.S. economy vis-à-vis the rest of the world. It is often argued that the improved outlook for the U.S. economy is a result of lower rates of inflation, the reduction of personal income tax rates, and the increased depreciation allowance for new capital—all developments that tend to increase the after-tax rate of return on capital.

The analytical refinements of the conventional view have added important dynamic considerations. They have helped to shift the debate away from a simple one-period flow analysis toward a more relevant multiperiod framework, which highlights the importance of such factors as the stock of assets and private sector expectations of the future course of the economy in determining the effects of budget deficits. They have also helped to focus attention on the long-run consequences of the current fiscal policy of the United States, which if unchanged will produce a string of large structural budget deficits.

In a dynamic long-run context, structural deficits are analogous to intertemporal transfers of income from future generations to the present generation. These transfers involve selling existing assets or incurring future liabilities in exchange for current spending. These are the means by which the excess spending reflected in the budget deficits and the current account deficits are financed. The transfers of wealth cannot continue indefinitely, however, but must eventually cease. The current account deficits must be reversed when the country exhausts its ability to borrow from foreign savers and when service payments on foreign liabilities start to accumulate. This reversal of the current account requires a fall of the real exchange rate below its long-run equilibrium level.

The certainty that at some time recent trends will have to be reversed is the source of the present concern over the sustainability of the U.S. budget and current account deficits and the basis for recent predictions of a future sharp decline of the dollar. But, as this paper shows, recent events in the United States may have increased the long-run real exchange rate; the future fall of the dollar may thus not be as large as expected.

In addition to analytical issues, the paper addresses several empirical questions. Data from European countries and Japan do not support the argument that the continuing rise of the dollar, despite falling nominal interest rates, reflected mainly political and safe-haven considerations. An analysis of the nominal interest rate differential and the forward premiums in the foreign exchange markets for the early 1980s reveals no significant increase of the political risk factor either in the United States or in those other countries. This is not surprising since few political, as distinct from economic, changes have taken place in those countries that would threaten the safety of financial investments there.

The same cannot be said for capital flows from Latin America, however. The recorded outflows from that region have been considerable in the last few *years, coinciding with heightened political threats to capital values. Thus some of the appreciation of the weighted value of the dollar may be due to political factors.*

Tests to determine whether the recent bilateral appreciation of the dollar is linked to the budget deficits or to the improved investment opportunities in the United States generated by the recent tax reductions yielded no conclusive results. The lack of an accurate measure of the long-run average real exchange rate precludes any definite answers. But an analysis of the recent movements of real interest rates, the spot exchange rate, the forward rates, and expected inflation differentials in various countries casts some doubts on the notion that the budget deficits are the sole reason for the appreciation of the dollar.

Another challenge to the conventional view that is tested here is the assertion that the recent deterioration of the U.S. trade balance is due mainly to the better performance of the U.S. economy and not to the real appreciation of the dollar. A simple test of this proposition based on an in-sample simulation of overall imports and exports shows that a significant portion of the deterioration of the trade balance in 1983 was caused by the rising value of the dollar.

Domestically, the internal adjustments in the United States to a higher dollar have been significant, with import-competing industries apparently more affected than export-competing industries. The appreciation of the dollar has led to sharp increases in the share of imports, particularly in apparels and machinery. The largest proportional loss of exports as sources of revenue occurred in the primary products and textile industries. These developments may have been aggravated by the movements of real wages in those industries. But an analysis of real compensation per employee adjusted for productivity changes reveals no systematic response across sectors to the increased competitive environment that has emerged in recent years.

Another popular contention is that the U.S. budget deficits are crowding out investment abroad while sustaining foreign income by boosting foreign exports. According to empirical evidence for Europe and Japan, this effect was not apparent until the end of 1983. Foreign performance in these areas was consistent with past cyclical fluctuations. This effect may have been more pronounced in 1984, but no data on it were available at the time of writing.

An analysis of the financial and physical transfers of capital reveals that, in contrast to popular perception, a significant portion of the capital flowing into the United States until early 1984 was diverted from Latin American countries. This shift occurred mainly because U.S. banks considerably reduced their lending abroad and lent instead to domestic businesses. The continuation of this means of financing the U.S. current account, however, depends on the ability of those countries to repay their foreign debts or on the ability of the banks to liquidate their holdings of foreign assets abroad. These sources are limited, and capital from other parts of the world will eventually

225

have to replace this flow if the current account of the United States is to remain at a high level.

The ability of the United States to finance its current account also depends on its net foreign investment position, the amount of net private saving in the world, and the willingness of foreign savers to hold dollar-denominated assets in their portfolios. According to existing projections, the net foreign investment position of the United States will become negative by the middle of 1985, making the United States a net debtor to the world. Given the loss of net foreign income and the eventual need to service its debt, the United States will have to absorb a larger share of foreign savings if the other components of its current account remain constant. Rough estimates of the available pool of world savings show that the U.S. current account absorbed 5 percent of the total in 1983 and approximately 12 percent in 1984. The rate of accumulation of dollar assets in 1984 is slightly larger than current proportional holdings of dollars by foreign residents. Thus a precipitous decline of the dollar exchange rate simply because of a saturation of dollar-denominated assets is not yet apparent, although the proportional holdings of dollars will have to increase if the United States continues, as expected, to run large current account deficits.

A continuation of current policies ensures that at some time the dollar will have to fall below its long-run average. But that could be far in the future, and the decline need not be sharp or, for that matter, large. A series of unexpected events, however, such as a highly expansionary monetary policy or an inability to lower the deficits in the near future, could lead to a negative reevaluation of the expected future return on dollar assets and precipitate a general and sharp decline of its value.

Introduction

Since the United States changed its fiscal policy in 1981, some important developments have occurred in the external sector of the U.S. economy: the dollar has appreciated substantially against other currencies; the U.S. trade deficit has widened; and a significant amount of foreign capital has flowed into the United States. According to most analysts, these events were not coincidental. They were the natural economic consequences of a fiscal policy that generated large budget deficits, whether intended or not.

The conventional view of these developments is based on the presumption that there are causal links between the budget policies of a government and developments in the external sector of the economy—in this case running from budget deficits to domestic interest rates, to exchange rates, and eventually to the current account. This chain of causation is a well-established proposition in economics and generally fits well with recent developments in the United States.

226

The conventional view has been challenged, however, as a proper depiction of recent events on the grounds that not all the links of the chain are well supported by the empirical evidence. According to some analysts, the lack of correlation among certain variables raises questions about the validity of the propositions put forth by proponents of the conventional view.

In addition to the empirical challenge, recent analytical developments have introduced some ambiguity to the analysis. These theoretical refinements of the framework underlying the conventional argument have revealed a possible multitude of results, depending on the environment within which deficits are generated and the policies and responses that accompany them. These developments, though not invalidating the original assertion that budget deficits affect the external sector, have shown a number of possible outcomes. As a result, a lively debate has ensued within political and academic circles about the effects of recent U.S. fiscal policies.

This debate has yielded a number of seemingly competing explanations of how a policy of growing budget deficits affects the movements of the exchange rate, the competitiveness of trade-related sectors, the flows of financial capital, and income and output abroad. In fact, recent disparate statements by government officials and economists have created the impression that there are several possible outcomes, none of which is a priori certain or even dominant.

Given the conflicting views on the role of deficits and the apparent confusion regarding some of their effects, the aim of this paper is to examine some of the explanations that have been presented and the extent to which they are supported by the recent empirical evidence. Three years have passed since the shift in fiscal policy in the United States occurred, and preliminary evidence of its effects is now available. This evidence should reveal whether the conventional propositions about the links between deficits and the external sector need qualification.

The paper focuses on the major links between the budget deficits and the external sector, such as the relation between interest rates and exchange rates, the link between the exchange rate and the current account in both the short and the long run, the connection between deficits and export- and import-competing industries in the United States, and, finally, the relation between budget deficits in the United States and economic activity abroad. The paper also addresses the issue whether the recent transfer of financial and physical capital to the United States can be sustained.

The first section describes the theoretical reasoning and the assumptions underlying the more conventional explanations for the

227

links between deficits and the external sector. The second section discusses several of the empirical challenges to the conventional view and analyzes the recent empirical evidence to examine the validity of those challenges. The third section examines the qualifications necessary for analyzing the long-run implications of a string of structural budget deficits. The fourth section reviews the economic performance of several sectors of the U.S. economy to determine which export- and import-competing industries have been most affected by the recent appreciation of the dollar. The fifth section analyzes the effects of the U.S. current account deficits abroad and the sources and methods by which those deficits have been financed. Finally, the sixth section discusses the long-run financial constraints facing the United States.

The Conventional View

Public discussion of the external effects of the budget deficit has focused on two main issues. The first is the relation between budget deficits, on the one hand, and the exchange rate, trade deficits, and the current account, on the other. The second, which is sometimes of greater interest in countries other than the United States, arises from concern over the financing and sustainability of the U.S. current account deficits and the net effect of high U.S. interest rates and a strong dollar on economic activity abroad.

In both issues the point of departure is the received doctrine from economic literature. It is a well-established proposition in economics that government budget deficits affect the external sector of an economy. The economic rationale for this proposition can be derived from a simple framework that incorporates the main links between the domestic economy and the foreign sector. A simplified example of this framework is depicted in figure 9–1.

Quadrant one displays the standard IS and LM schedules. They show the combination of interest rates (r) and income (Y) that would clear the goods market (the IS curve) and the money market (the LM curve). The underlying assumptions are that prices and wages are fixed and that investment and the demand for money (for a given supply) are interest elastic. Thus aggregate demand determines output.

Quadrant two shows the relation between interest rates at home (r) and the spot exchange rate(s)—here defined as the *foreign* price of a unit of the *domestic* currency. The relation is positive given the assumptions that the forward exchange rate and foreign interest rates remain constant. These assumptions mean that any changes in the interest rate differentials must be reflected in a change of the spot rate

FIGURE 9-1
THE LINK BETWEEN DEFICITS AND THE CURRENT ACCOUNT

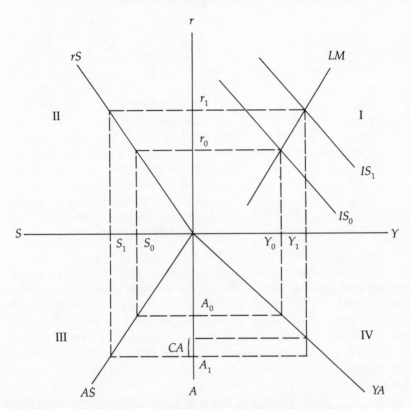

in relation to the fixed forward rate. If these assumptions were re-laxed, the relation would differ, as discussed later. Moreover, since prices of goods are assumed to be fixed, the nominal changes in interest rates and exchange rates are also real changes.

The reason that an increase in the yield on domestic assets leads to an appreciation of the spot rate is that when assets are substitut-able, a rise in interest rates in the United States, for example, will induce wealth owners to substitute dollar-denominated assets for for-eign assets in their portfolios. In attempting to change the composi-tion of their wealth, market participants will succeed only in raising the value of the dollar and in generating an increase in the forward discount. This in turn will offset the attraction of the initial difference in yields because the overall rate of return on all assets will be equal-ized and therefore will leave wealth owners content with their existing asset position.[1]

Quadrant three shows a simple linear relation between the exchange rate and aggregate spending, or absorption (A), for a given level of output. Aggregate spending is defined as

$$A = C + I + G$$

the sum of private consumption (C), investment (I) and government spending (G). Note that all these spending measures contain the consumption of both domestically produced goods and foreign goods and thus include imports. Unlike their role in the National Income Accounts, these measures represent spending rather than income. The relation between the exchange rate and spending is positive, because an appreciation of the currency leads to an increase in imports and so in domestic expenditures, when output is held constant.

The 45-degree line in quadrant four represents an equality between income and aggregate spending when the current account is zero. Any point above the line signifies a current account surplus (when income is greater than spending), any point below the line a current account deficit (spending greater than income). Thus:

$$Y - A = CA = X - M + rF$$

To show the relation between budget deficits and the external sector, we can start by using one of the narrowest definitions of the current account, that is, by letting it be equal to the trade balance, exports minus imports $(X - M)$ and the interest received (or paid) on the net foreign investment position of domestic residents (rF). Since the value of domestic output (O), where $O = C + I + G + (X - M)$, can be used for consumption (C), for saving (S), or for paying taxes (T), we can write

$$C + I + G + (X - M) = Y - rF = C + S + T$$

Subtracting spending and rearranging terms, we derive the simple identity for the national accounts:

$$Y - A = X - M + rF = (S - I) + (T - G)$$

Thus when the trade balance equals the service account, spending must equal income. The identity also shows that, when the current account deficit matches the government's budget deficit, domestic investment equals saving. More important, a current account deficit in the presence of a budget deficit means that investment is larger than it would otherwise be.

These relations in figure 9–1 provide the apparatus to trace the underlying adjustment to an exogenous increase in the budget deficit. Starting at the equilibrium point (Y_0, r_0) with domestic interest rates equal to foreign rates and the current account in balance, the increase in the budget deficit, represented by the shift in the IS curve to the right, will initiate a series of effects. At the initial level of exchange rates and interest rates, it will raise aggregate demand, income, and the demand for money. If the supply of money is unchanged, interest rates will rise to r_1 to clear the money market. This rise to r_1 will create an interest rate differential in relation to foreign rates that will raise the demand by foreigners for domestic financial assets. This rise in the yield of domestic assets, as noted before, will be associated with a higher spot exchange rate if the forward rate remains constant.

The appreciation of the currency in turn raises the demand for imports and lowers the demand for exports, generating a temporary current account deficit equal to the difference between A_1 and Y_1 in quadrant four. This deficit represents the actual inflow of capital, in both financial and physical terms, even though the failure to record all transactions often results in a statistical discrepancy between the current account and capital flows (see chapter 8 for a discussion of the discrepancy). The financial transfers take place as foreign residents purchase domestic interest-earning securities or stocks with the excess holdings of dollars obtained from the sale of goods to the United States. The transfer of physical capital, which exactly matches the financial transfers, occurs through the increase or at least the preservation of the existing levels of investment at home and lower investment abroad (assuming no change in foreign income, or saving, with the rise of foreign exports).

Figure 9–1 thus outlines a consistent set of links that trace the connection between an unanticipated increase in the budget deficit and a temporary increase in the current account. These outcomes depend on certain assumptions. If the level of domestic income at Y_0 were at full employment, for example, and could not rise in real or in nominal terms, since prices are assumed constant, the initial increase in interest rates and the exchange rate would be larger. Moreover, if financial assets were not substitutable, the rise in interest rates would not affect the exchange rate, and in time the higher level of income and the additional demand for imports would lead to an exchange rate depreciation. The same would be true if the budget deficit were initially financed by money creation instead of by bonds.

The important point to note from the standard results is that, in contrast to popular notions, the change in the exchange rate does not occur because of an inflow of foreign capital. In this framework the reverse is actually true: it is the change in the exchange rate that leads to an inflow of capital. The reason is that nominal interest rates and exchange rates move concurrently because of the high degree of substitution of financial assets in private portfolios, not because of the mobility of capital. Interest rates and the exchange rate are jointly determined at a point in time by the demand for and the supply of assets and are only affected over time by the flow of capital and the corresponding change in wealth. The actual net flow (or transfer) of capital takes place when financial assets are exchanged for real goods (or physical capital), that is, when there is a current account imbalance.

The current account imbalance occurs because of the appreciation of the spot exchange rate or, as discussed later, because of the rise of the *real* exchange rate above its long-run equilibrium value. In this framework, since prices are assumed to be constant, all the nominal changes are also changes in real values. Thus a change in the spot exchange rate, with a fixed forward rate, constitutes a rise in the current real exchange rate while the expected future real rate remains constant. This means that the rise of the exchange rate is expected to be reversed after all adjustments (including the flow of capital) have taken place. The discrepancy between the current real exchange rate and its long-run value emerges because the real interest rate in the home country has risen above foreign real interest rates as a consequence of budget deficits.

In equilibrium, the real interest rate should equal the real rate of return on capital, defined as the rental value of capital (adjusted for taxes) divided by its price. Thus a rise in the real interest rate, which reflects either an increase in the rental value of capital or a decline of its price, creates an incentive to shift capital to the home country. This is accomplished by a temporary real appreciation of the currency, which generates a current account deficit and its counterpart, a capital account surplus. Over time the net inflow of capital should reduce the real interest rate, if the marginal product of capital declines with an increasing capital stock, and should also lead to a return of the exchange rate to its long-run equilibrium level.

The distinction between asset substitutability and capital mobility, therefore, is important. A high degree of asset substitution ensures that nominal yields are equalized across all financial assets in the short run and that the existing stock of domestic and foreign assets is willingly held by the private sector. A high degree of capital mobility, however, ensures that the after-tax real rate of return on physical capital is equalized across countries over the long run.

This distinction is sometimes lost in public discussions of the effect of budget deficits on the external sector, just as several other aspects of the framework presented here have been misinterpreted. This is nowhere more evident than in the questions recently raised about the validity of this framework in explaining the events taking place in the United States. The accusations of its empirical failure have sometimes been based on incorrect links and, most important, have not taken into consideration the dynamic long-run consequences of a string of budget deficits. These issues are discussed next.

The Empirical Evidence and Competing Arguments

The Recent Experience of the United States. According to the conventional argument presented above, an increase in the budget deficit should be accompanied by an increase in the current account deficit. This has indeed happened. As shown in figure 9–2, the increase in the cyclically adjusted federal budget deficit of the United States from an average of 2.2 percent of GNP in 1980 to approximately 4.0 percent in 1983 was followed by a deterioration of the current account of a similar magnitude. The current account went from a small surplus in 1980 to a deficit equaling 2.1 percent of GNP in the first half of 1984.

The deterioration of the current account and the increase in the U.S. budget deficits were accompanied by a significant appreciation of

FIGURE 9–2

CURRENT ACCOUNT AND CYCLICALLY ADJUSTED DEFICIT, 1973–1984

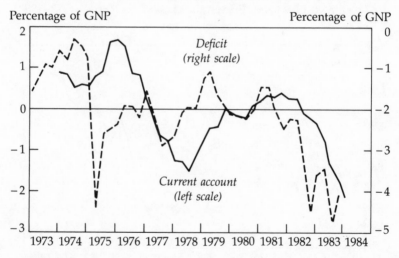

NOTE: The current account is a 4Q moving average of the U.S. nominal current account. The cyclically adjusted deficit is the measure derived by DeLeeuw and Halloway, available in the Federal Reserve Bank of Boston Conference Series No. 27, *The Economics of Large Government Deficits*, "Measuring and Analyzing the Cyclically Adjusted Budget Deficit." It measures the cycle-neutral path of the federal deficit.
SOURCES: International Monetary Fund and Board of Governors of the Federal Reserve System.

the dollar. As shown in figure 9–3, both the nominal and the real trade-weighted dollar exchange rates appreciated considerably over the period. The nominal rate rose 42 percent from its low point in the second quarter of 1980 to the second quarter of 1984, and the real rate rose approximately 36 percent over the same period.

Although the appreciation of the dollar was to be expected, it should have been accompanied by a rise of interest rates in the United States. As described in chapter 8, nominal interest rates did not rise persistently in the United States during this period. They in fact declined for most of the period, although real interest rates, by most measures, rose to unprecedented levels by the middle of 1982. For the purpose of examining the link between interest rates and the exchange rate, however, neither the nominal nor the real interest rate in the United States suffices. The appropriate measure is the interest rate differential or the movement of interest rates in the United States in relation to those abroad.

Since a weighted average interest rate is not available, this analy-

FIGURE 9–3

REAL AND NOMINAL EFFECTIVE EXCHANGE RATES, 1973–1984

(1980 = 100)

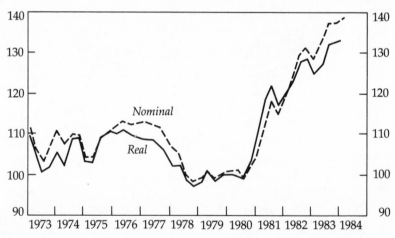

NOTE: The real effective exchange rate is the average exchange rate for thirteen industrial countries (in units per dollar) deflated by a trade-weighted index of their main indicators. The nominal effective exchange rate is the weighted average of nominal exchange rates for thirteen industrial countries (in units per dollar).

SOURCES: International Monetary Fund and Board of Governors of the Federal Reserve System.

sis focuses on bilateral movements of the exchange rate and the corresponding interest rate differentials. Figure 9–4 shows the movements of the nominal interest rate on twelve-month dollar-denominated Eurodeposits in relation to rates payable on Eurodeposits denominated in sterling, marks, francs, and yen.

Except for a short interlude in late 1981, the interest rate differentials for the pound and the yen rose significantly from the middle of 1980 until the middle of 1982. The mark-dollar interest rate differential also rose throughout this period but not by as much as the others and with less volatility while the franc-dollar interest rate differential declined for most of the period. Against all these currencies during that period the dollar gained strength, an outcome somewhat compatible with the movements in the interest rates.

The most interesting period for this analysis is that ranging from the middle of 1982 through the end of 1983. All the interest rate differentials, except for that of France, declined for approximately six months and remained relatively stable thereafter while the dollar continued to rise in relation to the other currencies. This is contrary to what would be expected in the conventional view of the effect of U.S. deficits. This rise of the dollar, in the presence of growing budget deficits but with a falling nominal interest rate differential, gave impetus to alternative explanations for the continuing strength of the dollar.

Alternative Explanations for the Appreciation of the Dollar. The inconsistency between the movements of exchange rates and those of interest rate differentials during the period from mid-1982 through 1983 led several analysts to suggest that other, more important factors were at work in determining the new value of the dollar. First, there was the safe-haven factor. That is, increased political turmoil and greater risks around the world were responsible for a flight of capital toward more secure U.S. assets. Second, the tax changes introduced in early 1981 substantially lowered the user cost of new capital (or increased the net-of-tax real rate of return on new capital). This, along with the deregulatory thrust of the Reagan administration, improved the environment for new investment and led to an increase in the demand for investment funds. Consequently, since saving did not rise concurrently, real interest rates in the United States rose in relation to those abroad, creating new incentives for foreign investment in the United States.

In response it can be argued that the developments of 1982 and 1983 are still consistent with the conventional emphasis on the role of budget deficits. The argument starts from the fact that the spot ex-

FIGURE 9–4
INTEREST RATE DIFFERENTIALS AND EXCHANGE RATES, 1973–1984

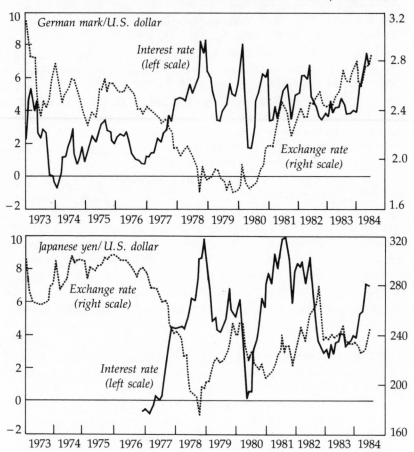

change rate is determined not by nominal but by real interest rate differentials. The explanation is that nominal rates were falling in the United States in relation to those abroad during that period primarily because of the magnitude of the recession in 1982 and the monetary policy pursued by the Federal Reserve. These two factors led to a significant downward revision of the long-run expected rate of inflation in the United States at a time when the real interest rate was rising because of the budget deficits.[2] In this view the appreciation of the dollar in late 1982 is not a puzzle at all. The dollar continued to appreciate because of the divergent policies being followed by the United States vis-à-vis other countries.

Another challenge to the link between budget deficits and current

FIGURE 9–4 (continued)

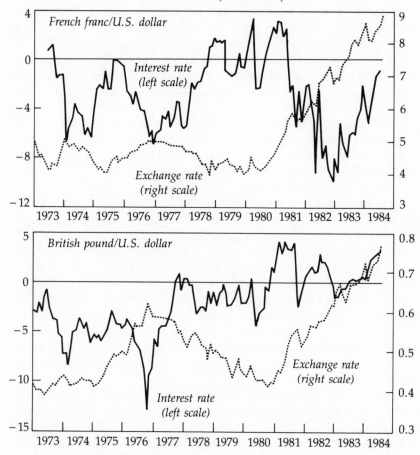

NOTE: Interest rates are end-of-period values based on the bid rates. Exchange rates are also end-of-month values expressed as natural logarithms.

SOURCES: International Monetary Fund and Morgan Guaranty Trust.

account deficits is made by questioning whether the main reason for the recent deterioration of the U.S. current account was the appreciation of the dollar. The question arises because the increase in the trade deficit occurred at a time when the economic performance of the United States was much better than that of the rest of the world. Some analysts have argued that a considerable portion (maybe two-thirds) of the recent increase in the trade deficit is due to the sluggish economic performance abroad and the vibrant economic recovery in the United States.[3] This argument is usually supported by partial-equilibrium estimates of income elasticities of foreign trade for the United States, which for exports tend to be lower, and for imports higher, than the average for the other major industrial countries. This means that the trade balance would therefore deteriorate even if incomes for the United States and these countries grew at the same rate and much more if they grew disproportionately in favor of the United States.

Determining the relative significance of each of these competing explanations is important because each carries different implications for the future course of the dollar if U.S. budget deficits are reduced. First, if the recent appreciation of the dollar and the deterioration of the current account are linked to the budget deficits, as in the conventional view, reductions of the deficits should bring down the dollar and alleviate the competitive pressures being placed on U.S. producers by the strong dollar.

Second, if tax advantages are the driving force behind the strength of the dollar, the dollar might return closer to its long-run value—which is presumably lower than the values prevailing today—only after the adjustment in the stock of physical capital is completed and the inflow of financial capital ceases. Once the new desired stock of capital has been attained and the net-of-tax marginal rate of return on capital is again approximately the same in the United States as abroad, the incentives to transfer capital to the United States would be greatly diminished. How long this process would take would depend on how fast the marginal productivity of capital declined over time, assuming that there will be no further changes in the taxation of capital.

Third, if political factors are responsible for the high value of the dollar, the dollar's movements are at the mercy of the whims of investors. Political conditions are generally perceived to be volatile and unpredictable; therefore a rapid and unforeseen reversal in the political climate could lead to a massive capital flight from the dollar and thus a large currency depreciation, unrelated to the deficits.

Finally, if it is true that the deterioration of the current account occurred mainly because of higher growth rates in the United States, a reversal of current budgetary policies would affect the external sector only if it altered the prospects for growth of the U.S. economy.

An empirical analysis of these issues is presented in the next section. On the basis of recent events, no strong reasons are found for rejecting the conventional view in favor of alternative explanations that the appreciation of the dollar occurred because of safe-haven considerations or that the current account deteriorated because of higher growth rates in the United States. Determining the relative importance of the changes in the taxation of capital and of the deficits is more difficult, however. Such a comparison requires analyzing the dynamic long-run effects of deficits, which depend in part on whether those deficits result from lower taxation of capital or higher transfer payments.

Evidence on the Interest Rate-Exchange Rate Link and the Safe-Haven Argument. This section examines the relationships among exchange rates and interest rates for evidence that would reject the conventional view of the recent appreciation of the dollar in favor of the safe-haven argument. The analysis is based on the behavior of monthly bilateral nominal spot and one-year forward exchange rates and the movements of the nominal interest rate differentials for one-year Eurodeposits in the relevant currencies. It compares the relationships for two periods: one from 1974 to 1981, a time when structural deficits were relatively constant; and the other from 1981 to 1984, when U.S. budget deficits rose rapidly.

It should be emphasized first that the conventional view cannot be rejected simply by noting that the changes in the spot exchange rate were not associated with changes in the domestic interest rate. As shown in table 9–1, a simple correlation analysis of these variables clearly indicates that, for the United States vis-à-vis the four currencies analyzed, the degree of association between exchange rates and interest rates was very low during both periods.[4]

The low correlation is not surprising since the link between interest rates and the exchange rate involves the covered-parity condition. The correct relation is based on the requirement that arbitrage among perfectly substitutable financial assets produces an equality of nominal yields. This can be represented by the simple covered-parity condition relating the yield on the domestic asset to the yield on a covered foreign asset:[5]

$$r = r^* + s - f \qquad (1)$$

where r = the natural log of 1 plus the domestic interest rate; r^* = the natural log of 1 plus the foreign interest rate; s = the log of the spot exchange rate, defined as the foreign price of a unit of domestic currency, for example, £/\$; and f = the log of the forward rate.

It is evident from equation 1 that the spot exchange rate would be expected to rise (or fall) commensurately with an increase (decline) of the nominal interest rate differential only when the forward exchange rate remains constant; that is, only when the exchange rate is expected to return to its initial level within the period of the cover. This occurs usually when the causes for the changes in the interest rate differentials are viewed as temporary and are expected to disappear within a

TABLE 9-1

CORRELATION BETWEEN RATE OF CHANGE IN THE SPOT EXCHANGE RATE
AND CHANGES IN NOMINAL INTEREST RATE DIFFERENTIALS, 1974–1984

Country	1974:2–1984:5[a]	1974:2–1981:4[b]	1981:4–1984:5
United Kingdom	−.019	−.013	.047
France	.271	.164	.456
West Germany	.080	.068	.151
Japan	.064	−.079	.341

NOTE: Correlation between $\Delta \log (S)$ and $\Delta (r - r^*)$, where $\Delta \log (S)$ = the rate of change of the spot exchange rate, and $\Delta (r - r^*)$ = the change in the interest differential on one-year Eurodeposits.
a. For Japan, 1977:2–1984:5.
b. For Japan, 1977:2–1981:4.
SOURCES: International Monetary Fund and Morgan Guaranty Trust.

short period of time—for example, when temporary and unexpected credit tightness raises the nominal (as well as the real) interest rate at home.

More frequently, however, the changes in the interest rate differential are not expected to be reversed within a relatively short period of time, particularly when they reflect basic policy changes or changes in expected inflation. Under these circumstances, the forward rate, as a measure of the expected future spot rate, will also vary along with the changes in the interest rate differential. Therefore, the changes in the spot rate must exceed or fall short of the changes in interest rates if the covered-parity condition holds, in which case their correlation is reduced.

In the framework presented earlier, the forward rate was assumed to be fixed; therefore all the changes in interest rates were associated with changes of the spot rate. Unfortunately, the reliance on this simple framework has led to a greater emphasis on the link between interest rates and the spot exchange rate than is warranted. Public discussion often overlooks the fact that a change in the interest rate differential is related to a change in the forward discount, not simply to a change in either the spot or the forward exchange rate.

An analysis of the covered-parity condition for recent periods reveals that the close correlation between the forward discount and the interest rate differential remained basically unchanged. In table 9–2, the regression results based on the first difference of the covered-parity condition are presented. They show a high degree of correlation between monthly changes in nominal interest rate differentials

TABLE 9–2
REGRESSIONS OF CHANGES IN THE FORWARD PREMIUM
ON THE INTEREST RATE DIFFERENTIALS, 1974–1984

Country	$\hat{a}$	$\hat{b}$	rho[a]	$\bar{R}^2$	Durbin-Watson Statistic	Standard Error of Regression
United Kingdom						
74:2 to 84:5	.01	.95	−.55	.84	2.17	.44
	(.42)	(28.70)	(−7.42)			
74:2 to 81:4	.01	.98	−.55	.90	2.14	.41
	(.41)	(30.49)	(−5.97)			
81:4 to 84:5	.00	.85	−.56	.63	2.14	.57
	(.07)	(9.91)	(−4.09)			
West Germany						
74:2 to 84:5	.00	.95	−.53	.89	2.09	.26
	(.16)	(36.58)	(−6.80)			
74:2 to 81:4	.01	.96	−.51	.91	2.08	.24
	(.29)	(34.87)	(−5.44)			
81:4 to 84:5	−.00	.92	−.57	.83	2.22	.29
	(−.01)	(13.53)	(−3.94)			
France						
74:2 to 84:5	.01	.97	−.35	.86	2.16	.51
	(.35)	(27.83)	(−4.00)			
74:2 to 81:4	.01	1.03	−.28	.87	2.15	.41
	(.28)	(24.50)	(−2.70)			
81:4 to 84:5	.00	.93	−.36	.86	2.15	.70
	(.05)	(14.34)	(−2.28)			
Japan						
77:2 to 84:5	.00	.92	−.46	.69	2.24	.58
	(.06)	(15.66)	(−4.59)			
77:2 to 81:4	−.00	.91	−.44	.66	2.18	.61
	(−.07)	(11.94)	(−3.38)			
81:4 to 84:5	.01	.94	−.45	.72	2.35	.54
	(.20)	(9.35)	(−2.83)			

NOTE: The coefficients are from the following regressions:

$$\left[\ln(S/S_{t-1}) - \ln(F/F_{t-1})\right] \times 1{,}200 = a + b\,\Delta(r - r^*) \times 100$$

where r, r^* = the natural logarithm of 1 plus the twelve-month Eurodeposit rates of the dollar and the respective foreign currency; and F = the forward exchange rate for one year. The dependent variable was multiplied by 1,200 to annualize the monthly rates of change and make them compatible with the one-year interest rate. Numbers in parentheses are t-statistics.

a. Regressions were corrected for autocorrelation by the Cochrane-Orcutt method, where rho is the autocorrelation coefficient.

SOURCES: International Monetary Fund and Morgan Guaranty Trust.

and the monthly changes of the difference between the spot and forward exchange rates. Additionally the coefficients of the interest rate variable, in most cases, did not vary across periods. This indicates that the high degree of substitutability among those assets remained fairly constant over time. These coefficients were also slightly less than one, which shows that the covered-parity condition does not hold perfectly. There is always a residual, which in this case, given the significant autocorrelation coefficient, also varied back and forth in a systematic fashion.

The regressions should not be viewed as implying causation, since all the variables are jointly determined. The results are shown to illustrate two main points. First, the forward premium is important, and it is incorrect to dismiss the relation between interest rates and the exchange rate solely on the basis of a lack of correlation between the spot rate and interest rate differentials. Second, Eurodeposits in these currencies are highly substitutable, and the close relation between interest rates and the forward premium did not change significantly in the latter period, when the United States ran fairly high budget deficits.

The second point suggests that, at least among these countries, political considerations have not altered the relationship and have apparently not contributed significantly to the recent appreciation of the dollar vis-à-vis these currencies. This can be inferred from the constancy of the interest rate coefficients across different periods.

This assertion, however, must be substantiated by a test, given that the residuals were autocorrelated and the regression coefficients are based on monthly changes of the covered-parity condition and not on its level. A measure of political risk would be captured, along with other factors, in the spreads between yields or in the residuals derived from the level of the covered-parity condition. That is because even when an investor has forward cover, he still faces the risk associated with a default or some other political measure during the interim period of the cover that could affect both the value of the capital invested and the expected returns from it.[6] Thus an approximate measure of political risk can be obtained from the residual, μ, derived from equation 1, as

$$\mu = r^* - r + s - f \tag{2}$$

This residual actually measures the degree of asset substitutability after adjusting for transaction costs. It reflects a series of factors, such as the effects of government capital controls and the relative risk preferences toward different assets. Therefore, if these factors remained relatively constant, a growing fear of political risks should have led to a growing divergency between interest rate differentials and the forward discount.

As shown in table 9–3, however, the average value of the residuals was not significantly different during the second period of analysis (1981:4 to 1984:5) from the value during the earlier period (1974:2 to 1981:4). Although the significance of the tests is reduced by the fact that the average values were small in relation to the standard deviations, in all cases the hypothesis that the sample means have changed over time cannot be rejected with a 95 percent level of confidence. These results suggest that the political risk premium (as distinguished from the currency risk premium) was not a factor in the appreciation of the dollar. Given the nature of the assets being analyzed and the political stability of the countries included, the results are not unexpected.

The results derived from the analysis of European currencies and

TABLE 9–3
AVERAGE VALUE AND STANDARD DEVIATION OF μ, 1974–1984

Country	Average μ and Standard Deviation of μ
United Kingdom	
74:2 to 84:5	0.023 (0.391)
74:2 to 81:4	0.121 (0.293)
81:4 to 84:5	−0.207 (0.479)
West Germany	
74:2 to 84:5	−0.048 (0.231)
74:2 to 81:4	−0.059 (0.220)
81:4 to 84:5	−0.021 (0.249)
France	
74:2 to 84:5	0.406 (0.452)
74:2 to 81:4	0.373 (0.354)
81:4 to 84:5	0.476 (0.612)
Japan	
77:1 to 84:5	0.236 (0.500)
77:1 to 81:4	0.380 (0.498)
81:4 to 84:5	0.061 (0.455)

NOTE: $\mu = (r - r^*) - [\log(\text{spot}) \times 100] + [\log(\text{forward}) \times 100]$, where spot and forward are both in units of foreign currency per dollar. A positive μ means that dollar-denominated assets offer better returns than covered foreign assets, when transaction costs are smaller than μ.

SOURCES: International Monetary Fund and Morgan Guaranty Trust.

the yen may not hold for other currencies. The nonavailability of developed forward markets for most of the currencies of the developing countries precludes a similar analysis of political factors in those countries. Some inference about those factors can be drawn, however, from recent changes in the flow of capital from the United States to other countries, particularly Latin America, and from the growing spreads charged on Latin American loans. As discussed later, since 1981 capital flows to Latin American countries have been significantly reversed, to the point that the United States is now a heavy net importer of capital from those countries. This shift was greater than required to compensate for the shift in the current account during the period. Also, during this period debt rescheduling and new loans carried larger spreads, which in many ways reflected the considerable political uncertainties affecting the region. These developments indicate that some purchases by foreigners of assets in the United States may have been motivated by the greater political stability in the United States.

Since political factors do not seem to be a major cause of the appreciation of the dollar with respect to the four currencies analyzed here, it remains to be determined whether the strength of the dollar can be linked to the increase in budget deficits or to the changes in the taxation of capital. Determining this requires first an analysis of the dynamic long-run effects of deficits, both when they are accompanied by changes in taxes and when they are a result of increased transfer payments.

Dynamic Adjustments and Long-Run Considerations

To understand the full effects of deficits on the external sector, we must know why deficits are being generated and the extent to which the factors and policies generating them are expected to persist. Not all deficits are uniform in their effects or elicit the same responses from the private sector. The environment within which a deficit is created has much to do with its effect on the economy.

A major drawback of the framework presented in the first section is that it addresses only the effect of an unexpected one-time increase in the deficit. It does not, for example, illustrate the current effects and the long-run consequences of a fiscal policy characterized by a continuous and indefinite string of structural deficits, as in the United States today. The framework is not inclusive enough to capture the effects of long-run budget constraints, changes in expectations, and the multitude of responses by the private sector that may evolve from the knowledge of such a fiscal policy. Moreover, the framework does not allow us to distinguish between those deficits generated by increases in government spending and those resulting from lower taxes. Nor does it reveal the effect that deficits will have over time on various sectors of the economy. In all, it lacks the dynamic characteristics necessary for a full analysis of current policies.

Introducing these dynamic characteristics produces a richer and more descriptive framework that better exemplifies the current situation. This dynamic framework reveals that the conventional explanations are still applicable but must be viewed in the context of temporary outcomes that may not hold in the long run, because the accumulation of effects over time sometimes reverses the initial effect and leads to long-run outcomes different from those outlined above. This is particularly true of the wealth effects created by deficits and the transfers that accompany them.

According to the projections presented in chapter 2, the current deficits of the United States are not expected to disappear in the near future unless there is a radical change in the budget. These deficits could thus be viewed as permanent until new policies are adopted. This means that their effects on allocative decisions will be different from the effects they would have if they were the result of a temporary cyclical downturn. Cyclically adjusted (or structural) deficits, by definition, raise the level of debt to income and thus have permanent wealth effects on spending and on the external sector. This holds true under any exchange rate system and whether or not the additional government spending or lower taxes raise permanent income.

These permanent effects reflect the fact that society faces an intertemporal (long-run) as well as a current budget constraint. The intertemporal budget constraint places a boundary on the level of aggregate demand over time and therefore prevents the citizens of the country from enjoying permanent levels of absorption higher than their permanent income. Given that a permanent increase in the cyclically adjusted deficit raises long-run aggregate demand without a compensating increase in permanent income, one of the other components of demand must be reduced over time to be consistent with the intertemporal budget constraint. That is, either consumption or investment as a share of GNP must decline to avert an explosive accumulation of debt.

Given a binding long-run income constraint, structural budget deficits merely shift the consumption of future income toward the present, through the transfer of resources from future generations. These transfers can take place either internally or across national borders. Transferring resources intertemporally across borders usually requires selling existing assets or incurring future liabilities to for-

245

eigners. This is the method of financing a current account deficit, which, as noted earlier, represents spending by the current generation in excess of its income. The foreign liabilities incurred by selling securities abroad, however, require an eventual stream of debt-servicing payments that can be satisfied only by current account surpluses in the future. In a world of no growth, these surpluses can be generated only if future consumption is lowered, that is, only if future generations reduce the purchase of imports or release domestically produced goods for export.[7] But future consumption can decline only so far, and future exports are limited by future income. Therefore, a country cannot run a permanent string of structural budget deficits and accumulate an unlimited amount of foreign debt.

The understanding that structural deficits are not sustainable indefinitely means that the private sector will adjust spending and investment decisions after an increase in these deficits. The response will vary according to the market evaluation of how long those policies are going to continue, the perception of the long-run effects of those policies, and the revisions of the future outlook of the economy and its major components. Determining the permanency of the situation requires evaluating the political factors influencing the policies being followed, while an evaluation of the long-run effects of the deficits requires an analysis of the policies and the circumstances that are generating the deficits and the types of transfers that are taking place.

Two important aspects of the current situation are that the structural deficits of the United States have been accompanied by a monetary policy that reduced short-term inflationary expectations and by a fiscal package that reduced taxes on income and on capital. These factors contributed, first, to a change of attitudes toward the dollar at the same time the deficits were being enlarged and, second, to a larger desired stock of physical capital in the United States at the time when capital inflows were rising. Both these factors should have led to a rise in the long-run equilibrium level of the dollar exchange rate—an outcome that has important implications for determining the effects of the deficits on the external sector, as well as the prospective future course of the dollar. If the recent rise of the dollar is not only related to the increase in the deficits but also reflects increases in its long-run real equilibrium level, elimination of the deficit will not completely reverse the recent appreciation of the dollar.

Deficits and the Long-Run Equilibrium Real Exchange Rate. The real exchange rate, Q, is defined as the nominal exchange rate, S, adjusted for the general price levels of the two countries; that is, $Q = S \cdot P/P^*$.

The adjustment by the price levels gives the relative command of the domestic currency over the bundle of goods covered by the price indexes or, put differently, the rate at which one country can trade its output for one unit of the foreign output. In the long run the real exchange rate is determined by real factors, such as relative real per capita income, relative saving rates, the effective tax rates on capital, and the elasticity of imports and exports. In the short run, though, it can fluctuate with nominal shocks.

The long-run *equilibrium* real exchange rate is the rate that would generate a trade balance that could be financed with the service income from a country's net foreign investments. That is, in equilibrium, when a country is a permanent net creditor, the interest payments it receives from abroad must be able to finance a continuous trade deficit without affecting the country's net investment position. In such a case the long-run equilibrium real exchange rate would be higher (as defined above) than if the country were a net debtor and had to generate a current account surplus to service a perpetual foreign debt. Thus, everything else being equal, the larger the average net foreign asset position of the country, the higher will be its long-run real exchange rate.

The effect of a string of structural budget deficits on the long-run equilibrium real exchange rate depends, among other things, on whether the capital inflows that accompany the budget deficits are being used to augment the capital stock or solely to finance higher consumption. If the budget deficits are a result of lower taxes that raise the desired stock of capital, the inflow of capital from abroad will help to attain this higher stock without larger domestic saving. If the budget deficits are a result of higher government transfer payments that raise the level of consumption, however, the capital inflows will only help to maintain previous levels of investment or the existing capital stock. In either case, assuming equal current account deficits, the deterioration of the net foreign investment position (the increase in the foreign debt) of the country will be the same, but the effect of the budget deficits on the long-run equilibrium real exchange rate will not.

In the case when the deficits are the result of higher consumption, the net foreign investment position of the country will be declining in relation to its capital stock; that is, its present valued domestic wealth will be falling. Therefore, the long-run equilibrium real exchange rate (as defined here) will have to fall. In the case when the deficits are the result of tax cuts that spur an increase in the desired capital stock, the effect on the equilibrium real exchange rate is ambiguous. If the internal capital stock is rising faster than the foreign

247

indebtedness, then the average long-run equilibrium real exchange rate will rise. The reason is that when a country increases its desired capital stock, it will generate a higher income in the future. With the higher income the interest on a larger foreign debt can be paid without curtailing future consumption, and the trade surplus needed to service the debt can be generated without a large depreciation of the domestic currency. In contrast, if the capital stock remains unchanged, the future debt servicing could be accomplished only by reducing future consumption in relation to income, which requires a future depreciation of the currency. Thus with a lower capital stock the required future real depreciation of the currency would be larger because a larger proportion of income would have to be diverted to exports.

The recent U.S. deficits have been accompanied by changes in tax policy that raised the desired stock of capital, and thus their overall effect on the long-run equilibrium real exchange rate is unclear. If the present value of the future income that will be generated by the higher stock of capital is greater than the decline in the U.S. net foreign investment position, the long-run equilibrium real exchange rate should be higher, at present, than it was before the policies were adopted. Therefore, some of the recent strength of the dollar could be due to an increase in the long-run equilibrium real exchange rate.

The Recent Real Appreciation of the Dollar. How much of the recent appreciation of the dollar can be attributed to changes in the long-run real exchange rate and how much to the budget deficits? This is an important question that cannot be easily answered. Unfortunately, the lack of a measure for the long-run real equilibrium exchange rate precludes any conclusive results with regard to the nature of the recent rise of the dollar. It cannot be shown with any certainty whether the higher value of the dollar is just a temporary aberration associated with the budget deficits, which cannot be sustained permanently, or whether it also reflects permanent changes in its values. Nevertheless, some tentative inferences can be drawn from the recent joint movements of the real spot rate, the expected future real spot rate, and the real interest rate differentials. Information may be extracted from the concurrent changes in these variables that could, at least, indicate whether an increase in the long-run real value of the dollar has actually occurred.

As noted earlier, the current value of the real exchange rate and its long-run equilibrium value are linked by the long-term real interest rate at home and abroad. As shown in more detail in the appendix, when the real interest rate is higher at home than abroad, the real exchange rate is above its long-run equilibrium level and is expected to depreciate in real terms over time by an amount proportional to the real interest rate differential. Therefore, any change of the current value of the real exchange rate can reflect a change in the real interest differential or a shift in the long-run equilibrium level of the real exchange rate or a combination of both.

To determine which of these two factors was associated with the recent changes in the value of the dollar, long-term interest rates on equally risky assets denominated in the domestic and foreign currencies are needed. Since these rates are not readily available, the analysis in this section relies on the changes in the interest rates payable on one-year Eurodeposits and the changes in the one-year forward exchange rates. Under certain circumstances, the joint movements of the real measures of these variables can yield information similar to that obtained from long-term real interest rates.

Since these variables must be measured in real terms, the nominal values of the changes in the interest rate differentials and the forward rates were adjusted for the expected change in the inflation rate differential. The measure of inflationary expectations used is a simple adaptive scheme based on a monthly moving average, with geometrically declining weights, of the inflation rates over the previous twelve months. The weights start with a 0.2 value for the current monthly observation and decline geometrically to zero within a year. The data are wholesale price indexes for each country. The changes in the forward rates adjusted for expected changes in inflation are used as a proxy for the changes in the expected future real spot rate, although they also capture the changes in the currency risk premium, which in this analysis is assumed to be constant.

The need to rely on proxy measures and simplifying assumptions restricts the analysis to a deductive instead of an inductive inquiry. That is, an explanation for the recent strength of the dollar cannot be obtained directly from the data used: at best, it can only be determined whether one of the two competing factors, deficits or lower taxes on capital, can be excluded as a possible reason responsible for the rise of the dollar. The analysis can be conducted only by following a process of elimination.

The first point to note is that the recent movements of the dollar have been accompanied by similar changes in the expected future real rate of the dollar. As shown in table 9–4, the changes in the nominal spot exchange rate, during the period of floating and the two subperiods shown, have been closely correlated with the movements of the one-year forward rates (line 1) and were mainly changes in the real

TABLE 9–4
CORRELATIONS BETWEEN NOMINAL, REAL SPOT, AND FORWARD EXCHANGE RATES, 1974–1984

Country	1974:2–1984:5[a]	1974:2–1981:4[b]	1981:4–1984:5
United Kingdom			
Correlation between			
1. $\Delta \log (S)$ and $\Delta \log (F)$	.934	.927	.947
2. $\Delta \log (S)$ and $\Delta \log (Q)$	.966	.953	.993
3. $\Delta \log (Q)$ and $\Delta \log (V)$	.893	.875	.929
France			
Correlation between			
1. $\Delta \log (S)$ and $\Delta \log (F)$	.901	.931	.834
2. $\Delta \log (S)$ and $\Delta \log (Q)$	.934	.924	.988
3. $\Delta \log (Q)$ and $\Delta \log (V)$	.822	.836	.809
Germany			
Correlation between			
1. $\Delta \log (S)$ and $\Delta \log (F)$	.971	.970	.970
2. $\Delta \log (S)$ and $\Delta \log (Q)$	.983	.983	.995
3. $\Delta \log (Q)$ and $\Delta \log (V)$	.947	.942	.964
Japan			
Correlation between			
1. $\Delta \log (S)$ and $\Delta \log (F)$	.962	.966	.959
2. $\Delta \log (S)$ and $\Delta \log (Q)$	.980	.975	.990
3. $\Delta \log (Q)$ and $\Delta \log (V)$	.931	.927	.942

NOTE: $\Delta \log (S)$ = the rate of change of the spot exchange rate; $\Delta \log (F)$ = the rate of change of the one-year forward rate; $\Delta \log (Q)$ = the rate of change of the real spot exchange rate; and $\Delta \log (V)$ = the rate of change of the forward rate adjusted for expected change in the relative price levels.
a. For Japan, 1977:2–1984:5.
b. For Japan, 1977:2–1981:4.

SOURCE: International Monetary Fund.

spot rate (line 2). More important, the fluctuations in the real spot rate have been highly correlated with the changes in the expected future real rate (line 3), measured by the forward rate adjusted for expected changes in inflation.

Although the results are sensitive to the method of measuring inflationary expectations and could be biased by the implicit assumption that the currency risk premium is constant, they nevertheless show that the expected future real value of the dollar was consistently revalued upward with the changes in the real spot rate. These concurrent revaluations reflect three possible outcomes: changes in the long-run real value of the dollar, changes in the long-run real interest rate differential, or changes in the expected length of time that it takes for the exchange rates to return to its equilibrium level (see appendix). Because the analysis is based on one-year forward rates, it cannot be concluded that the changes in the expected future real value of the dollar represent possible changes in its long-run real value. One year is too short a period of time in which to expect the real exchange rate to return to its long-run equilibrium level after a fiscal policy shock. Therefore, only if it can be shown that the last two factors were not associated with the comovements of the spot and expected real exchange rates can it be inferred that the recent rise of the dollar reflects mainly an increase in its long-run real value. Such an increase would have resulted mainly from lower rates of taxation on capital and not from the increase in the budget deficits.

A possible simple test of this is produced by the coefficient of the real interest rate differential variable in a regression relating the movements of the real spot rate to the changes in the real interest rates. If the coefficient is large and close to one, it means that most of the changes in the real spot rate were due to changes in the interest rate differentials. This would be inconsistent with the argument that the recent changes of the dollar reflect changes in its long-run equilibrium value. Moreover, if the coefficients remained constant over time, it would indicate that the markets did not change their evaluation of how long it would take for the real exchange rate to return to its long-run equilibrium value.

Regressions relating changes in the real spot rate of the dollar to movements in the real interest rate differential are presented in table 9–5 (the derivation of the equation is shown in the appendix). The interest rates are for one-year Eurodeposits. They are not long-term real interest rates. Therefore, to isolate the effect of the interest rates on the real spot rate, the concurrent movements of the adjusted forward rates were subtracted from both the changes in the real interest rate differential and the real spot rate. This approach was taken to avoid the serious problem of multicolinearity that would have been introduced by including the forward rates as an independent variable in the regression. The information from the identity in equation 2 (and the equations in the appendix) provided a way of avoiding the multicolinearity. By substituting the identity in equation 2 in equation A–1 and rearranging terms, it can be shown that the sum of the two coefficients in the regression for the real interest rate differential and the joint variable $v + \mu$ must add up to one (see note to table 9–5). This

251

TABLE 9-5

REGRESSIONS OF THE RATE OF CHANGE
OF THE REAL SPOT EXCHANGE RATE
ON CHANGES OF THE REAL INTEREST DIFFERENTIALS, 1974–1984

Country	$\hat{a}$	$(1-\hat{a})$	$\bar{R}^2$	Durbin-Watson Statistic	Standard Error of Regression
United Kingdom					
74:2 to 84:5	.21 (7.33)	.79	.30	2.27	1.27
74:2 to 81:4	.24 (7.62)	.76	.40	2.08	1.21
81:4 to 84:5	.11 (1.63)	.89	.06	2.56	1.38
West Germany					
74:2 to 84:5	.11 (4.90)	.89	.15	2.10	.90
74:2 to 81:4	.10 (3.79)	.90	.14	1.84	.89
81:4 to 84:5	.13 (2.89)	.87	.15	2.19	.94
France					
74:2 to 84:5	.31 (9.54)	.69	.42	2.31	1.44
74:2 to 81:4	.28 (8.08)	.72	.43	2.08	1.35
81:4 to 84:5	.36 (5.05)	.64	.39	2.44	1.65
Japan					
77:2 to 84:5	.16 (4.48)	.84	.19	2.32	1.35
77:2 to 81:4	.19 (4.46)	.81	.28	2.14	1.32
81:4 to 84:5	.10 (1.57)	.90	.06	2.61	1.37

NOTE: The coefficients are from the following equation:

$$\ln(Q/Q_{t-1}) \times 1{,}200 = a \{\Delta[(r - E_t(\dot{p}_{t+1}) - (r^* - E_t(\dot{p}^*_{t+1}))] \times 100\}$$
$$+ (1 - a)\left[\ln(V_t/V_{t-1}) - \dot{\mu}\right] \times 1{,}200$$

where Q = the real spot exchange rate and V = the forward real rate. $[r - E_t(\dot{p}_{t+1})]$ and $[r^* - E_t(\dot{p}^*_{t+1})]$ are real interest rates in the United States and the other countries. In running the regression, the equation above was rearranged because of imposed restric-

restriction of the coefficients was then used in running the regressions.

The results, though highly tentative, point to relatively low coefficients for the interest rate variable. The absence of high coefficients that are close to one, along with the apparent changes in coefficients in the 1980s for the United States and Japan, suggests that an increase in the long-run equilibrium value of the dollar, resulting from changes in the taxation of capital, cannot be ruled out as a possible reason for the recent strength of the dollar. The results also indicate that the effects of the changes in the real interest rate differentials on the spot rate were expected to be only partially eliminated within one year. This is not surprising inasmuch as it is commonly believed that these deviations of the real exchange rates from its long-run value will disappear only after two to five years.[8]

Although these results are not conclusive and do not invalidate the argument that the strength of the dollar is related to the budget deficits, they raise doubts about the magnitude of the decline in the dollar that could be expected from a deficit reduction package that did not affect the tax changes instituted in the early 1980s. The commonplace statement that the budget deficits have produced a dollar overvalued by about 30 percent is based on a definition of the long-run equilibrium value of the dollar derived from values that prevailed in the late 1970s. Such statements assume that a return to more normal conditions, such as lower budget deficits, would return the dollar to its earlier values. But the long-run equilibrium level may be higher today than it was before the recent tax changes were introduced; if it is, the fall of the dollar may not be as large as widely expected.

Nevertheless, the analysis of joint movements of interest rates and the exchange rate offers no strong support for any of the alternative explanations for the recent rise of the dollar. The burden of proof still lies with those who would assert that the deficits have not been the main reason for the rise of the exchange rate.

Recent Evidence on the Exchange Rate—Current Account Link. Another issue is whether the recent economic performance of the United

---

tion on the sum of the parameters. The actual regression used to derive the coefficient for the real interest rate differential was

$$\left[\ln(Q_t/Q_{t-1}) - \ln(V_t/V_{t-1}) + \dot{\mu}\right] \times 1,200$$

$$= a \left\{\Delta\left[(r - E_t(\dot{p}_{t+1}) - (r^* - E_t(\dot{p}^*_{t+1}))\right] \times 100 - \left[\ln(V_t/V_{t-1}) + \dot{\mu}\right] \times 1,200\right\}$$

SOURCE: International Monetary Fund and Morgan Guaranty Trust.

States in relation to its main trading partners is mainly responsible for the deterioration of our trade balance. This argument has recently been made to downgrade the possible contribution of the appreciation of the dollar to the increase in our trade deficit and to question the validity of the conventional view. The assertion that relative income growth has played an important role in shaping the course of the trade balance cannot be dismissed, since it is a long-established proposition in economics that income is one of the main determinants of trade activity.

To test the validity of this argument, it is necessary to estimate the net effect of the recent appreciation of the dollar on the decline of the trade balance and compare it with the estimated contribution of relative income growth. A method of obtaining such measures is to estimate export and import equations and generate in-sample simulations. Although this may not be the most satisfactory method, it does shed some light on the magnitudes involved.

Table 9–6 presents estimates of total export and import equations for the United States from the first quarter of 1971 to the third quarter of 1983. The data cover exports from the United States to sixteen industrial countries and imports from those countries. The specification differs slightly from more standard regressions in that a weighted value for the real exchange rate is used instead of a direct measure of relative prices. This directly tests the effect of the exchange rate on imports and exports. The measures of income used are real gross domestic product for the United States and the sixteen other countries. The foreign income figure is an aggregate measure of GDPs weighted by import shares. It is measured as a deviation of income from its trend, used as a proxy for capacity utilization.

As expected, both incomes and the real exchange rate are significant explanatory variables of exports and imports. An increase in the real exchange rate of 1 percent leads to an estimated total increase in real imports after two years of 1.5 percent and a decline in real exports of 0.67 percent over the same period. An increase in GDP of 1 percent in the United States and abroad will worsen the U.S. trade deficit, but only slightly. This result would of course be exacerbated by a higher growth rate at home.

To test the effect of the recent real appreciation of the dollar on the deterioration of the trade deficit, an in-sample simulation was carried out. The value of the real exchange rate was held constant, at its 1980 average value, for the period from the first quarter of 1981 to the end of 1983, and the simulated results were compared with the predicted values from the original regression. The simulation results (not shown in the table) indicate that, if the dollar had remained at its

TABLE 9-6
REGRESSION EQUATIONS FOR IMPORTS AND EXPORTS, 1971:I-1983:III

Import Equation[a]
Independent Variables

	Constant	$\sum_{t=1}^{8} \log\left(\text{weighted real exchange rate}\right)_t$[b]	$\log\left(\text{real GDP}_{US}\right)$	$\log\left(\dfrac{\text{aggregate GDP}/}{\text{trend GDP}}\right)$[c]	rho	$\bar{R}^2$	DW	SSE
Coefficients	-6.91	1.49	1.00	2.68	0.35	.75	2.17	.054
t-value	(-4.69)	(6.32)	(6.75)	(2.73)	(2.27)			

Export Equation[d]
Independent Variables

	Constant	$\sum_{t=1}^{8} \log\left(\text{weighted real exchange rate}\right)_t$	$\log\left(\text{aggregate real GDP}\right)$	$\log\left(\dfrac{\text{real GDP}_{US}/}{\text{trend GDP}_{US}}\right)$[e]		$\bar{R}^2$	DW	SSE
Coefficients	3.18	-0.68	0.97	0.74		.84	2.09	.061
t-value	(2.69)	(-4.38)	(6.61)	(1.27)				

a. The dependent variable is an index of the real value of U.S. imports from the sixteen industrial countries used in the aggregate GDP figure.
b. The exchange rate variable is the natural logarithm of the weighted real exchange rate compiled by the IMF. It is the real multilateral exchange rate model MERM measure reported on line L 63 ey 110. The coefficient is the sum of an eight-term second-degree polynomial lag structure without restrictions.
c. The variable (aggregate real GDP/trend GDP) is a proxy for excess capacity abroad. The aggregate measure was obtained by using import weights. The coefficient captures the supply elasticity of foreign export to the United States.
d. The dependent variable is an index of the real value of the U.S. exports from sixteen industrial countries used in the aggregate GDP figures.
e. The variable (real GDP$_{US}$/trend GDP$_{US}$) is a proxy for excess capacity in the United States. Its coefficient measures the supply elasticity of U.S. exports.

SOURCE: International Monetary Fund.

1980 value for the past few years, real imports would have been 27 percent below and real exports 16 percent above their predicted levels by the end of 1983. This would dramatically have reduced the U.S. trade deficit, measured in real terms. These results would have been even more pronounced if figures for 1984 had been available when the regressions were run. The assertion that the recent appreciation of the dollar is not largely responsible for the deterioration of the current account deficit does not seem, therefore, to be supported by these rough estimates. The decline in U.S. exports and the rise of imports can be traced mainly to the strength of the dollar.

Sectoral Influences

The emphasis on the macroeconomic effects of the budget deficits conceals the fact that the effect of the real appreciation of the dollar has not been uniform across all sectors of the economy. Certain industries have been affected much more than others, mainly because of their greater dependency on the external sector or, more specifically, their reliance on foreign markets for income or on foreign sources for their inputs.

In a system of flexible exchange rates, budget deficits, instead of crowding out investment, crowd out those sectors that compete directly with imports or depend heavily on exports. That is, deficits adversely affect those sectors sensitive to exchange rate movements more than those that are sensitive to changes in interest rates. As a consequence the recent budget deficits have placed several U.S. industries under international competitive pressures unmatched in postwar history. These pressures have led to a loss of markets and in some instances to a decline in real wages and in the return on capital. Some industries have adapted to the new environment much faster than others, by curtailing operations and by instituting new measures to enhance productivity.

A review of the recent performance of key industries of the U.S. economy shows that some characteristics, such as import penetration ratios, which are used as proxies for the degree of foreign competition, contributed to determining the relative magnitude of the losses suffered by different industries, while other developments, such as movements of real compensation per employee adjusted for productivity changes, may have averted even further losses of market shares worldwide.

The total volume of U.S. imports rose 51 percent from the beginning of 1980 to the middle of 1984 while the real volume of exports declined by 12 percent. The decline in U.S. exports was accompanied by a decline in total world exports, so that the U.S. share remained relatively constant. The ratio of imports to GNP in the United States rose from 7.7 percent to approximately 10.2 percent. These changes show that sectors highly dependent on exports may not have been as adversely affected as sectors that face strong foreign competition.

Sectoral evidence seems to provide further support for this assertion. As shown in table 9-7, industries with the highest ratio of imports to apparent consumption experienced the largest proportional decline in the ratio of exports to shipments.[9] Even before the recent appreciation of the dollar, two of the industries analyzed—primary metals and apparels—faced strong competition from abroad. As a result of recent developments, American producers in those industries not only have faced even stronger competitive pressures at home, with rising import penetration, but also have lost revenues from foreign markets.

Industries that were initially highly dependent on export earnings for revenues have not lost as large a share of export revenues as import-competing industries. Both the agricultural and the machinery industries have been adversely affected by recent developments, but not as much as textiles or transportation equipment. Apparently initial market dominance and perhaps product differentiation have lessened the effect of the real appreciation of the dollar on those industries.

It is misleading, however, to interpret changes in export revenues or import shares as showing the effect of a budget deficit or, more specifically, an exchange rate appreciation on these industries. Specific developments in each industry are also very important, particularly movements in real wages. The response of wage patterns to an appreciation of the currency, for example, can also determine the degree of competitiveness as well as the unemployment experienced in each industry and to some extent unemployment in the economy as a whole.

The reason is that an appreciation of the exchange rate reduces the home price of imports and raises the foreign currency price of exports. As a result, domestic producers of traded goods (of import-competing and export goods), in order to maintain their market shares and to remain competitive, must lower the dollar prices of their products. The lower prices in turn will reduce the demand for labor in those industries if wages do not fall proportionally, since a rise in the product wage (the money wage deflated by the price of the good) in relation to labor productivity decreases profitability and signals the need to shift resources elsewhere. The only way, therefore, of retaining market shares and avoiding the loss of employment, would be

TABLE 9-7

RATIOS OF EXPORTS TO SHIPMENTS AND OF IMPORTS TO APPARENT CONSUMPTION, BY INDUSTRY, 1979–1983
(percent)

Industry	1979	1980	1981	1982	1983
Agricultural, forestry, and fishery products					
Exports[a]	31.650	39.186	34.798	30.976	35.736
Imports	16.341	18.408	14.770	14.467	18.700
Mineral commodities, including petroleum					
Exports[a]	9.268	8.682	6.910	6.890	5.495
Imports	46.924	44.640	36.239	31.555	29.091
Textile mill products					
Exports[a]	14.045	16.691	14.640	11.527	8.902
Imports	12.250	14.007	15.386	13.972	13.658
Apparel and related products					
Exports[a]	9.041	9.743	9.054	6.930	5.533
Imports	29.323	30.364	31.844	33.073	34.222
Chemicals and allied products					
Exports	11.724	12.730	11.883	11.593	10.397
Imports	4.398	4.619	4.672	4.775	5.321

Primary metal products					
Exports[a]	21.571	25.949	17.836	15.315	13.245
Imports	30.853	35.473	33.611	35.757	33.797
Fabricated metal products					
Exports	5.040	5.908	6.398	6.793	5.672
Imports	3.741	3.833	4.145	4.656	4.498
Machinery, except electrical					
Exports	17.482	20.518	21.097	21.528	19.116
Imports	8.450	8.793	9.208	10.228	11.607
Electrical and electronic machinery					
Exports	11.359	12.338	12.876	12.874	11.612
Imports	11.276	11.737	13.143	14.081	15.214
Transportation equipment					
Exports	12.934	15.671	16.199	15.222	12.811
Imports	13.126	15.980	16.147	17.743	16.539

NOTE: Apparent consumption is defined as shipments (or GDP) plus the change in inventories minus net exports.

a. GDP used instead of shipments.

SOURCE: Department of Commerce, Bureau of the Census.

through a decline in the product wage.

The fall in the product wage means that workers would lose purchasing power, since the prices of other goods would not have declined as much as the price of traded goods. This industrywide loss cannot be avoided, because if wages do not fall, the employment levels in the industry cannot be preserved without significant changes in labor productivity. Therefore, either the loss is shared by all workers through a reduction of the product wage, or it is going to be borne by the few who become unemployed. The degree and the duration of unemployment depend on the degree and the durability of wage rigidity and factor immobility in the economy as a whole and in those industries in particular. If workers from the declining industries can be easily absorbed in other industries, overall employment would not be affected. It is therefore incorrect to assert that the real appreciation of the dollar itself has led to an export of U.S. jobs, since real wage adjustments and greater factor mobility could ensure the maintenance of existing employment levels.

Table 9–8 presents indexes of real compensation per full-time-equivalent employee for the same manufacturing industries as in table 9–7, adjusted for changes in average productivity in each industry during the period 1974–1981. The objective is to find whether patterns in real wage adjustments have been associated with losses of export market shares or increased import penetration.These figures are preliminary and should be viewed with caution given the nature of the data available. Furthermore, the productivity of many of these industries may have changed substantially since 1981; if it has, the figures for 1982 and 1983, which are based on the assumption that their productivity growth remained at the previous average value, may be biased.

The results show no systematic relation between the loss of market share or the increase in import penetration, shown in table 9–7, and the movement of real compensation. On one hand, the only industries where the loss of market shares appears to have been exacerbated by the higher real wages are primary metals and machinery. On the other hand, only in the chemical and transportation equipment industries has the loss of market shares been lessened by a decline in real wages. This divergent sectoral response means that, as observed, unemployment in certain sectors has been more pronounced than in others and that the reallocation of resources in the United States is occurring faster than it would otherwise.

The shift of labor and capital and the restructuring of the U.S. economy now underway are a significant result of the current U.S. fiscal policy. The recent strength of the dollar has accelerated some

TABLE 9-8

INDEX OF REAL PRODUCT WAGES, ADJUSTED FOR PRODUCTIVITY CHANGES, 1979–1983

Industry	1979	1980	1981	1982	1983
Textile mill products	1.000	1.033	1.010	1.019	1.041
Apparel and related products	1.000	1.012	0.987	0.938	0.941
Chemicals and allied products	1.000	0.984	0.942	0.921	0.957
Primary metal products	1.000	0.996	1.014	1.051	1.095
Fabricated metal products	1.000	0.999	0.993	1.000	1.060
Machinery, except electrical	1.000	1.010	1.040	1.058	1.118
Electrical and electronic machinery	1.000	1.003	1.002	1.034	1.049
Transportation equipment	1.000	1.044	0.975	0.944	0.975

NOTE: Total real compensation divided by number of full-time-equivalent employees. This is divided by the index of productivity for the various industries. The index is an extrapolation of the average productivity performance for each industry for the period 1973–1981.

SOURCE: Department of Commerce.

long-run structural adjustments that would have occurred anyway, albeit more slowly. The acceleration of these adjustments has made the transition period more difficult and has led to increased calls for protection, which have placed severe strains on our trade relations with other countries.

Moreover, the recent strength of the dollar may also be distorting investment decisions in the United States because of the diminished profitability of export and import-competing industries. The uncertainty about the future course of the dollar makes investors shy away from those industries and invest instead in nontradable service industries. This allocation of capital may not be as efficient as it would be if the dollar were closer to its long-run equilibrium real value. Conceivably, if the dollar declines, a partial reversal of the adjustments now taking place will have to occur. Such a reversal would once again raise the cost of the long-run structural adjustment of the U.S. economy.

Structural and Cyclical Deficits and Their Effects Abroad

In addition to their effects on the U.S. economy, the recent U.S. budget deficits have influenced economic developments abroad. In fact, much of the recent debate over the deficits has revolved around the issue of their net effect on foreign economies. As our demand for foreign goods has increased and our current account widened, many questions have been raised about the contribution of this increased demand to aggregate output abroad, since it has been accompanied by higher real interest rates worldwide and by an inflow of foreign capital into the United States.

Much of the debate has been based on generalizations that do not seem well supported by the available data. This is particularly true of the assertion that recent U.S. budget deficits were crowding out investments in Europe or Japan. This outcome was only marginally evident until the end of 1983, probably because most of the net effect of the U.S. deficits up to that time reflected differences in cyclical variations.

To understand the net effect of the recent U.S. deficits, we must distinguish between their cyclical and structural components, since each will have a different effect on economies abroad. Cyclical fluctuations tend to be important in generating deficits and have accounted for the largest portion of U.S. budget deficits during the postwar period. Even in the early 1980s the cyclical component remained relatively high because of back-to-back recessions and a generally stagnant level of income from 1980 till 1983.

The effect of cyclical deficits on the external sector of the economy is highly dependent on the phase of the cycle, the degree to which cycles are coordinated across countries, and the relevant income elasticities of such variables as government expenditures, taxes, savings, investment, the demand for money, and imports and exports. In a world where all economies have synchronous cycles and similar propensities to spend, tax, and import, there would be little discernible net external effect of a cyclical budget deficit. A decline in income worldwide would generate deficits of similar relative sizes abroad, which would create offsetting pressures in the financial markets. Relative interest rates and exchange rates would not change. Conversely, with an increased divergence between cyclical movements or a greater difference in income elasticities, the apparent net effect of a cyclical deficit on the external sector will be more pronounced.

Of course, the world economy is not synchronized with that of the United States, and the elasticities of imports and exports as well as the marginal propensities to save and invest are quite different among countries. It therefore becomes very difficult to predict the net effect of the U.S. deficits.

Several facts, however, might provide a guide to the direction of some of these effects. During the 1980s, for example, cyclical fluctuations have been more pronounced in the United States than in the other countries of the Organization for Economic Cooperation and Development (OECD). This has meant that a large part of the variation of U.S. deficits can be attributed to income movements. According to OECD estimates, "automatic stabilizing expenditures" were responsible for 42 percent of the deficit for 1982, or 1.6 percent of GNP, while the average for the other seven major OECD countries was approximately 30 percent, or 1.2 percent of their combined GNP. With the faster economic recovery in the United States than elsewhere, the automatic stabilizers were expected to be greatly reduced in the United States for 1984—actually to turn into a small surplus. But the automatic stabilizers still account for close to 13 percent of the deficits of other major OECD countries.

In relative terms, then, the cyclical deficits in the United States have been substantially reduced during the 1983–1984 recovery. This outcome may have had a positive effect abroad, since it has increased the marginal propensity to import by shifting the composition of spending toward foreign goods. The shift occurred because government consumption or the consumption of those receiving transfer payments during a recession is biased toward domestic goods. Although many other factors influence the composition of spending, in the recent cycle the marginal propensity to import declined from 1980 to 1982 (from 0.17 to −0.16) along with the U.S. economy, and by the first quarter of 1984 it had risen back to 0.30.

The major source of contention is not the cyclical component of the U.S. budget deficits, however, but the rise in the structural component. There are valid concerns that the positive effects abroad of an increase in the U.S. current account deficits are being offset by the inflationary pressures of a higher dollar and the contractionary effect of the propagation of higher U.S. real interest rates abroad.

It cannot be argued that exchange rate movements do not affect the inflation rate in the short run. Several empirical studies have shown a positive correlation, as would be expected.[10] The exchange rate is a relative price, however, and over the long run governments that allow it to float freely should be able to follow a relatively independent monetary policy and decouple their price level from any permanent effect of an exchange rate depreciation. The contractionary effects in the short run usually arise from the attempt of foreign monetary authorities to support their currency against depreciation. Such a policy invariably trades off short-run inflation for higher interest rates, which simply delay the flight of physical capital that will occur as long as real interest are higher in the United States than abroad.

Thus the argument that higher real interest rates in the United States lead to similar changes abroad and therefore depress investment and other economic activity there as well should also be viewed in the context of an attempt by the authorities to prevent the flight of capital from their countries, either through exchange controls or through tighter monetary policy. These short-run monetary responses abroad could be the reason for the high correlation among the changes in the short-term real interest rates in the United States and those abroad, as recently shown by Cumby and Mushkin.[11]

If real interest rates are depressing economic activity abroad and the higher dollar is working in the opposite direction, we should observe an increase in the contribution of exports to economic growth along with a declining contribution of investment, which is usually the most interest-elastic component of GNP. As shown in table 9–9, such a pattern is not wholly evident. In fact, it is apparent only in Japan, where it is consistent with the significant flows of capital to the United States from Japan. In none of the other countries has the ratio of investment to growth consistently declined, except cyclically, when the share of exports, or net exports, has increased over the period analyzed. A shift in the regional structure of exports seems to be taking place, the United States taking a larger share of the increased exports. But these are not dramatic shifts that reveal a clear effect of U.S. policies. These data offer no conclusive evidence on the net effect of the U.S. deficits on other countries, particularly in Europe. Prelimi-

TABLE 9-9
PART OF THE CHANGE OF GNP OR GDP ATTRIBUTABLE TO CHANGES IN INVESTMENT OR EXPORTS, 1970–1983
(percent)

Country	1970	1975	1980	1981	1982	1983
United Kingdom						
Gross capital investment	16.0	4.0	-3.0	-5.7	24.4	14.0
Total net capital investment	4.1	-7.4	-17.4	-15.5	11.9	5.7
Exports to the world	16.9	15.1	19.9	14.6	19.1	20.0
Exports to the United States	0.8	0.0	1.6	6.9	5.2	3.6
Net exports to the world	0.6	10.7	11.6	9.3	-5.5	-16.3
Net exports to the United States	-0.2	-0.4	-1.8	6.6	2.7	0.1
France						
Gross capital investment	26.2	-4.1	27.8	1.6	17.1	12.6
Total net capital investment	7.4	-18.7	12.8	-13.5	4.1	0.8
Exports to the world	25.7	3.0	18.9	25.8	12.5	23.9
Exports to the United States	1.3	-1.2	0.1	2.8	0.9	2.5
Net exports to the world	6.9	16.2	-16.2	0.2	-10.1	12.3
Net exports to the United States	-2.3	0.1	3.2	0.4	-0.5	1.9

(Table continues)

265

TABLE 9-9 (Continued)

Country	1970	1975	1980	1981	1982	1983
Germany						
Gross capital investment	38.7	-34.2	26.2	-30.3	-5.4	12.9
Total net capital investment	26.0	-56.1	7.3	-54.9	-26.7	-1.4
Exports to the world	13.5	-21.2	38.9	81.7	54.7	6.2
Exports to the United States	0.9	-9.8	0.8	7.8	3.9	6.2
Net exports to the world	-0.2	-31.0	-15.0	32.3	42.7	-12.4
Net exports to the United States	-1.3	-10.4	-5.2	3.0	4.4	6.9
Japan						
Gross capital investment	47.1	-11.3	29.2	16.4	5.3	-11.7
Total net capital investment	33.9	-20.7	13.2	-2.5	-18.0	n.a.
Exports to the world	10.8	2.3	42.3	23.7	8.4	4.4
Exports to the United States	3.2	-3.2	8.5	8.3	4.1	12.1
Net exports to the world	-1.7	9.2	-4.8	27.0	1.5	31.9
Net exports to the United States	-1.5	-1.3	1.9	8.3	0.6	13.4

n.a. = not available.

NOTE: Change in component/change in GNP/GDP, in local currency.

SOURCE: OECD, *National Income Accounts*, 1982, and Department of Commerce.

nary figures for exports in 1984 show a more pronounced change in European exports to the United States, but more time and data are needed to clarify the possible newly emerging trends.

One reason for the absence, to the end of 1983 at least, of a significant increase in European exports to the United States or of a decline in European investment at a time when there have been large capital inflows to the United States is that most of the shift in the U.S. current account did not occur with respect to Europe. It is misleading to draw inferences about the regional effects of current U.S. policies simply by looking at the overall U.S. current account deficit, since the increased demand associated with it has not been evenly divided among countries or regions. A bilateral analysis of the U.S. current account shows a fairly significant deterioration of our external balance with Latin America, and less so vis-à-vis Europe.

As shown in table 9–10, the shift of the U.S. current account from a $6.3 billion surplus in 1981 to a $41.6 billion deficit in 1983 has not been evenly distributed. Approximately 33 percent of this shift can be attributed to Western Europe. Japan has accounted for only 9 percent of our total current account change, Canada for 14 percent. The greatest change has occurred with respect to Latin America: 59 percent of the change in our overall current account balance is due to a shift of our current account balance with the region from a surplus of $20.1 billion in 1981 to a deficit of $8.2 billion in 1983. This reflects not only the weak economic conditions in Latin America, which have reduced its imports from the United States by $13 billion over the period, but also a change in the regional composition of U.S. imports, with Latin America now providing a larger share of our imports than in 1981.

A slightly different picture emerges with net capital flows. The largest recorded shift occurred in our accounts with Europe. But still, a significant share of the change in foreign capital flowing into the United States is due to a shift in capital transactions with Latin America. In 1981 the United States was a net exporter of capital to Latin America, and by 1983 that condition was dramatically reversed. This reversal reflects a retrenchment of lending to the region by U.S. banks and apparently a flight of capital due to political and economic instability there.

It is not surprising that the U.S. budget deficits have had a smaller effect on European economies than on other regions of the world. Most of the shift in U.S. trading patterns and a significant shift in the capital transactions have been with Latin America. But these trends must be reversed if the United States is to secure financing for its large current account deficits. Its growing indebtedness cannot be accommodated by capital flows from other regions of the world and

TABLE 9-10

U.S. CURRENT ACCOUNT, NET CAPITAL FLOWS, AND STATISTICAL DISCREPANCY, SELECTED COUNTRIES, 1981-1984

(billions of dollars)

	1981			1982			1983			1984:I		
	CA	NK	D	CA	NK	D	CA	NK	D	CA	NK	D
Western Europe	9.7	-13.8	4.1	3.1	1.7	-4.8	-6.4	28.9	-22.5	-11.7	11.7	0
United Kingdom	3.9	-7.4	3.6	-0.8	-0.4	1.2	-2.0	17.3	-15.3	-1.8	5.6	-3.9
West Germany	-4.2	-4.9	9.1	-5.9	1.6	4.3	-9.6	2.8	6.8	n.a.	n.a.	n.a.
France	1.1	-0.3	-0.9	1.8	-3.4	1.6	-0.2	1.2	-1.1	n.a.	n.a.	n.a.
Japan	-13.9	4.3	9.6	-15.5	-4.5	20.0	-18.3	3.7	14.7	-15.4	5.2	10.2
Canada	7.2	-5.0	-2.1	0.1	-0.2	0.1	0.6	-1.5	1.0	-0.8	-0.3	1.2
Latin America	20.1	-12.6	-7.5	8.0	-15.5	7.5	-8.2	16.7	-8.5	-7.6	14.3	-6.7
Rest of the world	-16.8	-2.6	18.2	-4.9	-5.2	10.1	-9.3	-15.6	24.6	-7.2	-7.7	14.9
Total	6.3	-29.7	-22.3	-9.2	-23.7	32.9	-41.6	32.2	9.3	-42.7	23.2	19.6

n.a. = not available.

NOTE: CA = current account; NK = net capital flows (− means outflow); and D = statistical discrepancy.

SOURCE: *Survey of International Business*, June 1984 and September 1984, tables 10–10A.

will have to draw more heavily on European and Japanese capital. Therefore, the key issues are the extent to which, and how long, savers in these countries are able and will be willing to absorb dollar liabilities into their portfolios.

The Foreign Financial Constraint

As noted in the discussion of the long-run effect of budget deficits, structural deficits constitute a transfer of future income to the present generation. As such they require a transfer of wealth, which can be carried out in many ways. Two methods of effecting the transfer are selling existing wealth abroad and incurring liabilities to (borrowing from) foreigners. The latter can be used indefinitely only if foreign savers are able and willing continually to extend credit to domestic residents.

Thus the crucial question is, How long can the current budget deficits of the United States continue to be financed by foreign residents before the risk premium they demand for holding additional dollar assets rises to levels that make it unattractive for U.S. residents to incur any more foreign debt? That is, how soon will they demand a rate of return on dollar assets that will reduce present consumption in the United States and generate sufficient domestic savings to finance the budget deficits internally?

A correct answer to this question is difficult to obtain since it depends on evaluating the rate at which U.S. foreign indebtedness is expected to occur, the available pool of world savings, and the preferences of foreign savers for their own assets.

The United States has so far been able to finance its budget deficits without major difficulties by relying on foreign savings. This pattern of financing means that its net foreign investment position must be deteriorating. As shown in table 9–11, the net foreign asset position of the United States in the first quarter of 1984 was still a positive $81 billion. Even though it has deteriorated sharply since reaching a peak of $149.5 billion in 1981, the United States remained a net creditor in the middle of 1984. But, according to projected current account balances, or given the current trend, this position shifts to net debtor by the first half of 1985.

In public discussions this deterioration is usually associated with the notion that foreign residents are buying Treasury securities. But a look at the figures shows that outright purchase of securities is not the main item in the rise in foreign assets in the United States. The increase in direct investment by foreign residents has been larger than the increase in the holding of Treasury securities. And the largest

269

TABLE 9-11
U.S. Net International Investment Position, 1979–1984
(billions of dollars)

	1979	1980	1981	1982	1983	1984:II
Net investment position	94.5	106.1	143.1	149.5	106.0	81.1
U.S. holdings of assets abroad	510.6	606.9	719.6	838.1	887.4	914.3
U.S. private assets	433.2	516.6	621.1	729.8	774.4	796.8
Direct investment abroad	187.9	215.4	228.3	221.5	226.1	227.7
U.S. claims by U.S. banks	157.0	203.9	293.5	404.6	430.0	452.2
Foreign holdings of assets in the United States	416.1	500.8	576.5	688.6	781.5	833.2
Private foreign assets	256.3	324.7	396.0	499.6	587.6	642.5
Direct investment in the United States	54.5	83.0	106.2	121.9	133.5	143.6
U.S. Treasury securities	14.2	16.1	18.5	25.8	33.9	41.8
Liabilities of U.S. banks	110.3	121.1	165.4	231.3	280.3	310.8

NOTE: Year-end figures except for 1984, which covers the first half of 1984 (1984:I + 1984:II).
SOURCE: *Survey of Current Business*, vol. 6 (June 1984) and vol. 9 (September 1984), table 1.

share of the increase in foreign assets is accounted by the rise in the liabilities of U.S. banks. That means that bank deposits, a portion of which are backed by the holding of a U.S. Treasury security, have been the means most frequently used to finance the U.S. deficits.

Looking at both sides of the ledger, we find that in addition to taking in more deposits from abroad, U.S. banks have severely curtailed their lending to foreign residents. As shown in table 9–12, the largest change in capital flows occurred as a result of the decline in annual lending by U.S. banks from a high of $111.1 billion in 1981 to $22 billion in the first half of 1984. This shift, along with the increase in banks' liabilities, more than explains the change in the U.S. net investment position over the past two years.

The shift of bank lending away from foreign and toward domestic loans, as well as the growing acquisition by foreigners of U.S. deposits, signifies a reversal with important implications for the future. The rate at which claims of U.S. banks abroad can be reduced is not known, particularly since most of them are loans to developing countries that are not well positioned to pay the principal. Little room may be available, therefore, to finance current account deficits by drawing down on U.S. loans abroad. This leaves the acquisition of liabilities as the main source of financing, and that means a greater reliance on foreign residents to acquire dollar deposits and a growing role for the international banking system.

The ability and willingness of foreign residents to purchase dollar-denominated assets depends heavily on world saving. Although measures of world saving are not readily available, some inferences about their relative magnitudes can be obtained. The net private saving of the largest OECD countries amounted to roughly $595 billion in 1982 according to the latest available information. These countries account for approximately 70 percent of total income; one can extrapolate that, assuming the marginal propensity to save is the same elsewhere as in the OECD, the available saving worldwide was about $850 billion in 1982. Since 1982 was a recession year and those countries are now expanding, saving today should be even larger. On the assumption that saving has grown by 10 percent since then, to roughly $935 billion in 1984 and that U.S. net private saving was approximately 20 percent of that, the current account deficits of the United States absorbed over 12 percent of total foreign net private saving. This compares with approximately 5 percent for 1983.

This allocation of world financial assets means that dollar-denominated assets are a growing component of financial portfolios. Even though we do not have measures of total net worth abroad, we know that recorded foreign holdings of dollar assets in 1983 were $781 bil-

TABLE 9-12
NET FLOWS OF CAPITAL, 1980–1984
(billions of dollars)

	1980	1981	1982	1983	1984:II
U.S. holdings of assets abroad	86.1	111.0	118.9	49.5	26.9
U.S. government assets and official reserves	13.4	10.3	11.1	6.2	4.5
U.S. private assets	72.8	100.7	107.8	43.3	22.4
Direct investment abroad	19.2	9.6	-4.8	4.9	1.6
Foreign securities	3.6	5.7	8.1	7.7	0.2
U.S. claims by nonbanks	3.2	1.2	-6.6	5.3	n.a.
U.S. claims by U.S. banks	46.8	84.2	111.1	25.4	22.2
Foreign holdings of assets in the United States	58.1	81.3	95.2	81.7	51.7
Foreign official assets	15.5	5.0	3.3	5.3	-3.4
Other foreign assets	42.6	76.3	91.9	76.4	54.9
Direct investment in the United States	16.9	23.1	14.9	11.3	10.1
U.S. securities other than Treasury securities	5.5	7.2	6.4	8.6	2.1
U.S. Treasury securities	2.6	2.9	7.1	8.7	7.9
Liabilities of U.S. nonbanking concerns	6.9	0.9	-2.4	-1.3	n.a.
Liabilities of U.S. banks	10.7	42.1	66.0	49.1	30.5

n.a. = not available.

NOTE: Year-end figures except for 1984, which covers the first half of 1984 (1984:I + 1984:II).

SOURCE: *Survey of Current Business*, vol. 6 (June 1984) and vol. 9 (September 1984), table 1.

lion, excluding net holdings of dollars by foreigners in the Eurodollar markets. In all likelihood these holdings constitute less than 10 percent of foreign wealth, on the assumption that the net worth of U.S. households, which was about $11.1 trillion in 1983, constitutes approximately 48 percent of the world's total wealth, as it did in 1979.[12]

Since foreign residents will always want to hold a portion of their wealth in domestically denominated assets, there is a point beyond which additional dollar assets will be held only if their relative yield continues to increase. The current proportional holdings of about 10 percent may not seem excessive, particularly if the current anti-inflationary policy of the United States is sustained. But a growing share of dollar assets in foreign portfolios ensures that sometime in the future a point of relative saturation will be reached, which will mean higher interest rates on dollar financial assets. Unfortunately, this point of saturation cannot be precisely determined.

Concluding Remarks

The impact of the recent budget deficits of the United States on the external sector has been significant and in line with standard economic theory. The deficits have adversely affected the export and import-competing industries, instead of crowding out domestic investment, and have been partially financed by an inflow of foreign capital. Although the budget deficits are expected to persist in the future unless there are major policy changes, the foreign capital inflow cannot continue. This would require a growing foreign indebtness by the United States that is not sustainable.

At this early stage of the large deficits, it is not yet clear how far the United States can go into debt. The lack of historical precedents, the relative size of the U.S. economy, and its future outlook make it difficult to determine the borrowing capacity of the United States. So far the current account deficits have been financed without any major financial disruptions. In fact, the absorption of foreign savings by the United States has not dramatically altered the relative size of dollar holdings in foreign portfolios. The rate at which the net foreign investment position of the United States is deteriorating, however, indicates that by the end of 1985 the United States will be the largest foreign debtor nation in the world. The wealth effects and the financial pressures resulting from the continuation of these trends ensure that at some point in the future the dollar will have to fall below its average long-run equilibrium level. This fall, however, may not be as large as expected by those who base their calculations of an equilibrium dollar on values that prevailed in the late 1970s. It is possible that the recent changes in the taxation of capital have led to an increase in the average long-run equilibrium value of the dollar.

Unless there is a sharp reversal of policies, particularly monetary policy, there is no reason to expect, at the beginning of 1985, a sharp decline of the dollar. One important factor contributing to the greater willingness of foreigners to hold dollar financial assets has been the anti-inflationary posture of the Federal Reserve. One factor that could expedite the fall of the dollar, however, is the failure to deal with the deficits in the coming fiscal year. It is generally perceived that 1985 is one of the most favorable political periods to institute policy changes that would place projected deficits on a more stable path. A political stalemate and a lack of progress could lead financial markets to reevaluate the future borrowing needs of the U.S. government and demand higher risk premiums for holding additional dollars.

Appendix

The Link between the Current Real Exchange Rate and Its Long-Run Equilibrium Value. The simple relation between the current real exchange rate and its long-run equilibrium level is shown in the figure below.

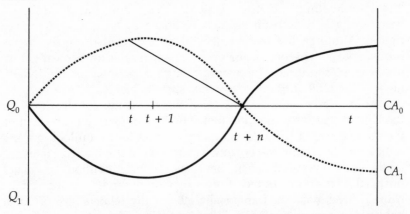

Also shown are the associated movements of the current account balance. The horizontal axis measures time and the vertical axis the current account on the right-hand side and the real exchange rate on the left-hand side. A balanced current account is shown by the line CA_0, and the equivalent long-run real exchange rate that would yield a balanced current account by the line Q_0. When the current account is in deficit, as shown at time t by the value CA_1, the real exchange rate will be above its long-run average, as shown by Q_1.

The figure also helps to show that at time t the real exchange rate is expected to return to its long-run equilibrium at time $t + n$, when the current account is expected to be in balance. As noted earlier, the expected real depreciation is equal to the current real interest rate differential. Thus any change in the real interest rate differential may affect the expected real exchange rate for $t + 1$—a year hence—even though the long-run rate has not changed. Similarly, any reevaluation of the necessary change in the real exchange rate that would bring about a balanced current account would also change the expected Q for $t + 1$. Finally, any change in the long-run equilibrium real exchange rate would also bring about changes in the expected Q.

Derivation of Equation Used for Regression in Table 9–5. Starting with equation 2 from the text and subtracting the expected inflation differentials from both sides, we can rewrite (2) as:

$$s - f - \left[E_t \left(\dot{p}_{t+1} \right) - E_t \left(\dot{p}^*_{t+1} \right) \right]$$

$$= \left[r - E_t \left(\dot{p}_{t+1} \right) \right] - \left[r^* - E_t \left(\dot{p}^*_{t+1} \right) \right] - \mu \tag{A-1}$$

where E is the expected operator. Since

$$E_t \left(\dot{p}_{t+1} \right) = E_t \left(p_{t+1} \right) - p_t \tag{A-2}$$

we can substitute (A–2) in the left-hand side of equation A–1 to obtain

$$s + (p - p^*) - \left[f + E_t \left(p_{t+1} \right) - E_t \left(p^*_{t+1} \right) \right]$$

$$= \left[r - E_t \left(\dot{p}_{t+1} \right) \right] - \left[r^* - E_t \left(\dot{p}^*_{t+1} \right) \right] - \mu \tag{A-3}$$

Letting $q = s + p - p^* =$ the real spot exchange rate, and $v = f + E_t \left(p_{t+1} \right) - E \left(p^*_{t+1} \right) =$ the expected real exchange rate, we can substitute these definitions in equation A–3, taking the first differences of the results to obtain the equation used for the regression in table 9–5:

$$\dot{q} = \Delta \left\{ \left[r - E_t \left(\dot{p}_{t+1} \right) \right] - \left[r^* - E_t \left(\dot{p}^*_{t+1} \right) \right] \right\} + \dot{v} - \dot{\mu} \tag{A-4}$$

Notes

1. Assuming that foreign interest rates are constant precludes the possibility of a shift in the relative price between domestic and foreign interest-earning assets. Thus only the relative price of the two currencies (the exchange rate) can change. If foreign interest rates were allowed to vary, the change in the exchange rate would be less than shown.

2. Paul A. Krugman, "International Aspects of Monetary and Fiscal Policy," *The Economics of Large Government Deficits*, Conference Series No. 27 (October 1983), Federal Reserve Bank of Boston, pp. 112–33.

3. For a fuller exposition of this argument, see Rajni Bonnie Ohri, "Delusive Trade Deficit," *Economic Outlook* (August/September 1984), pp. 9–12.

4. The interest rate series used here were not adjusted for changes in the effective rate of taxation of financial assets. Since both borrowers and lenders calculate their costs and returns on a post-tax basis, the interest rate series should have been adjusted for changes in the rate of taxation of income and capital gains. This correction was omitted here because of the limited information available on the average marginal tax rates for all countries, particularly on a monthly basis. For example, the latest data available for the United States are for calendar year 1982. The results reported in table 9–1 would not be greatly altered, however, if taxes were included. Even though income tax rates in the United States were reduced in 1981 by 25 percent over a three-year period, the changes in the interest rate differentials were of such large magnitudes that they may have overwhelmed the effect of the tax changes. For a good review of the tax treatment of foreign exchange transactions, see Vito Tanzi, ed., *Taxation, Inflation, and Interest Rates* (Washington, D.C.: International Monetary Fund, 1984).

5. The log form of the covered parity shown in equation 1 is derived from the natural logarithm of the covered-interest parity condition:

$$(1 + R) = \frac{S}{F} (1 + R^*)$$

where R = the domestic nominal interest rate over maturity t, R^* = the foreign nominal interest rate over maturity t, S = the spot exchange rate (the foreign price of domestic currency), and F = the forward exchange rate. It states that the total return on a domestic security must equal the return on an equally risky foreign security once an investor has covered his open position in the forward market.

6. As noted in Willem H. Buiter, "Implications for the Adjustment Process of International Asset Risk: Exchange Controls, Intervention and Policy Risk, and Sovereign Risk," *Research International Business and Finance: The Internationalization of Financial Markets and National Economic Policy* (Greenwich, Conn.: Aijai Press, 1983), pp. 69–100.

7. That assumes that the country is neither a permanent debtor nor a permanent creditor in present-value terms. Conceivably, a country could be a net debtor indefinitely, but it would still have to run future current account surpluses to meet its interest payments after reaching a certain threshold of debt, beyond which no further lending would be forthcoming.

8. Peter Isard, "An Accounting Framework and Some Issues for Modeling How Exchange Rates Respond to the News," in Jacob A. Frenkel, ed., *Exchange Rates and International Macroeconomics* (Chicago: University of Chicago Press, 1983).

9. The value of shipments, or in some cases GDP, was used because of the lack of available compatible data on the value of production.

10. Rudiger Dornbusch, "Equilibrium and Disequilibrium Exchange Rates," National Bureau of Economic Research Working Paper No. 983, September 1982.

11. Robert E. Cumby and Frederic S. Mishkin, "The International Linkages of Real Interest Rates: The European-U.S. Connection," National Bureau of Economic Research Working Paper No. 1423 (August 1984).

12. These figures were derived from the *Balance Sheet of the U.S. Economy, 1945-1983*, published by the Board of Governors of the Federal Reserve System, and *Measuring the Effects of Inflation on Income, Spending, and Wealth*, OECD publication, June 1983. These are very rough figures, to be sure, and are useful only for illustration.

Bibliography

Bank for International Settlements. *Fifty-fourth Annual Report, 1st April 1983-31 March 1984*. Basle (June 1984).

Bisignano, Joseph, and Kevin D. Hoover. "Monetary and Fiscal Impacts on Exchange Rates." Federal Reserve Bank of San Francisco. *Fiscal Policy: Influence on Money, Saving, and Exchange Rates*, (Winter 1982).

Branson, William H., and Willem H. Buiter. "Monetary and Fiscal Policy with Flexible Exchange Rates." National Bureau of Economic Research Working Paper No. 901 (June 1982).

Buiter, Willem H. "Implications for the Adjustment Process of International Asset Risk: Exchange Controls, Intervention and Policy Risk, and Sovereign Risk." In *Research in International Business and Finance: The Internationalization of Financial Markets and National Economic Policy*, 69-100. Greenwich, Conn.: Aijai Press Inc., 1983.

Caprio, Gerard, Jr., and David C. Howard. "Domestic Saving, Current Accounts, and International Capital Mobility." *International Finance Discussion Papers*, Working Paper No. 244 (June 1984).

Cohen, Darrel, and Peter B. Clark. "The Effects of Fiscal Policy on the United States Economy." *Staff Studies*, No. 136, Board of Governors of the Federal Reserve System (January 1984).

Cumby, Robert E., and Frederic S. Mishkin. "The International Linkages of Real Interest Rates: The European-U.S. Connection." National Bureau of Economic Research Working Paper No. 1423 (August 1984).

Cumby, Robert E., and Maurice Obstfeld. "International Interest Rate and Price Level Linkages under Flexible Exchange Rates: A Review of Evidence." National Bureau of Economic Research, Working Paper No. 1423 (August 1984).

de Leeuw, Frank, and Thomas M. Holloway. "Measuring and Analyzing the Cyclically Adjusted Budget." In *The Economics of Large Government Deficits*, 1–42. Conference Series No. 27 (October 1983). Federal Reserve Bank of Boston.

Dornbusch, Rudiger. "Equilibrium and Disequilibrium Exchange Rates." National Bureau of Economic Research Working Paper No. 983 (September 1982).

Dornbusch, Rudiger, and Stanley Fischer. "The Open Economy: Implications for Monetary and Fiscal Policy." Paper prepared for the National Bureau of Economic Research Conference on Business Cycles, March 1984.

Fair, Ray C. "Effects of Expected Future Government Deficits on Current Economic Activity." National Bureau of Economic Research Working Paper No. 1293 (March 1984).

Feldstein, Martin. "The Strong Dollar." *Challenge* (January/February 1984).

Feileke, Norman S. "The Budget Deficit: Are the International Consequences Unfavorable?" *New England Economic Review* (May/June 1984): 5–10.

Frenkel, Jacob A., and Razin Assaf. "Budget Deficits and Rates of Interest in the World Economy." National Bureau of Economic Research Working Paper No. 1354 (May 1984).

Giordano, Robert M., Kenneth C. Froewiss, and Andrea M. Sandor. "Financial Market Perspectives." *Economic Research in Goldman Sachs Economics* (May 1984).

Isard, Peter. "An Accounting Framework and Some Issues for Modeling How Exchange Rates Respond to the News." In *Exchange Rates and International Macro-economics*, edited by Jacob A. Frenkel (Chicago: University of Chicago Press, 1983).

Keran, Michael. "Budget Deficits and Foreign Savings." *Federal Reserve Bank of San Francisco Weekly Letter* (July 1984).

Krugman, Paul A. "International Aspects of Monetary and Fiscal Policy," 112–33. *The Economics of Large Government Deficits*, Conference Series No. 27 (October 1983). Federal Reserve Bank of Boston.

Kubarych, Roger M. "Financing the U.S. Current Account Deficit." *Federal Reserve Bank of New York Quarterly Review* (Summer 1984): 24–31.

Larsen, Flemming, John Llewellyn, and Stephen Potter. "International Economic Linkages." *OECD Economic Studies*, No. 1 (Autumn 1983): 43–91.

Modi, Jitendra R. "Survey of Tax Treatment of Investment Income and Payments in Selected Industrial Countries." International Monetary Fund Fiscal Affairs Department Working Paper (May 1983).

Mundell, Robert A. *International Economics*. New York: MacMillan, Co. 1968.

Niehans, Jurg. *International Monetary Economics*. Baltimore: Johns Hopkins University Press, 1984.

OECD Economic Outlook (Paris), vol. 34 (December 1983).

Ohri, Rajni Bonnie. "Delusive Trade Deficit." *Economic Outlook* (Washington, D.C.: U.S. Chamber of Commerce, August/September 1984): 9–12.

Penati, Alessandro. "Expansionary Fiscal Policy and the Exchange Rate; A Review." *International Monetary Fund Staff Papers*, vol. 3, no. 3 (September 1984).

Pigott, Charles. "Indicators of Long-Term Real Interest Rates." *Federal Reserve Bank of San Francisco Economic Review*, no. 1 (Winter 1984): 45–62.

Sachs, Jeffrey, and Charles Wyplosz. "Real Exchange Rate Effects of Fiscal Policy." National Bureau of Economic Research Working Paper No. 1255 (January 1984).

Tanzi, Vito, ed. *Taxation, Inflation, and Interest Rates*. Washington, D.C.: International Monetary Fund, 1984.

10
Tax Reform and Deficit Reduction

Edgar K. Browning and Jacquelene M. Browning

Summary

This chapter examines the ways in which federal taxes could be increased to reduce the federal budget deficit. It does not advocate an increase in taxes but instead evaluates the alternatives, assuming that a decision has been made to raise a given amount of revenue.

The simplest way to raise additional revenue would be to increase the tax rates of existing taxes. To eliminate the deficit fully, however, would require a very large tax increase; federal individual income and corporation taxes, for example, would have to be increased by approximately 50 percent. These taxes are already perceived to be inefficient, inequitable, and complex, and increasing their rates without changing their structures would severely aggravate these problems. For that reason, this seems an opportune time to consider options for more fundamental tax reform that may achieve revenue goals at lower cost.

One option that has attracted a great deal of attention is the flat rate tax. In its pure form, taxpayers would be taxed on a comprehensive measure of income, without any exclusions, deductions, or personal exemptions. On this broadly defined tax base, a flat rate of about 12 percent would raise the same revenue as the present individual income tax. The flat rate tax would be a more efficient revenue raiser than the present tax: it would distort work and savings decisions less, reduce the misallocations due to the channeling of recourses into nontaxable forms, and simplify the compliance problems of taxpayers. We estimate that the efficiency gain of a flat rate tax would be approximately 20 percent of tax revenue. In other words, a flat rate tax could raise the same revenue at 20 percent less cost than the present tax.

The primary disadvantage of the flat rate tax is that it redistributes the tax burden from upper-income to lower-income households. According to the Joint Economic Committee, in 1981 taxpayers with incomes below $30,000 would have paid $31 billion more in taxes under a flat rate tax. This calculation, however, ignores the efficiency gains that would accompany the flat rate

281

tax; we estimate that the loss in real income for lower-income families would be substantially less (though probably still positive) when these gains are taken into account.

Modified flat rate tax plans, such as the Kemp-Kasten and Bradley-Gephardt proposals, broaden the tax base somewhat and move toward a smaller number of rate brackets, but stop short of a comprehensive tax base and a single rate. According to their sponsors, these plans would not substantially change the distribution of tax burdens by income class. To the extent that this is so, we show that the potential efficiency gains of such tax reforms would be significantly less than the gains under a true flat rate tax.

Another option is a personal consumption tax, a tax on household consumption rather than on income. Such a tax can be levied at graduated rates to maintain approximately the progressivity of the present system. Some economists have argued that consumption is a fairer tax base than income. In addition, taxing consumption may lead to increased savings, since saving is deducted from income in calculating consumption. There are, however, some practical and transitional problems in implementing a personal consumption tax.

Another way to tax consumption is with a value-added tax, a tax similar in its economic effects to a national sales tax. A value-added tax would produce substantial efficiency gains in relation to the present system, but it would suffer from the same distributional problem as a flat rate tax: it would shift the tax burden toward lower-income classes.

A central finding of this study is that most of the efficiency gains possible from tax reform can be realized only if the tax system is made less progressive. That is, it is simply unrealistic to expect a tax that maintains the progressivity of the present income tax to produce much improvement in work and savings incentives.

One way to reduce federal budget deficits is to increase federal tax revenues beyond the amounts the current tax system now produces. Additional tax revenue could be raised in a variety of ways, from an increase in the tax rates of existing taxes to a thoroughgoing reform of the federal tax system. In this chapter we examine the major options being discussed. We will not attempt to describe or to evaluate specific legislative proposals in any detail, but, instead, will emphasize the broad issues related to each of the general types of tax changes that have received the most attention.

Before examining the options available for increasing taxes, we believe it will prove helpful to discuss briefly the current federal tax system and its defects. Indeed, dissatisfaction with federal taxes, especially the individual income and corporation income taxes, seems to have grown in recent years, and many favor reforming these taxes even if no additional revenue will be generated. The necessity of raising large amounts of additional revenue has only increased the importance of careful consideration of fundamental reform measures.

The Federal Tax System

Table 10-1 provides some summary data concerning the federal tax system and its projected revenue yield during the next several years, according to the Congressional Budget Office's baseline projection. If current tax laws remain unchanged, the relative contributions of the various taxes are expected to remain about the same as in 1984, with the individual income, corporation income, and social insurance taxes contributing approximately 90 percent of the total revenue. Since social insurance tax receipts are earmarked to finance social security benefits, that tax is not generally considered a possible source of any additional revenues to close the deficit. Thus, attention has tended to concentrate on the individual and corporate income taxes, which provide the bulk of federal general purpose revenues.

Federal tax revenue as a percentage of gross national product peaked in 1981 and then gradually declined to an estimated 18.7 percent in 1984 largely as a result of the phasing in of the tax rate reductions of the Economic Recovery Tax Act (ERTA) of 1981. Although real tax revenues are projected to grow as the economy expands during the remainder of this decade, revenue relative to GNP is expected to rise only slightly, reaching 19.4 percent of GNP in 1989. At the same time, budget outlays are projected to rise from 23.5 percent of GNP in 1984 to 24.3 percent of GNP in 1989, implying a deficit of about 5 percent of GNP in each year if there are no changes in tax and expenditure policies. To eliminate this deficit through tax changes, federal taxes would have to be increased by almost 30 percent. If only individual and corporate income taxes are increased, these two taxes would have to be increased by nearly 50 percent. The prospect of a 50 percent increase in each taxpayer's burden under the income tax should put in perspective the magnitude of the problem we confront in trying to eliminate the deficit.

Now let us take a closer look at some characteristics of the federal government's largest revenue raiser, the individual income tax. Table 10-2 provides estimates of average and marginal tax rates at selected relative income positions for families of four with typical deductions. The average tax rate is the family's tax liability as a percentage of its adjusted gross income (AGI). As can be seen, higher-income families pay a larger percentage of their income in taxes, the defining characteristic of a progressive tax.

TABLE 10-1

SOURCE OF FEDERAL REVENUES, 1980–1989
(percentage of GNP)

	Actual		Estimated	Baseline Projection		
Tax	1980	1983	1984	1985	1987	1989
Individual income	9.5	9.0	8.4	8.7	8.9	9.3
Corporate income	2.5	1.2	1.7	1.7	1.9	1.8
Social insurance	6.1	6.5	6.7	6.8	6.8	6.9
Excise	0.9	1.1	1.0	1.0	0.8	0.6
Estate and gift	0.2	0.2	0.2	0.1	0.1	0.1
Other	0.8	0.8	0.8	0.8	0.7	0.7
Total	20.1	18.6	18.7	19.1	19.2	19.4

NOTE: Data may not add to totals because of rounding.
SOURCE: Congressional Budget Office, Baseline Budget Projections, July 1984.

Although it is widely believed that the wealthy have used special tax provisions, or "loopholes," to avoid paying a fair share of the income tax burden, note that upper-income families provide the bulk of income tax revenue. In 1982, for instance, taxpayers in the top 1.4 percent of the adjusted gross income distribution (those with AGIs above $80,300) paid 21.8 percent of all federal income taxes. The top 25 percent of taxpayers paid 73 percent of total federal income taxes, while the bottom 50 percent paid only 7 percent.[1]

Although the distribution of individual income tax burdens is highly progressive, it is important to keep in mind that the income tax is the most progressive tax used in the United States. While the bottom 50 percent of families pay only 7 percent of all federal income taxes, they bear about 16 percent of the burden of all other federal, state, and local taxes combined. Thus, the use of the individual income tax to raise additional revenues would concentrate more of the burden on upper-income families than would other taxes, at least if the degrees of progressivity of the various taxes are not altered.

The average rates of a tax tell us something about the distributional effects of the tax (who pays the tax), but the marginal tax rates are most relevant in assessing the effects of the tax on the productive incentives of households. The marginal rate of tax is the rate that applies to an additional dollar of income; it indicates how the tax will affect disposable income when the amount of income changes. If, for example, the marginal tax rate is 40 percent, the taxpayer will keep

TABLE 10-2

AVERAGE AND MARGINAL INDIVIDUAL INCOME TAX RATES, 1965-1984

Year	25 Percent of Median Income	50 Percent of Median Income	Median Income	Twice Median Income	Five Times Median Income
		Average Rates			
1965	0.0	2.8	7.4	12.2	20.5
1978	−7.3	3.4	11.6	17.3	30.9
1981	−8.4	5.7	13.3	18.5	31.7
1984	−5.4	5.9	11.9	16.0	26.1
		Marginal Rates			
1965	0.0	14.0	17.0	22.0	39.0
1978	10.0	16.0	22.0	36.0	55.0
1981	12.5	18.0	24.0	43.0	59.0
1984	12.5	14.0	22.0	33.0	45.0

NOTE: Computed for families of four with typical standard or itemized deductions. The negative average rates for lower-income families reflect the refundable earned income tax credit.

SOURCE: Congressional Budget Office, *Reducing the Deficit: Spending and Revenue Options*, February 1984, table VI-3.

sixty cents of each additional dollar of earnings, or will save forty cents in taxes, if he reduces his taxable income by a dollar. The way high marginal tax rates are likely to affect the economy will be discussed later.

Table 10-2 also gives the estimates from the Congressional Budget Office (CBO) of marginal tax rates for various incomes for selected years. In 1984 a family with median income will pay about 11.9 percent of its income as individual income taxes, but its marginal tax rate is nearly twice as high, 22 percent. Under a progressive tax, the marginal tax rate is above the average tax rate for each income group; for the U.S. income tax, table 10-2 suggests that marginal tax rates are typically about twice as high as average rates. Also note that marginal rates are substantially higher in 1984 than in 1965. Although marginal rates were reduced somewhat from 1981 to 1984, they are about the same today as they were in 1979. A significant part of the 1981 cut in rates was effectively repealed by inflation, which continued to push taxpayers into higher-rate brackets over the three-year period when the tax cut was being phased in.

Today, many middle- and upper-middle-income taxpayers face marginal income tax rates that were until quite recently reserved for the wealthy. In 1965, for example, only 3 percent of taxpayers filing joint returns were in marginal rate brackets of 28 percent or higher; by 1979, 35 percent of taxpayers were in this category. In 1965, only 1 percent of taxpayers were in marginal brackets as high as 37 percent; in 1979, 13 percent were.[2]

These figures pertain to the marginal rates of the federal individual income tax. For some purposes, it is more important to consider the combined marginal tax rates that result from all the taxes in the U.S. system. Unfortunately, accurate estimates of combined marginal tax rates for various incomes for recent years are not available. Recently, however, Barro and Sahasakul have developed estimates of a weighted average marginal tax rate for taxpayers as a group under the federal individual income tax and the social security payroll tax.[3] In 1965 the combined average marginal tax rate was estimated to be 23 percent; by 1980 it had risen to 36 percent, a 50 percent increase. Moreover, these estimates do not take account of state income taxes or other taxes that also fall on individual taxpayers.

It seems clear that marginal tax rates are now significant for most taxpayers and that they have risen sharply during the past two decades. This change has given impetus to reform proposals designed to lower marginal tax rates, some of which will be discussed in subsequent sections of this chapter.

Shortcomings of Present Federal Income Taxes

A significant first step in evaluating the advantages and disadvantages of various tax reform proposals is to understand what is wrong with present federal taxes. Any brief catalogue of defects, or undesirable effects, of current taxes is certain to be incomplete; but several features of the present system are especially relevant to reform proposals, and we will focus on them.

Effects on Labor Supply, Saving, and Investment. The economy's output, and hence the incomes of households, depends on, among other things, the quantities of labor and capital that households choose to supply. Households' decisions regarding resource supplies are guided by the net, or after-tax, remuneration they receive. By reducing the net returns for supplying productive resources, taxation may lead taxpayers to reduce the quantities they supply. The result would be lower total output, and therefore lower average incomes.

The marginal tax rate that applies to the earnings of productive resources can be expected to have adverse effects on resource supplies. If the marginal tax rate on labor earnings is 40 percent, for instance, a person who has the opportunity to earn an extra $100 will decide whether the extra effort is worth the additional $60 that he gets to keep. Similarly, reducing one's earnings by working less is not as costly when marginal tax rates are high. If the marginal tax rate is 45 percent, then earning $100 less costs the taxpayer only $55 in disposable income.

Thus, the higher the marginal tax rate on labor earnings, the lower is the net rate of pay received and the more adversely labor supply is likely to be affected. The recently rediscovered "supply-side" school of economics emphasizes this effect: with high marginal tax rates, people keep only a small fraction of any additional output generated by working more, so they tend to work less. Some feel, therefore, that the steady rise in marginal tax rates applying to labor earnings may have something to do with the estimated 16 percent reduction in lifetime labor supply of a typical worker since the late 1940s. The quantitative effect of taxes on labor supply, however, is difficult to estimate and so is not known with any precision. Recent empirical research suggests, however, that the effect is large enough to be of concern, and that is one reason for the dissatisfaction with the recent increases in marginal tax rates.

Saving can also be adversely affected by taxation. High marginal tax rates applied to the interest on saving sharply reduce the net rate of return received by savers. If, for example, the interest rate a taxpayer can earn on his saving is 10 percent and the marginal tax rate that applies to interest income is 50 percent, then the net rate of return the taxpayer receives is reduced to 5 percent. If people tend to save less when the net rate of return is lower, then the tax system reduces the supply of saving. A reduction in the supply of saving implies that the rate of capital accumulation is diminished, and along with it the amount of real capital per worker, so output per worker will be lower in future years.

The way the tax system affects saving and investment is both complex and controversial, and so cannot be dealt with here in great detail. It is complicated because saving and investment are affected by interactions between the corporate and individual income taxes, as well as by inflation and many special tax provisions that apply to investment income. It is important, however, to recognize that these taxes adversely affect the allocation of capital resources in two ways. First, they reduce the aggregate supply of capital by depressing saving. This effect depends on how much on average the rate of return is depressed. Second, the allocation of capital to different uses is believed to be adversely affected by the very uneven taxation of investment income. Some types of investment income are extremely heavily taxed, while some are lightly taxed, and a few are even subsidized. The result is that capital may be invested in lightly taxed areas even when it would be more productive (before-tax) if invested elsewhere. Thus, the tax system is believed not only to affect the quantity of capital adversely but also to lead to an inefficient allocation of the capital stock.

Effects of a Narrow Tax Base. Ideally, a tax on individual income will base the amount of tax people pay on a comprehensive measure of income. All types of income, whether capital gains, fringe benefits provided by employers, or government transfers, would be equally subject to tax, and the tax due would not depend on the way taxpayers spend their incomes. The U.S. income tax falls far short of this ideal. Because of deductions, exemptions, exclusions, and other special tax preferences (or tax "loopholes"), income subject to taxation at positive rates is only about half of total personal income.[4] Among other things, the use of a narrow tax base means that higher marginal tax rates must be applied to the smaller base to generate a given amount of revenue.

This "erosion of the tax base" is not new to the income tax. In fact, in the 1950s a smaller percentage of personal income was subject to tax than is now the case. During the 1950s, an average of 40 percent of personal income was subject to tax; this percentage rose to a high of 51.5 percent in 1969 and declined slightly to 48 percent in 1981. The aggregate tax base has shown no systematic tendency to erode over time. What has changed significantly over this period, however, is the composition of this untaxed income. In 1947, 46 percent of untaxed income was in the form of personal exemptions and standard deductions, but by 1979 this share had fallen to 26 percent, largely because inflation reduced the real values of these items. By contrast, in 1947 only 21 percent of untaxed income took the form of exclusions, itemized deductions, and tax credits; by 1979 this share had increased to 58 percent.[5]

The significance of this change is that the amounts of exclusions, itemized deductions, and tax credits generally reflect choices by taxpayers to channel resources into these untaxed forms, while personal exemptions and standard deductions are fixed in amount and therefore do not influence economic choices. In short, tax preferences are having a larger influence on the allocation of economic resources today than in the past, and the effect is probably undesirable.

When high marginal tax rates are applied to an emasculated definition of income, taxpayers are encouraged to channel part of their incomes into untaxed forms. This change in the composition of income reflects a loss in economic productivity as taxpayers devote resources to lower-valued uses simply because they are not taxed. Consider a person in a 50 percent marginal tax bracket. An additional $100 of taxable income produces benefits for him of only $50 since the government collects $50 in taxes. If the taxpayer can transfer the $100 in taxable income to an untaxed use, he will be better off even if the untaxed use of $100 produces benefits worth only $51. In this instance, the taxpayer benefits by $1 while the government loses $50 in revenue: $49 is wasted. This type of waste, or efficiency loss, reflects a misallocation of resources caused by the existence of many untaxed sources and uses of income.

The use of a narrow tax base also has implications for the fairness of the distribution of the tax burden. Taxpayers who are able to shift large portions of their incomes into untaxed forms end up paying less in taxes than those with equal incomes who are unwilling or unable to make as much use of tax preferences. The result is a wide dispersion in effective average tax rates for taxpayers who are equally situated—at least as indicated by equality in incomes comprehensively defined. In 1969, for example, 77 percent of those with adjusted gross incomes of $15,000 to $20,000 paid taxes between 10 and 20 percent of their AGIs; another 22 percent in the same income class paid between 20 and 30 percent, and 1 percent paid less than 10 percent.

Tax preferences can also lead to inequities in the distribution of taxes among different income classes. The situation is complicated by the multiplicity of tax preferences, some of which work to the advantage of lower-income families (like the exclusion of government transfers from the tax base), while others tend to benefit primarily higher-income families (like the preferential treatment of capital gains). When all tax preferences are considered as a group, however, there does not appear to be any tendency to favor higher-income taxpayers. In 1977, for taxpayers with AGIs over $100,000, total nontaxable income was 31 percent of their income, comprehensively measured. For taxpayers with AGIs between $10,000 and $100,000, untaxed income was also 31 percent of their comprehensive income, while for lower-income taxpayers a substantially higher share of their income was in untaxed forms.[6] These average figures probably mask greater disparities among individuals; undoubtedly some higher-income taxpayers are able to shelter a larger share of their income from taxation than some lower-income taxpayers.

Complexity. Another cost of the present tax system is its complexity. Tax returns require a good deal of time to fill out correctly, and additional time is needed to keep the necessary records. The time required to comply with the tax laws is a socially unproductive use of resources: if a taxpayer could pay the same final tax without spending thirty hours locating records and filling out forms, he would be better off. In the same sense, payments for professional tax assistance also are unproductive. Today, nearly half of all taxpayers use professional tax preparers, up from 10 to 15 percent thirty years ago. Of taxpayers with only an elementary school education, 92 percent seek professional help with their tax returns. High percentages of upper-income taxpayers also obtain professional assistance though probably for different reasons: the tax savings from locating tax shelters is greater for those in higher tax brackets.

Understandably, the size of the compliance costs tax payers bear is not known with any certainty. Slemrod and Sorum have recently estimated that taxpayers spend 1,800 million hours during the year on tax matters, or about 20 hours per tax return.[7] Based on this figure, they estimate the dollar value of this time to be about 5 percent of tax revenue. To this must be added the costs firms bear in administering withholding and the costs the Internal Revenue System bears in collecting taxes; a rough estimate of these costs is 2 percent of tax revenue. Thus, total collection costs may be on the order of 7 percent of tax revenue. No feasible tax could reduce collection costs to zero, but a simpler tax would lower these costs substantially.

Complexity exacts another cost in addition to these outright resource costs: it makes the consequences of the income tax more difficult for the public to understand. Consider, for instance, the widely held view that wealthy taxpayers largely avoid paying taxes through ingenious and excessive use of tax loopholes, perhaps even to the extent of paying a smaller share of their incomes in taxes than middle-income taxpayers. Although the evidence shows this view to be untrue on average—only a tiny percentage of wealthy taxpayers accomplish this feat—one must have a fairly sophisticated knowledge of the present complex system to recognize how tax burdens are really distributed among income classes.

Closing the Deficit without Tax Reform

Certainly the simplest way of raising tax revenue to reduce the deficit would be to raise the existing tax rates and not bother with changing or reforming the tax system. This option, however, has some serious problems that for many make fundamental tax reform more attractive. One problem is whether it is even possible to raise more revenue by increasing the rates of existing taxes. The Laffer curve illustrates that as tax rates rise, they ultimately reach a point where further increases yield less revenue because the incentive effects of higher rates cause taxable income to fall sharply. The question is whether we have gone beyond that point in the United States.

For the effects on the labor supply, this question can be answered fairly definitely: higher tax rates will produce more tax revenue. Every major study agrees on this point.[8] This is not to say that higher tax rates will not cause labor supply to fall—they probably will—but the magnitude of the reduction is not likely to be large enough to negate the revenue-enhancing effects of higher rates.

This conclusion is, however, subject to two qualifications. First, tax rate increases could cause taxable income to fall in ways other than reducing labor supply. Most important, when marginal tax rates rise, the relative cost of converting income into nontaxable forms through the use of tax preferences falls. Even if gross earnings do not fall, taxable income could decline if higher tax rates encourage sufficiently greater use of tax loopholes. In addition, higher tax rates could divert income into the underground economy where it illegally avoids being taxed. Most economists do not, however, believe that taking these effects into account would alter the general conclusion that higher rates will produce more revenue.

A second qualification is that although across-the-board tax rate increases will raise more revenue in total, it is not clear that more tax revenue can be raised from every income class. There is some evidence that higher marginal tax rates on the wealthiest 1 or 2 percent of taxpayers will reduce tax revenues from these taxpayers. Gwartney and Long have estimated that this is true even if gross income is unaffected, because the use of tax preferences is so sensitive to marginal tax rates.[9] In addition, gross income itself is likely to change and to reinforce this conclusion. It is suggestive that the real wage and salary income of the top 1.4 percent of taxpayers rose by 4.2 percent from 1981 to 1982 following the sharp reductions in top bracket rates, while the real wage and salary income of the remainder of the population fell.[10] These findings, though tentative, do suggest that it may not be possible to squeeze much more revenue from the very top brackets.

Another simple option for reducing the deficit would be reducing government expenditures rather than, or in addition to, raising taxes. Deciding whether government expenditures should be cut lies beyond the scope of this study, but it may be worthwhile to explain the aspect of tax analysis that bears on the choice between spending cuts and tax increases. The Congressional Budget Office explains that "it is necessary to decide whether an additional dollar spent by government can be put to better use than an additional dollar spent by the taxpayer."[11] Actually, this is not quite correct, for when the government spends an additional dollar, the cost to the public is greater than a dollar. This is due to the efficiency costs of taxation discussed in the preceding section. Government spending should be cut back unless the marginal benefit of spending a dollar on any program exceeds the marginal cost of raising a dollar in revenue, where the marginal cost includes the efficiency losses imposed on the private economy by the tax.

How much does it really cost the public when the government raises an additional dollar of tax revenue under existing taxes, specifically the individual income tax? That question has been the subject of several recent papers.[12] Although no definite answers are available, it appears that the marginal cost of raising tax revenue is quite high—somewhere in the range of $1.25 to $1.60 per dollar of revenue. In other words, unless spending programs generate benefits greater than $1.25–1.60 per dollar spent, the public would be better off if the government cut spending rather than increased taxes. Moreover, these estimates consider only the effects of higher tax rates on labor supply and saving; when the efficiency losses due to tax preferences are taken into account, the cost is likely to be higher.

So far, we have argued that the cost of raising more revenue from the present income tax is quite high. The cost of raising more revenue from a reformed income tax or from some new tax may, however, be a good bit lower. Indeed, many people who believe this favor tax reform, rather than just higher tax rates, to raise more revenue. In addition, simply raising the rates of the present system will aggravate the inequities of the tax system. As we have seen, higher rates are likely to lead to greater use of tax preferences, which is certain to intensify the impression that the system is unfair. Therefore, for reasons of both efficiency and equity, this seems an opportune time to consider fundamental reform of the federal tax system.

Income Tax Reform: The Major Options

Any proposal for reforming the individual income tax can be classified by the way it deals with two issues: the definition of the tax base and the structure of tax rates applied to this base. Most proposals agree on the desirability of expanding the tax base, that is, using a more comprehensive definition of income for tax purposes. In addition, there is agreement that reducing the number of separate marginal tax brackets is desirable, but disagreement over whether there should be only one marginal tax rate that applies to all taxable income or a small number of graduated rates.

Broadening the tax base and simplifying the rate structure can be combined in a wide variety of ways. We believe it will clarify the issues to consider one specific type of reform in some detail before turning to an analysis of other types. Specifically, we will consider the proposal for a flat rate tax applied to a comprehensive measure of income. This tax will be analyzed on the assumption that it raises the same total amount of revenue as the present income tax. Of course, it should be recognized that if the reform is advantageous at the current yield, it would also be advantageous if the goal is to raise more revenue to close the deficit.

In 1982, the Joint Committee on Taxation estimated that a flat tax rate of 11.8 percent would raise the same amount of revenue in 1984 as the present tax (assuming income levels were the same in 1984 as in 1981) if the tax base were expanded by eliminating all exemptions, deductions, and tax credits and all capital gains were taxed. While it would be possible to use an even more comprehensive measure of income, and thus a lower rate, we will examine this 11.8 percent tax because of the availability of data on its effects on various income classes.

Table 10–3 shows how the Joint Economic Committee estimates that the distribution of tax burdens would be affected by substituting a flat rate tax of 11.8 percent for the federal income tax in 1984. (Incomes are for 1981; although incomes and tax revenues would be higher in today's dollars, the general pattern of effects should be about the same.) Note that tax liabilities rise for incomes up to $30,000 and fall for incomes greater than $30,000.[13] Any income tax levied on a comprehensive base can be expected to increase taxes for lower-income classes because many households currently pay no taxes since their incomes fall below the amount allowed for personal exemptions and for the standard deduction (zero bracket amount). In total, the 77 percent of taxpayers with incomes below $30,000 would pay $31 billion more in taxes, while higher-income taxpayers would pay this much less in taxes. In 1981, $31 billion was about 1 percent of GNP and about 14 percent of income tax revenue.

Advantages and Disadvantages of the Flat Rate Tax. The advantages of the flat rate tax are the elimination or mitigation of the shortcomings of the present tax, discussed earlier. Several beneficial effects should flow from the sharp reduction of marginal tax rates. Lower marginal rates should increase incentives to work, to save, and to invest. They should also reduce the incentive to avoid paying taxes, legally or illegally, since the tax savings from doing so would be reduced.

293

TABLE 10-3

DISTRIBUTION OF TAX LIABILITIES: FLAT RATE TAX
COMPARED WITH 1984 TAX LAW FOR 1981 INCOMES

Expanded Income (thousands of dollars)	Number of Taxable Returns (millions)	Tax Liability 1984 Law (billions of dollars)	Tax Liability Flat Rate Tax (billions of dollars)	Change in Tax (dollars per return)
0– 5	6.48	0.40	5.48	783
5– 10	15.06	5.77	14.28	565
10– 15	13.09	12.53	19.70	548
15– 20	10.74	17.46	22.50	469
20– 30	16.80	44.08	49.70	335
30– 50	13.57	63.83	60.58	– 240
50–100	3.58	38.69	27.39	– 3,156
100–200	0.63	18.66	9.87	– 13,921
200 and up	0.16	16.39	7.68	– 53,107
Total	80.11	217.80	217.17	
Average				– 8

NOTE: Data may not add to totals because of rounding.
SOURCE: Congressional Budget Office, *Revising the Individual Income Tax*, July 1983, table 7.

The way the flat rate tax would affect supplies of labor and capital depends on how much effective marginal tax rates would be reduced. It is important not to overstate how much effective marginal rates would fall. Current marginal bracket rates apply only to increments in taxable income (after any deductions or exclusions), while the 11.8 percent rate would more nearly apply to increments in total earnings. To see the significance of this point, consider how a taxpayer now in a 30 percent bracket might be affected when his gross earnings rise by $100. Part of this $100 is likely to be received in nontaxable forms, like fringe benefits, and part is likely to be devoted to outlays that are deductible, such as state and local taxes. Thus, taxable income would rise by less than $100, perhaps by $80, and the 30 percent rate applied to this amount results in $24 in taxes. In this example, the effective marginal tax rate is really 24 percent, not the statutory 30 percent rate bracket. If a flat rate tax of 11.8 percent that applies to all income at the margin is substituted for the present tax, the effective marginal tax rate for this taxpayer would fall from 24 percent to 11.8 percent, and it is this change that creates the incentive to work and to save more.

Therefore, looking only at current statutory marginal bracket rates tends to overstate the advantage of the 11.8 percent tax since the 11.8 percent tax would apply to a broader base at the margin than do current rates. Nonetheless, there is no doubt that effective marginal tax rates will drop significantly for most, if not all, taxpayers.

Since the tax base of the flat rate tax is a more comprehensive measure of income, many of the misallocations due to the channeling of income into untaxed or sheltered forms will be avoided. There would be fewer nontaxable uses or types of income so the artificial incentive to misdirect resources into lower-valued uses is diminished. In addition, the lower marginal rate gives less incentive to taxpayers to search out tax shelters or to exert political pressure to create new tax preferences. (Here, it is the comparison of statutory marginal rates that is relevant.) It may be that only with a single, low flat rate can we avoid the proliferation of tax loopholes. It is instructive, we think, to note that with the social security payroll tax—which is a flat rate tax up to a ceiling amount on labor earnings—there has been no significant erosion of the tax base.

The use of a more comprehensive measure of income should improve the horizontal equity of the tax. Taxpayers with the same incomes would pay the same tax.

Finally, a flat rate tax of this type is also potentially less complex than the present tax. Compliance costs for taxpayers would be lower, as would collection costs for the IRS and for firms. Of course, these costs would not fall to zero, but they would be reduced. For most taxpayers, the process of tax compliance would be no more involved than the determination of AGI on present tax returns.

There are some disadvantages to the flat rate tax. First, it would increase marginal tax rates for lower-income households. These taxpayers are now in zero rate brackets because of the various exclusions, personal exemptions, and deductions, and their marginal tax rate would rise from zero to 11.8 percent. It should be noted, however, that the total income of taxpayers affected in this way is only about 5 percent of national income. Marginal tax rates will fall for the remaining 95 percent of national income. There is little doubt, therefore, that in the aggregate, incentives will be improved. Nonetheless, the higher rates for lower-income families pose a serious problem since many of these families already face high marginal tax rates because of the implicit marginal tax rates in several welfare programs.

A second disadvantage is the short-run effects of the tax change on taxpayers who have large amounts of untaxed income that would become taxable. Those, for example, who have recently borrowed at high interest rates to finance homes on the expectation that the interest costs will be deductible could be harmed. It should be recalled, however, that the tax rate falls significantly, so the net cost would not be high except for taxpayers who use many tax preferences.

Finally, the objection perhaps most frequently made to the flat rate tax is the redistribution of the tax burden. Lower- and middle-income families would pay higher taxes while upper-income families would pay lower taxes. To many people, this disadvantage is the overriding one; for that reason, we will examine it further a bit later.

The Efficiency Gains of a Flat Rate Tax. Data like those in table 10–3 that show the changes in tax liabilities when a flat rate tax is substituted for the present tax are generally interpreted as measuring the gains and losses realized by various income classes. Such calculations, however, are based on the assumption that the economic behavior of taxpayers will remain unchanged when one tax is substituted for another. In other words, it must be assumed that every person's earnings would be the same under either tax, which is unlikely given the substantial changes in tax rates involved.

As we have seen, some benefits are likely to result from improvements in resource allocation when the flat rate tax is used instead of the present income tax. In this section we will try to put a dollar price tag on these efficiency gains. Making this estimate will require some heroic assumptions, but the economics literature provides us with some guidance concerning the relative magnitudes that we need to use. We caution, however, that this exercise does not purport to provide definitive answers; instead it is intended only to indicate the orders of magnitude involved.

Consider first the gains from increased labor supply under the flat rate tax. How much labor supply increases depends on how much after-tax rates of pay rise because of the lower marginal rates and how responsive workers are to changes in after-tax wage rates. The rise in the after-tax rate of pay depends on how much the overall marginal tax rate (from all federal, state, and local taxes) falls under the flat rate tax. Based on other research, it is reasonable to take 44 percent as an economy-wide average value for the marginal tax rate when all taxes are considered.[14] According to Barro and Sahasakul a weighted average marginal tax rate for the individual income tax alone was 29 percent in 1979 (which should be about the same as the rate in 1984). This may seem to suggest that a flat tax rate of 12 percent would reduce marginal rates by seventeen percentage points. Seventeen points is more, however, than the reduction in the effective marginal rate: the Barro-Sahasakul estimate is of the average statutory marginal rate that applies to taxable earnings and consequently overstates the effective marginal rate on a comprehensive measure of earnings. Instead of assuming a seventeen-point drop in the effective marginal rate, we assume it would fall only eight percentage points. Although this is largely conjecture on our part, we do not believe we are overstating how much marginal rates would typically fall.

Thus, on average the marginal tax rate would fall from 44 to 36 percent when a flat rate tax applied to a comprehensive base replaces the present income tax. This drop in the marginal rate means that the after-tax rate of pay would rise from 56 percent of the before-tax rate of pay to 64 percent, a 14.3 percent increase in the net rate of pay applying to changes in labor supply. How much labor supply would increase depends on how responsive workers are to changes in net wage rates at the margin, something again not known exactly but extensively studied and summarized in the form of labor supply elasticities that relate the percentage change in labor supply to the percentage change in the wage rate. Based on available evidence, an economy-wide average value for the labor supply elasticity of 0.3 is reasonable.[15] This implies that labor supply would rise by 4.3 percent, a result that does not seem excessive given a 14.3 percent increase in the net rate of pay.

With such an increase in labor supply, labor earnings would rise by about $86 billion. This increase in labor earnings does not, however, constitute a net gain to taxpayers since they would be working more (consuming less leisure) to produce the additional $86 billion. The net gain is the extra earnings less the value of leisure given up, which can be estimated as $52 billion using the after-tax rate of pay to value leisure.[16] Thus, we arrive at a net gain to taxpayers as a group of $34 billion from the improved incentives of the flat rate tax.

We can roughly estimate two other efficiency gains. First is the gain from a broader tax base, which avoids the uneconomic shifting of income to lower-valued uses because of tax advantages. The efficiency cost of these distortions under the present tax has been estimated to be 7 percent of revenue, or a total of $15 billion for the base used in table 10–3.[17] Not all loopholes can realistically be avoided under a flat rate tax, so suppose we assume a gain of only $10 billion on this count. Finally, the costs of complying with the tax laws and the costs of collecting taxes would be lower. These costs have also been estimated to be about 7 percent of revenue, or $15 billion. Let us assume that the simpler flat rate tax would reduce these costs by $5 billion.

Combining these three gains in efficiency yields a total annual net gain of $49 billion. Again, we emphasize that this is only a rough estimate, but the assumptions on which it is based are entirely reasonable given the available evidence. What this gain means is that shifting to a flat rate tax of equal yield will increase the real income of the community by $49 billion. Stated differently, the real burden of a flat rate tax that raises the same revenue as the present tax would be about 20 percent less.

Recognizing this efficiency gain does not mean that everyone benefits from the flat rate tax. Determining exactly who would receive the benefits of this efficiency gain is a difficult question, but one way to approach it is to note that governments (federal, state, and local) would receive additional revenue from the $86 billion in additional earnings. Indeed, this revenue is the tangible representation of most of the net gain from the higher earnings. If the government returned the revenue to the public by reducing the tax rate on income, the gain would accrue to people in proportion to their incomes. Even if not returned in this way, taxpayers would benefit from government's spending this amount. So let us assume that the efficiency gain is distributed among taxpayers in proportion to their incomes, an assumption that permits us to use the data in table 10–3 to estimate how the flat rate tax would affect the real income, or well-being, of each income class.

The results are shown in table 10–4. To the change in tax liability of each income class under the flat rate tax, we add the efficiency gain realized by that class. The sum of the changed tax liability and the efficiency gain, shown in the last column, is our estimate of the amount that the real income of each income class is changed by substituting a flat rate tax for the present income tax. Instead of lower-income classes bearing a burden of $31 billion from this tax reform, we see that the actual burden is only $11.8 billion. Families with incomes above about $15,000 gain a total of $61.5 billion. (Fifty-seven percent of tax returns are filed by income classes that gain from the reform, and these would include about two-thirds of the population.) Put differently, the use of the present tax with its high rates, distorting loopholes, and costs of compliance benefits lower-income classes by $11.8 billion, but at a cost of more than five times as much for the higher-income classes. Income redistribution through the tax system is a costly endeavor.

Another type of potential efficiency gain, which has been neglected in this analysis, is the gain from increased saving and investment stimulated by the flat rate tax. Because there are many special tax provisions in the present tax that already favor saving and investment, it is not clear whether or by how much saving would be increased. Several consequences of the flat rate tax—the lower effective marginal tax rates, the higher labor earnings out of which to save, and the higher incomes of upper-income families who tend to save more—all

TABLE 10–4

DISTRIBUTIONAL EFFECTS OF SUBSTITUTING FLAT RATE TAX FOR PRESENT INDIVIDUAL INCOME TAX

Expanded Income (thousands of dollars)	Change in Tax Liability (billions of dollars)	Efficiency Gain (billions of dollars)	Change in Real Incomes (billions of dollars)
0– 5	5.08	1.23	−3.85
5– 10	8.51	3.23	−5.28
10– 15	7.17	4.46	−2.71
15– 20	5.03	5.10	0.07
20– 30	5.62	11.22	5.60
30– 50	−3.25	13.67	16.92
50–100	−11.30	6.17	17.47
100–200	−8.78	2.25	11.03
200 and up	−8.71	1.72	10.43
Total	−0.63	49.05	49.68

SOURCE: Table 10–3 and calculations explained in text.

suggest that saving will increase under the flat rate tax. If saving does rise, the efficiency gains will be larger, and the conclusions above will be strengthened.

As we mentioned earlier, the most common objection to the flat rate tax is its distributional effects: it harms the poor and helps the rich. It is probably true that lower-income classes will be harmed by this tax reform if no other policy change is made, but the harm is much less than the conventional estimates suggest because they ignore all efficiency gains. In addition, it should be realized that many lower-income persons are not permanently at the bottom of the income distribution. Considerable mobility occurs over time within the distribution, and some of those who appear to be harmed when only one year's data are considered may actually benefit when a longer-run accounting is made. Finally, the possibility of using government transfer programs to mitigate some of the harm done to the neediest households should be considered. The existence of a well-developed (if not well-designed) welfare system reduces the importance of distorting the entire income tax system to avoid any taxes on the poor.

A final point concerning the efficiency gains from tax reform should be mentioned: these gains will not materialize instantaneously. It takes time for taxpayers to change their economic behavior. Work habits and labor market institutions, for example, will not respond immediately when marginal tax rates are lowered. The skimpy evidence available suggest that it would take several years for workers to adjust fully to improved work incentives. The benefits from increased saving, if it occurs, also stretch out many years into the future. What this means is that the immediate, albeit temporary, effects of this tax reform may be more closely approximated by the data of table 10–3 than by those of table 10–4. Lower-income classes will be harmed much more in the short run than they will be after the flat rate tax has been in place for several years. The high losses in the short run may be the biggest obstacle to achieving a meaningful reform of the tax system.

Other Options for Income Tax Reform. Most major reform proposals combine some form of base-broadening with reductions in statutory marginal tax rates. Two types of tax preferences that are almost always retained, however, are personal exemptions and zero bracket amounts (or standard deductions). The intention of retaining these tax preferences is to avoid levying any taxes on those with very low incomes, but their use has other consequences that are less favorable.

Figure 10–1 illustrates some important differences between taxes that exempt some fixed amount of income and those that do not. With family income measured on the horizontal axis and the amount of tax paid on the vertical axis, the line OA shows a flat rate tax on total income like the one described in the previous section. The slope of the line equals the marginal tax rate, which in this case is the same for all incomes. If an exemption equal to OE is granted to each taxpayer, the amount of taxable income will be reduced; and a higher marginal tax rate must be used to raise the same revenue. This is illustrated by the line EB, which shows a flat rate tax applied to income above the exempted amount. The slope of the line is steeper, illustrating the higher marginal tax rate. In addition, note that the exemption benefits (relative to the flat rate tax) not only those with incomes below OE but also those with incomes in the EF range, while applying higher taxes to those with incomes above OF. In short, an exemption coupled with a flat rate makes the tax progressive, with the average tax rate rising with income.

Figure 10–1 also illustrates the effect of using a set of graduated tax rates above an exempted amount. This is shown by the segmented line EC, which has three marginal tax brackets. The graduated rate tax benefits middle-income families (over the range EF) at the expense of higher-income families; the tax is more progressive than a flat rate tax applied above an exemption. In addition, the weighted average marginal tax rate is now higher than it was when a flat rate is used above

FIGURE 10–1

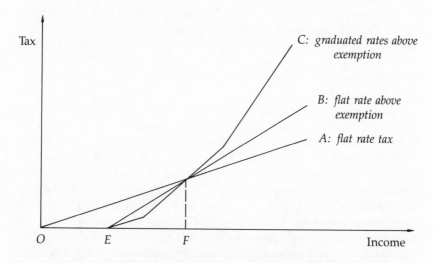

the same exemption. This is not shown by the diagram, but recall that Barro and Sahasakul found that the weighted average marginal tax rate from the present income tax is about 29 percent. A flat tax rate of 18.5 percent, however, applied to the present tax base would yield the same revenue.[18] The use of graduated rates on the same tax base sharply increases the average marginal tax rate that applies to income, even though it may mean lower marginal rates over certain income ranges.

Therefore, the use of an exempted level of income will increase the effective marginal tax rate, and the use of graduated rates will increase it even further. The need to use higher rates means that the efficiency advantages of moving to a flat rate tax above an exemption will be less than those of moving to a flat rate tax on all income. The use of graduated rates will reduce the efficiency gains further. To put this in perspective, introducing current exemptions and zero bracket amounts into the tax described in the previous section raises the required marginal tax rate from 11.8 percent to 15.7 percent. We estimate that this would reduce the efficiency gains that depend on the effective marginal tax rate by half. (Recall that we assumed the effective marginal tax rate fell by eight percentage points—from 19.8 percent to 11.8 percent; if the rate falls only to 15.7 percent, the reduction is only half as large.) Use of graduated rates would reduce the gains even further and could eliminate them entirely. A more redistributive

301

tax, however, is the result.

These observations are highly relevant to evaluating the likely effects of several actual tax reform proposals, particularly the Bradley-Gephardt and Kemp-Kasten proposals. Both proposals involve increasing exempted income and eliminating several other tax preferences. On the redefined tax base, Bradley and Gephardt would levy three graduated rates—14 percent, 26 percent, and 30 percent. On a tax base redefined somewhat differently from the Bradley-Gephardt base, the Kemp and Kasten would levy marginal rates of 20 percent, 28 percent, and 25 percent.[13]

Most notable about these proposals is their sponsors' claims that they would not produce any significant change in tax liabilities by income class. These proposals, as well as several others, take it as a political fact of life that the tax must retain approximately its present degree of progressivity. If the same degree of progressivity is maintained, however, the *effective* marginal tax rates will not be reduced at all. This is simply a matter of arithmetic. If the current and new tax is $3,000 at an income of $30,000 and $5,000 at an income of $40,000, the effective marginal tax rate applied when income increases from $30,000 to $40,000 must be 20 percent under both taxes since the additional tax liability is $2,000. It makes no difference whether the statutory marginal tax rates are lower; the point is that they are applied to a broadened measure of income at the margin, which they must be if actual tax liabilities remain unchanged. Consequently, the effective marginal tax rates will not be lowered.

Since the Bradley-Gephardt and Kemp-Kasten proposals do not reduce effective marginal tax rates, they will not realize the efficiency gains that depend on lowering these rates. Thus, we would not expect much, if any, improvement in the incentives to work, to save, and to invest from these plans. There may still be some efficiency gains because the base of the tax is broadened and the tax is less complex, but the estimates presented earlier suggest that these are only a small part of the total efficiency gain possible from a movement to a true flat rate tax that actually reduces effective marginal tax rates.

Taxing Consumption: Two Options

Rather than taxing income to close the deficit, many favor taxing consumption. There are two major options.

Personal Consumption Taxation. Many tax specialists have come to favor substituting a personal consumption tax for the income tax. Support for this reform has come from the U.S. Treasury Department itself, as well as from the Brookings Institution and from several influential private economists, including a former chairman of the President's Council of Economic Advisers, Martin Feldstein.

All of a person's uses of his income can be classified as either consumption or saving. A personal consumption tax (also called a "cash flow tax" or an "expenditure tax") has as its base the consumption of the taxpayer and therefore differs from a pure income tax by not taxing saving. Each person would be required to fill out a tax form that gives his total consumption expenditures during the year, which would then be subject to the tax rate or rates in the law. It would not be necessary, however, for every consumption outlay to be recorded and added; instead, we can determine consumption by starting with the taxpayer's income and then deducting from it all saving since income minus saving is consumption. Several people who have studied the matter have concluded that the compliance and collection costs of such a tax would not be more than the costs of the present income tax, and might even be less.

A fundamental question is whether income or consumption is the more appropriate base for taxation. Income has enjoyed wide support for many years because it seems to be a comprehensive measure of a person's ability to pay taxes. Proponents of consumption taxation, however, argue that a tax on income is intrinsically unfair in a way that is corrected by a tax on consumption. The following simple example can illustrate the difference between these views. Consider two persons who have the same earnings, and no other income, in one year and no income the following year. If these two people are considered to be equally able to bear a tax burden, they should pay the same tax. Under an income tax, however, the one who saves more of his income in the first year will pay more in taxes over the two-year period, because the interest earned on the savings is considered income. Thus, if one person saves and the other does not in the first year, they will pay the same income tax in that year, but the saver will pay an additional tax on the interest income the following year. Although the two taxpayers have the same opportunity to consume over their lifetimes, an income tax will place a larger tax burden on the one who saves more. According to supporters of the consumption tax, this is unfair.

Supporters of the income tax maintain that whether income is consumed or saved is irrelevant to a person's ability to pay a tax; all income represents the power to consume, and it is potential consumption rather than consumption itself that should be taxed. We cannot evaluate these arguments fully in this study, but we can mention three points suggesting that a consumption tax is more equitable than it might seem. First, savers do not avoid paying taxes under a consumption tax; they simply postpone paying the tax on their savings until the time it is consumed.[20] Second, a personal consumption tax need not be regressive even though higher-income households do consume a smaller portion of their incomes. One of the advantages claimed for this tax is that, in contrast to a sales tax, it can be levied at graduated rates with higher rates applied to those with more consumption. Third, if the long run is considered, the consumption tax appears fairer compared with an income tax. In any one year, it may appear unfair for those who save to pay less in taxes, but taxes are paid later on both the sums saved and the interest earned on the savings.

Many people favor a consumption tax because they believe it will stimulate savings. Because an income tax is levied on the return to savings (interest income, dividends, capital gains, and so on, are part of the income tax base), the saver's net rate of return is reduced. The corporation income tax compounds this problem. Investors in corporations find their income reduced first by the corporate income tax and then a second time by the individual income tax on dividends and capital gains. A consumption tax does not reduce the rate of return received by savers since saving is deducted from income before the tax is applied. If a consumption tax is substituted for the personal income tax, the net rate of return received by savers would be increased, and that should improve incentives to save. Moreover, if the corporation tax is eliminated at the same time, as some supporters of the consumption tax feel it should be, incentives to save would be improved even more.

The differences between a consumption tax and the present income tax, as they affect both savings incentives and equity, are probably much less significant than might be imagined. Our current income tax has a great many special provisions that grant preferential treatment to income that is saved. Employer contributions to pension plans, all income earned in pension accounts, and deductions for individual retirement accounts (IRAs) shelter at least part of the taxpayer's savings from taxation. A consumption tax would allow the same deductions from income in determining the tax base. The current income tax, therefore, is really not a pure income tax at all but a combination of elements of income and consumption taxation. For many people, moving to a consumption tax would not produce that significant a change. The incentives to save may not significantly improve under a consumption tax since some saving is already not taxed.

Whether or not, and by how much, saving could be expected to increase after a change to a consumption tax is controversial. Many of the provisions in the income tax that treat saving preferentially are not well designed as incentives to save.[21] The ceiling on contributions to IRAs, for example, means that for those who would save more than the maximum amount, there is no effective improvement in incentives at the margin. A shift to a consumption tax should, therefore, increase the net return received by savers, but how much this would affect saving is unclear. We would expect savings to rise somewhat, and that would increase the rate of economic growth, which benefits most people.

Although a consumption tax should increase the incentive to save, it could have an adverse effect on the incentive to work. Since consumption is less than income, higher statutory marginal tax rates must be applied to consumption to raise the same revenue an income tax would raise. Some fear that these higher rates may further weaken incentives to work. Insofar as people work for present consumption, this is a possibility, but the return for working for future consumption is increased. A consumption tax taxes present consumption more heavily than an income tax does, but future consumption less heavily since saving is deductible. For this reason, we suspect that an income tax and a consumption tax would have about the same effect on labor supply.

A consumption tax could be riddled with loopholes just as easily as an income tax, and the implications for equity and efficiency would be the same. In principle, most proponents of a consumption tax favor a comprehensive measure of consumption, which, if achieved, would be a gain in relation to our current tax system. The higher statutory marginal tax rates required for a consumption tax would, however, create even greater incentives for taxpayers to seek out and politically promote tax preferences than under the present tax, especially if graduated rates are used. Realistically, we expect the problems associated with a narrow tax base to be just as great under a personal consumption tax as under the current income tax.

One serious problem in the transition to a consumption tax would be the treatment of wealth already accumulated. Under a consumption tax, a retired person financing consumption by drawing down his savings account would be taxed on his consumption. That would be fair if he paid no tax on his savings in the past, but if the savings were accumulated out of after-tax income, to tax it again would constitute double taxation. There are ways to mitigate this problem, but they would complicate the administration of the consumption tax and still probably treat some unfairly.

To sum up, it would be practical to substitute a personal consumption tax for the individual income tax. A consumption tax would improve incentives to save and would have a debatable effect on equity. If levied at graduated rates, it would probably have a negligible effect on work incentives. If levied at a flat rate on a comprehensive base, it would probably improve work incentives as much as the flat rate tax discussed earlier.

Value-added Taxation. A value-added tax (VAT) is levied on the difference between the sales receipts of a firm and its purchases from other firms. Assuming that purchases of capital goods are deductible, the total tax base of such a tax is equal to the total consumption of the nation. A uniform tax rate applied to all firms would therefore be quite similar in its effects to a national retail sales tax.

A VAT is generally thought to be regressive in relation to income in the distribution of its tax burden since lower-income families spend a larger fraction of their incomes on consumption. Poor families, however, finance a large part of their consumption out of government transfers. If transfers are indexed to prices, as many are by law, then the regressivity of a VAT would be mitigated, and the tax would actually be progressive at the lowest income levels. If the tax produces a one-time increase in the price level, for example, a family living on its social security check would find the transfer increased in proportion to the increase in prices and would therefore bear no burden at all. Since consumption that is financed by transfers and indexed to prices would be insulated from the tax, the alleged regressivity of a VAT is probably less than popularly imagined.[22]

In its pure form, a VAT would be levied at a uniform rate on all goods and services. It is possible, however, to exclude some goods and services from taxation, and some people favor this approach. Total consumption in the United States in 1985 is expected to be about $2,800 billion. A 5 percent rate, for example, applied to this base would produce $140 billion in additional tax revenue, as a first approximation. If housing, food, and medical care were excluded from taxation, the tax base would shrink to $1,200 billion, and the yield of a 5 percent levy would be $60 billion. Two reasons are given for favoring excluding some items from taxation. The first is administrative difficulties in taxing some types of consumption, such as owner-occupied housing. Second, it is felt that exempting necessities would make the tax less regressive. It is possible to go even further and tax items at different rates—perhaps higher rates on luxury goods—in an effort to shift more of the tax burden to upper-income groups. Most tax specialists believe, however, that the complexities and administrative costs of exemptions and different rates are not worth the effort.[23]

In contrast to the other proposals we have discussed, the VAT is usually not proposed as a substitute for the individual income tax; instead, it is intended to be a new tax added to the present system. Viewed in this way, the VAT would not correct any of the deficiencies of the present system, but it would probably not aggravate them as much as some other proposals for raising more revenue. For reasons of efficiency, for example, raising more revenue with a VAT would almost certainly be preferable to raising the rates of existing taxes. The reason is that effective marginal tax rates would not rise as much under the VAT as they would from an expansion of the highly progressive income tax. The VAT would also not reduce incentives to save since it is a tax on consumption, but it would not improve incentives either since it would leave the present tax structure intact. By adding the VAT to the present system, however, we lose the opportunity to realize what may be quite substantial productivity gains from reform of existing taxes.

Part of the attraction of a VAT is that the public generally views sales taxes in a favorable light. Opinion surveys show that retail sales taxes are a significantly more popular form of taxation than the federal income tax.[24] Since the federal income tax raises three times as much revenue as retail sales taxes, people may simply be expressing an aversion to higher taxes. Even lower-income groups, who probably bear a greater burden under sales taxes than under the income tax, favor sales taxes by a margin of 1.75 to 1. These attitudes may make adding a VAT more politically feasible than raising some other tax, regardless of the objective merits of the other proposals.

Related to the public's perception of the VAT is the possibility that it will prove to be too easy for the government to use it to finance new spending programs. The VAT, like other taxes collected from firms, ultimately falls on individual taxpayers, but the burden may be effectively concealed by its method of collection. Almost all countries that have adopted a VAT have increased its rate over time.

Conclusion

Tax reform now offers greater potential benefits than at any time in our history simply because the present tax system is so complex, inefficient, and inequitable. Although the current tax system could be used to raise more revenue to close the deficit, doing so would make the shortcomings of the existing system even greater. In contrast, some tax reforms do hold out the promise of substantial productivity and efficiency gains even if they are used to raise additional revenue.

Unfortunately, most of the productivity gains realizable from tax reform are inversely related to the degree of progressivity of the tax. It is simply not realistic to expect a tax that maintains the progressivity of the present income tax to produce much improvement in work and saving incentives. A flat rate tax on personal consumption or a flat rate tax on income, however, could produce substantial benefits in these areas. They also would increase the real tax burdens on lower-income families, though by less than numerical calculations that take no account of efficiency gains might suggest. Moreover, because the advantages from improved work and saving incentives would probably not be fully realized for several years, the choices facing us are especially difficult.

Notes

1. James Gwartney, "Tax Rates, Taxable Income and the Distributional Effects of the Economic Recovery Act of 1981," testimony before U.S. Congress, Joint Economic Committee, June 12, 1984, exhibit 5.

2. Ibid., exhibit 1.

3. Robert J. Barro and Chaipat Sahasakul, "Average Marginal Tax Rates from Social Security and the Individual Income Tax," National Bureau of Economic Research, Working Paper No. 1214, October 1983.

4. Personal income is the most comprehensive measure of the income of families and of persons available from the national income and product accounts. Although more comprehensive than adjusted gross income, it still falls short of a truly comprehensive measure of income.

5. Eugene Steuerle and Michael Hartzmark, "Individual Income Taxation, 1947–1979," National Tax Journal, June 1981, pp. 161–62, 165.

6. Edgar K. Browning and Jacquelene M. Browning, Public Finance and the Price System, 2d ed. (New York: Macmillan, 1983), table 11–4.

7. Joel Slemrod and Nikki Sorum, "The Compliance Cost of the U.S. Individual Income Tax System," National Bureau of Economic Research, Working Paper No. 1401, July 1984.

8. For a survey of the evidence, see Don Fullerton, "On the Possibility of an Inverse Relationship between Tax Rates and Government Revenues," Journal of Public Economics, October 1982, pp. 3–22.

9. James Gwartney and James Long, "Income Tax Avoidance and an Empirical Estimation of the Laffer Curve," workshop paper, Department of Economics, Florida State University, July 1984.

10. Gwartney, "Tax Rates," exhibit 4. Gwartney gives the data on nominal wages and salaries; we have used the consumer price index to convert to real magnitudes.

11. Congressional Budget Office, Revising the Individual Income Tax, July 1983, p. 10.

12. Charles L. Ballard, John B. Shoven, and John Whalley, "The Welfare Cost of Distortions in the United States Tax System: A General Equilibrium Approach," National Bureau of Economic Research, Working Paper No. 1043,

December 1982; and Charles Stuart, "Welfare Costs per Dollar of Additional Tax Revenue in the United States," *American Economic Review*, June 1984, pp. 352–62.

13. We are puzzled by the large increase in taxes shown for the under $5,000 class. Note that if every family had income at the top of that class, $5,000, the total tax per family from an 11.8 percent levy would be $590, but the table shows an increase of $783.07, which appears impossible. The problem may be that the change in tax is given per tax return under the present system, and there would be many more tax returns under the flat rate tax.

14. Browning and Johnson give weighted average marginal tax rates for each quintile of households in 1976. By weighting each of these rates by the share of labor income earned by each quintile, we get an overall weighted average marginal tax rate of 43 percent. Since both social security and income taxes are higher today, we think 44 percent is a conservative figure. See Edgar K. Browning and William R. Johnson, "The Trade-off between Equality and Efficiency," *Journal of Political Economy*, April 1984, table 3.

15. Strictly speaking, we should use compensated labor supply elasticities for the computation of welfare costs, and values exceeding 0.3 could be supported from the literature. See the discussions in ibid. and Stuart, "Welfare Costs."

16. The after-tax rate of pay rises from 56 percent to 64 percent of market pay, so averages 60 percent for the $86 billion in additional earnings. Thus, 60 percent of $86 billion, or $52 billion, is necessary to compensate workers for the leisure they give up.

17. Jacquelene M. Browning, "Estimating the Welfare Cost of Tax Preferences," *Public Finance Quarterly*, April 1979, pp. 199–219.

18. Testimony of Joseph Minarik before U.S. Congress, Subcommittee on Monetary and Fiscal Policy of the Joint Economic Committee, July 27, 1982; cited in Congressional Budget Office, *Revising the Individual Income Tax*, p. 52.

19. The Kemp-Kasten plan has a nominal marginal tax rate of 25 percent that applies to all taxable income. It allows, however, an earned income exclusion of 20 percent of earnings up to $40,000, which makes the net marginal tax rate 20 percent up to that amount. The exclusion is gradually phased out for earnings between $40,000 and $100,000, which makes the net marginal tax rate 28 percent for this range. For incomes above $100,000, only the 25 percent rate applies.

20. Taxpayers could avoid paying the tax altogether if they die without consuming their savings. For this reason, many proponents of a consumption tax favor treating bequests as consumption at the time of death and collecting the tax then. If graduated rates are used, it would probably be appropriate to have some sort of averaging provision.

21. Galper and Steuerle give a lucid discussion of why most provisions designed to stimulate saving probably have little effect. See Harvey Galper and Eugene Steuerle, "Tax Incentives for Saving," *The Brookings Review*, Winter 1983, pp. 16–23.

22. For a detailed discussion of this argument, see Edgar K. Browning and William R. Johnson, *The Distribution of the Tax Burden* (Washington, D.C.:

American Enterprise Institute, 1979).

23. Charles E. McLure, Jr., "Value Added Tax: Has the Time Come?" in Charls E. Walker and Mark A. Bloomfield, eds., *New Directions in Federal Tax Policy for the 1980s* (Cambridge, Mass.: Ballinger, 1983).

24. Advisory Commission on Intergovernmental Relations, *Changing Public Attitudes on Governments and Taxes* (Washington, D.C.: ACIR, 1982).

11

The Politics of the Deficit

Norman J. Ornstein

Summary

Federal deficits have been an issue of the politics of American elections at least since the first party platform on record, in 1840; deficits have been a preoccupation of the politics of governing at least since the days of the Founding Fathers. The Founding Fathers set up a structure of government to prevent a powerful central government from exercising undue control, first and foremost, over the power of the purse. To restrain government power over spending and taxing, they deliberately and explicitly gave more control to the Congress of the United States than to the president, expecting that the direct representatives of the people, in a system of checks and balances, would be more restrained.

In this paper, a historical review of deficits and the responses of government to them suggests that the Founding Fathers' assumptions were, and remain, fundamentally accurate. Through nearly 200 years, Congress has not acted in a basically irresponsible fashion, spending more money than it took in to satisfy short-term and parochial political needs. To the contrary, through the broad sweep of American history, Congress has struggled to restrain the growth of federal spending and to limit deficits and the public debt, through direct action and through periodic adjustments of its own structures to minimize the deleterious effects of political pressures. Indeed, the great growth in federal debt and the periodic problems with deficits are much more the result of massive expenditures to support major wars and the activist policies of presidents striving to make their mark on American society and in American history.

An examination of the problems of the 1960s through the 1980s confirms this judgment. Proposals, like the line-item veto, that would give more power to the president and weaken the hand of Congress to restrain the growth of federal spending and deal with the deficit are, upon analysis, misguided and

---

Portions of this essay appeared originally in a presentation for the Fourth Annual Donald S. MacNaughton Symposium, "What Should Be Done about the Federal Deficit?" (May 15-17, 1984), and in "Veto the Line-Item Veto," *Fortune* (January 7, 1985).

311

might well have the opposite effect. The conclusion of this paper is that the best way to deal with contemporary deficits is by having two strong and confident political institutions, not by weakening the powers of the Congress. Some relatively minor institutional changes might well help, but there is no institutional or structural panacea. Finally, the paper argues, the solution begins not with the institutions but with the public. Meaningful action on the deficit requires public pressure for urgent action and public agreement to waive deep-seated individual policy preferences for a greater goal. Action by elites to encourage that set of responses will help in turn to encourage the appropriate institutional responses to the immediate deficit problems.

When Walter F. Mondale made the federal deficit the centerpiece of his presidential campaign in his acceptance speech at the 1984 Democratic convention in San Francisco, it was perhaps the first time that a major party presidential candidate had based his campaign on this issue. But of course it was by no means the first time that deficits and their corollaries, government spending and taxation, had been a part of American political debate. The question of government deficits was raised in the first party platform on record, that of the Democratic party in 1840; the fifth of nine planks in that platform read: "Resolved, that it is the duty of every branch of government, to enforce and practice the most rigid economy, in conducting our public affairs, and that no more revenue ought to be raised, than is required to defray the necessary expenses of the government."[1]

In virtually every campaign since then, both parties have gone on record against deficits, for restraint in government spending, and for limited taxation. But in very few campaigns has the consequence of too much spending or too little taxation—that is, large government deficits—been a major issue. Some parties, notably the Republicans in the 1930s and 1940s, tried to make deficits the major issue but failed to penetrate the public consciousness. Evidence from the November 6 election suggests that Mondale also failed to do so. Although deficits have been important but not decisive in the politics of elections, they have been much more of a preoccupation in the politics of governing.

A Historical Review of Deficits and Government in the United States

When the Founding Fathers deliberated over the American form of government, they were concerned with the accumulation of power and its irresponsible use by individuals and institutions of government. Nothing concerned them more than the power to tax indiscriminately—a root cause, of course, of the American Revolution—and the power of government to spend money to advance its own causes. For these reasons the Founding Fathers divided the power of the purse, as they did all other government powers, creating a series of checks and balances. But they very deliberately and very carefully gave the fundamental power of the purse to the institution of government most directly connected to the public at large: Congress. And they gave a greater share of this power, the power to initiate revenue measures, to the House of Representatives. No appropriation from the public treasury could be accomplished without the approval of both houses of Congress and the signature of the president; no revenue could be raised unless the action was initiated by the House of Representatives, approved by both houses of Congress, and signed by the president. Although the president could veto any money measure, as he could veto any piece of legislation passed by Congress, Congress was made the ultimate arbiter; presidential vetoes could be overridden by two-thirds votes in both houses, with no legal recourse by the president.

The founders believed that the greatest forces of restraint on governmental power over spending and taxing were in the public at large, through their representatives. They had trepidations, of course; they recognized the political interests of individual representatives and the power of factions but believed that checks and balances would provide some solution for these problems.

During the early years of American government, the founders' schema worked largely as they had intended. Saddled with a large revolutionary war debt of about $80 million, the political actors in the federal government struggled to keep the debt from getting worse and to reduce it. They had remarkable success, cutting the debt nearly in half by 1811. But then came a problem that was to be recurrent: war.

The War of 1812 brought four years (1812–1815) of big deficits. By its end the federal debt had tripled. Redoubled efforts by government in the next quarter-century and more reduced the debt once again—almost, in the 1830s, to zero. It rose again during the war with Mexico in 1847 to 1849 but was reduced steadily once more in its aftermath.

Then came a war that brought, by any standard, enormous economic costs: the Civil War. Whereas the four years of the War of 1812 produced a total deficit of $68.5 million, the four years of the Civil War increased the debt of the national government by nearly $2.6 billion, as federal spending soared (to $1.3 billion in 1865) without, of course, a corresponding rise in federal receipts.

The Civil War created a crisis in the federal government and an unprecedented debt, which first went over $1 billion in 1863 and over $2 billion two years later and came dangerously close to $3 billion. The government responded to this crisis with both institutional reform

313

and fiscal restraint. Immediately after the Civil War, the House of Representatives created a unified Appropriations Committee; the Senate followed two years later. These committees took over some of the responsibility that had been handled by the House Ways and Means and the Senate Finance committees, which had managed both appropriations and revenue measures. But the Civil War had placed enormous burdens on these two committees. The war required, for example, dramatic changes in tax laws, including three major tariff bills and the first federal tax on incomes, as well as major acts authorizing new government bonds and the first national banking system. This put too much work in the hands of a single committee; the response of Congress was to create new committees to handle the burdens of appropriations and spending more responsibly.

That process worked remarkably well in the years following the Civil War, when the federal government ran an almost incredible string of surpluses. As Thomas Wander has noted, "In the 31 years between 1867 and 1897 there were 27 years of budget surpluses at the federal level. In 13 of those years, revenues exceeded expenditures by more than 25 percent; only one year saw expenditures exceed revenues by as much as 10 percent."[2]

The restraint on spending that this record of prudence demonstrated was driven by the two penurious Appropriations committees, aided, at least in the House of Representatives, by a change in House rules in 1876. This change, the so-called Holman rule, allowed general legislation in appropriations bills if the result was to reduce expenditures. The result *was* reduced expenditures but also a tremendous expansion of the legislative power of the Appropriations Committee. With years of big surpluses, the political interests of individual members of Congress began to come to the fore, and resentment over both the tremendous power wielded by the Appropriations Committee and its pruning-knife attitude led in the 1870s and 1880s to a near revolt in the House. That revolt ultimately crippled the appropriations process and the Appropriations Committee, sending spending bills to a number of other committees more interested in logrolling than in spending restraint.

These other committees, from Agriculture to Commerce to Post Offices and Post Roads, participated actively in expanding the role of the federal government during the 1880s and 1890s. But the changes did not bring federal deficits—not until the Spanish-American War, coupled with the recession of 1896, created another cycle of large federal deficits.

Through the 1890s and in the early twentieth century, when the federal government had become a major force in American society with expanded responsibilities and activity, federal decision makers grappled with a new set of problems, and the federal budget results demonstrated this change. Wars, recessions, and other economic problems and the less disciplined approach by Congress to federal spending brought more erratic budget behavior. In the twenty years from 1896 to 1916, the federal government experienced eleven years of deficit to only nine of surplus; the net effect, however, was a national debt in 1916 almost the same as it had been twenty years earlier.

But 1917 brought a new and more severe crisis, World War I. This war, like the Civil War, brought staggering deficits greater than all others in the history of the country combined. In 1916, after 127 years, the total public debt stood at $1.23 billion; by 1919 it had increased twentyfold, to $25.5 billion. The deficit in 1919 alone was over $13 billion. Congress and the executive branch, suddenly faced with a national debt much greater than they could comprehend, once again turned to institutional reform in search of solutions. On June 1, 1920, the House restored exclusive spending power to its Appropriations Committee and enlarged the committee from twenty-one to thirty-five members. On March 5, 1922, the Senate also concentrated spending powers in its Appropriations Committee (although it left the membership at sixteen). And in the largest single reform up to that time, the Budget and Accounting Act of 1921, Congress reformed the executive branch, unifying the federal budget under the president's control and creating the Bureau of the Budget and the General Accounting Office (GAO). The bureau was created as an arm of the executive branch for fiscal management; the GAO was intended to be an arm of Congress, strengthening the oversight of federal spending. With the economic expansion that followed World War I, these reforms contributed to another string of federal surpluses, which gradually whittled the public debt back, to only $16 billion by 1930.

The depression that followed, with a sharp decline in federal revenues and the increase in expenditures that accompanied New Deal programs, led to new deficits through the 1930s. Those deficits were moderate compared with the staggering deficits of World War II, which totaled $211 billion dollars through six war years. Once again a massive war took the federal budget problem to an unprecedented level. Once again the response of Congress was to attempt a reform that would consolidate and tighten up its spending process: a federal legislative budget proposed, and passed, as part of the overall Legislative Reorganization Act of 1946.

The legislative budget did not last, and the era following World War II was marked by attempts on the part of government to adjust to a very new and complex economic and political situation, that of post-

New Deal and postwar America. Even though federal outlays dropped after World War II, they were still far greater than they had been before the war. In 1952, for example, federal spending was $67.7 billion—compared with only $9.5 billion in 1940, the year just before the war. The Legislative Reorganization Act of 1946 had dramatically reduced the number of committees in Congress and had provided some restraint on logrolling; but the activist programs of presidents, combined with economic conditions and congressional spending habits, led to several years of deficit to go with periodic surpluses during the late 1940s and 1950s. In dollar terms, the gross federal debt grew during these years, but, with economic expansion, it declined considerably as a proportion of gross national product. The national debt on the eve of the depression was $16.8 billion, or 33 percent of GNP; by 1940, on the eve of our entry into World War II, it was $43 billion, or 43 percent of GNP; in 1946, after the economic drain of the war, it was a staggering $269 billion, or 128.5 percent of GNP. Through congressional restraint on expenditures, however, the debt declined steadily to $253 billion, or 98 percent of GNP, in 1949; with continued restraint and economic growth, it was down to 56 percent of GNP by 1961.

In sum, a historical overview of government spending, government actions, and government deficits from the beginning of the American republic to the 1960s shows a strong concern in government about spending restraint and fiscal responsibility, with overall results that match. Our national debt to this point was built very largely on intervals of war. Without the deficits caused by the War of 1812, the Mexican War, the Civil War, and the Spanish-American War, the federal government would have had a $1.6 billion surplus at the beginning of the twentieth century. Without the deficits caused by the two world wars, it would have had a gross debt of under $30 billion—or less than 5 percent of GNP—in 1961. When faced with the fiscal crises caused by war, American policy makers found ways, through institutional devices and internal control, to create budget surpluses and retire substantial portions of the colossal debt they had incurred through war expenditures.

Since the 1960s, however, we have seen a somewhat different pattern of politics and economics. In the quarter-century since 1961, we have had only one year of surplus—a relatively modest $3.2 billion in 1969. In all other years the federal government has run deficits, and the volume of deficits has grown, particularly during the administration of Ronald Reagan. From 1960 to 1980 our national debt grew from $293 billion to $993 billion; in the first Reagan term it nearly doubled again. Despite signs that Congress has responded to this budget stress much as it has in the past—for example, by enactment of the Budget and Impoundment Control Act of 1974 in the aftermath of the Vietnam War, a reform that once again consolidated and centralized budget authority in Congress—we have become increasingly critical of our policy makers, especially Congress. In the Reagan years particularly, attacks on Congress and sweeping proposals for constitutional revision to restrain Congress have increased dramatically.

The concern over deficits and their political causes is understandable; our contemporary situation is unprecedented, particularly in the last several years, when ballooning deficits have in no way been caused by a large-scale war. But is the problem an institutional one, most particularly a congressional one? Can sweeping institutional change that would limit the powers of Congress solve these problems? It is to these questions that I now turn.

Congress, the President, and Deficits: From the 1960s to the 1980s

The contemporary problem of deficit spending dates from about 1965—the beginning of Lyndon Johnson's elected presidential term. The causes were a combination of stagflation, Great Society programs, and the Vietnam War. In the early 1960s budget growth was relatively low; from 1960 through fiscal 1966 it averaged only 2 percent a year. But from 1966 to 1970, the Johnson years, the average was 10 percent. Contemporary wisdom would have it that this was Congress's fault, but even a cursory glance at the data suggests a different interpretation. Certainly Congress agreed to the increased budgets of the Johnson years, often (especially in the Eighty-ninth Congress) with enthusiastic support for the new Great Society programs. But growth in the late 1970s was greatest in national defense, averaging 12.1 percent, to only 7.3 percent in other federal expenditures. Congress was much less enthusiastic about defense increases. The engine of rapid governmental growth was President Johnson's driving demand for guns and butter together. Congress was certainly an accomplice—but the president was the mastermind. No doubt, as analysts have repeatedly stressed over the years, Johnson's desire to have his cake and missiles too encouraged the stagflation that bedeviled us for over a decade and, by depressing tax receipts, worsened our deficit problem.

Although today's deficit problem dates from the Johnson years, the economic difficulties triggered by Johnson's policies did not alone create it. Nor did we come to our current state of affairs through simple accident or inadvertence. A number of conscious policy decisions, some in the 1970s and others in the first year of the Reagan

317

presidency, created the large and growing gap we now face between federal revenues and federal expenditures. Once again Congress has been an accomplice. But once again the problems can be traced, at least in part, to other sources as well.

One key decision, reached in the wake of the Johnson Vietnam policy and concurred in by the public and the Congress, was to make a major change in priorities, sharply away from defense and toward social spending. In fiscal 1966 outlays for national defense totaled 40.7 percent of the federal budget. A decade later, through actions taken by Presidents Richard M. Nixon and Gerald R. Ford in concert with the Congress, defense had dropped to 24.5 percent of the budget. Concomitantly, of course, domestic spending proportionately rose—especially spending for benefit payments to individuals. These payments, popularly labeled entitlements, went from 26.9 percent of budget outlays in 1966 to a staggering 48.5 percent in 1976. Entitlements, especially social security, rose absolutely and comparatively throughout this period, but the greatest increases came in the first term of President Nixon. The Democratic Congress, competing with Nixon for political advantage, under intense pressure from interest groups and public opinion, and spurred by the political ambitions of Chairman Wilbur Mills of the Ways and Means Committee, increased social security—the largest entitlement by far—in 1969, 1971, and 1972 by a full 45 percent (20 percent in 1972 alone). These huge increases were *double* the cost of living.

The increases also gave individual members of Congress a political advantage. Nevertheless, in 1973 Democrats and Republicans in Congress, concerned that the entitlement programs were getting out of hand, joined to tie social security to the consumer price index. They did so both to save money and to insulate the process from intense special interest pressure. In so doing, they fulfilled a pledge made in the 1968 Republican party platform. They also recognized full well that indexation of social security would inevitably lead to indexation of other entitlement programs. This decision came at some considerable long-term cost to the individual members of Congress. Lawmakers voting each year or two on a cost-of-living increase for social security could go back home and claim credit with elderly citizens for a concrete action taken in their behalf. Making the increase automatic through indexation removed that advantage.

The motives for indexing entitlements, then, were largely positive and fully consistent with the long history of congressional concern for out-of-control spending. As inflation took over under President Jimmy Carter in the late 1970s, however, the consequences of indexation were not positive. Benefits, now beyond the reach of normal congressional discretion, increased at an accelerating pace. So, too, did interest rates and thus federal expenditures for interest on the national debt, which, of course, was also outside direct congressional control. These increases, combined with a faltering economy, gave rise to contentiousness over the fate of the dwindling elements left in the federal budget that could be altered directly each year.

In sum, by the end of the 1970s—the end of the Carter years—we had a defense budget that had dropped dramatically over a decade as a share of the total budget, a domestic budget that had risen sharply at the same time, especially in entitlements and net interest, and sharp conflict over these and other budget priorities—all fueled by a sagging economy. The budget deficit was viewed by politicians as only one of several problems. It was not seen as uncontrollable or even worsening, mainly because high inflation had cushioned it, swelling tax revenues more than increased budget outlays and cheapening the value of the dollars in the national debt.

To his credit, President Carter tried in both 1979 and 1980 to grapple with many of these problems. He proposed significant increases in defense spending and significant cuts in the domestic arena, while pledging to move toward balancing the budget. Congress, though preoccupied with the political fallout of these economic problems, nevertheless responded. In 1980, relying in part on reconciliation—a device created in the 1974 Budget Act—Congress took a series of painful actions to accommodate the Carter goals.[3] But Carter's sentiments and the actions he proposed were clearly not enough. They made him ever more unpopular within the Democratic party and were not convincing enough to the electorate at large.

To be sure, the problems of the 1960s and 1970s were not just the result of poor economic performance, presidential programs and misfeasance, and such noble but misguided actions as indexing entitlements. Congress itself contributed to the deficit problem, through institutional reforms that removed many of its traditional restraints on federal spending. Since the 1920s—the period following the major reforms, which included the Government and Accounting Act of 1921—Congress had relied on tough-minded, institution-oriented, and strong-willed Appropriations committees to put brakes on the natural political impulses to spend more money for individual political advantage. During the 1940s and 1950s such important Appropriations Committee chairmen as Representative Clarence Cannon (Democrat, Missouri) and Senator Carl Hayden (Democrat, Arizona) erected internal incentives and restraints on their committee members to keep the committees acting as guardians of the federal treasury. But reforms in the late 1960s and early 1970s diluted the role of the Appropriations committees and, by democratizing and decentralizing power to a large number of subcommittees, to rank-and-file members, and to staff, removed many of the existing restraints on the growth of federal spending. Individual members and subcommittees, led by entrepreneurs seeking political advantage, reputation, and power, came up with new ideas for more spending and accelerated the problems of the 1970s. But although these congressional reforms have contributed to the growth in spending, their effect has been relatively small compared with the magnitude of the problem. The largest single policy result of congressional reforms during this era was an expansion of economic regulation, not of concrete spending programs.

Regardless of the cause, actions of the federal government and the course of the economy in the 1970s aroused growing public discontent. When the American public chose Ronald Reagan on November 4, 1980, they were signaling their displeasure with the economic performance of Carter and Congress and their desire for a change. Public opinion surveys tell us that substantial public support existed for the three main legs of the Reagan economic program—more defense, less domestic government, and a reduced tax burden. But there was *also* deep public support for a continuing strong federal role in nearly every area of public policy (save welfare and foreign aid) and evidence of public willingness to accept sacrifices—including taxes—to solve our economic difficulties, such as a deficit projected to reach $60 billion in President Carter's last budget year. Overall, clearly, the public wanted a change in 1980 but was willing to leave the specifics up to its political leaders.

Ronald Reagan took that mandate for change and moved swiftly in 1981 to implement his program: sharp increases in defense spending; slowdowns and some significant cuts in domestic spending (except in entitlements); and deep tax reductions, led by a 25 percent across-the-board cut in tax rates over three years. Assisted by yeoman work and shrewd strategy by his key lieutenants in the newly Republican Senate, Reagan was able to move his budget plan nearly intact through the Senate early in 1981. Virtually perfect Republican unity and some key Democratic votes gave the president budget victory over the House and its Democratic leaders by midyear.

The House Democratic leaders were stung by Reagan's successes—and their defeats. They were determined to avoid further humiliation when the tax component of the Reagan plan came up for consideration in July or August 1981. Chairman Dan Rostenkowski (Democrat, Illinois) of the Ways and Means Committee tried to achieve a compromise with the president's forces but was rebuffed. So Rostenkowski, encouraged by Speaker Thomas P. ("Tip") O'Neill, began to develop his own own tax-cut alternative. Eager to win at all costs, the House Democrats put together a package incorporating most of the Reagan plan, while adding additional tax breaks attractive to conservative Democrats and Republicans: greater depreciation, reduction of maximum taxes, indexing of brackets, and other components. Reagan's forces retaliated by sweetening the pot with even more tax cuts to lure back their natural allies. The bidding was intensified through the summer; in the end, however, the president once again prevailed. The "victory" meant a much deeper tax cut than originally envisioned.

There was an electricity in Washington and around the country during 1981, but it had little to do with substance. The question was, Would Reagan win or lose? Many Democratic and Republican legislators, along with serious economists and other observers, were raising serious questions about the Reagan program, especially about the combined cumulative effect on future federal deficits of deep tax cuts, large defense spending increases, and modest domestic spending reductions; but the questions were largely lost or ignored in the uproar over who would win. The rhetorical response from the White House reinforced the rosy economic assumptions and projections of the Office of Management and Budget: no need to worry, the tax cuts will raise more revenue than they will lose, and the package will stimulate instant economic boom, sustain prosperity, and bring a budget surplus by 1985. The same public arguments were made during the tax-cut battle, although they were a sideline to the clash of wills between Reagan and the House Democratic leadership. "It had nothing to do with good or rational public policy; it was simply a macho contest between Reagan and Tip O'Neill," said one disgruntled observer at the time, "and it really compounded the deficit."[4]

The deep tax cut did compound the deficit. And behind the scenes the people around Reagan clearly knew that it would. In the middle of the tax-cut war, a key Reagan lieutenant candidly assessed the situation:

> We're well aware that tax cuts at the level we're discussing will add tremendously to future deficits. Most of us, to be frank, don't buy the extreme supply-side line. Regardless, Reagan's main goal is not to balance the budget—it is to reduce the role of government. How do we best do this? In our view, if we don't cut taxes and generate big deficits, spending will never come down. Congress will just spend the revenues and more . . . but with huge deficits, their choices are tougher . . . they'll *have* to cut spending.[5]

President Reagan may have believed that the more massive the tax cuts, the greater the ultimate revenue gain (although his belated support for large tax increases in 1982 and 1984 belies that notion). More likely Reagan, too, saw the specter of mammoth deficits as a price worth paying to get Congress, under extreme duress, to cut government.

Of course, the president and his lieutenants were wrong, and for several reasons. First, the public mandate for change—with details left up to the political leaders—would clearly be short-lived (as any major mandate for change has been in American history). In 1981 public sentiment was to give the president a chance and never mind the details, but it was evident that this sentiment would fade and the details would sharpen by 1982. Interest groups caught off balance by Reagan in 1981 would by the next year be better able to mobilize. They did—and stiffened Congress's resolve against further deep domestic cuts.

But it was not simply, or primarily, special interest pressure or congressional stubbornness that brought domestic budget cutting largely to a halt by 1982. Public opinion also played a role. Budget director David Stockman, early in 1984, put it best:

> People want to have mass transit subsidies and middle class subsidies for education. And the agricultural sector wants all those benefits . . . You are now at the point where you are reaching the legislative hard core of the budget. The budget system is not the problem. The problem is that this democracy is somewhat ambivalent about what it wants. It wants low taxes and substantial public spending.[6]

In the same interview Stockman made clear the consequences of the limits of public tolerance for spending cuts. When he was asked about the Reagan administration's goal of cutting federal spending to 19 percent of GNP, he commented, "The minimum size of government achievable appears to be 22 percent to 23 percent of GNP."[7]

The Reagan administration can perhaps take credit, as Stockman noted, for keeping federal spending from going above 25 percent of GNP as it would otherwise have done, but the key point is that the administration deliberately helped to negotiate a tax package that simultaneously brought federal revenues down to 19 percent of GNP. Whether the administration's "plan" for domestic spending cuts in 1982 and beyond failed through miscalculation, overoptimism, or sheer folly, the result, built into the Reagan policies, was a chronic and huge deficit problem.

Washington policy makers, it is true, did not deal sweepingly or effectively with this problem in 1982 and beyond. But once again the blame could not be laid in major part at the feet of Congress. Congress, to its credit, began to grapple on its own with each of these areas. In taxes and defense, at least, the president was of little help. In 1982, after his unrealistic first budget proposal was rejected across the board in Congress and after the collapse of the informal budget negotiations known as the Gang of Seventeen, President Reagan essentially withdrew from the budget policy process. The Republican Senate moved in unilaterally to fill the policy vacuum. It passed its own budget, calling for smaller defense increases than the president had requested and building in a tax increase that he had flatly opposed. It is true that the president belatedly endorsed both budget and tax proposals, helping to steer them through the Democratic House of Representatives. But it was Congress, in an approximation of congressional government, that defied conventional wisdom in an election year by slowing defense and raising taxes to reduce the deficit.

Late in 1982 Congress and the president acted together to save social security, legislating a major plan that raised social security taxes and shaved future benefits. At the same time, of course, the plan reduced future deficits from what they would otherwise have been. (Moreover, it included a delay in cost-of-living adjustments in social security that would inevitably lead to similar delays in the other entitlement programs and thus reduce deficits further.)

In 1983 Congress initiated an energy tax increase. In 1984 the Republican Senate once again moved into a policy vacuum, proposing a "down payment" on the deficit, including another significant tax increase, which the president once again belatedly endorsed.

These actions may be too little, too late. But in the absence of strong presidential economic leadership, in the face of presidential opposition to tax increases or defense slowdowns, and in the absence of any strong public mandate comparable to that of 1981, it is surprising that any significant actions at all were taken in 1982, 1983, or 1984.

In 1984, although Congress did no more than propose and implement another incremental down payment on the deficit, it took other steps intended to set the stage for more significant action in 1985 and beyond. Proposals were floated that were designed not to be implemented immediately but to be injected into the policy debate for future use. The most significant of these was the budget freeze, proposed by a triumvirate of senators who spanned the ideological spectrum, from liberal Democrat (Joseph Biden, Delaware) to centrist Republican (Nancy Kassebaum, Kansas) to conservative Republican (Charles Grassley, Iowa). These senators proposed that the budget for fiscal 1985 be frozen at the level of the 1984 budget. The freeze was attacked from many quarters, including the White House, which noted its dramatic effect on the defense budget. But it was widely viewed on Capitol Hill as a device that could be explained more easily than selective budget cuts to a wide range of Americans and perhaps be accepted by them. As one participant noted at the time, "The freeze means fairness. I can tell my constituents nobody suffers very much—everyone simply gets what they got last year—and the burden is borne to some degree by everybody."[8]

Although the freeze was ignored in the budget battles of 1984, it was an idea that was certain to rise again when Congress was ready to take more serious action on the budget and the deficit in 1985. One reason was the deficit-related debate that dominated the 1984 campaign—especially the presidential campaign. During the campaign President Reagan directly and explicitly precluded any changes in social security benefits or outlays for current or future recipients. That pledge, combined with firm pledges not to increase taxes and to continue to push for defense increases comparable to those requested in the past (14 percent or more in real terms), doubled the difficulty faced by Congress in grappling with the deficit, especially on the spending side.

Walter Mondale's campaign ploy of pledging a tax increase to deal with the deficit and challenging political debate on that basis further complicated the prospects for 1985. Mondale made taxes a centerpiece of the campaign and forced the White House to take a much more explicit stance against a tax increase for political purposes, than it would otherwise have liked. It also altered the tactics for congressional campaigns, precipitating a nationwide Republican congressional television advertising campaign that focused on one theme: Democrats in Congress will raise your taxes; Republicans will not. This theme hardened Republican positions against tax increases and forced many Democrats, in the heat of election campaigning, also to pledge not to increase taxes.

In the days after the election, most politicians faced the new reality. The deficit was still there; the president's campaign theme that economic growth would eliminate the problem was accepted by fewer and fewer observers; and the savings available in direct budget cutting—given a large defense increase and exemption from cuts of the largest domestic program by far—were clearly not enough to take care of the deficit problem.

The stage was set for confrontation on domestic spending, a confrontation that would be over the same areas of spending about which President Reagan had clashed with Congress in 1981 and throughout his first term. But political forces in Washington were searching for devices to move the battleground beyond those increasingly fruitless political disputes to a common ground that would yield larger savings and broader action to grapple with out-year deficits.

The problem was complicated by the political dynamics of a two-term president in his fifth year. Two-term presidents since the Twenty-second Amendment to the Constitution have started their final terms at a political disadvantage, whatever their reelection margin. The disadvantage begins with the lame-duck status of the president and is reinforced by the political dynamics of the off-year election to take place two years hence. For many reasons, including the six-year senatorial terms, the way congressional candidates are recruited, and the typical pattern of economic performance, the election in the sixth year of a two-term president almost inevitably results in significant losses for the president's party in both houses of Congress. For 1986 Republicans face the prospect of having many more vulnerable Senate seats than the Democrats (twenty-two to twelve), largely because of the great Republican success in the Senate in the sweeping Reagan victory of 1980. Democrats who held Senate seats in that Republican year are not likely to face as severe a challenge six years later; many Republicans who won needed the boost of an enormous Reagan tide, a boost that will be absent in 1986.

Republicans in the Senate will be particularly nervous about the political prospects of 1986, therefore, particularly concerned about protecting their own electoral interests first, and considerably more independent of the president and his desires than they have been in the past. They want action now that will preclude an economic disaster in 1986.

All these difficulties suggest the need for quick steps on the deficit, a need that has been acknowledged by the overwhelming majority of lawmakers. The likelihood of quick action is enhanced by the scarcity of other significant items on the political agenda for 1985. Before the end of November 1984, lawmakers were searching for an appropriate way to put together the package that many, if not most, acknowledge is necessary: a combination of domestic spending slowdowns, reductions in the rate of increase of defense, and tax increases.

Clearly, the president's commitment to tax simplification and the Treasury Department's tax reform proposals were bound together in this process of negotiation and strategy. At this writing, in late November 1984, no explicit vehicle, like a bipartisan commission on the deficit, a bipartisan commission on tax simplification or reform, or an informal working group such as the Gang of Seventeen, had emerged. But with the selection by Senate Republicans of Robert Dole

(Kansas) as their new majority leader and the related accession of Robert Packwood (Republican, Oregon) to the chairmanship of the Senate Finance Committee, the Republican Senate was controlled by men who set their first priority on deficit reduction and who have made clear their preference in the past for a combination of spending reductions and tax increases. And the early maneuvering after the election suggested that, as in 1982 and 1984, the Congress, most particularly the Republican Senate, would be likely to take the lead in acting to reduce the deficit, pulling a reluctant president along.

Is Congress to Blame for the Deficit?

The history I have recounted suggests that Congress, though a key participant in budget decisions, is not inherently inclined, for political reasons, to spend federal dollars at will or to pile up injudicious deficits. Still, a substantial literature in political science casts doubt on Congress's institutional abilities, given the demands and incentives of its individual members. Political scientist David Mayhew, in his classic book *Congress: The Electoral Connection*, eloquently described the kinds of parochial, particularized benefits reelection-minded legislators would seek—and we regularly see them doing so on the House floor.[9] Kenneth Shepsle and Clifford Hardin of Washington University in St. Louis have further claimed that the contemporary rise of subcommittee government, by reducing the internal restraints that had earlier existed in Congress, has greatly exacerbated the spending problem.[10]

Although both lines of argument are credible, a wholesale acceptance of them would lead us to expect congressmen to have increased the share of pork-barrel type programs in the past few years and to have at least protected these beneficial programs for the future. The opposite is true. By indexing first social security and then other entitlement programs, congressmen consciously reduced their ability to use federal budget dollars in the interests of their reelection. In the future, as entitlements grow automatically, defense skyrockets, and the interest on the national debt accumulates, the share of the budget devoted to the rest of government—which includes most of the items we think of as special interest or parochial pork—will decline markedly.

Consider the component parts of the federal budget from 1966 to 1986. Grants to state and local governments together with other federal operations—the category that includes the programs congressmen can boast about when they run for reelection—constituted 25.3 percent of the budget at the height of the Great Society. Entitlement indexing began in 1973; by 1976 other domestic spending was only

19.7 percent of the budget; in the first Reagan year, it was down to 17 percent; by 1986 it will be less than 14 percent. The number, in other words, has regularly and significantly declined. In short, Congress has directly and greatly reduced the areas where congressmen could use spending to their individual advantage. As political scientist Douglas Arnold has noted, Congress has moved dramatically in the past two decades toward formula grant programs that remove the discretion from individual congressmen to affect or claim credit for particular benefits.[11] Economist Gardner Ackley offers additional, macroeconomic evidence that raises doubts about the thesis that our government structures inevitably swell federal programs and national debt.[12]

The Congress of the United States is not, of course, a selfless and noble institution. Members of Congress have other ways to secure their enormous electoral advantages. Defense has become a major focal point for particularized benefit giving, a direction encouraged by actions taken by major military manufacturers in the private sector. Rockwell International, for example, explicitly ensured that subcontracts for the B-1 bomber were spread to nearly every congressional district, so that Congress would view funding for the bomber favorably and would see electoral debits in cancellation or slowdown. Moreover, many members of Congress have found that the tax code, through tax expenditures, is an efficient and little noticed way to spread benefits to important groups and to keep economic perquisites flowing to constituencies.

Nevertheless, a look at the components of the federal budget shows a decline in constant dollars through the 1980s in domestic spending other than social security and Medicare, great increases in formula programs, and reductions in growth of the so-called pork-barrel programs. These facts must give pause to those who would place all blame for federal spending increases and expanding deficits on the venal political habits of individual congressmen.

A closer look at our political institutions and relations casts doubt on the efficacy of some of the major proposals that have been advanced to clean up our deficit problems once and for all. Institutional devices *can* matter, and, as we have seen, Congress has repeatedly responded to budget stress through internal reform, usually to centralize its own budget processes. When public attitudes and larger events—like a demand for spending or a change in priorities or a large war effort—do not intervene, these institutional devices can be meaningful and important. But some work better than others.

For many decades the main institutional device Congress relied on to limit deficits was the requirement of periodic votes to increase the national debt limit. This device had been expected to restrain spending and force Congress to pay serious attention to growing deficits. But, driven by the demands of presidents and limited by the constraints of public and interest group pressure, Congress has viewed the votes on the debt limit largely as nuisances. When for any reason Congress has been unable to agree to increase the debt limit, a game ensues in which the government comes perilously close to being brought to a halt, until common sense prevails and the limit is finally raised. Indeed, this device has proved to be a wonderful way for many members of Congress to eat their cake and have it too: voting consistently both against increases in the debt limit, to demonstrate to their constituents their concern for fiscal responsibility, and for programs and appropriations that increase federal spending and the debt, thus requiring the votes to increase the debt limit.

The proposal for a constitutional amendment to balance the budget has served a similar purpose for many politicians. It enables proponents to show how deeply concerned they are about federal deficits without having to propose or vote for the specific programs that might bring the budget into balance and therefore incur the wrath of the large majority of Americans who are protecting most existing federal expenditures from the legislative scalpel.

Some limited reforms would help; I return to them at the conclusion of this essay. But the history of budgeting in America suggests that constitutional change would be both unnecessary and ineffective, and perhaps even detrimental.

Institutional Change and the Deficit

So far I have tried to debunk the conventional wisdom that lays the blame for outrageous deficits and uncontrollable spending entirely at the feet of an irresponsible Congress. A serious movement, however, is afoot to deal with this problem through institutional change that would curtail the power and the role of Congress.

One major proposal that was a dominant theme of the 1984 presidential campaign is a constitutional amendment to give the president line-item veto authority. President Reagan first framed the issue in his 1984 State of the Union message:

> Some 43 of our 50 states grant their governors the right to veto individual items and appropriations bills without having to veto the entire bill . . . It works in 43 states. Let us put it to work in Washington for all the people.
>
> It would be most effective if done by constitutional amend-

ment. The majority of Americans approve of such an amendment, just as they and I approve of an amendment mandating a balanced federal budget. Many states also have this protection in their constitutions.

Throughout the campaign President Reagan and Republican senators and congressmen made the line-item veto a major theme, they suggested that the president could deal with the deficit if only he had the tools—that the most effective, most efficient, and least onerous way of dealing with federal spending is through a constitutional amendment to give the president line-item veto authority.

As a political theme this is an understandable one. But its main drawback, as the preceding pages demonstrate, is that it starts with the basic premise that the president is better than the Congress at controlling government spending. A line-item veto would give the president more authority and take away some of the basic powers that have resided in Congress since its beginning.

There is a fundamental flaw in this premise. Over time any executive-centered political system will almost certainly spend more and enlarge the scope of government more than one with substantial legislative power; witness the fate of nearly all our European allies that rely on parliamentary systems with strong executives and weak legislatures. Compared with nearly all of them, the United States, in size of government and taxation as a proportion of GNP, is small indeed. Political scientist Michael Malbin, after a recent visit to France, made the point especially well:

> The French budget system clearly favors the executive. Party discipline rules our log-rolling, and voting on the budget by department cuts down on localism. But one thing the system does not do, according to figures compiled by the Organization for Economic Cooperation and Development, is to produce a lower rate of government budgetary growth in France than in the United States. For 14 of the 20 years from 1961 to 1981, under Presidents Charles deGaulle (1958–1969), Georges Pompidou (1969–1974), Valery Giscard d'Estaing (1974–1981) and Mitterand, government spending went up at a faster rate, as a percentage of gross national product, than it did in the United States in the same period.[13]

The line-item veto, of course, is more a political ploy than a comprehensive proposal for reducing or eliminating deficits. For one thing, the veto as proposed aims exclusively at appropriations bills, while most spending, as the Office of Management and Budget has pointed out, is not directly in the hands of the Appropriations Committee or funneled through individual appropriations bills. Consider, for example, the $926 billion in the 1985 fiscal budget. Some $188 billion goes for social security, handled separately through social security legislation. Another $116 billion is for net interest payments, which the president could not item-veto. Medicare and Medicaid get $90 billion, also handled through formulas; the formulas can be changed by law, but the items in the existing law are virtually immune from veto. Another $123 billion is for other mandatory programs handled through existing legislation. Commitments made in prior years for which contractual obligations exist total $97 billion for defense and $74 billion for domestic programs. We are left with $237 billion—but $175 billion of that is for defense. That leaves, in other words, $62 billion in nondefense, discretionary spending as the main potential for line-item vetos. That includes the general operating expenses of the federal government—Central Intelligence Agency, Federal Bureau of Investigation, the mint, the national parks, and so on. A very small proportion of those expenses could be effectively vetoed if the president had the desire.

Most presidents, however, including Reagan, do not really have that desire. Driven by the same political considerations as members of Congress, presidents generally support, even when they have an opportunity to veto, the kinds of programs that clearly stand out as wasteful federal spending. One very solid example is the subsidization of electric power in the West, Reagan's strongest political base and the base of his closest supporters. Time after time, when bills calling for continued large federal subsidies of power rates in western states have been sent to the president, he has, without protest, signed them and, with conservative Republican senators and congressmen, taken credit for them. He has done the same thing with subsidized grazing lands in western states. Even a lame-duck president, ineligible for reelection, will not chance damage to his political base.

President Reagan is also not immune in other areas. He has supported nearly all the water projects that Jimmy Carter tried to veto when he was president. He supported the Clinch River Breeder Reactor. He supported swollen farm subsidies and generous farm loan guarantees. And during the campaign he pledged to protect the benefits not only of existing social security recipients but also of future recipients. These are not the habits of a president who would wield the item-veto pen mercilessly.

I do not mean to single out Reagan; he has been more courageous than nearly any other president in modern memory in attempting to cut back domestic federal spending. The problem is not President

Reagan—it is presidents in general. Every president, including Reagan, wants to make his mark on the country. Some significant part of that mark depends on proposing new programs and allocating resources for them. Part of Reagan's ambition has been to strengthen our national defenses, and he has pushed hard for the additional federal dollars to do so. These dollars may be justified; they are federal spending nevertheless. Moreover, Reagan has proposed such new deficit enhancers as tuition tax credits, enterprise zones, and a permanent manned space station.

Presidential power—in whatever form—will be used to advance all presidential interests. That means, ironically, that the line-item veto, over the long run, would probably *increase* spending, not cut it. Beyond any doubt, if the line-item veto had been available to President Reagan in 1984 when the MX missile was under fire in Congress, a number of calls would have been made to recalcitrant legislators from the White House, suggesting that a favored dam or federal building would be item-erased if the lawmaker did not reconsider and support funding for the MX. We would have paid for all those dams and buildings—along with more MXs.

Moreover, there is little to the claim that the item veto exists and has worked well in forty-three states. States, of course, are different; comparing the role, powers, and range of state governors and legislatures with those of the president and Congress is like comparing apples and oranges. Additional powers might well be desirable for state governors, who do not have the sweeping responsibilities in foreign affairs, among other areas, that the president has. Still, we have significant evidence that the line-item veto is not very effective in the states. As Benjamin Zycher has noted in the *Wall Street Journal*, per capita spending in the seven states whose governors lack line-item veto authority is no higher—and in some is lower—than in states with some form of line-item veto. After a systematic look at state and local spending patterns, Zycher concludes that the data "do not support the conclusion that the item veto power provides an effective constraint on government spending."[14]

Put simply, the problem is not an institutional one—it is a political one. No institutional solution, from a constitutional amendment to balance the budget to a Congress-crippling device like a line-item veto, will solve a long-term deficit problem. Indeed, a "solution" that would weaken Congress only to strengthen the presidency would be more likely, over the long run, to exacerbate the problem. A political problem requires a political solution. The solution begins, naturally, in the two national political institutions: Congress *and* the presidency. This historical review makes it clear that, despite Congress's premier power over federal money, it rarely, if ever, takes significant sweeping policy actions without presidential pressure—or at least presidential concurrence. Presidential opposition to tax increases or budget cuts dooms them (so, too, of course, does congressional opposition). Thus give is needed on both sides to form a common ground for compromise. The best environment for this is *two* strong and confident institutions.

Some limited institutional changes might help ensure that our two political institutions are stronger, more confident, and more willing to engage in the kind of political compromise that can lead to control of the federal deficit. Congress can and should strengthen the hand of Appropriations committees, returning to them both the strong ethos to act as guardians of the federal treasury and the institutional tools to aid their decisions on their way through the House and the Senate. In the House of Representatives, some greater control by the chairman over Appropriation subcommittee positions and chairmanship would be desirable. So, too, would somewhat tighter rules under which appropriations bills are considered on the House floor, to discourage the wholesale practice of legislating on appropriations bills and offering dozens of amendments that are difficult to vote against politically and that add to spending pressures.

Some sensible and limited changes could also be made in the congressional budget process. The House of Representatives should abandon its practice of rotating membership and chairmanship on the Budget Committee, the only committee on which it does so. The Budget Committee has no chance of developing either a core of experienced and continuing legislative support or the enduring bipartisan relationships that could make the passage of a budget resolution more likely. The Senate could enforce its rules limiting membership on committees so that the Budget Committee would become more of a core assignment for its members, instead of being third or fourth among the four or five committees that most of its members serve on. Eliminating the two-step budget resolution process and adopting a single binding budget resolution would also be useful.

Both the president and Congress should explore the possibility of more frequent bipartisan commissions or informal working groups early in the budget season, to seek a broad consensus on the rate of growth of big domestic programs and of defense as well as on the need, if any, for a tax increase. If broad guidelines can be agreed on early in a process of give-and-take among both parties, both houses, and both branches, it will be at least somewhat easier to enact a budget that incorporates restraint in all spending and revenue areas.

As with any fundamental political problem in America, however, the solution begins not with the institutions but with the public. Public pressure for urgent action and public agreement to waive deep-seated individual policy preferences for a greater goal are necessary conditions for meaningful action on the deficit. When that public response emerges, we are likely to see both significant tax increases and budget slowdowns.

The public response is conditioned by the response of opinion leaders, who are no doubt partially responsible for the flaccid state of public opinion. If a Treasury secretary proclaims across the country that deficits do not matter, or a president blames an increase in the prime rate solely on the Federal Reserve, or Wall Street sends a mixed message about the deficit and the strength of the economic recovery, we will not find an aroused public demanding drastic action by policy makers to eliminate future deficits.

Notes

1. Donald Bruce Johnson and Paul H. Porter, *National Party Platforms*, 5th ed. (Champaign: University of Illinois Press, 1975), p. 2.

2. Thomas Wander, "Patterns of Change in the Congressional Budget Process, 1865–1975," *Congress and the Presidency*, vol. 9, no. 2 (Autumn 1982), p. 48.

3. Allen Schick, *Reconciliation and the Congressional Budget Process* (Washington, D.C.:American Enterprise Institute, 1981).

4. Comment to author.

5. Interview with author.

6. Interview with David Stockman, *Fortune*, February 6, 1984.

7. Ibid.

8. Comment to author.

9. David Mayhew, *Congress: The Electoral Connection* (New Haven, Conn.: Yale University Press, 1974).

10. Kenneth Shepsle and Clifford Hardin, "Government by Subcommittee," *Wall Street Journal*, June 24, 1983.

11. R. Douglas Arnold, "The Local Roots of Domestic Policy," in Thomas E. Mann and Norman J. Ornstein, eds., *The New Congress* (Washington, D.C.: American Enterprise Institute, 1981), pp. 250–87.

12. Gardner Ackley, "Leviathan Revisited: Macroeconomic Evidence on the Relative Size of Government," *Rackham Reports* (Fall 1984).

13. Michael J. Malbin, "Plus Ça Change," *National Journal*, April 14, 1984, p. 729. See also Ackley, "Leviathan Revisited."

14. Benjamin Zycher, "An Item Veto Won't Work," *Wall Street Journal*, October 24, 1984.

CONTRIBUTORS

Phillip Cagan—*Editor*
Professor and chairman of the Department of Economics, Columbia University; former senior staff economist for the Council of Economic Advisers. Visiting scholar with the American Enterprise Institute.

William J. Beeman
Assistant director—fiscal analysis, Congressional Budget Office; former assistant professor of economics, University of Maine.

Edgar K. Browning
Professor of economics, Texas A & M University; former professor of economics, University of Virginia.

Jacquelene M. Browning
Visiting associate professor, Texas A & M University; former associate professor and chairman, Department of Economics, Sweet Briar College.

Jacob S. Dreyer
Deputy assistant director—fiscal analysis, Congressional Budget Office; former deputy assistant secretary for international economic analysis, Department of the Treasury; and former assistant professor of economics, New York University.

Gottfried Haberler
Galen L. Stone Professor of International Trade Emeritus, Harvard University, and past president of the American Economic Association and of the International Economic Association. Resident scholar with the American Enterprise Institute.

John H. Makin
Director of Fiscal Policy Studies and resident scholar with the American Enterprise Institute. Former professor of economics and director of the Institute for Economics Research, University of Washington.

Norman J. Ornstein

Professor of political science (on leave), Catholic University; regular contributor to the "MacNeil/Lehrer News Hour" (PBS); series editor for "Congress: We the People." Resident scholar with the American Enterprise Institute.

Eduardo Somensatto

Assistant director of Economic Policy Studies, American Enterprise Institute; former instructor of economics, Georgetown University.

Vito Tanzi

Director, Fiscal Affairs Department, International Monetary Fund; former professor of economics, the American University.

Paul N. Van de Water

Chief, Projections Unit, Congressional Budget Office; former acting director for policy analysis, Social Security Administration.

Alan Walters

Personal economic adviser to the prime minister of the United Kingdom, 1981–1983, and subsequently part-time consultant; economic adviser to the World Bank; professor of economics, the Johns Hopkins University; former Sir Ernest Cassel Professor of Economics in the University of London at the London School of Economics; knighthood June 1983. Senior fellow with the American Enterprise Institute.

John C. Weicher

Resident fellow and first scholar named to the F. K. Weyerhaeuser Chair in Pubic Policy Research at the American Enterprise Institute; former deputy assistant secretary at the U.S. Department of Housing and Urban Development and past president of the American Real Estate and Urban Economics Association.

A NOTE ON THE BOOK

This book was edited by
Gertrude Kaplan and Ellen Dykes, with
Donna Spitler and Margaret Benjaminson.
Pat Taylor designed the cover and format,
and Hördur Karlsson drew the figures.
The text was set in Palatino, a typeface designed by Hermann Zapf.
Hendricks-Miller Typographic Company, of Washington, D.C.,
set the type, and R. R. Donnelley & Sons Company,
of Harrisonburg, Virginia, printed and bound the book,
using permanent, acid-free paper made by the S. D. Warren Company.

SELECTED AEI PUBLICATIONS

Essays in Contemporary Economic Problems: Disinflation, William Fellner, project director (1983, 324 pp., cloth $19.95, paper $10.95)

Trade in Services: A Case for Open Markets, Jonathan David Aronson and Peter F. Cowhey (1984, 46 pp., $3.95)

High-Technology Policies: A Five-Nation Comparison, Richard R. Nelson (1984, 94 pp., cloth $13.95, paper $4.95)

Controlling the Cost of Social Security, Colin D. Campbell, ed. (1984, 269 pp., $26.00)

Maintaining the Safety Net: Income Redistribution Programs in the Reagan Administration, John C. Weicher, ed. (1984, 204 pp., cloth $17.95, paper $9.95)

The R&D Tax Credit: Issues in Tax Policy and Industrial Innovation, Kenneth M. Brown, ed. (1984, 47 pp., $4.95)

Changing Utilization of Fixed Capital: An Element in Long-Term Growth, Murray F. Foss (1984, 128 pp., $14.95)

• *Mail orders for publications to:* AMERICAN ENTERPRISE INSTITUTE, 1150 Seventeenth Street, N.W., Washington, D.C. 20036 • *For postage and handling, add 10 percent of total; minimum charge $2, maximum $10 (no charge on prepaid orders)* • *For information on orders, or to expedite service, call toll free 800-424-2873 (in Washington, D.C., 202-862-5869)* • *Prices subject to change without notice.* • *Payable in U.S. currency through U.S. banks only*

AEI ASSOCIATES PROGRAM

The American Enterprise Institute invites your participation in the competition of ideas through its AEI Associates Program. This program has two objectives: (1) to extend public familiarity with contemporary issues; and (2) to increase research on these issues and disseminate the results to policy makers, the academic community, journalists, and others who help shape public policies. The areas studied by AEI include Economic Policy, Education Policy, Energy Policy, Fiscal Policy, Government Regulation, Health Policy, International Programs, Legal Policy, National Defense Studies, Political and Social Processes, and Religion, Philosophy, and Public Policy. For the $49 annual fee, Associates receive
• a subscription to *Memorandum,* the newsletter on all AEI activities
• the AEI publications catalog and all supplements
• a 30 percent discount on all AEI books
• a 40 percent discount for certain seminars on key issues
• subscriptions to any two of the following publications: *Public Opinion,* a bimonthly magazine exploring trends and implications of public opinion on social and public policy questions; *Regulation,* a bimonthly journal examining all aspects of government regulation of society; and *AEI Economist,* a monthly newsletter analyzing current economic issues and evaluating future trends (or for all three publications, send an additional $12).

Call 202/862-6446 or write: AMERICAN ENTERPRISE INSTITUTE
1150 Seventeenth Street, N.W., Suite 301, Washington, D.C. 20036